Software Engineering and Knowledge Engineering: Trends for the Next Decade

SERIES ON SOFTWARE ENGINEERING AND KNOWLEDGE ENGINEERING

Series Editor-in-Chief
S K CHANG (*University of Pittsburgh, USA*)

Vol. 1 Knowledge-Based Software Development for Real-Time Distributed Systems
Jeffrey J.-P. Tsai and Thomas J. Weigert (Univ. Illinois at Chicago)

Vol. 2 Advances in Software Engineering and Knowledge Engineering
edited by Vincenzo Ambriola (Univ. Pisa) *and Genoveffa Tortora* (Univ. Salerno)

Vol. 3 The Impact of CASE Technology on Software Processes
edited by Daniel E. Cooke (Univ. Texas)

Forthcoming titles:

Acquisition of Software Engineering Knowledge
edited by Robert G. Reynolds (Wayne State Univ.)

Intelligent Image Database Systems
edited by S. K. Chang (Univ. Pittsburgh), *E. Jungert* (Swedish Defense Research *Establishment*) *and G. Tortora* (Univ. Salerno)

Monitoring, Debugging, and Analysis of Distributed Real-Time Systems
Jeffrey J.-P. Tsai, Steve J. H. Yong, R. Smith and Y. D. Bi (Univ. Illinois at Chicago)

Series on Software Engineering and Knowledge Engineering

Vol. 4

Software Engineering and Knowledge Engineering: Trends for the Next Decade

Series Editor

S K Chang

Editor

W David Hurley

University of Pittsburgh, USA

World Scientific

Singapore • New Jersey • London • Hong Kong

Published by

World Scientific Publishing Co. Pte. Ltd.

P O Box 128, Farrer Road, Singapore 9128

USA office: Suite 1B, 1060 Main Street, River Edge, NJ 07661

UK office: 57 Shelton Street, Covent Garden, London WC2H 9HE

SOFTWARE ENGINEERING AND KNOWLEDGE ENGINEERING: TRENDS FOR THE NEXT DECADE

ISBN 981-02-1911-3

Printed in Singapore by Uto-Print

PREFACE

The papers collected in this book are either updates or reprints of selected papers that appeared originally in the *International Journal of Software Engineering and Knowledge Engineering.* These papers were selected because they examine current and future trends in the interplay between software engineering and knowledge-based systems. The aim of this book is to inform the reader of the issues and which research directions seem most promising.

Software system artifacts are produced within the framework of a software production process. Active research issues include specifying and mechanically supporting these software processes. Chapter one clarifies the issues concerning software process representations, reviews the main approaches, and analyzes the desirable features for future process languages. Chapter two considers the problems inherent in providing a sofware infrastructure to support software production processes, and examines the emerging trend toward meta-environments for constructing more powerful infrastructures. Chapter three examines interactive software environments in which the system artifacts being manipulated have some definable structure; the scope of such systems is much wider than one might at first imagine.

Key to successful software construction is specification of what is to be built. Chapter four discusses knowledge-based support for requirements engineering: it reviews the kinds of knowledge involved, the different ways each kind of knowledge can be used, and the considerable work that remains to be done.

Software is pervading nearly every human endeavor, including those in which failure of a software system could result in personal injury, loss of life, or significant material loss. Chapter five presents a comprehensive research agenda for these safety-critical systems, examining issues related to every aspect of the software process. Chapter six considers the use of formal methods to address reliability issues; it surveys the merits and demerits of various formal techniques and analyzes the emerging trends.

Two areas in which technology is exploding are software reuse and the information superhighway. Chapter seven takes an interesting look at how these areas overlap when information retrieval systems are used as software reuse repositories.

Of course, system developers cannot control what they cannot measure. Chapter eight looks at the trend towards supporting measurement of product and process in software engineering environments, detailing several research and commercial systems. Chapter nine examines the utility of software engineering metrics to problems in artificial intelligence, applying it in particular to expert systems development. Chapter ten examines software productivity measurement, including the current state of the art, open challenges, and ways to use knowledge-based systems technology to address these challenges.

Dave Hurley

CONTENTS

A SURVEY AND ASSESSMENT OF SOFTWARE PROCESS REPRESENTATION FORMALISMS*

SERGIO BANDINELLI

CEFRIEL and Politecnico di Milano Dip. di Elettronica,
Piazza Leonardo Da Vinci, 32,
I-20133 Milan, Italy

CARLO GHEZZI and ANGELO MORZENTI

Politecnico di Milano Dip. di Elettronica,
Piazza Leonardo Da Vinci, 32,
I-20133 Milan, Italy

Process modeling is a rather young and very active research area. During the last few years, new languages and methods have been proposed to describe software processes. In this paper we try to clarify the issues involved in software process modeling and identify the main approaches. We start by motivating the use of process modeling and its main objectives. We then propose a list of desirable features for process languages. The features are grouped as either already provided by languages from other fields or as specific features of the process domain. Finally, we review the main existing approaches and propose a classification scheme.

1. Introduction

Industrial products are produced following a set of pre-established methods and procedures, integrated in a production process. The goal of production processes is to produce quality artifacts in a reliable, predictable, and efficient manner. Software artifacts are the result of software production processes, which involve a number of steps and activities from the conception of an idea to the delivery of the system and its evolution. There is a wide consensus that the overall quality of these artifacts depends on the process through which they are produced [16, 28, 40, 47].

Traditional industrial production processes may be (and have been) applied to software in order to help improve software processes and support the

*This work is partially supported by CNR Progetto Finalizzato Sistemi Informatici e Calcolo Parallelo.

production of high quality software systems. But software has distinguishing characteristics that make traditional production processes inadequate. Indeed, the software production process is a multiperson, largely intellectual design activity, that can only be partially automated. Cooperation among humans and coordination of human activities play a fundamental role. Moreover, it is an evolutionary activity, in that not only software products are subject to continuous modifications, but also the software process itself is likely to be modified while it is being executed, since process and product requirements are highly unstable.

The focus on software processes as a relevant research theme is quite recent, but has quickly drawn considerable interest within both academia and industry. A series of *International Workshops on Software Processes* has been organized, and an *International Conference on Software Processes* has been launched.

It is possible to group current work on software processes into two broad areas. The first focuses on managerial issues and aims at improving current industrial practices by focusing on organizational issues. The most relevant work here is done at the Software Engineering Institute (SEI), Carnegie Mellon. [28] describes the methodology developed by SEI for software process assessment, known as the"maturity framework". Work in this area also includes criticism of the conventional waterfall process and study of new paradigms.

The second research area addresses technical issues involved in specifying and mechanically supporting software processes. The starting point is the recognition that there is no universally valid software process that can be automated once and for all, and then replicated for any new application development. Rather, the process should be tailored to possibly each new application development. The process model definition can be used as a configuration parameter of development environments. In this way, users (programmers, designers, managers, etc.) may receive support and guidance from the development environment, consistently with the process model specification. These environments, in which the process model plays a central role, are generally called Process-centered Software Engineering Environments (PSEE).

Clearly, within this latter area, software process representation notations play an important role. A representation formalism for describing software processes should serve not only to improve communication among people both at the technical and the managerial level but also as a code to a process interpreter to automate (parts of) the process.

There is no general agreement, however, as to whether it is possible to describe real and practical software processes in a completely formal way. The advantages of a partial formalization, however, would still be valuable.

A successful modeling requires the use of an adequate notation or language. Notations can be either textual or graphical or mixed text and graphics. Some notations have a well-defined syntax and thus qualify as languages. Some languages have formally defined semantics and therefore are amenable to formal reasoning. In this paper we will use the terms "notation" and "language" interchangeably, concentrating on the facilities offered to describe software processes. The primitives of a software process modeling language have to be chosen so that process concepts can be naturally expressed. Nevertheless, we should be aware that probably "the" process language will never be defined. Quoting Rombach [42]:

> "The effectiveness of a tool in general and a process description language in particular, depends on the context in which it is used, the objectives it is used for and the degree to which its features are understood and used."

The paper organization is as follows. In Sec. 2, we identify the general objectives of software process modeling. In Sec. 3, we derive a list of desiderable properties and requirements for a software process representation language. In Sec. 4, we provide a classification of different process language approaches and we evaluate these approaches. Finally, in Sec. 5, we draw some conclusions.

2. Software Process Modeling Objectives

Process modeling is a relatively new research area and consequently, there is no general consensus on its final objectives. Its main goals may be classified as follows.

Communicating. The software process is the framework in which interacting agents cooperate to develop software applications, support their evolution, produce and maintain reusable components, etc. Different kinds of roles may be involved, and different people may be interacting in the process: managers, software engineers, end-users, etc. The software process is the common ground on which these individuals work cooperatively. Despite its importance, however, the process is normally left implicit and little or no attention is paid to making it clearly understood by all participants in the process. By providing an explicit representation, the process becomes more clearly understood, and this helps improve communication among people.

Estimating and planning. An engineering project is expected to produce a reliable product within a limited time using limited resources. In the initial part of a project, it is the manager's responsibility to estimate the resources needed to accomplish the task, in terms of both man-months and total expected duration. Based on the initial estimate, a plan must be constructed for the utilization of resources during the process, the milestones to be met, the deliverables to be produced, the controls to be accomplished, etc. The explicit representation of the software process provides a rigorous framework for both estimating and planning. Indeed, explicitly represented processes may be formally analyzed in order to complement the manager's judgement and intuition. For example, managers may simulate the effect of decisions, evaluate their implications, or examine past decisions taken in similar circumstances.

Managing and replanning. Process descriptions help managers to monitor the project with respect to the plan and to react to the deviations that may occur by replanning and re-estimating. Some forms of change might be anticipated in the defined software process (e.g., in the form of possible iterations); other forms might require the structure of the process to be more deeply modified. Changes, however, are quite critical to deal with. After a change is applied, the process resumes its execution in a state that may be inconsistent with the change and, ideally, the system should tolerate inconsistency and possibly return to a consistent state in a gradual fashion.

Measuring. Measures provide quantitative assessments of the process and of the product qualities. They can be used to assess an on-going process, and to decide whether a modification should be applied to the process in order to improve it. By having an explicit representation of the software process, one may precisely define where and how to perform measurements. Some measures may be even collected automatically. Measures, in turn, may provide a quantitative evidence of the merits or weaknesses of the different processes, and this helps improve the processes via experimentation.

Configuring. A main assumption behind software process work is that no blanket process model exists, but rather the most suitable process model must be defined depending on the nature of the project being developed. A process must be adapted to the organization and the project at hand. By providing a notation for explicit process representation, in principle one may configure the desired process and its support environment. Within the defined process, some activities are performed by humans, others are mechanically supported by the tools provided by the environment. A number of process-centered software development environments are currently being designed (e.g., Arcadia [46] and ESF [20]). Consequently, one may view the software process description as a specification of the environment configuration.

Reusing. Processes do not need to be defined from scratch every time. Rather, process descriptions should help materialize previous experiences in terms of knowledge, which may be reused as a basis of new processes for new projects. Presently, the most widely practiced form of process reuse is through personnel reuse. Software specialists are transferred from one project to another, so that they may apply their previous experience to a new development. By providing explicit process representations, knowledge becomes independent of the individuals and process reuse may become a company standard.

Executing. The process description defines the activities performed in the software engineering environment: both management and technical activities. Such activities are performed concurrently, perhaps by geographically dispersed work units. Depending on the level of formality of the notation used for process representation, one may derive an interpreter of the notation. The notation would then be executable, at possibly different levels of completeness. This is exactly what happens in the aforementioned process-centered environments. Actually, the word enactment (instead of execution or interpretation) is used in the process modeling area to mean that the execution of the process is done not only by machines but by a symbiosis of human beings and computers.

Verifying. The use of a formal notation for process specification provides powerful ways of process verification. For example, process specifications based on finite-state machines or Petri nets may be verified by showing that certain properties hold (e.g., certain desirable states are reachable, no-deadlocks arise in the Petri net behavior, etc). Another form of process verification may be provided by simulation. Simulation may be obtained via execution of the process language and may be used to generate process scenarios that support a form of "what if" analysis (e.g., what happens if certain activities are executed in parallel instead of sequentially, etc). Finally, as we said under "executing", it is also possible for the interpreter of the notation to act as the run-time engine of the development environment. In this last case, the explicit and formal process description may become the input to the environment's configuration activity, which provides a communication infrastructure supporting cooperative work of the individuals involved in the process, consistent with the process description. Such infrastructure might be (in part) automatically derived from the process formal description. This would be a significant step towards tailoring the process-centered environment to the needs of the specific project being developed.

Evolving. Software processes are by no means static entities. During their long lifetime, processes must be allowed to evolve, in order to cope with a variety of change requests. Changes may arise for quality improvements, for example, by incorporating new tools and techniques, because of restructuring in the organization, because different strategies are introduced, etc. Processes may be changed *off-line*, before they are actually started, hopefully reusing previous experiences of the organization. Process change also occurs *on-line*, i.e., during enactment. Thus, suitable mechanisms have to be provided by PSEE to support process evolution. In particular, changes in the process have to be dynamically reflected in the model that describes it.

3. Software Process Language Features

Based on the objectives presented above, we present here some desirable features for a process language. These features will be used to evaluate various proposed approaches to process modeling.

The software production process may be addressed from many points of view. It seems unlikely that a single approach will be able to adequately capture the multiple aspects of process modeling [35]. Indeed, the software process field may be viewed as a synthesis of diverse areas of research and application with, in addition, its own peculiarities.

Software process languages profit from previous linguistic approaches, borrowing language features from other areas and adding new features specific to software process applications. Following this idea, we classify software process language features as either already provided by languages of other fields or as specific features of the process domain.

3.1. *Features inherited from general-purpose sequential programming languages*

These features are present in different ways and extents in modern programming languages. Their applicability, however, is not limited to the development of programs: they implement general principles that also apply to process modeling. Among these we mention:

- abstraction;
- modularity;
- genericity;
- nondeterminism.

An *abstraction* mechanism allows one to focus on the important aspects of a system while irrelevant details remain hidden. Abstraction is important in process modeling because it helps in mastering the complexity of the process by allowing the designer and user of the process to concentrate on what is important on each phase of software development.

A feature related to abstraction is *modularity*, which provides the possibility of structuring a specification or program in many logically independent units, called modules. *Genericity* provides the way of describing a general solution for a set of related problems, by parameterizing it with respect to its possible instantiations. Before being used, a generic solution has to be instantiated for a specific problem. Modularity and genericity features are of great importance for process languages, since they are essential for reusability and evolvability.

At certain levels of abstraction in the description of a process, it may be useful not to specify how the choice among several open alternatives is actually performed. This kind of underspecification is called *nondeterminism* and it should be supported by a process modeling language.

3.2. *Features inherited from concurrent, reactive, and real-time system languages*

Concurrency is becoming an increasingly important programming language feature. Software processes are intrinsically concurrent because the members of a software development team concurrently interact in accomplishing their tasks. The language should therefore provide mechanisms for specifying concurrent activities and synchronizing their evolution.

Furthermore, software processes have much in common with reactive real-time systems [3]. In fact, software processes may be viewed as a set of activities that proceed in parallel and react to external events which may occur at unpredictable times. These activities must be be scheduled in a way that respects logical precedence relations, and yet meets their required deadlines. The overall correctness of a process depends not only on correct execution of individual steps but also on meeting time constraints. Time constraints in process modeling are of different order of magnitude than the ones we find in critical real-time systems; however, the basic characteristics of being time-dependent are shared by both kinds of systems.

In conclusion, in order to appropriately model the software production process, process modeling languages should include features inherited from concurrent real-time languages such as:

- parallelism;
- time constraints specification;
- description of interaction with the environment.

3.3. *Features inherited from database languages*

The influence of databases on software processes is not new. Databases have been used as part of software engineering environments to provide a repository in which persistent data could be stored and accessed concurrently by multiple users.

The application of databases to software processes, however, has brought new problems into the database field. The traditional database technology is not able to efficiently deal with objects of different degrees of granularity, as needed in software development environments. For example, one needs to represent large objects, such as programs, manuals, or executable code at very fine-grained levels (e.g., an individual node of a parse-tree representing a statement). In addition, traditional databases do not provide specific facilities to deal with versioned objects. Conversely, software artifacts are subject to continuous evolutionary changes, and their development history must be stored and maintained in different versions.

The traditional transaction model is also inadequate for software process applications. Transactions may have a long duration, may require user interaction, and even multiuser synergistic efforts. Sample software engineering transactions may correspond to building a new release, performing regression testing, or performing corrective maintenance. Therefore, it is not acceptable, nor even possible, to lock all accesses to the involved data or to roll back a transaction, when, for some reason, it could not commit.

The development of advanced, nonconventional database systems is presently a very active research topic [6], which spans a variety of applications areas such as CAD and software engineering environments. The process language must be integrated with the underlying software engineering database in order to support cooperation within a project group, while controlling access to different versions of different documents. The following points summarize required process languages features, coming from the database field:

- to provide a conceptual data model (independent of the physical model);
- to efficiently handle persistent objects of different granularity;
- to support very long transactions;
- to support versioning.

3.4. *Software process specific features*

Software processes have characteristics that make them different from processes in other endeavors. First, software production is a creative, intellectual activity and, therefore, it is not completely formalizable. Thus, software process modeling languages should support incomplete, ambiguous, and informal descriptions as well as formal ones. They should describe interactions with (and among) humans as well as interactions with automatic tools.

As a consequence, the execution of the activities involved in a software process cannot be done entirely by computers. In fact, the partially formalized or not formalizable activities require human intervention. Therefore, process languages should be able not only to describe the binding of activities to computer devices, but also to model human intervention and tool invocation — if a tool is required to carry out a task.

It is true that the fact of materializing the process by simply writing it down is a big step towards making the process explicit, rather than implicit, and thus repeatable, understandable, and transferable. But an additional — and perhaps more substantial — advantage of a precise description is that it can be analyzed and enacted, and thus the people involved in the process would be constrained to follow it.

Analysis of the process may be performed by simulating the execution. By analyzing the results of simulation, one may evaluate the effect of certain process design decisions or the implications of certain managerial decisions, or perform any other kind of process assessment before actually enacting it. Other forms of assessment can be performed during enactment by providing process measurements so that process features (e.g., process productivity, cost, risk) can be assessed later. Measurement should be integrated in the software process, so that it can provide on-line feedback to managers to improve or correct the development while it is being carried out, or advice on the structuring of future processes. Process languages offering measurement and analysis facilities effectively contribute to a good management of a software project.

In a process-centered environment, the process model is the "code" to be executed by the process interpreter (as we said, the interpreter consists of a mixture of machines and humans). Automation may be obtained by using the process language interpreter to integrate individual tool fragments in larger grain tools. In addition, enactable process models help control the evolution of the process and support the coordination and cooperation of people working in a software project by providing guidance and assistance during the whole development cycle.

A software production process may take a long time and is subject to changes during this time. Thus, a software process language should be flexible enough to allow dynamic process modification, i.e., while it is being enacted. The modifications may be caused by deviations from the manager's plans and may range from changes in the assignment of tasks to persons to more serious changes regarding, for example, the precedence relation between activities. The process language should impose some restrictions on the kinds of allowed modifications to guarantee, for example, that consistency is preserved or that certain desiderable properties are maintained.

The whole software production process should be representable with a process language. This includes not only technical activities, but also management activities. Management is a basic problem of software production. Management decisions have a strong impact on the technical aspects of a project. A project may fail because of poor management, even if it is correct from the technical point of view. Management activities include resource management, planning, and controlling.

To satisfy management requirements, a process language should offer tools to build schedules so that resources are used in an efficient way, assist the manager in making estimates and previsions (for example, by simulating the process, as it has already been said), notify managers as soon as technical steps are accomplished, and provide adequate policies for exception handling, i.e., detect and correct deviations from the plans.

The distinctive features required for process modeling languages may be summarized as follows:

- permit coexistence of both formally described parts and informal, incomplete, or ambiguous parts in the same process specification;
- support the binding of the execution of the different parts of a process to computing devices, human beings, or predefined tools;
- support controlled modification during enactment;
- represent both technical and nontechnical activities;
- provide analysis tools, including process and product measurement facilities, scheduling and planning tools;
- represent what is to be done when a certain activity fails.

4. Classification and Assessment

The purpose of this section is to give a succinct overview of some of the most relevant approaches to software process languages presented in the literature. Since the area is still in rapid evolution and the languages are still evolving, the overview may be inaccurate or incomplete on some points. This overview, however, illustrates the main directions being followed by research in the area of software process modeling and describes the main benefits that may be expected in the future.

In Table 1, we show a classification of some of the most relevant approaches. For each considered process language, the representation styles are indicated. Actually, most languages combine different representation styles, and therefore, cannot be classified under just one style. This is a consequence, at least in part, of the fact that process modeling languages inherit features from various linguistic approaches.

The considered styles are *logic rules* (Ru), which denotes *ruled-based* and *logic language*-based approaches; *attribute grammars* (Gr); *automata* (At), which includes finite state automata and Petri nets; *imperative programming languages* (Ip); *artificial intelligence* (AI), which refers to those languages using *AI techniques* or knowledge-based systems; *event-triggering*-based formalisms (Et); and *abstract data types* (adt), including object-oriented approaches for structuring data.

In the following, sample process modeling languages are surveyed in order to discuss some pros and cons of the different approaches. In some cases, we include a small example to give a more concrete flavor of the language.

Table 1. Classification of software process languages.

	Language style						
	Ru	Gr	At	Ip	AI	Et	adt
Adele						X	X
ALF	X					X	X
APPL/A				X			X
Entity			X				
EPOS	X			X	X		X
FUNSOFT			X	X			X
HFSP		X					
Marvel	X				X		
Merlin	X						
Oikos	X				X		
PADM	X				X		
SMART	X			X	X		X
SPADE	X		X				X
PROCESS WEAVER			X	X			

4.1. *Adele and Adele-TEMPO*

The Adele environment [8] is built around a central versioned database in which all components of the environment are stored. The Adele database is based on the entity-relationship model extended in an object oriented fashion and supporting long transactions, user defined commands and activities.

Tasks having a long duration are not performed directly on the database, but on *workcontexts*. A workcontext is an Adele (mono-version) subdatabase and is associated with a user, a set of directories and files, a set of tools, and a task to do. The coordination between workcontexts is managed by the *activity manager* using a trigger mechanism. *Triggers* are actions to be executed automatically when some condition holds. The trigger mechanism has been used as a support to process-specific actions, such as constraint integrity checking, propagating updates, etc. For instance, when an interface module is modified, the trigger mechanism may be used to evaluate the impact of the modification on other related modules, causing the affected modules to be notified and/or recompiled, if necessary.

Adele has been specifically designed to manage activity coordination in a software production process. Currently, the intention is not to offer a mechanism for a complete formalization of software processes, but to help control software production processes.

Recently, a higher-level language called TEMPO [9, 10] has been constructed on top of Adele with the purpose of improving the support for cooperative work and favoring the proper sharing of resources among sets of processes. A role concept has also been introduced to facilitate the managing of software process evolution by allowing an instantiated object to dynamically change its static and behavioral properties. TEMPO also provides facilities for working with object history and process evolution. Adele's triggering mechanism has been extended to support temporal event interpretation by augmenting trigger conditions with (implicit) temporal logic predicates. For instance, the following clause:

```
ON modify-code(O) AND testRegression(O)
DO testPerformance(O)
WHEN testPlan.state=finished
```

defines a software process policy specifying that if modify code and test regression have been executed (sometimes in the past) on object `O` then the test performance will be executed when (sometimes in the future) the test plan will be in the finished state.

4.2. *ALF*

In ALF [13, 38], a software process model is described as a hierarchy of MASPs (Model for Assisted Software Processes). Each MASP describes a software process model fragment, which in turn, can be detailed by others MASPs and so on. This permits a structured description at different levels of abstraction.

Actually, a MASP is a generic description that must be instantiated before being executed. The instantiation need not be completed before enactment begins. Instead, instantiation and enactment may interleave so that the part of the development that has already been executed may be taken into account to instantiate a further part.

Each MASP is described as a 5-tuple (Om, OPm, Rm, ORm, C). Om, the *object model*, provides a conceptual data model based on ERA (Entities, Relationships, and Attributes), which is basically the PCTE [18] model extended with multivalued attributes. OPm is a set of *operator types*, which are abstractions of tools with a profile and pre-/postconditions. Actually, an operator type represents a generic tool and it has to be linked (statically or dynamically) to a concrete tool satisfying the operator type specifications. *Rm* is a set of rules of the type event-condition-action, saying how to react to some predefined events. *ORm* is a set of *ordering constraints*, represented using path expressions, that specify whether operators must be executed in parallel, alternatively or sequentially. Finally, *C* is a characteristic, i.e., an expression specifying invariant constraints on the reachable process states; if they are not satisfied, they raise an exception condition. In this case, the process execution state has to be fixed with the intervention of a human agent.

One of ALF's main goals is to provide assistance during software development. The user receives guidance about what to do next, how a certain process works or how to perform a certain action. In addition, explanations are given when the invocation of an operator is rejected, when the system takes an initiative on its own, and when an operation invocation would violate the characteristic.

4.3. *APPL/A*

APPL/A [39, 44] (Ada Process Programming Language based on Aspen) is a process programming language developed as part of the ARCADIA project [46]. Basically, APPL/A is a superset of Ada, which has been extended to include abstract persistent relations, relation attributes that may be composite and derived, and triggers that react to relation operations. Aspen is a data model for software engineering supporting relations among software objects.

Being based on Ada, APPL/A inherits from the language basic features, such as its type system, the module definition style (packages), and task communication paradigm (rendezvous).

In APPL/A, process descriptions are given in a procedural way. However, certain aspects, such as consistency conditions, may be specified using optionally-enforcible predicates on relations.

Figure 1 presents an APPL/A function (which is obviously part of a larger program) telling whether the result of a test is OK. The function checks if the result satisfies the needs (this is computed by function `fcnOK`) and if the test execution time for the test case is less than or equal to the execution time needed.

4.4. *Entity model*

The entity model, described in [29], is mainly intended to provide a support to some key managerial activities such as planning, monitoring and record-

```
Function resultOK(result, needed);
declare
     result derived_result,
     needed req_output;
if fcnOK(result.fcn_output, needed) OR
     (result.observ_timing > needed.time)
     then resultOK := False;
     else resultOK := True;
endif
endresultOK;
```

Fig. 1. An APPL/A example (from [39]).

ing progress, and dynamic replanning. The modeling of software processes is centered around *entities* considered as persistent, nontransient objects, whose existence is not limited to some phase of the software process but spans through all its entirety. Examples of entities are the requirements document, the finished programs, the documentation, the design or, in general, any artifact that is produced during the process execution.

The entities that are involved in the modeled process are then described by means of the states they successively undergo and the events that trigger transitions among such states. States are characterized by the fact that they last for nonzero length time intervals, while transitions among states are considered to be instantaneous. The overall software process is thus described as a set of cooperating finite state machines by using STATEMATE [27] facilities for parallel composition of the system subcomponents and communications among them. Each entity has a number of states, and is represented by an orthogonal component; these orthogonal components represent entities evolving concurrently.

For instance, Fig. 2 depicts the Entity-Process description of a sample software process consisting of three entities: module code, module unit tests, and test execution. The entities are represented as high-level orthogonal state components corresponding to the filled-in quadrants of the figure (upstream and downstream entities, in the lower right quadrant, are temporarily left unspecified). The states in the quadrants depict the possible states of the entities, while transitions are represented by the lines, whose labels define the triggers which cause the transition. Default transitions (beginning with a small dot) lead from the outer state into the initial states "none" (for a nonexisting

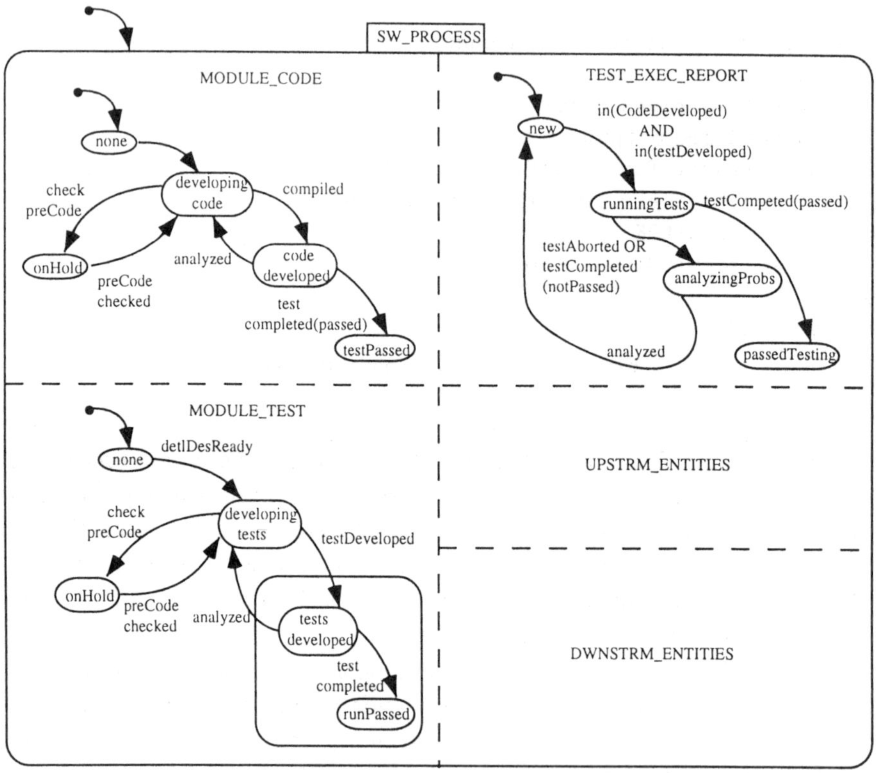

Fig. 2. Entity model example (from [29]).

entity) and "new" (for a newly produced entity), thus indicating that the process begins with the entities in those states. It can be noted that transitions in one component may be labeled by events occurring in another parallel, orthogonal component, and that such labels may be boolean compositions of elementary events.

The facilities of STATEMATE are also exploited to perform schedule planning and analysis of the modeled process. An initial idealized model, called Unconstrained Process Model, is obtained by assuming unconstrained availability of resources for supporting the tasks and the transitions among states of the process. Analysis is thus based exclusively on the logical interconnections of transitions and events. By providing some additional information like the number of times the loops are performed and the time length of each iteration, some estimates of the possible evolutions of the process, in the form of Gantt charts, are derived. The second model, called the Constrained Process Model, takes into account the limitations on the available resources typical of real software organizations, where personnel or computing resources may not always be available in the desired quantities. The analysis of the constrained model also results in Gantt charts, which permits a more realistic and accurate simulation of the process, and can be used in practice during process enactment. The most recent versions of the entity model environment [34] include the possibility of providing, besides the behavioral view of the modeled process by means of a Statechart, also functional view composed of Activity charts (basically, an enriched version of data flow diagrams) and an organizational perspective composed of a Module chart. The uncertainty on the values of the parameter adopted in the software process model and the difficulty in their prediction can be dealt with by considering, in a more realistic view, probability distributions for their expected values instead of point estimates, thus obtaining a stochastic model where the individual outcomes are drawn from the probability distribution of the input values.

4.5. *EPOS*

EPOS [30, 31] is a multiparadigm system, which combines in a unified framework many characteristics of distinct language approaches. Process models in EPOS are described in SPELL, a persistent object-oriented language.

SPELL supports several levels of abstraction and composition. In particular, it is possible to define a task hierarchy. Task types express knowledge about a development step and consists of an activation rule (associated with an executable program or script) together with PRE- and POSTconditions. These conditions can be used for analysis purposes (forward and backward reasoning) without execution of the activation rule. Tasks instances (or simply tasks) are part of a network, defining a plan for the automatic activation of tasks.

In EPOS, the descriptions of both the process model and the data on which the process operates are stored in a unique object-oriented repository based on the entity-relationship data model. This makes it possible to describe simultaneously and in an integrated framework both the management of the successive product versions and process model versions. In addition, relationships in the database are "active", so that creation and update of related objects can be performed upon interrogation or search in the data base, using either a lazy

```
RootER                          (root type)
      PersistentObj             (persistent objects)
      VersionedObj              (version groups)
      GenRelationship           (general relationships)
      GenEntity                 (general entities)
         DataEntity             (software component)
         ProcEntity             (passive procedure)
         Actor                  (manual or automatic agent)
            Tool                (automatic tool)
            Role                (generic person)
         Task                   (active process)
            TaskNode            (chained task)
```

Fig. 3. EPOS type hierarchy fragment (from [15]).

or an eager strategy. Database (sub)transactions are connected to a task. Information exchange among transactions is regulated by an inter-transaction task network, where communication exchange is regulated by communication protocols.

The various elements of the process (tasks and procedures, tools, roles etc.) are modeled by a set of types organized into an object-oriented hierarchical inheritance structure. As an example, consider Fig. 3, which shows a fragment of the EPOS type hierarchy.

EPOS offers a set of process tools which make part of the process support environment. The *SPELL interpreter* and the *Execution Manager* constitute the EPOS process engine. The *Planner* is invoked by the Execution Manager to incrementally generate the network of subtasks from a composed task. The *Schema Manager* is responsible for browsing and editing the set of types.

The EPOS process environment possesses a very rich variety of features, borrowed from nearly all approaches that are present in the literature, and seems to allow a very dynamic and flexible management of processes. However, due to its complexity and superposition of features and mechanisms, it is quite difficult to get an overall picture of the system.

4.6. *FUNSOFT Nets*

FUNSOFT nets [17, 25] are based on a high-level Petri net notation built on top of Predicate/Transition nets [23]. They provide extensions that proved to

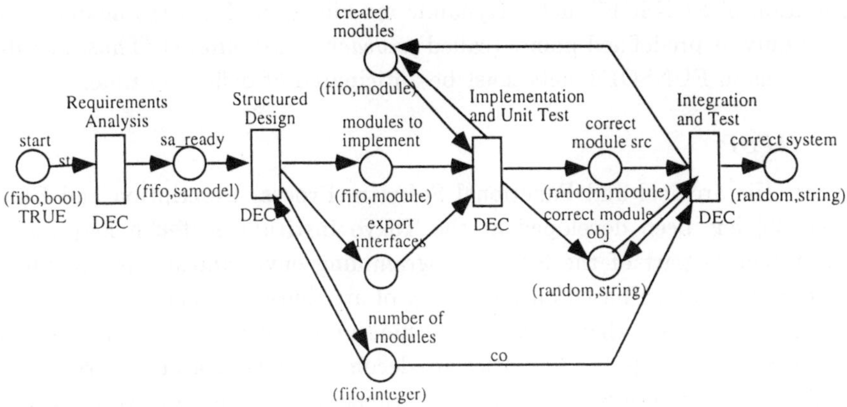

Fig. 4. A FUNSOFT net modeling a waterfall-like software process (from [17]).

be useful to support software process modeling, including, for example, the ability to associate a policy with places (random, fifo, lifo), different firing behaviors with respect to the number of consumed and produced tokens (all, mult, complex), etc.

Being a Petri net-based formalism, FUNSOFT nets naturally represent nondeterminism and parallelism. It is also possible to associate a value to a transition, in order to model the duration of the activity represented by that transition. This information is then used in simulation mode to animate the behavior described by the net. The objects involved in the process are described using an extensible set of object types.

The example in Fig. 4 illustrates a waterfall-like process modeled with FUNSOFT nets. Each place is annotated with the policy and object type. Transitions marked with "DEC" are further detailed using a subnet.

FUNSOFT nets are suitable for the representation of complex activities. They have been developed paying special attention to simulation and validation capabilities; i.e., they support the analysis of properties of the modeled process. It is also possible to translate first the model to the underlying Predicate/Transition net and then perform some analysis on them (e.g., invariant analysis).

Simulation and enactment of FUNSOFT nets is done within the software process management environment MELMAC [26]. It provides a FUNSOFT net editor and an analysis component, called ANAMEL, for verification and validation of FUNSOFT nets. Dynamic modification of process models is allowed only at predefined points (called *feedback modifications*). Thus, possible evolutions in FUNSOFT nets must be anticipated at definition time.

4.7. *HFSP*

HFSP (Hierarchical and Functional Software Process Description and Enaction) [33] has been developed at the Tokyo Institute of Technology and is prototyped as part of the SAGE programming environment. It provides a functional approach based on the theory of attribute grammars.

The basic idea is that activities are functions that produce output objects from given input objects. Activities are decomposed using grammar rules, and attribute rules describe input-output relationships in terms of those associated with subactivities. Finally, like any functional language, HFSP is reflective, i.e., the execution status is treated as a basic data type that can be handled by the formalism. This means that a process may be modified during the process itself.

In particular, the language also includes an ad hoc construct, called redoing, to handle dynamic run-time reconfiguration of the software process [45]. This operation cancels a part of the process enactment structure which is polluted by erroneous and incomplete activities and performs that part again. Detection of the cause of errors is obtained through dependency analysis.

Let us give a glimpse at how the attribute grammar formalism is used to model software processes. An activity A with inputs x_1, x_2, …, x_n and outputs y_1, y_2, …, y_m may be represented by the grammar nonterminal A with inherited attributes $x_1, x_2, \ldots, x_n$ and synthesized attributes y_1, y_2, …, y_m (as shown in Fig. 5).

Activities may be decomposed into subactivities by using grammar rules. For example, the following rule gives a high-level description of the JSP function, which describes how a specification is transformed into a program by the JSP methodology [12].

```
JSP(spec, progOut) ←
          MakeProgTree(spec, progTree)
          EnumerateOp(spec, operators)
          MakeProg(operators, progTree, progMid)
          DoInversion(progMid, progOut)
```

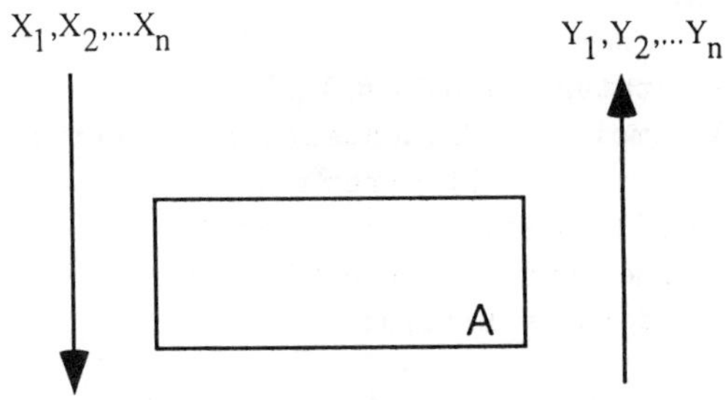

Fig. 5. An HFSP activity.

The rule describes the subactivities `MakeProgTree`, which makes a program tree, `EnumerateOp`, which lists the operators needed for the program; `MakeProg`, which produces an intermediate program; and `DoInversion`, which performs a specific JSP function that does program inversion.

HFSP is intrinsically concurrent, i.e., unless there are explicit dependencies among attributes, they may be evaluated in parallel. It can also describe nondeterminism, by having two rules for the same activity. The language may also interact with an object base, i.e., in $A(x_1, x_2, \ldots, x_n | y_1, y_2, \ldots, y_m)$, input objects may be extracted from the database, and output objects may be inserted in the database.

There are published examples of the use of HFSP, and the theory underlying the language is rather clear. What is not clear from the papers is how human interaction in the process is modeled and handled by the environment.

4.8. *Marvel*

MARVEL [7, 36] is a PSEE developed at Columbia University. Process models in MARVEL are written in a rule-based language, called MSL (MARVEL strategy language). In addition, the environment provides a language to interface external tools, called SEL (shell envelope language), based on an extension of the Unix shell language, and a language to manage conflicts during concurrent execution, called CRL (coordination rule language) [7].

MSL allows the process administrator to describe the data model and the process model. The data model is described in terms of a set of object-oriented class definitions. Persistent objects are class instances. All objects are kept in MARVEL Objectbase. Process models are described in terms of rules. Rules

```
compile[? f:CFILE]:
        :
        (?f.compile_status = NotCompiled)
        { COMPILER compile    ?f.contents ?f.object_code
                              ?f.error_msg ''-g'' }
        (and (?f.compile_status = Compiled)
        (?f.object_time_stamp = CurrentTime));
        (?f.compile_status = Error);
```

Fig. 6. A MARVEL activation rule (from [7]).

can be of two kinds: *activation rules* and *inference rules.* Activation rules control the initiation of development activities, and typically involve the invocation of a tool. They generally have multiple mutually exclusive sets of effects, that is, they may end with different conditions. For example, a rule modeling the invocation to a compiler may end with success producing object code or may fail producing a set of error messages. Inference rules, instead, only define relations among attributes of objects, the activity invocation part is left empty and they have a single effect.

As an example of an activation rule, consider the compile rule shown in Fig. 6. It has a typed object `?f:FILE` as the parameter (each parameter has a name beginning with "?"). Then follows a condition that has to be satisfied for the rule execution. Between curly braces follows an activity invocation, which contains the invocation to tools (in this case the invocation to the C compiler). The rule finishes with a list of exclusive sets of effects. Each set of effects is a conjunction of logical predicates that assign values to the attributes of the parameter objects.

Rules may be executed by applying forward and backward chaining. If the user wants to execute a rule whose condition is not satisfied, backward chaining is applied to fire other rules whose effect might satisfy the condition. The result of backward chaining is either the satisfaction of the action or a notification to the user that the command cannot be executed. If the condition is satisfied, the activity is initiated and, after it terminates, one of the rule effects is asserted. This may enable the execution of other rules causing a forward chaining.

To support process model evolution, the MARVEL system provides a tool called *evolver.* Given a change in the process model, the evolver analyzes the consistency of the change with respect to the current state. The evolver, however, requires the enactment to be suspended and proceeds "off-line".

4.9. *MERLIN*

MERLIN [19] is a software process modeling language whose main purpose is to assist its users (the software developers) by displaying all the activities that can or must be carried out at the current project status, and to provide all the necessary information to perform these activities. MERLIN supports the basic abstractions of any software process, such as roles (e.g., project manager, technical leader, programmer), activities (e.g., specify, test, compile, edit), software objects (e.g., modules, specifications, test plans), and resources (e.g., people and tools). Software processes are represented in a knowledge base by means of a rule-based technique. Rules and facts in the knowledge base may be interpreted in two ways: by backward and forward chaining. Backwards rules and facts are given in a Prolog-like notation and are interpreted in a Prolog-like manner. The backward mechanism is exploited to select the roles and the activities a user may perform. It is also used to collect information in order to answer queries on the process state. On the other hand, forward chaining is applied when explicit guidance is to be provided by the system. The rules being interpreted by forward chaining consist of a precondition, a list of activities, and a postcondition. A key feature of the knowledge base is that it is stored in an object-oriented database, and the changes occurring runtime are recorded persistently, so that process execution may be interrupted and later restarted from exactly the same point. Since rules and facts may be dynamically inserted and deleted from the knowledge base, the model exhibits a great flexibility in representing changes that occur during process enaction.

To give a flavor of MERLIN, let us consider a scenario where the roles *designer*, *programmer*, and *tester* exist. The association of people to these roles is described by facts of the form: `has_role(Role, Name)`. Figure 7 shows that when a user starts working with MERLIN, the rule `execute_job` is executed. Suppose that the user in this case has a role tester. Consequently, it will unify with "`tester`" and the `test` rule will be called. The tester selects an item from a list of items to be done. Every item in the list corresponds to one rule. Now suppose that the item `work_on_test_environment` is chosen. It is checked that the person has been assigned to test module "`Module`" in project "`Proj`" and that the testing of that module is incomplete. Then, the `do_test` rule is executed and finally the test menu is displayed again. Up to now, the described mechanism corresponds to backward chaining. The execution of `do_test` instead, is done using forward chaining, which provides an explicit guidance for the user through the possible activities. Note that, as shown

```
execute_job:-
       check_identification(Name),
       select_task(Name).
...
select_task(Name):-
       has_role(tester, Name),
       test(Name),
       display_menu(check_continuation, Item),
       test_item(Item).
select_task(Name):-
       DISPLAY(''There is nothing to do yet'').
test(Name):-
       display_menu(test, Item),
       do_item(Name, Item).
do_item(Name, work_on_test_environment):-
       is_tester(Proj, Module, Name),
       tested(Proj, Module, incomplete),
       do_test(Proj, Module),
       test(Name).
do_test(Proj, Module):-
IF     exist_test_environment(Proj, Module, incomplete)
THEN   CALL (editor, Proj, Module, Status)
       INSERT(exist_test_environment(Proj, Module, Status))
...
```

Fig. 7. MERLIN example (from [19]).

by the last rule in Fig. 7, forward chaining rules have a different syntax and provide a way to test for preconditions, perform some action, and then insert postconditions in a knowledge base.

Recent research in the MERLIN project [32, 41] has been devoted to the solution of problems that had been left unsolved in the initial versions of the environment, namely, the use of a graphical interface for the knowledge base, the introduction of structuring mechanisms for large rule sets, and the definition of mechanisms to support concurrency and parallelism in accessing the knowledge base. The user interface has been improved by displaying on the screen a working context, which reports, for a given user and depending on its role, the documents to be manipulated (represented as boxes), their dependencies to other documents (depicted as labeled arrows), and the activities to be performed on each document (to be triggered by means of context sensitive menus associated with boxes).

To facilitate the construction of large rule sets for the definition of software processes, structuring mechanisms are now being defined, based on a combination of Extended Entity Relationship (EER) diagrams and Statecharts. EER diagrams are used to specify the static part of software processes (types of documents and their attributes, the relationship types, the tools classes, and the roles), while Statecharts are used to specify the dynamic part, i.e., the allowed transitions between states and the conditions under which a transition may occur.

The process enactment engine can manage the parallel work of several developers when they access concurrently a given document through their working contexts, thus providing a support for cooperative work. To synchronize concurrent access to documents both by the user and by the process engine, a transaction mechanism is provided which avoids or solves the conflicts.

4.10. *Oikos*

Oikos is designed and developed at the University of Pisa. An enactable process model in Oikos [1, 2] consists of a hierarchy of interacting reactive entities. There are different kinds of entities (processes, offices, environments, desks, clusters, sessions, roles, service instances, and coordinators), which may be simple (leaves of the hierarchy) or structured (internal nodes of the hierarchy).

In order to specify a process model and describe its entities, Oikos provides two languages: a specification language, called *Limbo*, and an enactment language, called *Paté*. Actually, *Paté* is a sublanguage of *Limbo*. In *Limbo*, for example, it is possible to leave underspecified some parts of a process model. Both languages are derived from ESP (Extended Shared Prolog) [14]. ESP combines logic programming with the blackboard paradigm. In an entity, coordinators are concurrent agents connected to blackboards; each blackboard represents a shared space of facts. The behavior of coordinators is defined as a set of reaction rules (patterns), with a condition, a computation, and an action. If the condition unifies with the agent's state, these facts are deleted from the blackboard, the computation (a Prolog goal) is executed, and the facts specified in the action are added to the blackboard. When more than one condition is enabled, the system choses one nondeterministically.

The run-time system in the Oikos environment, called Expo, supports the distributed execution of *Paté* systems. In addition, Expo permits the integration of off-the-shelf tools by means of customizable shell scripts.

4.11. *PADM*

PADM (Process Analysis and Design Methodology) [11] is a comprehensive methodolgy and tool environment for the acquisition, modeling, and enactment of Software Processes, developed at the University of Manchester on top of preceding research results in Process Modeling, like the IPESE 2.5 experimental system [43], and now marketed by ICL. The distinctive feature of this approach is that the method and environment are based on two principal technologies: The Base Model (BM) specification method, a language to specify the abstract requirements of the software process using a descriptive notation whose semantics is ultimately provided in terms of a linear time temporal logic, and the ProcessWise Integrator (PWInt) and its Process Management Language (PML), evolved from the corresponding PML of IPESE 2.5, which is more devoted to the implementation of processes by means of a (process) programming language having distinct imperative features. A tool for animating the BM specifications, called the stepper, has been developed, which allows the user to generate possible evolutions of the specified process that are consistent by construction with the specified requirements, thus obtaining a form of validation of specification through their execution. Operational descriptions of processes written in PWInt/PML can be executed in a rather direct way, thus obtaining process enactment thanks to the possibility of integrating the process modeling environment with a software development environment. Execution of the PML results, among other things, in the production of entries for the agendas of the software development group members. These entries may be compared with the results of the animation of the BM process specification, thus obtaining some form of verification of consistency among the specification and its implementation. Although the idea of separating a descriptive specification part of the process model from an operational implementation part with the purpose of supporting specification validation and verification of implementation wrt specification is certainly interesting and useful, it seems that the support provided by the PADM environment is still rather limited and needs some extension and improvement to become effective in practice.

4.12. *SMART*

The SMART approach [22] to process modeling combines an object-oriented knowledge-based formalism and an imperative-style programming language. Processes are initially modeled using Articulator [37], an object-oriented knowledge representation scheme for process modeling. This formal model is used for analysis purposes and, in particular, for simulation. In order to enact process models, it is necessary to transform them into an imperative-style programming language. This transformation is partially done automatically, by generating process templates, which are then completed by the process engineer. Process templates are written in an extended Bourne shell script language. This language is understood by SynerVision, an HP product that supports the process model execution within SMART.

Articulator provides a meta-model, stored in a knowledge-base, which defines a web of resources and situations to describe software processes. The web consists of clusters of attributed objects and relations linking them. Each of the objects is defined as an instance of a class. Classes are divided into subclasses in an object-oriented fashion. Examples of predefined concepts in the Articulator meta-model include more than 500 objects classes and more than 2000 relations. The top abstraction level consists of resources, agents, and tasks.

A very simple example is presented in Fig. 8. The example provides the specification of two objects, representing two persons (`Mary` and `Joe`) both belonging to `Team-A`, and the assignment of task `Architecture-design` to `Mary`. Tasks are defined as a hierarchy of task decompositions (not shown here). The leaves of this hierarchy are actions, which are basic processing units, linked to some procedural specification.

In brief, SMART covers the different stages of the software life-cycle by combining the modeling features of Articulator and the execution capabilities of SynerVision. Moreover, modifications to the process that occur during enactment are automatically captured by the system and used as feedback to improve future process models. Process model evolution, however, is done "off-line".

4.13. *SPADE*

SPADE [4, 5] is a PSEE developed at Politecnico di Milano and CEFRIEL. SPADE goals are to support Software Process Analysis, Design, and Enact-

```
(define-object Mary
      (is-a PEOPLE)
      (individual-in-collective-agent Team-A))

(define-object Joe
      (is-a PEOPLE)
      (individual-in-collective-agent Team-A))

(define-object Architecture-design
      (is-a TASK-CHAIN)
      (task-force-assigned-to-agent Mary))
```

Fig. 8. A part of an Articulator process model, within the SMART approach.

ment. Process models in SPADE are specified using SLANG (Spade LANGuage), which is a process modeling language based on an extension of a high-level Petri net formalism, called ER nets [24].

A SLANG process specification is composed of a set of activities. An activity encapsulates a set of logically related process operations and may include invocations to other activities. Tokens in the net may be arbitrarily complex object structures that model documents, tools, resources, data, programs, plans, etc. Places are viewed as distributed persistent object containers. Places are typed and every place may contain only tokens of its associated type. Transition firings represent the occurrence of events. The net topology describes precedence relations among events; it also describes parallelism and conflict situations. Each transition is associated with a *guard* and an *action.* The guard is a condition on the transition input places, that indicates whether the event may occur in a given state. The action represents the reaction to the event. An activity definition has an interface part and an implementation part. The activity interface includes a set of *starting transitions* and a set of *ending transitions*, that represent respectively the starting and ending events of the activity.

Tools are integrated in the environment and their invocation can be described in the process model. SLANG provides a special kind of transitions and places, called respectively, *black transitions* and *user interface places*, to manage interaction with tools in the user environment. A black transition represents the execution of any external tool (i.e., the C compiler `cc`, or a tool service request such as `openfile` for a text editor). The notification to the process enactment environment of relevant events that occur in the external environment, generated by users or by tools, are accomplished in SLANG through *user interface places* — depicted with a double circle. These events are communicated to the process enactment environment by "translating" them into tokens that are stored in appropriate user interface places. Based on these features, the semantics of the interaction among tools and human beings can be described in SLANG, as part of the process model.

Figure 9 presents the SLANG specification of an activity to modify a program unit. The part inside the dashed box corresponds to the activity implementation, while external places and transitions represent the activity interface. The description of the activity is completed by a textual part (not shown here) with guard and action specifications. The activity shows an edit-save-compile cycle that is terminated when no compilation errors are obtained. At that point the file being edited is closed and the activity finishes.

The SPADE environment provides multiuser support and exploits parallelism among activities by associating different activities with different concurrent process engines, i.e., instances of the SLANG interpreter. These process engines may be distributed over a net of workstations. In order to support process evolution, SLANG provides reflective features (e.g., activities and types can be manipulated as any other data). This allows us to manage process model modifications "on the fly", by specifying the meta-process as part of the process.

4.14. *PROCESS WEAVER*

PROCESS WEAVER [21] is one of the few examples of industrially engineered and commercially available tools that provide a support to process modeling and enactment. It was developed by Cap Gemini, and runs on UNIX-based environment and may operate on a network of UNIX servers and PC workstations, with a graphical interface built on top of OSF Motif.

Process modeling is performed in terms of a static hierarchical decomposition of activities coupled with a description of procedures to be applied at each activity. In the hierarchical decomposition of activities, the activities at any level of granularity are described by including information on input and output artifacts of the activity and roles of people involved in its performance. The procedures to be applied at the activities are described in terms of high-level Petri nets where transitions represent elementary operations and include a condition part specifying the circumstances in which the transition

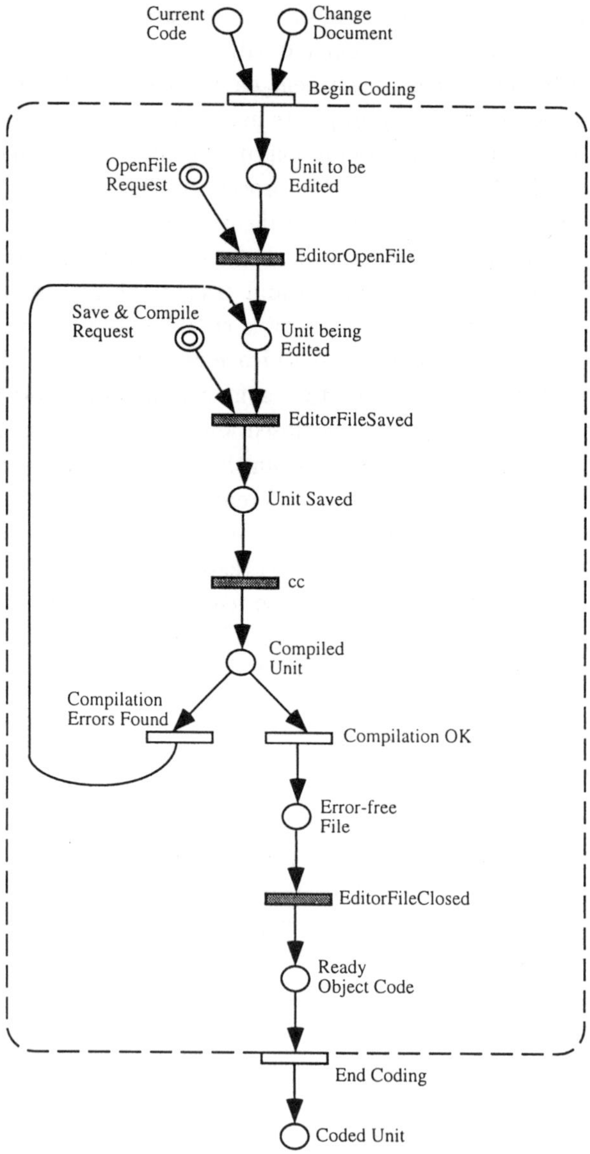

Fig. 9. An example of a SLANG activity.

may be activated, and an action part describing the concrete operations that correspond to the transition.

Process enactment is basically obtained through the execution of high-level Petri nets: Transition activation eventually results in tools being executed or people performing manual or intellectual activities, these operations being performed in a cooperative fashion according to the information attached to the hierarchical decomposition of activities. The PROCESS WEAVER environment also provides support for communication among members of the project group and for the coordinated management of agendas.

5. Open Issues and Conclusions

The immaturity of the process modeling field is still manifest in the high level of semantic ambiguity and in the lack of consolidation in software representation languages. It is a young area with many open issues, especially in the following areas:

- representation of interaction with humans;
- mechanisms to manage failures and unforeseen events;
- mechanisms to guarantee that the modification of the process "on the fly" is done in a disciplined and controlled way;
- integration between process modeling and process management (planning, monitoring, etc.);
- integration between process and data modeling (software engineering databases, long transactions, etc.).

In the introduction of this paper we said that no existing paradigm seems to be expressive enough to adequately model all the aspects of a software process. To tackle this problem, most of the languages have indeed adopted a multiparadigm approach. The expressive power provided by the different languages in order to describe software processes has been demonstrated so far on several case studies (e.g., in the context of the exercises proposed by the *International Software Process Workshops*). These case studies have also been the source of inspiration for many of the extensions that have been incorporated in the various language proposals. Since most of the existing languages are still evolving, both the syntax and the semantics are seldom defined in a precise (let alone formal) way. This makes comparisons and evaluations difficult and not based on firm grounds. Eventually, when the languages are consolidated, a formal definition shall be given. Otherwise, we will end up with notations lacking precise meaning.

Languages based on Petri nets are able to model parallelism and nondeterminism naturally and explicitly. This is not true for rule-based languages, where the execution control is implicit. On the other hand, in a rule-based system, the dynamic modification of the process is dealt with in a more natural and homogeneous way.

Presently, no software process language provides a satisfactory solution for all of the required features, especially for the distinctive features for process models. Much experimentation and research are needed before the required language features will be identified.

References

1. V. Ambriola and C. Montangero, "Modeling the software development process", *Advances in Software Engineering and Knowledge Engineering*, eds. V. Ambriola and G. Tortora (World Scientific, 1993).
2. V. Ambriola and C. Montangero, "Hierarchical specification of software processes", *Proc. 1st European Workshop Software Process Modeling*, Milan, Italy (May 1991).
3. R. Balzer, "What we do and don't know about software processes", *CQS European Observatory on Software Engineering: CASE and Software Quality*, Milan, Italy (October 1990).
4. S. Bandinelli and A. Fuggetta, "Computational reflection in software process modeling: the SLANG approach", *Proc. 15th. Int. Conf. Software Engineering*, Baltimore, Maryland, USA (May 1993).
5. S. Bandinelli, A. Fuggetta, and C. Ghezzi, "Process model evolution in the SPADE environment", *IEEE Trans. Softw. Eng.* **19**, 12 (1993).
6. N. Barghuti and G. Kaiser, "Concurrency control in advanced database applications", *ACM Comput. Surv.* **23**, 3 (1991).
7. N. Barghuti and G. Kaiser, "Scaling up rule-based software development environments", *Proc. 3rd European Software Engineering Conf., ESEC '91* Milan, Italy (October 1991).
8. N. Belkhatir, J. Estublier, and W. Melo, "Adele 2: an approach to software development coordination", *Proc. 1st European Workshop Software Process Modeling*, Milan, Italy (May 1991).
9. N. Belkatir, J. Estublier, and W. L. Melo, "Adele-TEMPO: an environment to support process modelling and enaction", in *Software Process Modelling and Technology*, eds. A. Finkelstein, J. Kramer, and B. Nuseibeh (Research Studies Press Ltd., 1994).

10. N. Belkatir and W. L. Melo, "TEMPO: a software process model based of object context behavior", *Proc. 5th Int. Conf. Software Engineering and its Applications*, Toulouse, France (December 1992).
11. R. F. Bruynooghe, R. M. Greenwood, I. Robertson, J. Sa, and B. C. Warboys, "PADM: towards a total process modelling system", in *Software Process Modelling and Technology*, eds. A. Finkelstein, J. Kramer, and B. Nuseibeh (Research Studies Press Ltd., 1994).
12. J. R. Cameron, *JSP & JSD: The Jackson Approach to Software Development* (IEEE Computer Society Press, 1983).
13. G. Canals, N. Boudjlida, J.-C. Derniame, C. Godart, and J. Lonchamps, "ALF: a framework for building process-centred software engineering environments", in *Software Process Modelling and Technology*, eds. A. Finkelstein, J. Kramer, and B. Nuseibeh (Research Studies Press Ltd., 1994).
14. P. Ciancarini, C. Montangero, and A. Bucci "Extended Shared Prolog, Reference Manual 1.1", *Technical Report N 6/61, Progetto Finalizzato Sistemi Informatici e Calcolo Parallelo*, Dipartimento di Informatica, Università di Pisa (June, 1992).
15. R. Conradi, O. Solberg, V. Ambriola, and M. L. Jaccheri, "Software process management in EPOS", *IFIP WG2.4 Meeting* (September 1989).
16. M. Dowson, ed., "Proc. 3rd Int. Software Process Workshop", Beckenridge, Colorado, USA (November 1986).
17. W. Emmerich and V. Gruhn, "FUNSOFT nets: A Petri-net based software process modeling language", *Proc. 6th Int. Workshop Software Specification and Design*, Como, Italy (September 1991).
18. ECMA, "Portable Common Tool Environment (PCTE)", *Abstract Specification*, Standard Ecma-149 (European Computer Manufacturer Association, 1990).
19. W. Emmerich, G. Junkermann, and W. Schafer, "MERLIN: knowledge-based process modeling", *Proc. 1st European Workshop Software Process Modeling*, Milan, Italy (May 1991).
20. C. Fernström, "The Eureka software factory: concepts and accomplishments", *Proc. 3rd European Software Engineering Conf., ESEC '91*, Milan, Italy (October 1991).
21. C. Fernström "PROCESS WEAVER: adding process support to UNIX", *Proc. 2nd Int. Conf. Software Process*, Berlin, Germany (February 1993).
22. P. K. Garg, P. Mi, T. Pham, W. Scacchi, and G. Thunquest, "The SMART approach to software process engineering", *Proc. 16th Int. Conf. Software Engineering*, Sorrento, Italy (May 1994).
23. H. J. Genrich, "Predicate transition nets", *Advances in Petri Nets 1986*, LNCS 245-255 (Springer Verlag, 1987).
24. C. Ghezzi, D. Mandrioli, S. Morasca, and M. Pezzé, "A unified high-level petri net formalism for time-critical systems", *IEEE Trans. Software Engineering* (February 1991).
25. V. Gruhn, "Validation and verification of software process models", *Proc. European Symp. Software Development and CASE Technology*, Germany, (Springer-Verlag, 1991) LNCS 509.

26. V. Gruhn, "The software process management environment MELMAC", *Proc. 1st European Workshop Software Process Modeling*, Milan, Italy (May 1991).
27. D. Harel, H. Lachover, A. Naamad, A. Pnueli, M. Politi, R. Sherman, and A. Shtul-Trauring, "Statemate: a working environment for the development of complex reactive systems", *Proc. 10th Int. Conf. Software Engineering*, Singapore (1988).
28. W. Humphrey, *Managing the Software Process, SEI Series in Software Engineering* (Addison-Wesley, 1989).
29. W. Humphrey and M. Kellner, "Software process modeling: principles of entity process models", *Proc. 11th Int. Conf. Software Engineering* (1989).
30. M. L. Jaccheri and R. Conradi, "Techniques for process model evolution in EPOS", *IEEE Trans. Softw. Eng.* **19**, 12 (1993).
31. M. L. Jaccheri, J. Larsen, and R. Conradi, "Software process modeling and evolution in EPOS", *Proc. 4th Int. Conf. Knowledge Engineering and Software Engineering*, Capri, Italy (June 1992).
32. G. Junkermann, B. Peuschel, W. Schäfer, and S. Wolf, "MERLIN: supporting cooperation in software development through a knowledge-based environment", in *Software Process Modelling and Technology*, eds. A. Finkelstein, J. Kramer, and B. Nuseibeh (Research Studies Press Ltd., 1994).
33. T. Katayama, "A hierarchical and functional software process description and its enaction", *Proc. 11th Int. Conf. Software Engineering*, Pittsburgh, USA (1989).
34. M. I. Kellner, "Software process modeling support for management planning and control", *Proc. 1st Int. Conf. Software Process*, Redondo Beach, California, USA (October 1991).
35. C. Liu and R. Conradi, "Process modeling paradigms: an evaluation", *Proc. 1st European Workshop on Software Process Modeling*, Milan, Italy (May 1991).
36. "Marvel 3.0 administrator's manual", Technical Report, Department of Computer Science, Columbia University (October 1991).
37. P. Mi and W. Scacchi, "A knowledge-based environment for modeling and simulating software engineering processes", *IEEE Trans. Knowl. and Data Eng.* **2**, 3 (1990).
38. F. Oquendo, J. Zucker, and P. Griffiths, "The MASP approach to software process description instantiation and enaction", *Proc. 1st European Workshop Software Process Modeling*, Milan, Italy (May 1991).
39. L. Osterweil, "Software processes are software too", *Proc. 9th Int. Conf. Software Engineering* (1987).
40. D. E. Perry, ed., *Proc. 5th Int. Software Process Workshop*, Kennebunkport, Maine, USA (September 1989).
41. B. Peuschel, W. Schafer, and S. Wolf, "A knowledge-based software development environment supporting cooperative work", *Int. J. Softw. Eng. Knowl. Eng.* **2**, 1 (1992) 79–106.
42. D. Rombach, "A framework for assessing process representations", Internal Report University of Maryland (1990).

43. R. A. Snowdown, "An introduction to the IPESE 2.5 Project", *ICL Tech. J.* **6**, 3 (1989) 467–478.
44. S. Sutton, D. Heimbigner, and L. Osterweil, "Language constructs for managing change in process-centered environments", *Proc. 4th ACM SIGSOFT Symp. on Software Development Environments*, Irvine, California, USA (December 1990).
45. M. Suzuki, A. Iwai, and T. Katayama, "A formal model of re-execution in software process", *Proc. 2nd Int. Conf. Software Process*, Berlin, Germany (February 1993).
46. T. Taylor, F. Belz, L. Clarke, L. Osterweil, R. Selby, J. Wilden, A. Wolf, and M. Young, "Foundations for the Arcadia environment architecture", *Proc. ACM/SIGSOFT/SIGPLAN Software Engineering Symp. Practical Software Development Environments* ACM (November 1988).
47. C. J. Tully, ed., *Proc. 4th Int. Software Process Workshop*, Moretonhampstead, Devon, UK (May 1988).

META-ENVIRONMENTS FOR SOFTWARE PRODUCTION

ANTHONY S. KARRER
Computer Science Department, Loyola-Marymount University,
Los Angeles, CA 90045-2699, USA

WALT SCACCHI
Information and Operations Management Department,
and Center for Software Engineering, University of Southern California,
Los Angeles, CA 90089-1421, USA

Researchers who create software production environments face considerable problems. Software production environments are large systems that are costly to develop. Furthermore, software production environments which support particular software engineering methods may not be applicable to a large number of software production projects. These conditions have formed a trend towards research into ways which will lessen the cost of developing software production environments. In particular, the trend has been towards the construction of meta-environments from which specific software production environments can be created. In this paper, we attempt to categorize more than 60 meta-environment efforts. For each of the categories, we review research efforts which illustrate different approaches within that category. We conclude by presenting an emerging common thread of requirements which links this field together.

1. Introduction

Software engineering addresses the complex problems associated with software production. Many software engineering methods, such as structured design and object-oriented analysis, have emerged to ease these problems. Recently, there has been considerable attention paid to the application of these methods through software production environments in order to evaluate the effectiveness of each method [11, 44, 67]. A *software production environment* (SPE) is a system consisting of a software infrastructure providing a common operating environment for software tools, a set of tools, and an interface which provides users with access to the environment's capabilities.

Both software production organizations and research organizations have found that there are considerable problems in using SPE technology. One underlying problem is that software production environments are large systems and, without sufficient support, are costly to engineer and build. This result is not surprising, especially given that software production environments are large software products. Coupled with this problem, researchers have found that little is known about the requirements for a good SPE. Many researchers believe that the only way in which the requirements can be found is by developing, using, and evolving environments. Unfortunately, such an evolutionary approach will be costly because of the time and effort required for creating new SPEs, and because as better SPEs are developed, users are likely to change the manner in which they use the SPE [67]. Worse yet, each software production project may have different requirements for an SPE [14]. These factors imply that in order to research the requirements for SPEs and to support the requirements of individual projects we must reduce the cost of creating SPEs.

Because SPEs are themselves software products, we can consider the software production process used to construct SPEs. SPE construction processes have taken many forms, with early SPEs being constructed using a simple program-debug-test process based on a single programming language. *Meta-environments* [53, 55, 80] are emerging as a means of constructing SPEs with significantly more powerful constructs than are generally available in programming languages. Meta-environments have also been called generic environments [37] and environment generators [27, 32, 95]. The distinction between these terms is somewhat vague. As such, we will use the term *meta-environment* to include generic environments, environment generators, and other approaches to environment construction.

We find a meta-environment consists of a *construction model*, a *transformation* of instances of the model into an SPE, and a *process* for using the construction model and transformation to create an SPE. An *environment specification* is an instantiated construction model which specifies the intended environment. A *meta-environment construction process* is the collection of tasks, agent roles, resources, tools, and their relationships which specifies the procedures used to create viable software production environments.

In general, meta-environments are designed to overcome two major issues. The first issue is that SPEs are themselves large software systems and are extremely costly to create without the support provided by meta-environments. The second issue is that a high level of assistance in reducing the cost of environment creation often requires assumptions about the form of the resulting environment. These assumptions reduce the ability of a meta-environment to support many different kinds of software engineering methods.

In the rest of this paper, we examine the trend for creating meta-environments. First, we attempt to categorize current meta-environment approaches. For each of the categories, we review research efforts which illustrate different approaches within that category. We conclude by presenting the common thread which links this field together.

2. Related Research

Software engineering environments were initially constructed as monolithic systems, using a programming language as the construction model. Two of the more notable examples of this approach are the programming support environments for Smalltalk [38] and Interlisp [88]. Both environments support a single method of software production: interpretive, incremental program development. While the monolithic approach can be applied to construct environments which support virtually any software production method and programming language, the cost of producing an environment using this approach is generally prohibitive for most research organizations.

Since the monolithic approach, a variety of methods have been suggested for lessening the cost of construction and improving the utility of environments. We have categorized the approaches to environment construction into the following five classes:

- *Environment frameworks* support a set of low-level services including object management, control management and sometimes user-interface management.
- *Customizable environments* provide high-level core environment capabilities and a means of customizing those capabilities.
- *Process modeling* provides a meta-model which can be instantiated to specify the activities, developers, resources, artifacts, and their relationships which together form the processes of the environment.
- *Process programming* provides a programming language oriented towards the description of processes as the basis of constructing process-driven environments.
- *Tool integration* provides the means to combine tools into an integrated set of environment capabilities.

In the following sections, we further define each of these categories. We also present several research efforts in each category which serve both to give further insight into the basic category and also to illustrate the main issues which separate researchers within a category. Most research efforts in meta-environments actually combine technology from more than one category. For example, many environment frameworks provide support for tool integration. Nonetheless, we have categorized and presented these efforts in order to illustrate the meta-environment trend as a whole.

2.1. *Environment frameworks*

One of the recent trends in the commercial and government sectors has been the development of environment frameworks which provide a set of computational services as a basis for environment construction. As a starting point for a survey of this research, it is a good idea to mention that considerable attention is being directed to the definition of the kinds of services which environment frameworks should address. Much of this work has been done by creating reference models including the Conceptual Environment Architecture Reference Model (CEARM) [70], the ECMA Reference Model [26], and the NIST Reference Model [94]. Karrer and Penedo [48] used one of these reference models to survey current environment framework research. This survey showed the usefulness of a reference model as a conceptual framework for comparing the capabilities of frameworks. Much of this section is derived from that study.

These reference models suggest that frameworks should address Object Management Services, User-Interface Management Services, and Life-cycle Process Management Services (also called Environment Management [70] and Task Management [26]). The Object Management Services (OMS) provide for persistent objects and relationships as opposed to files and directories traditionally supported by operating systems. The Life-Cycle Process Management Services (LCPMS) provide a means for enacting change upon the current state of life-cycle objects. Most LCPMS are based on the operating system process. However, the LCPMS combines operating system processes with additional modeling services to provide a more powerful control mechanism. The User-Interface Management Services (UIMS) provide basic mechanisms for defining user-interfaces and associating objects graphically depicted with objects and actions within the environment.

These reference models suggest that environment frameworks must provide construction models for modeling data, control, and user-interface. While other meta-environment approaches require, for example, some kind of translation of a language or environment specification into an environment, a similar transformation of the framework's models is not needed since the framework models are used as the architectural basis of the environment. The examples that we present next show a variety of data and control models.

Atherton Technology's Software BackPlane [68] is an integration and portability framework designed to assist in building SPEs independent of tools, methodology, or languages. It provides a generic operating system, an object-oriented OMS and a Macintosh-like user interface. The Software BackPlane's OMS provides an object-oriented software interface and a set of predefined classes which give the database its form. The OMS uses the concept of Generic Messages to invoke methods for new/free, open/close, checkin/checkout, and others which are applicable to virtually all objects. This approach allows users to invoke similar tools using identical messages.

Some tool integration is addressed through the object-oriented integration techniques for defining new classes or attaching existing tools to previously defined classes as methods. Tools created without using the Software BackPlane as its persistence mechanism store their data using the native operating system. Translation of their data and rehosting to the Software BackPlane can be accomplished by creating a method which does both a translation from a file into a set of objects and tool invocation over those objects.

Atherton has also provided a high-level specification of an environment construction process called the "Environment Customization Plan". This process suggests the creation of user-defined methods as a form of process programming, tool definition, data definition, and user/role definition.

Gaia [90] embodies an approach similar to the Software Backplane by providing an object-oriented OMS as its cornerstone. It lacks some of the integration techniques present in the Software Backplane. It also lacks a plan for using object-oriented technology to instantiate an environment.

CAIS-A [4, 60, 71], the latest version of CAIS, is defined in the military standard report MIL-STD-1838A, under the control of the Ada Joint Program Office (AJPO) within the U.S. Department of Defense. CAIS-A is a set of Ada interfaces which are designed to act like a high-level virtual operating system. It provides an object management system (OMS) and process control based on the OMS. The OMS is a distributed database providing a node model which is similar in flavor to an entity-relationship-attribute (ERA) model with type inheritance. The node model is used to formalize the structures and capabilities of the OMS. Processes in CAIS-A form a tree of parent-child processes. All process information is kept in the OMS. Processes can communicate through special OMS-based queues.

The Portable Common Tool Environment (PCTE) [89] is a Public Tool Interface (PTI) which can be used as a basis for integrating tools as part of the development of an SPE. The PCTE PTI consists of software interfaces to services of an OMS, LCPMS, and UIMS. The Object Management System is a distributed database based on an ERA model with multiple type inheritance. The object types are modeled by a single overall schema which is actually comprised of a set of possibly overlapping Schema Definition Sets (SDS). PCTE models the static context of processes which are used to control process invocation. Inter-process communication is achieved through the OMS, message queues, pipes and signals. Monitoring of process execution is also available. PCTE has defined a set of user-interface management primitives, as well as extensions to support production of real-time software through the PCTE+ and PACT versions of PCTE.

The Sun Network Software Environment (NSE) [5] is a network-based object manager and tool integration facility. NSE is primarily a Unix environment with additional support for object management, configuration management, version management, distribution, environment management, target generation, and environment front-ends. The object manager is oriented around a specific view of version and configuration control based on an optimistic concurrency control mechanism. Tools are integrated into NSE by using NSE to control their objects (files) and by adding the tools to the NSE environment front-end. More recently, an object-based tool integration facility called ToolTalk has been introduced to support this capability

The NSE object manager is not a general purpose object manager in the same vein as PCTE, CAIS, and the Software BackPlane. It provides no extensibility of the base classes. It does support an extension to Unix process management by allowing triggers associated with NSE commands to perform some of the environment tasks.

The Software Life-Cycle Support Environment (SLCSE) [84] is a framework which provides a common database, a set of common schemata, and tools. The common schemata and tools are designed to support a MIL-STD 2167A model for documenting the software production life-cycle. The 2167A model is based on the waterfall model of software production based primarily on the production of documents after each step in the life-cycle. The SLCSE framework also supports specification of alternative schemata and alternate life-cycles.

RDPE3 [65] is a programming environment which is primarily oriented around the support of adaptation and extension of environments. RDPE3 uses an extended object-oriented, fine-grained programming paradigm to represent program fragments. Thus, RDPE3 focuses on a smaller component size as compared to PCTE, CAIS-A, etc. Furthermore, RDPE3 suggests a different integration scheme than those suggested by other frameworks, one in which the function of the integrated components must be accessible.

The ALMA [55] generic environment provides the capability to define a life-cycle support database schema based on the entity-relationship model. While the ALMA environment has capabilities similar to other frameworks, it specifically presents a plan for the use of the framework as both a meta-environment and a software production environment.

The Distributed System Factory (DSF) project is developing a multilayer infrastructure of software services which can integrate multiple data, control, presentation, and process models that can span a distributed wide-area network [77]. The DSF infrastructure provides a distributed hypertext (DHT) framework to integrate heterogeneous software object repositories (e.g., those with different data models) [63] with forward and reverse software engineering tools [20], graph-based editors and user interfaces [49], process-driven user interfaces with partially order tool invocation sequences [59], and a knowledge-based process modeling and simulation environment [58]. Using these mechanisms and components, it is possible to semi-automatically generate multirole, process-driven software production environments for a hierarchy of concurrent production processes [32, 59].

The EUREKA Software Factory (ESF) [3] is a large-scale pan-European research effort aiming at the development of an integration framework for a meta-environment that can accommodate the interoperation of various tools and the interactions of people working together with these tools according to a process meta-model [6]. The heart of the ESF architecture is a Software Bus (SWB), which is an abstract communication channel hiding distribution and supporting the exchange of data and control information using abstract data type interfaces. User-interaction components (UIC) and service components (SC) communicate across the SWB. UIC, which have no persistent data, communicate with the user and make requests on service components across the SWB.

SC may not have a user-interface. One UIC and one SC taken together are essentially a tool in current environments.

The ESF kernel, K/2r [6], is not tied to the use of a central OMS as the basis of integration. Rather, the ESF project uses process models as the basis of tool integration, although different schemes [22, 31] and modeling formalisms [24, 29] are being investigated. In this way, the ESF and DSF projects share many common goals, although their approaches differ.

Each of these environment frameworks provides services which are needed in virtually all software production environments. Access to an implementation of these services assists environment construction. In general, environment frameworks are intended to maintain independence from any particular software production method. While environment frameworks provide some support to environment construction, the services they provide are generally low-level functions. There is a considerable gap between these services and the services provided by a full software production environment.

Existing environment frameworks seem to be split on the kind of data and control models to provide. The object-oriented camp with Atherton and Gaia suggest a single model for both data and control. The extended ERA camp with PCTE, CAIS-A, SLCSE, ALMA, DSF-DHT, and ESF-K/2r suggest a data model based on the ER or object-based model, and a control model based on concepts which are similar to operating system processes.

2.2. *Customizable environments*

Customizable environments are based on the existence of a high-level, fixed core of services or capabilities. Different customizable environments will provide different methods of customization and different core capabilities. The construction method provided by a customizable environment allows the user to specify a set of extensions or changes to the core capabilities. This specification is then combined with the core capabilities to form an environment. This approach is very similar to the approach used in most tool generators, such as those used for parser generators [92], language-directed editor generators [20, 64, 76], or extensible graph editors [47, 69, 79].

Customizable environments differ from frameworks in that they trade ease of instantiation for less generality. In other words, customizable environments will support a model which can be used to describe only a small portion of the entire environment. The remainder of the environment is fixed by assumptions built into the customizable environment. In particular, customizable environments will fix the process supported by the environment, but will allow particular parts of the process to be subsequently modified.

Several researchers have developed customizable environments centered around the use of structured editors. These customizable environments provide a construction model which can be used to describe the grammars for the languages which will be manipulated in the environment. The fixed part of the environment is the process of using a series of editors. For example, the Mentor programming environment [25] is founded on an abstract syntax tree representation of the program as the common information base. This syntax tree can be annotated by means of other abstract syntax trees in specialized languages. By allowing arbitrary annotations of nodes in the syntax tree, Mentor allows the extension of the environment.

GANDALF [64], the Synthesizer Generator [76], and SOFTMAN [20] provide customizable structure/text editors which allow an environment to be constructed as a suite of tightly integrated editors. Editors are customized through the specification of (a) the grammars of the languages which they edit, and (b) the attributes or action routines which support incremental semantic checking. GANDALF also provides for the specification of commands which invoke external tools integrated around centralized parse tree representations, while SOFTMAN provides for the integration of generated multilanguage editors with an OMS.

TRIAD [51] is a customizable environment which supports a set of form-based, methodology-driven tools designed to operate over an extendible attribute grammar. This grammar is used to encode process information as well as syntax information. The grammar is used by TRIAD to construct various portions of the environment including a syntax-directed editor.

DRACO [62], Popart [92], GEM [39], KIDS [78], and Centaur [53] are generators of grammar-based or notation-based meta-programming environments. A meta-programming environment is an environment which assists in the creation of parsers and related tools which manipulate a particular language. Each generator accepts the specification of a language, then assembles a library of routines which can be used to operate over a parse tree or similar internal form of a program in the manipulated language. DRACO, Popart, KIDS, and Centaur are designed to support the development of domain language definitions using either (a) patterns, transformations, rules, or annotations for DRACO, Popart, and KIDS, or (b) algebraic and syntactic specification formalisms for Centaur. In addition, Popart is used in conjunction with Common Lisp Framework [8] and a generic process engine developed at USC/ISI [9], which accomodates the generation of rule-based programming and transformational implementation environments. The DRACO and KIDS environments provide similar capabilities, although they lack integration with a process engine. However, DRACO also supports the integration and composition of reusable components or tools, as described later.

Another approach to customizable environments is to provide a model which supports the specification of the objects to be manipulated during a software life-cycle process. The SOFTMAN environment [20] provides core capabilities which enforce a particular model of incremental software development and verification across life-cycle activity boundaries. It allows customization based on the specification of the formal attributes of life-cycle objects and specification of tools which operate on these objects. Thus, the specification refers to objects beyond those directly tied to the programming language. However, the primary tools in a SOFTMAN environment are customizable structure editors interfaced to a constraint-based OMS. The combination of the tools and the object repository can then track and verify the correctness attributes of objects that have been created or modified [18].

ISHYS [35] provides an interface to a hypertext-based information storage structure and to a structured documentation process. ISHYS supports the specification of the type, attributes, and composition of hypertext-based life-cycle documents based on the DIF software hypertext system [34]. It also supports the specification of a process model which describes the production and use of the documents by collaborating agents. The document formats and process model support multiple forms of group-based or team-based interaction and communication structures within a project and support multiple simultaneous projects.

META/GA [95] is a Life-Cycle Support System generator based on the specification of the format of information which must be processed in the generated environment. META/GA-generated environments support a specific life-cycle approach to the creation of information processing systems. However, the META/GA user, the environment constructor, is able to specify the type of information which will be processed. This customizable environment attempts to help standardize the type of information and leave the life-cycle as general as possible.

The Metaview project [15, 82] takes an approach that is a hybrid of framework approaches and customizable environments. The models provided are based on an ERA model extended with constraints, transformations, and a graphical interaction model. These models are used to describe the data manipulated by the environment as a whole and by generic tools. So both the environment framework as well as tools which operate over the environment are specified using this model.

There is growing interest in developing structure- or language-based editors for manipulating graph-based or graphic software specification notations. EDGE [69], TGE [49], MetaEdit [79], VSF [44, 72], and GEDL [47] are recent examples. In contrast to structured-text editors and related functionality generated by GANDALF or Synthesizer Generator, these graphic meta-editors provide multiple layouts of graphic information [47, 69], allow the specification or redefinition of user interface functionality [49, 47], and support a variety of object modeling, software process [49, 47] and method notations [44, 72, 79]. Each meta-editor employs a language-based specification notation for describing the iconic syntax and composition semantics to be supported in the target editors that are generated or instantiated. Finally, TGE, VSF, and GEDL have specification-level interfaces which allow them or their derived editors to be integrated with one or more repositories and environments, such as SOFTMAN's use of TGE-based graph editors [20, 77]. Subsequently, this provides another dimension for the extension of resulting meta-environments.

Overall, the primary advantage of customizable environments is the speed and relative ease of constructing high functionality environments. However, most customizable environments have lessened the burden of environment construction by adopting a particular approach to software development. This means that a customizable environment may only support certain kinds of software processes or development methods. Environments centered or driven by software production process models thus represent an alternative to this situation.

2.3. *Process Modeling*

In environments based on process models, a software process meta-model is used to circumscribe the family of processes the environment supports. Thus, a process model-based construction method must provide a *process meta-model* as the basis of implementing a specific life-cycle model. Instances of a meta-model describe active and inactive objects in an environment. Further, an instance of a meta-model allows the execution of a process-centered environment.

The GENESIS (from UC Berkeley) [73], Marvel [46], and Merlin [29] environments are among those that provide production rules and rule interpreters as the means for specifying and enacting software processes. A production rule has (1) a precondition, (2) an action part which is executed when the precondition is true, and possibly (3) a postcondition which becomes true once the action is executed. Environment construction using these systems consists of specifying the production rules for all of the activities or events which the environment should support.

PRISM [56], IPSE 2.5 [91], and its successor, PSS [16], provide process meta-models similar to Marvel and GENESIS. However, these efforts suggest a particular execution of the process models, which provides the environment to the user. In these environments, a process model execution facility serves as the means of invoking tools and presenting choices to environment users.

MELMAC [24] is a software process management environment based on the execution of high-level Petri-net representations of software process models [28]. The MELMAC research effort has led to the development of a prototype capable of enacting a software process model on top of a framework similar to the ones described in Subsec. 2.1. A major part of this prototype is the graphical user-interface, which depicts the Petri-nets and allows both the specification of process models and the enaction of process models.

The Software Designer's Associate (SDA) project [52] is a software design environment in which the executable process descriptions are specified as a process model consisting of activities, composite activities, products and tools. SDA is unique in that it only addresses the early phase of design and that it uses a model-based approach to the design and construction of an environment.

The DSF project has been developing and using the Articulator [57], which is a knowledge-based environment for modeling, analyzing, and simulating software production processes. The Articulator uses a hierarchical object-oriented representation of agent roles, products (or resources), and tasks, which can be either partially ordered or triggered through rule-based mechanisms. Modeled agents communicate process task status and resource availability to one another through queries and messages. These queries can entail direct or deductive retrieval of process enactment information, or trigger either the symbolic execution of new processes or replay processes already enacted. Multiple concurrent processes can be enacted and agents can interact across processes. In addition, the environment maintains persistent information about the state of enacted processes as process transitions occur. This information is used to track the execution history of planned activities, and to facilitate incremental process rescheduling and replanning when unplanned or dynamic changes in the process occur [58].

The Articulator has been integrated with a process-based user interface and a process model interpreter (together called PBI) to provide a framework for developing process model-driven environments [59]. The Articulator, PBI, and an open software environment or set of software tools can the be used to construct and instantiate process-driven software production environments. That is, process models created with the Articulator are automatically transformed into process programs that can be enacted by PBI's process interpreter. When the process models specify tool bindings to process pre- or postconditions, data objects, and object repositories, then process-driven software environments can be automatically produced. In one study [59], the SOFTMAN environment [20] was used as the base environment, and a software life-cycle process model that guides a user in their invocation of SOFTMAN tools was developed using the Articulator. The SOFTMAN process model was then transformed and loaded into the PBI process interpreter. This interpreter drives the process-based user interface by structuring access to which SOFTMAN tools can be invoked on the designated objects. This in turn depends on the development process history and process enactment status at that time. In order to do this, the pre-existing top-level user interface for SOFTMAN had to be disabled and redirected to the new process interface, while the tool-specific interfaces and object repository for SOFTMAN remained intact and unmodified. With the new PBI interface, a user is presented with a visual representation of the development process currently assigned to them. Users can then select the next process task or action to perform. In this way, we can say that a *process integration* interpreter and user interface enable knowledge-based process models to guide user invocation of tools within a software production environment, such as PBI-SOFTMAN [59].

The Articulator has also been integrated with the Matisse team programming environment [33] and the SynerVision process execution engine [43] in place of PBI. The resulting composite environment is called SMART [32]. SMART supports the modeling, analysis, enactment, measurement, and improvement of software processes utilizing encapsulated CASE tools that communicate messages and tool invocations across the SoftBench BMS [17], and that manipulate data stored in networked repositories. Since SMART can configure commercially available CASE tools, and as most Unix-based CASE tools have SoftBench encapsulations, then the number and configuration of process-based CASE environments that can be generated using SMART is very large. Finally, the Articulator has similarly been integrated with the generic process engine developed at USC/ISI [9], which supports the refinement of generic process descriptions into concrete instantiations during its enactment. Thus, the Articulator environment successfully demonstrates the power of software process meta-models as a basis for integrating and interoperating independently developed tools within generated process-driven environments.

Last, the SPADE environment [10] is similar in scope to the Articulator in that it supports the design, analysis, and enactment of software process models. Its process representation is based on extended Petri-nets, and the environment includes functional mechanisms for accommodating dynamic changes to a process description during its enactment. However, it does not utilize a process simulation facility, nor does it include inferential mechanisms for diagnosing and repairing process faults, as does the Articulator.

2.4. *Process programming*

Process programming environments use a programming language to describe the processes that form the capabilities of the environment. The goal of process programming-based systems is to provide a highly flexible, process-oriented environment construction mechanism. Process programming differs from process modeling in the form of the meta-model provided for environment construction. However, we can view process programming as process modeling where the meta-model is a programming language.

The Arcadia Research Project [87] consists of a collection of loosely coordinated research and development projects conducted by the Arcadia Consortium. Like ESF, Arcadia could also be categorized as an environment framework, but the architecture of the Arcadia framework is centered on the capability to execute process programs. In this manner, users interact with an Arcadia-based environment by executing parts of the process. The Arcadia environment is a process-centered environment. The form of the environment which the users see is wholly determined by the processes which are executed to form the environment.

Arcadia is currently a collection of many partially integrated components including a UIMS, an OMS, an Ada-based Process Programming Language (APPL/A), a Measurement and Evaluation (M&E) system, and a Process Administration System. The UIMS is based on Chiron [50], an Ada UIMS based on a very strong separation of functionality from interaction. The OMS in Arcadia is viewed as possibly many different object managers combined through a common underlying type model where data is combined through interoperability mechanisms. Triton [42] and PGraphite [93] are two OMSs which have been used as a basis of object management in the Arcadia project. APPL/A [86] is a process programming language which consists of extensions to Ada that include the notion of persistent relations associated with the OMS. The Process Administration System is a run-time support interface for executing processes based on a corporate metaphor. This metaphor has been suggested as a basis for the specification of environment characteristics.

Environment adaptation is the primary focus of the Arcadia architecture. Data and processes can be directly defined using the software interfaces provided by the Arcadia infrastructure. Further adaptation can be built up by creating processes which act like virtual architectures. In other words, a process could be defined which would allow the specification of user-role definitions. This mechanism would not be part of the Arcadia infrastructure, but it would be part of the virtual environment created by the definition of the process which allows user-role specification.

In contrast, the Adele-2 environment [61] utilizes a special-purpose persistent database and programming language, Adele, to describe and implement enactable processes. Adele-2 provides support for multiple work environments (i.e., tool, policy, and method configurations) that are coordinated and coupled through an activity manager and a task manager. Coordination and coupling, as well as activity and task specification, are all realized using the Adele-2 language.

Process WEAVER [30] and SynerVision [43] are commercially available process execution engines. Each provides a process programming language based on the Unix shell command langugage. Their use is similar in scope to Adele-2, but they both lack support for a persistent object store, other than the underlying file system. However, the SMART environment [32] can semi-automatically generate SynerVision process program code via transformations on Articulator-based software process models [57], while Process WEAVER allows modeled process states to be attributed with Unix shell commands, which can subsequently be executed under user direction.

Last, both OIKOS [7] and OPM [85] propose object-oriented approaches to process programming. The idea in these two efforts is to show how object-oriented views of process programming and software development environments can be united into a single view in which both the process model and programming environment can be dynamically modified. Thus, object-oriented process programming seeks to provide an object-oriented process model (or meta-model), process programming language, and meta-environment framework where the environment data, control, and presentation models all share a uniform object-oriented representation and interpretation scheme.

2.5. *Tool integration*

A primary concern for environment creators is the integration of existing tools as part of the capabilities of an environment. Because tool integration provides the ability to invoke other tools, the technology described in this section is often applied in each of the previous meta-environment construction approaches. For example, a process model-based environment can be based on a special tool which is in charge of executing a process model and in turn invokes other tools. However, we have split tool integration into a separate category because a large body of efforts have a distinct model, transformation, and process from any of the previous categories. In particular, tool integration meta-environments provide a model based on an interface between a set of connected tools. The execution or use of the interface to the tools is the transformation of the model into an environment.

Basically, two paths towards easier integration have been suggested. One path is the development of standards which tools must use in order to be integrated. Some standards are merely standards of data-exchange, while others are standards which affect all data storage. The other path is to build technology which can use tools developed prior to or outside of the standards. In the remainder of this section, we will consider examples of both approaches.

2.5.1. *Standards*

A Tool Integration Standard (ATIS) [13] and its more recent name, Component Integration Standard (CIS), is a proposal for an object-oriented approach to the integration of tools that provides a set of interfaces that support schema-driven dispatching of behavior. ATIS/CIS is presented in terms of a hierarchy that specifies and interrelates abstract data types, their properties, and their methods. In other words, ATIS/CIS proposes an instance of an object-oriented model which defines a set of classes and their properties. This model is designed to provide services to tools which promote integration and make tool development easier.

The IRDS [40] is an ANSI Standard (ANSI X3.138). The IRDS standard defines a meta-model using an ERA model. Instances of the meta-model are models which describe data. IRDS allows access to schema definitions through access to instances of meta-entities. The meta-entities define the types of entities, relationships, and attributes.

The IRDS/ISO is the IRDS Rapporteur Group of the ISO/IEC JTC1/SC21 WG3 (International Standards Organization, International Electotechnical Commission Joint Technical Committee 1 / Subcommittee 21 Working Group 3). The IRDS/ISO uses a model similar to the relational model as an approach to representing data. Information is stored at two levels, the definition level and the IRD level. The definition level defines the tables and the functions which manipulate the tables. The IRD level contains the application data. This is analogous to class and instance levels of an object-oriented model.

CDIF [2] is a definition of a common data transfer format which supports many data models and the transfer of data between CASE tools or frameworks. The CDIF approach is based upon the concept of a Meta-Meta-Model. In order to describe the conceptual models for each of these domains, a model (i.e., the meta-meta-model) which can describe data models for different application domains was developed. The Meta-Meta-Model is similar in form to an Entity-Relation-Attribute (ERA) model. Various proposals for how to best implement CDIF-based data transformations, however, seem to focus on batched monolithic transformation of large data sets. In contrast, the DHT approach noted earlier also incorporates modeling formalism similar in power to a meta-meta-data model, but does not require transformation of data sets to support access to heterogeneous data repositories [63]. In addition, DHT implements a persistent hypertext-based object management service using a persistent programming language, while CDIF lacks such a service and programming language.

The P1175 reference model for interconnections between computing system tools [1] is a tool-integration standard being developed by the IEEE Computer Society's Task Force on Professional Computing Tools. The approach taken in P1175 is to define reference models for tool-to-organization and tool-to-platform interconnections, and a language for the transfer of data between tools. The tool to organization interconnection defines roles, life-cycle phases, and support elements which relate to a tool. The tool to platform interconnection describes various interconnections which must be supported by the platform and by the tools to effectively integrate the tools into the platform. These interconnections consist of the Data Base Manager, Communication Network Manager, O/S Service Manager, and the User Interface Manager interfaces.

The Object Management Group (OMG) [81] is an international organization of more than 50 information systems vendors, users, and research organizations with diverse backgrounds. The basic technical approach being followed in OMG is an object-oriented layer of services which exists above various implementations of object managers, user-interface facilities, and environment managers. This layer defines a set of network transparent protocols for message-oriented common service requests.

The Product Data Exchange using STEP (PDES) is a US organizational activity that supports the development and implementation of STEP (Standard for the Exchange of Product Model Data — ISO TC184/SC4). STEP is a neutral mechanism capable of completely representing product data throughout the life-cycle of a product. This representation is suitable for neutral file exchange and as the basis for sharing product databases and archiving.

The Engineering Information System (EIS) [54] is a vast undertaking addressing heterogeneity of hardware and software platforms, data formats, tools, site-specific policies and methodologies, and interfaces primarily oriented around the computer-aided engineering (CAE) domain. Within the CAE community, the EIS program is intended to produce a consolidated approach to a broad set of functional and other requirements. This approach consists of proposed standards and guidelines for services which enable and accelerate a trend toward uniform engineering environments and information exchange. The EIS framework contains automated services which support and control the data and activities of the engineering process. The framework is composed of an OMS, Application Object Model (AOM), and Engineering Environment Services (EES). The OMS is composed of a meta-model, schema management, execution control, object identification support, and data access facilities. The AOM uses the OMS to create higher-level constructs which provide object-oriented capabilities. The EES is a large collection of types, operations, and default policies that support the engineering and administration processes built on top of the AOM. The EES addresses configuration management, access control, audit trails, backup and archival, inter-EIS exchange, user environment services, e.g., login, and rule processing (data-driven triggers). The UIMS is a family of guidelines and candidate standards for an interface to a CAE system. The UIMS design not only concentrates on interfaces for interactive EIS applications and tool adapters, but also provides interfaces for tying in external tools.

Any standardization approach to tool integration will work only if a significant number of tools use the standard. At this point, most of these standards are unaccepted, either by the national or international standards organizations, e.g., ISO, NIST, or by software tool vendors. One of the problems facing standardization efforts is the vast number which apply to tool integration. We have only presented a small subset to give some flavor of this approach. The IEEE P1175 effort cites around two hundred standards efforts, many of which overlap or compete with one another.

Another problem facing standardization efforts is the large number of existing tools which cannot be brought up to par with most standards efforts. While some standards do address this problem by considering approaches to data transfer which do not require changing storage formats of existing tools, many of the standards fall short in this area. The following section considers various technologies which address issues similar to the standards efforts, but do not assume prior knowledge of their technology.

2.5.2. *Integration technologies*

Tool integration environments began with the Unix operating system. The Unix pipe facility allows the combination of tools into larger tools through the interconnection of tool outputs to tool inputs through standard typeless I/O facilities. However useful this simple piping mechanism may be, it falls short of the kind of tool integration that other efforts have demonstrated.

DRACO [62] is an approach to the construction of software by organizing reusable software components or tools according to a specific problem area or domain. DRACO uses a domain language for describing programs in each domain. Statements of programs in these domain languages are then optimized by source-to-source program transformations and refined into other domains. A single reusable component corresponds directly to each object and operation in the domain language. Given the domain of software production environment construction, DRACO effectively provides a tool composition language based on a module interconnection language paradigm. GENESIS (from UT Austin) [12] is similar in purpose to DRACO, but specialized to a domain for constructing and generating of special-purpose database management systems.

Toolpack [67], and later Odin [21], support the construction of an environment based on the specification of software objects, tools, and relationships between objects and tools. Environments integrated through the use of Odin can be thought of as collections of tools which are satellites around a large structured repository of software data. Both Toolpack and Odin are ancestral predecessors to the Arcadia environment described earlier.

The Hewlett-Packard SoftBench product [17] is a tool integration framework comprised of several components including the Broadcast Message Server (BMS) that functions as a software bus, a Motif-based user-interface, the Encapsulator [23], and some integrated CASE tools. In the HP integration model, each tool makes changes to global information and informs other tools about its actions via the BMS. The BMS uses a broadcast paradigm via the software bus which is different from the point-to-point paradigm offered by object-oriented systems. The broadcast nature of the BMS communication allows the set of tools managed by a BMS and interested in a particular message to be extended without requiring any change in the tools that send the messages. The Encapsulator [23] provides a means of integrating tools into the HP SoftBench user-interface and BMS. The encapsulation consists of the Encapsulation Description Language (EDL) which describes a user-interface and corresponding communication across the BMS. The communication information consists of messages which it will respond to and messages it will generate in response to user-interface events. The message model [45] which is suggested as a basis of the environment definition is very primitive and will be too limited for environments consisting of a very large number of tools. A "multi-cast" messaging paradigm which transmits strongly typed messages may provide an alternative. Accordingly, a combination of SoftBench and SUN's ToolTalk tool integration mechanisms have been proposed as the basis of a new "standard" for open tool integration, as part of the Common Development Environment (CDE) now being investigated by the Open Software Foundation (OSF).

Field [74, 75] provides an integration framework very similar to the BMS using a communication mechanism called selective broadcasting. Field has extended the HP Softbench approach by passing all data through the message server rather than relying on a common database. Additionally, Field supplies an editor which provides consistent access to source code in multiple contexts and a set of analysis tools.

Forest [36] has extended the Field communication mechanism with an additional decision mechanism based on policies. Policies are rules that determine how and when tools are invoked. This approach represents a hybrid between process modeling mechanisms and frameworks.

The Common Lisp Framework (CLF) [8] is an incremental integration, development, and evolution environment. Tools and applications are programs written in an extension of Common Lisp called AP5. AP5 provides a persistent virtual database of relations, objects, and rules. The rules connect tools through triggering upon detection of changes to data or calling procedures. The Scorpion Meta-Environment [80] uses a specification of tool topology using a module interconnection language and a specification of the level of trade-off between evolution support and efficiency. This approach is different from the previous approaches in that it primarily addresses the use of a tool integration technology based on the module interconnection language rather than addressing the integration technology itself.

Last, the Matisse team programming environment [33] builds upon concepts previously demonstrated in the CLF and Odin. Matisse provides a multiuser programming support environment where user functionality and data object representation are managed by an intepreted, rule-based, persistent programming language. In this manner, shared objects or software components can be cached into a user's local address space from a networked object repository, to realize a user-configurable or user-extended workspace.

Overall, tool integration construction methods address the important problems of integrating externally developed tools into an environment. However, because tool integration construction is usually based on a limited control policy, they represent only a partial solution to the problem of environment construction. Generally, tool integration methods must be used in conjunction with other environment construction methods in order to support the construction of a full environment. Thus, it should be no surprise to find that many of these tool integration mechanisms are being extended or combined with environment frameworks or process support technologies.

2.6. *Summary of meta-environment research*

In Table 1, we briefly summarize the categories of meta-environments in terms of their models and transformations. For some of the categories, we have shown subcategories which arise based on differing approaches. Given these various approaches, we will now consider the more general question of what requirements must a meta-environment address.

Table 1. Summary of meta-environment research.

Category	Model	Transformation	Examples
Frameworks	ERA data model process-based control model	Used directly	PCTE, CAIS, SLCSE, ALMA, DHT, ESF K/2r
	Object-oriented data and control model	Used directly	Atherton, Gaia, RDPE3
Customizable	Grammar-based	Language-oriented Environment-generated	Mentor, GANDALF, Synthesizer Generator TRIAD, GEM, EDGE, TGE, VSF, GEDL
	Life-cycle objects	Generates environment which is specific to the information domain	Softman, ISHYS, META/GA, MetaView
Process modeling	Process meta-model	Executed directly	ESF, Genesis, Marvel, Merlin, PRISM, IPSE 2.5, PSS, MELMAC, SDA, Articulator, PBI-Softman, SPADE, SMART
Process programming	Process-oriented programming language	Compiled to generate environment	Arcadia, Adele-2, OIKOS, OPM, Process WEAVER, SynerVision
Tool integration	Standards and tool interface	Tools used directly according to tool interface	ATIS, IRDS, IRDS/ISO, CDIF, P1175, OMG, PDES, EIS
	Tool integration technology and tool interface	Tools used directly according to tool interface	Unix, DRACO, Toolpack, Odin, HP SoftBench, Field, Forest, CLF, Scorpion, PBI, Matisse

3. The Meta-Environment Problem

In the previous section, we presented a variety of approaches to lowering the cost and improving the efficiency of environment construction. While we have found that the approaches taken are not similar, the problems they address are. In particular, the common thread among these efforts is that all attempts to address the problems are associated with environment construction. Thus, to present this trend, we will attempt to give further insight into the problem area and, in particular, to the functional requirements which form the common thread.

Considerable work has been done in the area of defining the requirements for software production environments [66, 82, 83]. That is, a meta-environment must be capable of producing environments which satisfy these requirements. In this section, we will first present the kinds of roles environment builders must play and the processes they must perform which are the basis for meta-environment technology. These roles, processes, and related research are used as the basis of the requirements presented in the next section.

3.1. *Meta-environment roles*

One of the best ways to understand the problems which are to be addressed by meta-environment technology is to look at the various roles played by environment builders. A complete meta-environment process must account for the roles of the environment integrator, component builder, and component model manager among others.

The *environment integrator* is responsible for creating an environment specification and controlling the associated construction of an environment. This role has been the focus of this paper so far. In particular, developers acting in this role utilize meta-environment technology for environment construction, build a specification of the environment in terms of the meta-environment's construction model, and then generate and refine the specified environment. In general, the generation part of the process is an automated, or at least semi-automated, task. However, the task of specifying the environment's characteristics in terms of the construction model is a demand often requiring the environment integrator to be a software process architect, tool integrator, data modeler, control modeler, etc.

The *component builder* is responsible for creating, providing, or automatically generating new components which will be used in SPEs. This role has not been considered to this point. In general, the environment integrator does not create all of the environment components from scratch. Instead, the environment integrator relies on existing frameworks, process execution mechanisms, tool integration technology, generated or acquired tools, and schemata. The component builder is responsible for creating this technology, as well as the other software components which may be incorporated into them. This may entail selecting from existing components available within some reusable component repository, or extracting (and restructuring if necessary) candidate components from existing software systems [19, 59]. Note that there can be many component builders building products which are completely incompatible. The fact that they assume the same role does not imply that they work together. Nonetheless, once the component builder has created or acquired a new component, that component is potentially available for use in an environment or meta-environment.

The *component model manager* is responsible for the creation and evolution of models of component characteristics. Presently, the models are very simple and the description of characteristics is in natural language. However, as meta-environment technology becomes more prevalent and sophisticated, there will be a need for more sophisticated models to allow for automated and semi-automated selection of environment components as part of the environment integrator's role. An emerging line of research has begun to explore and develop such models using module/component interconnection formalisms and interaction protocols. Thus, the component model manager can be seen as a mediator between the component builder and the environment integrator, where the model is the language of discourse between these two roles.

Given these roles, we will now present a set of requirements which meta-environments must attempt to satisfy.

3.2. *Meta-environment requirements*

Environment specification. The fundamental requirement that a meta-environment must satisfy is that it should be able to support the construction of software production environments in accord with their specifications. This implies that a constructed environment must support desired software production methods and the process which controls the application of these methods. Furthermore, a constructed environment must have the characteristics of a "good" environment: it must be fast, provide a high level of functionality in a consistent and coherent manner, provide a consistent "look and feel" graphical user interface, etc. [66, 82, 83]. A meta-environment should provide a construction model able to express policies or methods for dealing with security, integrity, reuse, process, etc. Furthermore, the construction model should be general enough to express any of the mechanisms which can be chosen within any of these categories. This includes the ability to specify data models, data repositories, tool bindings and control message invocations, graphic and textual presentation displays, and multiple process model descriptions or notations, while accommodating one or more operating systems, computing hardware platforms and network communication protocols. Finally, either an (i) empirically tested, (ii) experience-based, or (iii) analytically robust process (or meta-model) should define the procedures for creating an environment.

Ease of use. The construction method supported by a meta-environment should be easy to use in the following ways:

- *Multiple levels of support.* The users of a meta-environment are likely to have different levels of expertise in dealing with the meta-environment. For this reason, a meta-environment should support multiple levels of interaction which give greater power to expert environment constructors, e.g., via process programming, and easier interaction for nonexpert environment constructors, e.g., by specifying parameter values in a process model.
- *Understandable.* A meta-environment should provide support in understanding the construction model through visualization, query, and browsing of process, control, and data model representations that will be embodied in the resulting environment. In addition, the process by which a specific environment is constructed should be able to be recorded, analyzed, replayed, simulated, reconfigured, and reused.
- *Selection assistance.* The number of possible software production methods and environment specifications which provide support for these methods is likely to be very large. A meta-environment should assist users in the selection of desired software production methods and corresponding environment specifications. Meta-environments might include reusable or extensible "starter kits" [41], or complete working examples of the kinds of environments that can be readily produced.
- *Automatic error checking.* A meta-environment should support automatic error checking in order to prevent the creation of environments with significant bugs in compilation, execution, or execution semantics. Language-directed text or graphic editors that can detect and prevent the entry of syntactically or semantically incorrect descriptions are typical tools to support this. In addition, mechanisms for analyzing, simulating, replaying, or repairing environment specifications or process models will be helpful.

Evolution support. Alterations are likely to occur in response to evolution in both the needs of a project and available technology. Both the environments created by a meta-environment and the meta-environments themselves must be capable of supporting evolution. A meta-environment should support evolution in the following ways:

- *Data continuity.* Changes to environments are likely to be required during the lifetime of the project which an environment supports. Therefore, a meta-environment should prevent the loss of project data during the evolution of environment specifications and the corresponding software production environment.
- *Incremental specification.* It is likely that only part of the complete environment specification will be available or known at the start of a project. A meta-environment should support the incremental construction of an environment based on partial specifications.
- *Environment versions.* As the environment evolves, it is important to control its evolution in a systematic manner. Therefore, a meta-environment should support version and configuration control over environment specifications.
- *Open for new technology.* When new technology such as better tools, frameworks, user interfaces, or methods becomes available, the meta-environment and the environments constructed by the meta-environment should be able to take advantage of this new technology. This requirement affects both the form of the environments and the meta-environment itself. The environment should be open such that new technology can be included. A meta-environment should be able to make the new technology available to environment specifications, and thus integrate and interoperate heterogeneous software data objects, components, tools, repositories, and process modeling notations.

Adopt existing capabilities. One of the primary means for making significant gains in environment construction capabilities is to adopt existing technology, such as currently available tools, frameworks, and user interfaces. A meta-environment should support the use of existing technology, where appropriate, in order to leverage the power of the construction method and correspondingly, the constructed environments. A meta-environment should also support, where possible, the use of environment capability generators or tool-building tools, such as editor generators or other application generators. Environment capability generators do not have the same characteristics as the capabilities themselves, but meta-environments should provide an effective means of utilizing this power.

4. Conclusions

Research on meta-environments for software production is following a number of alternative paths, representing a focus on either environment frameworks, customizable environments, process modeling, process programming, or tool integration. These paths represent both competing and complementary alternatives to the challenging problem of how to rapidly produce standardized or customized environments for engineering software applications. Clearly, no one path, nor any single meta-environment architecture, represents the best choice in all circumstances.

While we have examined dozens of efforts aimed at developing meta-environments, it should be clear that most of these efforts combine techniques and mechanisms employed in other categories. Further, we may expect to see a trend toward new or increased combination of techniques and mechanisms across these efforts. Accordingly, we think that further study in this field and further development of meta-environments is an important stepping stone in the creation of effective software production environments.

Finally, we have attempted to summarize and synthesize an emerging set of requirements that should be satisfied or addressed by meta-environments in the time ahead. These requirements outline a bold agenda for research and development in the area of meta-environments. Meta-environments have emerged as a key strategy for reducing the cost, time, and effort of constructing software production environments. If these requirements can be met, researchers will be able to use meta-environments to learn a great deal more about the requirements for environments themselves. Furthermore, meta-environments will enable the production of a new generation of large-scale software applications that are engineered using domain-specific environments constructed from meta-environments. Thus, the ultimate payoff from meta-environments will lie in the domain-specific environments and applications that can most readily be produced and supported.

Acknowledgements

Preparation of this report was supported in part through contracts and grants to the USC System Factory Project from AT&T Bell Laboratories, Hewlett-Packard, Northrop Corporation, the USC Center for Operations Management, Education and Research (COMER), and others. No endorsement implied.

References

1. *A Standard Reference Model for Computing System Tool Interconnections*, IEEE Computer Society's Task Force on Professional Computing Tools, p1175/d6 edition (February 1990) (Draft).
2. *CDIF Organization and Procedure Manual*, EIA, cdif-doc-n2-v1 edition, Electronics Industry Association Project No.: EIA/PN-2329, USA (January 1990).
3. *ESF Technical Reference Guide*, ESF - Eureka Software Factory (1989).
4. *Introduction to CAIS*, Common ADA Programming Support Environment (APSE) Interface Set, MIL-STD-1938A (September 1989).
5. E. W. Adams, M. Honda, and T. C. Miller, "Object management in a CASE environment", *11th Int. Conf. Software Engineering* (May 1989) pp. 154–162.
6. R. Adomeit, W. Dieters, B. Holtkamp, F. Schulke, and H. Weber, "K/2r: a kernel for the Eureka software factory support environment", *Proc. 2nd. Int. Conf. Systems Integration* (IEEE Computer Society Press, 1992) pp. 325–336.
7. V. Ambriola, P. Ciancarini, and C. Montangero, "Software process enactment in OIKOS", *Proc. 4th ACM SIGSOFT Symp. Software Development Environments* (December 1990) pp. 183–192.
8. R. Balzer, "A 15-year perspective on automatic programming", *IEEE Trans. Softw. Eng.* **11**, 11 (1985) 1257–1267.
9. R. Balzer and K. Narayanaswamy, "Mechanisms for generic process support", *Proc. 1st ACM SIGSOFT Symp. Foundations Software Engineering, ACM Software Engineering Notes* **18**, 5 (1993) 21–32.
10. S. C. Bandinelli, A. Fuggetta, and C. Ghezzi, "Software process model evolution in the SPADE environment", *IEEE Trans. Softw. Eng.* **19**, 12 (1993) 1128–1145.
11. V. R. Basili and H. D. Rombach, "The TAME project: towards improvement-oriented software environments", *IEEE Trans. Softw. Eng.* **14**, 6 (1988) 758–773.
12. D. S. Batory *et al.*, "GENESIS: an extensible database management system", *IEEE Trans. Softw. Eng.* **14**, 11 (1988) 1711–1731.
13. H. R. Beyer, K. Chapman, and C. Nolan, *The ATIS Reference Model* (June 1990) (Draft).
14. B. W. Boehm, "Software engineering environments in the United States (Plenary Talk)", *Proc. 4th ACM SIGSOFT Symp. on Software Development Environment* (December 1990).
15. G. Boloix, P. G. Sorenson, and J. P. Tremblay, "On transformations using a metasystem approach to software development", *Softw. Eng. J.* **7** (1992) 425–437.
16. R. F. Bruynooghe, J. Parker, and J. S. Rowles, "PSS: a system for process enactment", *Proc. 1st Int. Conf. Software Process* (1991) pp. 128–141.
17. M. Cagan, "The HP SoftBench environment: an architecture for a new generation of software tools", *Hewlett-Packard J.* (June 1990) pp. 36–47.
18. S. C. Choi and W. Scacchi, "Assuring the correctness of configured software descriptions", *Proc. 2nd. Int. Work. Software Configuration Management, ACM Software Engineering Notes* **17**, 7 (1989) 67–76.

19. S. C. Choi and W. Scacchi, "Extracting and restructuring the design of large systems", *IEEE Softw.* **7**, 1 (1990) 66–73.
20. S. C. Choi and W. Scacchi, "SOFTMAN: an environment for forward and reverse computer-aided software engineering", *Information and Software Technology* **33**, 9 (1991) 664–674.
21. G. Clemm and L. Osterweil, "A mechanism for environment integration", *ACM Trans. Programming Languages and Systems* **12**, 1 (1990) 1–25.
22. J. Cramer, H. Hunnekens, W. Schafer, and S. Wolf, "A process-oriented approach to the reuse of software components", Technical Report 43, Dortmund University (March 1990).
23. H. Davidson, "Encapsulator: the plug-in Compatibility tool for SoftBench", SoftBench Technical Note Series SESD-89-11 Revision 1.1, Hewlett-Packard, Software Engineering Systems Division, 3404 E. Harmony Road, Fort Collins, Colorado 80525 (June 1989).
24. W. Dieters and V. Gruhn, "Managing software processes in the environment MELMAC", *Proc. 4th ACM SIGSOFT Symp. Software Development Environments* (December 1990) pp. 193–205.
25. V. Donzeau-Gouge *et al.*, *Programming Environments Based on Structured Editors: The Mentor Experience* (McGraw Hill Book Co., 1984) pp. 128–140.
26. A. Earl, "A reference model for computer assisted software engineering environment frameworks", Hewlett-Packard Laboratories, Fort Collins, CO., USA (May 1990).
27. R. J. Ellison, "Software development environments: research to practice", *Int. Work. Advanced Programming Environments* (Springer-Verlag, 1986).
28. W. Emmerich and V. Gruhn, "Software process modeling with FUNSOFT nets", Technical Report Technical Report 47, University of Dortmund (1990).
29. W. Emmerich *et al.*, "Merlin: knowledge-based process modeling", *Proc. 1st European Work. Software Process Modeling*, Milan, Italy, (1991) pp. 181–186.
30. C. Fernstrom, "Process WEAVER: adding process support to Unix", *Proc. 2nd. Int. Conf. Software Process* (IEEE Computer Society Press, 1993) pp. 12–26.
31. C. Fernstrom and L. Ohlsson, "Integration needs in process enacted environments", *Proc. 1st Int. Conf. Software Process* (1991) pp. 142–158.
32. P. K. Garg, P. Mi, T. Pham, W. Scacchi, and G. Thunquest, "The SMART approach to software process engineering", *16th. Int. Conf. Software Engineering* (IEEE Computer Society Press, 1994) pp. 341–350.
33. P. K. Garg *et al.*, "Matisse: a knowledge-based team programming environment", *Int. J. Softw. Eng. and Knowl. Eng.* **4**, 1 (1994) 17–89.
34. P. K. Garg and W. Scacchi, "A hypertext system to manage software life-cycle documents", *IEEE Softw.* **7**, 3 (1990) 90–99.
35. P. K. Garg and W. Scacchi, "ISHYS: designing an intelligent software hypertext system", *IEEE Expert* **4**, 3 (1989) 52–63.
36. D. Garlan and E. Ilias, "Low-cost, adaptable tool integration policies for integrated environments", *Proc. 4th ACM SIGSOFT Symp. Software Development Environments* (December 1990) pp. 1–10.

37. J. L. Giavitto, A. Devarenne, G. Rosuel, and Y. Holvoet, "Adage: new trends in CASE environments", *Proc. Int. Conf. Systems Development Environments and Factories* (May 1989).
38. A. Goldberg and D. Robson, *Smalltalk-80: The Language and Its Implementation* (Addison-Wesley, 1983).
39. A. V. Goldberg and K. J. Lieberherr, "GEM: a generator of environments for metaprogramming", *COMPSAC 85* (1985) pp. 86–95.
40. A. Goldfine and P. Konig, "A technical overview of the information resource dictionary system", Technical Report NBSIR 88-3700 (supersedes NBSIR 85-3164), U.S. Department of Commerce, National Bureau of Standards, Institute for Computer Sciences and Technology, Gaithersburg, MD 20899 (January 1988).
41. M. L. Griss, "Software reuse – from library to factory", *IBM Systems Journal* **34**, 4 (1993) 548–566.
42. D. Heimbigner, "Triton reference manual", Technical Report CU-CS-483-90, Department of Computer Science, University of Colorado (July 1990).
43. Hewlett-Packard, "Developing synervision processes", HP Palo ALto, CA, part number: b3261-90003 edition (May 1993).
44. M. Heym and H. Osterle, "Computer-aided methodology engineering", *Information and Software Technology* **35**, 6&7 (1993) 345–354.
45. B. T. Jenings, "The HP SoftBench message model: concepts and conventions used by the HP SoftBench tools", SoftBench Technical Note Series SESD-89-21 Revision 1.2, Hewlett-Packard, Software Engineering Systems Division, Fort Collins, Colorado 80525, USA (September 1989).
46. G. E. Kaiser and P. Feiler, "An architecture for intelligent assistance in software development", *Proc. 9th Int. Conf. Software Engineering* (February 1987) pp. 180–188.
47. A. S. Karrer, "Generating graph editors", Ph.D. Thesis, Computer Science Department, University of Southern California (May 1993).
48. A. S. Karrer and M. Penedo, "A survey of native environment framework architectures", TRW Corporation Note Arcadia-TRW-90-002, El Segundo, CA (August 1990).
49. A. S. Karrer and W. Scacchi, "Requirements for an extensible object-oriented tree/graph editor", *ACM SIGGRAPH Symp. User-Interface Software and Technology* (October 1990) pp. 84–92.
50. R. K. Keller, M. Cameron, R. N. Taylor, and D. B. Troup, "Chiron-1: a user interface development system tailored to software environments", Technical Report UCI-90-06, Department of Information and Computer Science, University of California, Irvine (June 1990).
51. J. D. Kiper, "The ergonomic, efficient, and economic integration of existing tools into a software engineering environment", Ph.D. Thesis, Ohio State University, USA (1985).
52. K. Kishida, T. Katayama, M. Matsuo, I. Miyamoto, K. Ochimizu, M. Saito, J. Saylet, K. Torii, and L. Williams, "SDA: a novel approach to software environ-

ment design and construction", *Int. Conf. Software Engineering* (April 1988) pp. 69–79.
53. P. Klint, "A meta-environment for generating programming environments", *ACM Trans. Softw. Eng. Methodology* **2**, 2 (1993) 176–201.
54. J. W. Krueger, "Application object model for engineering information systems", Honeywell Systems and Research Center, Minneapolis, MN (October 1989).
55. A. Van Lamsweerde *et al.*, "Generic lifecycle support in the ALMA environment", *IEEE Trans. Softw. Eng.* **14**, 6 (1988) 720–740.
56. N. H. Madhavji *et al.*, "Prism = methodology + process-oriented environment", *Proc. 12th Int. Conf. Software Engineering* (1990) pp. 277–289.
57. P. Mi and W. Scacchi, "A knowledge-based environment for modeling and simulating software engineering processes", *IEEE Trans. Knowl. and Data Eng.* **2**, 3 (1990) 283–294.
58. P. Mi and W. Scacchi, "Modeling articulation work in software engineering processes", *Proc. 1st Int. Conf. Software Process* (1991) pp. 188–201.
59. P. Mi and W. Scacchi, "Process integration for CASE environments", *IEEE Softw.* **9**, 2 (1992) 45–53.
60. R. Munck, P. Oberndorf, E. Ploedereder, and R. Thall, "An overview of DOD-STD-1838A (proposed), the common APSE interface set, Revision A", Technical report, Department of Defense, USA (1988).
61. W. L. Melo, N. Belkhatir, J. Estublier, and L. G. I. France, "Adele-2: a support to large software development processes", *Proc. 1st Int. Conf. Software Process* (1991) pp. 159–171.
62. J. M. Neighbors, "The DRACO approach to constructing software from reusable components", *IEEE Trans. Softw. Eng.*, **10**, 5 (1984) 564–573.
63. J. Noll and W. Scacchi, "Integrating diverse information repositories: the distributed hypertext approach", *Computer* **24**, 12 (1991) 38–45.
64. D. Notkin, "The GANDALF project", *J. Sys. Softw.*, **5**, 5 (1985) 91–105.
65. H. Ossher and W. Harrison, "Support for change in RDPE3", *Proc. 4th ACM SIGSOFT Symp. Software Development Environments* (December 1990) pp. 218–228.
66. L. Osterweil, "Software environment research: directions for the next five years", *IEEE Comput.* **14**, 4 (1981) 35–43.
67. L. Osterweil, "TOOLPACK - an experimental software development environment research project", *IEEE Trans. Softw. Eng.* **9**, 6 (1983) 673–685.
68. W. Paseman, "The Atherton Software BackPlane – an architecture for tool integration", *Unix Review* (April 1989).
69. F. Newbury Paulisch and W. Tichy, "EDGE: an extendible graph editor", *Software Practice and Experience* **20**, S1 (1991).
70. M. Penedo and W. E. Riddle, Guest editors' introduction to software engineering environment architectures. *IEEE Trans. Softw. Eng.* **14**, 6 (1988).
71. E. Ploedereder, T. C. Harrison, P. Oberndorf, C. Roby, F. Belz, J. F. Kramer, and J. Clouse, "Rationale for DOD-STD-1838 (CAIS)", Technical Report, Department of Defense, USA (August 1988).

72. J. N. Popcock, "VSF and its relationship to open systems and standard repositories", *Software Development Environments and CASE Environments*, Lecture Notes in Computer Science, Vol. 509 (Springer-Verlag, 1991) pp. 53–68.
73. C. V. Ramamoorthy *et al.*, "GENESIS: an integrated environment for supporting development and evolution of software", *COMPSAC '85* (October 1985) pp. 472–479.
74. S. P. Reiss, "Connecting tools using message passing in the field environment", *IEEE Softw.* **7**, 4 (1990) 57–66.
75. S. P. Reiss, "Interacting with the field environment", *Software Practice and Experience* **20** S1 (1990) 89–115.
76. T. Reps and T. Teitelbaum, "The synthesizer generator", *Proc. ACM SIGSOFT/SIGPLAN Software Engineering Symp. Practical Software Development Environments* (April 1984).
77. W. Scacchi, "The software infrastructure for a distributed software factory", *Softw. Eng. J.* **6**, 5 (1991) 355–369.
78. D. Smith, "KIDS: A semi-automatic program development system", *IEEE Trans. Softw. Eng.* **16**, 9 (1990) 1024–1044.
79. K. Smolander, P. Marttiin, K. Lyytinen, and V.-P. Tahvanainen, "MetaEdit – a flexible graphical environment for methodology modelling", *Advanced Information Systems Engineering, Lecture Notes in Computer Science*, Vol. 498 (Springer Verlag, 1991) pp. 168–193.
80. R. Snodgrass and K. Shannon, "Fine grained data management to achieve evolution resilience in a software development environment", *Proc. 4th ACM SIGSOFT Symp. Software Development Environments* (December 1990) pp. 144–156.
81. R. M. Soley, "Object management group standards manual", Draft 0.1 OMG TC Document 90.5.4 (May 1990).
82. P. G. Sorenson, J. P. Tremblay, and A. J. McAllister, "The Metaview system for many specification environments", *IEEE Softw.* **5** (1988) 30–38.
83. V. Stennig, "On the Role of an Environment", *Commun. ACM* (1987).
84. T. Strelich, "The Software Life Cycle Support Environment (SLCSE): a computer based framework for developing software systems", *Proc. ACM SIGSOFT/SIGPLAN Software Engineering Symp. Practical Software Development Environments*(November 1988) pp. 35–44.
85. Y. Sugiyama and E. Horowitz, "Building your own software development environment", *Softw. Eng. J.* **6**, 5 (1991) 317–331.
86. S. M. Sutton, D. Heimbigner, and L. Osterweil, "Programmable relations for managing change during software development", Technical Report CU-CS-418-88, University of Colorado, Boulder, CO 80309-0430 (September 1988).
87. R. Taylor *et al.*, "Foundations for the Arcadia environment architecture", *Proc. 3rd ACM Symp. Software Development Environments*, (November 1988).
88. W. Teitelman and L. Masinter, "The Interlisp programming environment", *IEEE Comput.* **14**, 4 (1981) 25–33.
89. I. Thomas, "PCTE interfaces: supporting tools in software engineering environments", *IEEE Softw.* **6**, 11 (1989) 15–23.

90. D. Vines and T. King, "Gaia: an object-oriented framework for an Ada environment", *3rd Int. IEEE Conf. Ada Applications and Environments* (May 1988) pp. 81–90.
91. B. Warboys, "The IPSE 2.5 project : process modeling as the basis for a support environment", University of Manchester, UK (September 1989).
92. D. Wile, "Program development: formal explanations of implementations", *Commun. ACM* **26**, 11 (1983) 902–911.
93. A. Wolf, J. Wileden, C. Fisher, and P. Tarr, "Pgraphite: an experiment in persistent typed object management", *Proc. ACM SIGSOFT/SIGPLAN Software En-*

TRENDS IN STRUCTURE-ORIENTED ENVIRONMENTS

BENJAMIN R. WHITTLE*, ROBERT J. GAUTIER† and MARK RATCLIFFE†

Department of Computer Science, University of Wales,
Penglais, Aberystwyth, SY23 3BZ, UK

The term "Structure Editor" (structured environment, structure-oriented environment) is widely used and has been defined, and redefined, many times since the first recognised structure editor, Emily [49]. This paper follows the trends in this field, over the last decade, in the following areas: environment parameters, environment architectures, tools and the uses of environments, textual manipulation, internal (structure) representation, conceptual programming, and environment evaluation. This chapter contains an historical perspective of technological events shaping this field and concludes with a unifying summary.

1. Introduction

The term "Structure Editor" (structured environment, structure-oriented environment) is widely used and has been defined, and redefined, many times since the first recognised structured editor, Emily [49].

> An interactive software development environment can be viewed as a structure-based editor, provided that *structure* is broadly interpreted. [3]

This is the view expressed by Alpern [3], and forms the link in the development of our theme from simple editors through to the complex environments which form the latter part of the study. The Cornell Program Synthesiser [105] has been referred to, by Minör [79], as a benchmark within structured editing; this editor forms the lower historical bound of the area which we study here.

The term structure-oriented, as it appears in the title of this chapter, refers to the object, whether it be code, picture, text, or any other "structured entity", that the user manipulates through the tool(s) provided. The emphasis

*Ben Whittle works in the Department of Computer Science, University of York, Heslington, York, Y01 5DD, UK.

†R. J. Gautier and M. B. Ratcliffe are with the Department of Computer Science, University of Wales, Aberystwyth, Dyfed, Wales, UK.

on structure manipulation (editing) is a common thread in all of the environments in this survey, from simple text editors, to complex environments for the complete software life-cycle.

In the structured environment community, work on many projects has occurred concurrently, on different sites, by teams with different backgrounds and research goals. In some instances individual projects and papers have a marked influence on the whole field; in other cases, techniques evolve simultaneously as a result of increased technological support or the adaptation and application of methods assimilated from other research, in this case, often in compiler writing. Similarly certain themes and methods become "fashionable" and this *de facto* standard may become pervasive to the extent that its status is raised from a method of implemeting the process to a desired feature.

A basic historical context is necessary so that the fashionable and practical, as well as innovative, trends in each of the areas can be shown. It is also necessary to emphasize the status of certain features in particular papers so that themes can be brought out. This paper therefore provides a panoramic view of the field, rather than an in-depth study of any one particular environment or author's work. The sheer volume and diversity of subject matter within this field has meant that this chapter will cover a large area. It should be noted that this chapter is intended to show the trends in the field; any references to environments are made as commentaries in this context and should not be taken as either full or precise description.

1.1. *An historical perspective*

Taking a broad historical perspective we discover that within the area of structured environments the change in emphasis of research and in the application of that research are linked. Environment goals are not always explicitly stated and often include the need to improve or upgrade existing facilities. As certain practices become outmoded, or accepted as either *de facto* standards, or a problem solved, these goals become redundant. By looking at the change not only in the actual and implied goal statements for structured environments, but also at their relative importance, it is possible to gauge developments and progress in the field.

The definition of structure editing for the purpose of this paper, would include text editors (such as *vi*) as a structured environment with the target object being text. However, most of the discussion will be limited to the more mainstream definition of a structured environment, as the majority of the source material is in this area. Some text editors may be enhanced (e.g., Emacs [116]) to form syntax-oriented editors, often containing parsers. Syntax-directed editors could also be used for other structured objects which have some language-type representation. Structures such as programs, represented to the user as text but based on an underlying tree structure, fall into this category. This was the approach taken by Teitelbaum *et al.* in the Cornell Program Synthesiser (CPS) [105] structured environment which marks the start of the period of study.

With the advent of increasing Personal Computer (PC) technology and its accompanying graphics capacity, many diagram-oriented structured environments became available. The WIMP interaction capabilities of the PC/workstation were also used in the interface to program language editor environments with an integral structured environment capacity [45]. More recently [92] these areas of graphics and WIMP interfaces have been combined to provide integrated environments for program design [71].

Structures can be represented in more ways than one; it is important to distinguish between the representation presented to the user, the external representation, and the representation manipulated within the environment, the internal representation. Much of the development within this topic area is technology led [111], for example, the movement from single text-like representations [114] and their associated paradigms, to a multiple window, graphic and textual representation of a structured object. A command line interface has been complemented, or superseded, by WIMP interfaces and an array of menus and buttons, providing options consistent with the appropriate view of a structure.

The mechanisms behind the on-screen representation contain a host of incremental and batch tools. These could perform continual validations between the external and internal representations, as well as other structure specific tasks, for example, think-time throw-away compilation [30].

The advent of the generic, or at least the nondedicated, structured environment [6, 93] also formed an important watershed. The increasing size and complexity of the structured environment can be seen as the major contributing factor to this movement. This is in addition to the general increase in interest in reuse as a concept, due to its financial as well as epistemological software engineering benefits. Structured environments have become easier to build as a nondedicated capability has become available; this could be inversely linked with the increased cost of development of the structured environment [19]. The structured environment has become a tool which is generated from parameters, often themselves constructed within a structured environment, and with their own dedicated languages.

2. Trends in Structure-Oriented Editing

The Cornell Program Synthesiser is used to introduce some of the themes of this section and to provide a starting point for the investigation. This section continues to look at various trends under seven themed subsections:

1. *Environment parameters*: an environment builder's changing inputs, the development from language dependence, to independence, in both syntactic and semantic terms; the emergence of graphics;
2. *Environment architectures*: support for extensibility, focusing on: rule-based, message passing, and process models;
3. *Tools and the uses of environments*: configuration, management and industrial tools; a commentary on CASE and IPSE, definitions and directions;
4. *Internal representation*: the shift from a tree-based structure, through decorated trees, to directed graphs;
5. *Textual manipulation*: syntax-oriented directed editing, hybridization;
6. *Conceptual programming*: breaking the traditional edit compile mould, using multiple representation paradigms and knowledge-based tools;
7. *Environment evaluation*: the attempts to establish an objective environment evaluation;

each of which has an introduction and conclusion.

The Cornell Program Synthesiser (CPS) [105] provided a usable interface, supported good software engineering techniques, and combined extensive debugging facilities with a freedom from syntax details. Teitelbaum's rationale for the structured perspective was:

> Programs are not text; they are hierarchical compositions of computational structures and should be edited, executed and debugged in an environment that consistently acknowledges and reinforces this viewpoint. The Cornell Program Synthesiser demands a structured perspective at all stages of development. [105]

The CPS editor utilizes the grammatical structure of the target language, grammatical syntax units are treated as the basic units in early structure editing (syntax-directed editing). Using a textual editor the primary units would be words, lines and characters; in the same way that words are composed of characters, syntax units can be composed of other terminal, or nonterminal, syntax units (syntax objects). Thus, the operations provided are applicable to the units upon which the editor operates.

The CPS uses a tree structure for its internal representation, the external textual representation is consistent with that of source code. In the CPS, syntax-directed editing is used for high-level statements; at a lower level, such as expressions and assignments constructs, this becomes tedious and uneconomic because the user has to make a complex selection from menus.

2.1. *Environment parameters*

For an environment to be provided for a particular structure some notion of that structure must be present in that environment. We follow the development of that "notion" from hard-coded grammar rules, to instantiable environments and the parallel development from syntax-directed to full semantic support. The latter portion of the section contains a discussion on other notions of structure such as graphics.

The CPS utilizes the grammatical structure of its target language as a rule base. A grammar provides a basis for representation in terms of the syntactic units, formalised in the grammar rules. This syntactic base is used as the basis for an interaction mechanism, the representation structure of the target object. Syntax structure-directed environments allowed the language programmer to interact in terms of the syntactic representation of the object structure; a move thought to supersede textual editors where the underlying structure was for nonprogramming languages.

Morris and Schwartz [84] consider a language-directed editor as combining "the textual manipulation functions of a general purpose editor with the syntax checking functions of a compiler". This type of editor is referred to as syntax-oriented, rather than syntax-directed, as the editor checks the input with reference to the syntax, rather than operating with respect to it. This approach is less ambitious than that of the CPS and indicates an intention that editors move back towards enhanced text editors, such as [116]. A similar approach is taken by Allison in SED [2], an editor developed for Pascal at the University of Western Australia. Allison distinguishes between short and long distance syntax; only short distance syntax, such as the structure of an If statement, is checked within SED. The manipulation of a language-based structure is discussed in more detail in the section on textual manipulation (see Subsec. 2.5).

The advent of language independence is an important point in the development of the structured environment. Syned [58] is an early attempt at an instantiable environment and its facilities are somewhat limited. The environment requires two grammars: one for its internal representation, the other to support the generation of a (YACC) parser. A more consistent approach is provided by the synthesizer generator [93], which broadens the concepts of the CPS [105] into a system for generating "CPS-like" editors from language descriptions. The synthesizer generator utilizes both an abstract and concrete syntax, for internal and external representation respectively.

Early editors such as SED [2] are relatively simple syntax editors with separate tools for semantic analysis; in some structured editors such as ALOE (Gandalf [86]) the user can provide semantic check routines. A more complete approach is provided in Pecan [91], where a statement oriented-language is used for semantic descriptions. The Programming Systems Generator (PSG) [6] is used to generate language independent interactive environments from formal language definitions. This formal definition involves three major components: the syntax, and the contextual and denotational semantics of the language. Only the syntactic element is mandatory; to instantiate an editor for the syntax takes approximately two weeks [6]; for a full editor (Modula 2) this period is extended to eight months. Bahlke and Snelting comment on the inadequacy of attribute grammars for content evaluation, even with incremental attribute evaluation. They support the use of the context relation concept, introduced in [56], to compute the set of "still possible" attribute values for each node of an incomplete fragment. The denotational semantics for the PSG are defined using the Vienna Development Method (VDM) [9,10]. The meta-language which results is translated at run-time by an interpreter; incomplete program fragments cause a halt in run-time execution, which can continue when the user interactively completes the fragment.

The development of structural environments has progressed from extended textual editors with some syntax checking, to full structural environments defined to the level of denotational semantics. These changes can be broken into several stages:

- a textual editor with additional syntax checking functions,
- editors based on the structure of the language syntax using grammar productions,
- editors are enhanced by semantic checking functions, first as separate functions, then using statements-oriented language,

- the editor environment is instantiated for both syntactics and semantics using formal techniques.

An editor based on "structure" can be seen as a resultant point (ignoring all factors of usability), the intermediate editors are trends in that development. The problems of achieving an appropriate level of interaction, management resistance, and the prohibitive cost of implementation of these environments have reduced their widespread acceptance and use.

The Ipser [61] environment presents a possible next step in this process. Ipser uses a multi-information approach to integrate modules written in different languages. This is achieved using a grammar framework, combining descriptions in these different formalisms, for the construction and integration of interpreters for specifications. The use of multiple paradigms can provide a close fit of the model to the problem, a basis for describing an application and an easily extensible, domain-structured, model base.

The Lilac [13] system is also concerned with multiple representations in a structured form, particularly with textual objects. In the two views provided by Lilac, the user can interact with both What You See Is What You Get (WYSIWYG) and source representations; they are concurrently viewed. Updating occurs from WYSIWYG to source, and vice versa; enabling the construction of more complex features to be defined in the source. This structured environment is targetable during use, in that the user can define a structure interactively on screen, the source code for which appears as a direct result in the adjacent window. The user invents the hierarchy used in the document on the fly, this can then be "copied" as a skeletal structure to be used in the same or another document.

These two (Ipser and Lilac) environments exhibit a move towards extensibility at a fine-grained level, where the internal structure of the target of a tool is itself extensible. This can be seen as a part of the overall trend to extensibility most readily seen in environment architecture (see Subsec. 2.2).

The development of graphical-based representation lagged behind textually-based environments; the reasons for this were partly technological, but also because of the problems presented by representation and interaction issues. These issues had been encountered earlier in developments for text such as editors and compilers. The development of graphic-based and multiview editors follows a similar pattern to that of language-based editors. Early graphical environments represented pictorially the syntax of a method or a control flow diagram. However, the introduction of semantics was achieved more quickly in graphical environments, probably forced by the developments occurring at the time in language-based environments. Software Through Pictures [111] was an early graphics-based program development system. Other early systems include Kookabura [4] and Tinkertoy [38]; an environmental editor for programming languages, which used an icon-based representation. The underlying representation for languages edited graphically remained a syntax tree. The CAEDE environment [15] used Buhr's diagramming technique to represent Ada, to enable design and visual reasoning about programs. Many of these environments remain language- or method-specific because of the problems involved in extensibility and the complexity of instantiating such an environment.

Dannenberg [28] identifies six problems in graphical editors: incremental redisplay, granularity, i.e., whether to treat a box as a set of lines or as one object, efficient access to information, multiple views, to be able to undo, and to meet all of these goals without losing the modularity of information. Dannenberg concentrates on the undo mechanism; this is implemented by keeping a version list of changes, and allowing movement through the list. The benefit of this mechanism is that in an undo operation the current state of all other objects may be retained, so that all other changes may be kept whilst one object reverts to a previous version. This mechanism is extended to a multiple view scenario, where an item list is maintained of those views which must be informed, when a "shared" item is updated.

Dora is an environment generator in which graphical and textual views are edited within the same frame. This approach is based on an object-oriented paradigm with multiple views, complimented by a hierarchy of editors which work at the level of a single semantic unit within the target structure.

Graphics-based environments present facilities which are useful for visualization in a method or design. Their use is unlikely to replace textual representation for language except as a means of representation, for example, to support reuse of code or documentation text. It is also unlikely that graphic methods will be used for what has until now been language-based programming, the main reason is the difficulty in interacting with diagrams for low-level operations. At present many of the extensibility problems of graphically-based editors still exist.

2.2. *Environment architectures*

In early structure-oriented environments that were language specific, the environment could be written as a single piece of code. With the advent of the generic, or targetable, environment, a two-tier system developed. This comprised a kernel, with the language independent facilities of the target environment and the language-specific elements of the environment generated from a language description. The amount of target structure knowledge needed by the instantiator varied depending on the environment generator and the facilities it would provide. Examples of language-based architectures are the Synthesizer Generator [93]; and the Programming System Generator [6]; a bad example of architecture is provided by Centaur [11]. Previously targetable environments of this size have two elements: a kernel providing the central functionality and the user interface manipulation, which is generic and sometimes extensible. Unlike this architecture, Centaur [11] is split into three classes of functions, a kernel for the representation and manipulation of structured objects, a specification level to support the syntactic and semantic aspects of languages, and a user interface to deal with the interactive communication between the system and its users. Instantiating Centaur requires a knowledge of a variety of languages including Metal [62], a formalism developed for its direct ancestor Mentor [33]. A structured editor with associated parser can be formed using a combination of the parser and a pretty printing formalism [89], although the editor is not provided as a standard feature and the difficulty of achieving an "attractive" editor is emphasized. The Dora environment generator [89] uses an object-oriented representation of structure to form a tool comprising a hierarchy of independent cooperating editors. In this architecture each structure is seen as an object and an editor is individually provided. These editors form an hierarchy of independent (in operation) but interdependent (in structure) agents. It is possible to have more than one editor on one structure; editors can be both textual and graphical, and coexist within one window frame. Cooperation between editors is achieved through update lists and message passing, similar to Dannenberg [28] and Field [90] respectively.

At the architectural level of the project environment, several problems began to emerge as the environments comprised a greater number and variety of tools. To achieve integration in the environment many of the environments tools worked on a shared underlying repository. ISDE [19] was an example of an early environment that dealt with the problems of integration and representation. ISDE was an instantiable environment which used a grammar in part for both syntax and semantics. Chesi *et al.* [19] identify the basic features necessary in tools as: integration, open, openendedness, granularity, interactivity, and ease of use. ISDE allows the definition and implementation of a unique internal representation of a program, to allow complete integration among tools. Tool integration is carried out by an integrator unit, each tool registers its functionality with the integrator, which gives users tool access through a standard menu system. Functionality can also be built into meta commands by the integrator.

In the mid-1980s, three approaches began to emerge for environment architecture: process modeling; rule-based systems, and message-based systems. The remainder of this section comprises an introduction to the themes and systems of each paradigm.

Process modeling represents one of the most contentious contributions to many areas and could be said to have its roots in the issues of environment architecture; early attempts include Jasmine [74] and ISTAR [34] (a contractual approach). Taylor *et al.* in a paper on the architecture of the Arcadia [103] environment, comment on the problems of the disparity in environment architectures:-

> ... it seems that a well-integrated environment is easier to achieve if the environment is limited in scope and static in its concept and organization, conversely, broad and dynamic environments are typically loosely coupled and poorly integrated. [103]

This implies that a burden of poor integration is imposed on users in poorly integrated environments, whereas well-integrated, but static environments, can be outgrown or superseded. Arcadia aims to study the tension between the diverging aims of the two identified environment trends. The Arcadia environment uses a Process Description Language (PDL) to achieve flexibility and extensibility within the environment. The user of Arcadia is able to specify the action of the environment, by programing the environment and its constituent tools in the PDL. Flexibility is facilitated by allowing alteration to these PDL programs and extensibility by enabling the user to write new process programs, which indicate how the tools interact with each other.

The Software Life-Cycle Support Environment (SLCSE) [100] is a process-based environment that was delivered to the US Air Force in 1988. In the SLCSE, operational concepts such as agents, roles, and their associated tools can be accessed through a common user interface. The process model is hidden to the user, who interacts with this via an interface.

The difference between these two environments (Arcadia and SLCSE), where one explicitly represents the process in language form and the other where the process is hidden, is explained by the SLCSE being a commercial tool where a more attractive and user-oriented front end is necessary. Although process modeling now encompasses many more areas of the software life-cycle, as noted by the discussions of Osterweil in [87] and [70], it has not produced a satisfactory working answer to the problems of environment extensibility.

The second possible approach is that of a set of rules. Several rule-based systems emerge for environment architecture; these claim to be very simple with little overheads and therefore of little burden to the environment. The Workshop System [24] was designed to support teams of programmers working concurrently on large scale software projects. Clemm states that the workshop system is economically viable, unlike other systems which claim practicality with little chance of economic or technical enactment as "benefits to the user outweighs the costs". The system uses a knowledge representation language to specify, in a rule-based paradigm, the relationship between the software objects in the environment. The environment is designed to be extensible, comprising initially a kernel with a read-only rule base for the central system concepts. The system combines a knowledge-based software environment with an extensible object manager system named Odin. Other examples include the action sequence plans of Huff and Lesser [59].

Minsky [82] enters what has become an established rule-based arena, with a further paper on the law-based Darwin environment, previously seen in [80]. He comments that a law-based system is regulatory, he contrasts this with the replacement of natural program operation and evolution that he contends occurs within rule- and constraint-based systems. A law-based system is "meant to provide some of the 'ground rules' under which the system is to operate and evolve" [82]. The evolution of the "law set", is subject to the law, and unless specified in the rule base, cannot be changed once the creator entity (perhaps project manager) is released. The system is a hierarchy of two levels: the top level is the law system, the underlying level is a system working within the law. In the Darwin system, objects communicate with messages governed by the law. The law is interpreted by intercepting the messages and evaluating the ruling of the law with respect to the message in question. Evaluation is carried out in both the static and dynamic semantic domains, with as much evaluation as possible in the static domain to avoid run-time computation.

Garlan and Illias' Forest environment [43] was based on the work of Reiss in Field [90]. Garlan and Ilias address the problem of adjusting the environment so that tools can interact in different ways. The system Forest is represented as a set of *policies* — "rules" in which the condition is expressed as either the value of some variable or a function/system call. The user can change a policy or alter the state of a variable to alter the state of the environment; the user can also write new policies. Garlan and Ilias suggest, for example, that this system could be used to trigger automatic compilation, this action could be suppressed if the system load were too great. Obviously, they claim that in a multiuser environment a single policy set would be used as a standard, and the individual would not be allowed to amend rules. Garlan and Ilias suggest a hierarchy within which the rules written by those at higher levels take precedence; for example, a manager or administrator, similar to Darwin's creator entity, could make a rule which no-one could override. Rules of this type are "required"; other rules can act as defaults which individuals are allowed to override. A parallel is drawn between this environment and the system used in Darwin [80,82] (see above), where instead of the condition-action pair, a Prolog program is used to encapsulate the "rules".

Sullivan and Notkin [101] are also interested in the problems of developing an environment in which component tools can have increased independence. This approach is similar to that of Forest [43] (above). This approach differs in that, although both consider events, Sullivan and Notkin use a mediator system, rather than an event manager. Unlike Forest's policy modules, mediators are first-class components; they can maintain state and call other components in such a way as to produce side effects so that relationships can be maintained efficiently. Mediators represent a "design technique"; they are also independent of the relationships in which they participate; this aids in the evolution of the environment.

The third architecture mechanism identified is that of message passing. Essentially this can occur in several ways: all tools receive all messages and decide which ones they want, a broadcast to only those interested tools or a mail master system is used where the environment has control, as a central agent in the message system.

In the ISM post-implementation paper [95], Rodden *et al.* describe their rationale for a new knowledge-based architecture for support environments.

> The design of the next generation of IPSE will differ greatly from that of previous generations. The evolutionary design which has led to the development of current IPSEs from programming environments is not capable of accommodating the emerging technologies which simplify automation of the whole software process. [95]

This environment uses knowledge-based programming techniques to create a high degree of integration. The architecture consists of a "federation of intelligent, cooperating agents". The extensible open architecture enables the incremental addition of agents. The system uses a mailer as a consistent communications medium between its various agents. The user interface could also be tailored to the individual requirements of an agent. Rodden *et al.* distinguish between the new systems and previous passive systems, in which systems *support*, rather than *participate* in, the development process. An active environment supports active integration between the user and system in a cooperative paradigm with knowledge of system components on both sides. Information regarding interdependence of tools and actions is used to initiate actions automatically. The active system requires a declarative interface, rather than the imperative interface of the passive system. A similar technique is used in Kookabura [38], a multiview environment that utilizes a collection of parallel processs communicating via a message passing system over a network of Sun workstations.

Field also uses a message system to integrate tools. Reiss [90] attempts to show that highly integrated environments like those on PCs can be implemented on workstations and that these can be used for classical language and programming in the large. Field uses a loosely coupled message system to integrate the tools. Reiss states the advantages of this approach as simplicity, ease of reuse of existing tools, and ease of extensibility. The main contribution of Field is as an integration framework, which allows tools to be tied together with minimal effort. This is achieved by a "selective broadcasting" mechanism in which a central message server controls the flow of messages between the cooperating tools. Tools send messages to the server and receive messages which correspond to registered patterns. Field includes many other tools, such as editors, debuggers, and graphical interfaces to a variety of other programming tools and data structure displays. Reiss defines the forms of integration which are facilitated by this environment: tool interaction, so that the facilities of one tool are available to other tools; the sharing of dynamic information, so that different environments can know the execution context and state of the other components.

The message system was initially weakened by the free-for-all nature of the broadcast approach. With the selective broad cast mechanism and an environment-centered control structure many of these problems have disappeared. However, the emphasis of the message passing systems is still very much on the tools rather than the environment. These three areas (process-based, rule-based and message passing) dominated the development of environment architecture although other alternatives did occur such as those put forward by Clement for a distributed architecture [23].

The trends in architectural style that have been described present alternatives to the designer of an environment. The question is whether one of these will become dominant and if so why? The last few years have seen the area of process modeling become a very exciting arena. The process model provides a central means of control through a process description. This concentration on the process itself, rather than a rule system for that environment or a consideration of a mail system, is advantageous. However, the weakness of the process model is in its complexity, and thus, very few working process models exist [70]. The process model is seen to be the best way of describing the interaction among tools, tasks, and actors within a system but an adequate and workable means of describing this "system" is not yet available.

A rule-based architecture is not easily extensible, as many systems rely on the order in which rules are triggered. This architecture is suitable for small domain environments where extensibility is unlikely and a known series of actions will occur. A message-based system is very useful for loosely coupled systems. A central messaging system with a registration of interest would seem more intuitively efficient than a broadcast mechanism. The environment builder must also provide some means of enveloping tools so that messages can be triggered and received. Applications of this type of system are likely to be distributed.

The process model has the greatest potential and is attracting the most interest [70]. The many problems of definition that the achievement of an effective solution presents once solved will become the model's strengths.

2.3. *Tools and the uses of environments*

A great many editors and environments have been produced in the last decade, this section will highlight several areas of use or targets for these systems. The vast majority of systems are oriented towards software production in one way or other. Six themes will be explained briefly with examples; these themes are: life-cycle support, language and method support, concurrent computing, tools and toolsets, support for object-oriented paradigms and configuration, planning, and management. The section will conclude with a comparison of Case and IPSE developments.

2.3.1. *Life-cycle support*

Support [119] was one of the first environments to consider more of the wider issues than simply providing editing tools. It integrated development programming and execution environments to increase the connectivity between design and code, leaving more scope for maintenance and re-engineering.

The Acturus environment [104] was targeted at analysis, testing, and debugging of concurrent programs. This strategy involved a combination of static and dynamic analysis together with an interactive debugger. The Team [22] support environment was part of the Arcadia [103] project, it was designed "to create an automated testing system for demonstrating the feasibility of many advanced testing techniques".

The ABE environment [40] provides facilities to build and test systems in multiple languages on a virtual machine. The system has a multilevel architecture; the Mop virtual machine encourages deeply composed systems in the multiple (modular) languages which ABE supports. ABE also has a framework for reuse, in a module-based paradigm and component library.

2.3.2. *Language and method support*

The majority of environments are created in an academic environment and therefore teaching languages, such as Pascal, are often supported in language-based environments. It is easier to instantiate environments for well-defined languages; those that are used in industry are not always so precise. For example, Ross [96] comments: "writing in C is a hazardous duty. The language is lexically terse, syntactically sparse and semantically loose." Integral C provides an integrated environment for C.

In a similar way, the IR^n [27] environment is for Fortran. It uses a module interconnection language which allows the specification of both modules and source. Modules can be edited with regard to the self content (members) and to their import and export sets. The design rationale of IR^n is obviously linked to its target usage in its mathematically styled notation.

Ipsen [68] provides a "coherent" set of incremented and integrated tools for programming in the large. The environment is directed at Modula 2 with all tools operating incrementally at a fine-grain level. Ipsen aims to support the whole of the project life-cycle as one integrated unit. The system also includes a diagramming tool although this is noninteractive. The Software Through

Pictures [111] environment supports analysis, design, and code generation, through a graphical rather than textual medium.

The trend in language and method support as per an "appropriate" environment, for example, IR^n for Fortran, has a mathematical style of interaction and Ross describes Integral C as "industrial grade". The trend towards appropriate environments will increase; the environment whether hardcoded or instantiable will introduce more tailoring for the requirements and rationale of languages. Environments will also be used for more rapid and flexible prototyping [61].

2.3.3. *Concurrent computing*

A number of environments are directed towards supporting concurrent and communicating sequential processes. These environments are particularly concerned with animated representation and good-user interaction.

In the environment CSP [31], Delisle and Schwartz are concerned with implementing an environment for Communicating Sequential Processes [57]. The user interface paradigm is to support user interaction and provide a unifying interface. As the interactive communication between events is not decidable, the user interacts with the environment to steer this course when prompted at appropriate points. The animation window technique represents each process as a box containing information about the current state of a process. Processes can in this way be represented as a tree. A process box is highlighted when it is active, as is an event. The state transition diagram window shows a partial state transition diagram for the process (again the active state is highlighted). The comparatively rapid prototyping of the environment is achieved through the use of multiple languages; these include Smalltalk [47] for the user interface.

Starlite [26] provided a visual simulation environment for prototyping concurrent software. The environment provides a standard interface to hardware devices thus easing problems of prototyping.

The use of visual animation techniques is also new to the hardware field. More recent developments include the Voyeur [99] system which provides an aid to debugging parallel programs, allowing the user to view the output graphically. A further tool for parallel programming is provided by Hvannberg and Krishnamoorthy [60]; they provide a parallel programming assistant which identifies areas in code that are suitable for parallel operations.

2.3.4. *Tools and toolsets*

In the mid-1980s, research into single tools and suites of software that would fit into the new generation of environments was increasing. The AWB-ADE [21] system consists of three packages which represent collections of utilities brought together under one "umbrella" so that they can be exported and managed. Childs hopes that this will encourage rapid prototyping and reuse. The Dost [32] environment provides facilities for the automatic generation of user interfaces. The underlying structures are organized into objects which communicate with each other through a messaging system and the user through an interface (another object).

In the late 1980s, several tools and toolsets were being constructed to be compatible with programming environments although they were not aimed at any one environment. These typically show some incremental capability in program development and provide additional facilities and tools for use in other tools, for example, the tree transformation facilities of [44], graphics in AdaPIC [117], and tools of CATS [118]. CATS is designed to be a suite of software for analyzing software systems, for the purpose of decomposition, and subsequent independent analysis.

The increasing extensibility in tool set architecture and size of environments would suggest that there is more likelihood of tools being designed and developed to be compatible with existing and future environments.

2.3.5. *Support for object-oriented paradigms*

The area of object-oriented design and notation particularly with respect to programming languages led to a number of environments concerned with the object-oriented paradigm. Tenma [118] *et al.* show the advance in the object-oriented paradigm in the field of generating language-oriented editors. Using a class hierarchy and structural links, this leads to a highly modular and extensible editor, with, however, no textual capability, which is unusual.

Wasserman *et al.* [112, 113] define the concepts needed in an object-oriented architectural design method. An editor for this method is being developed as part of the Software Through Pictures[111] family. The editor is configured for the language by associating a set of language-specific templates with the editor, and thus users are prompted with the appropriate language structure.

Magnusson *et al.* [71] describe the Mjølner/ORM Environment which includes "a direct manipulation graphical user interface that is consistently used in program manipulation, observation of program execution, and when defining program grammars". This environment requires grammars for abstract and concrete syntax, semantic checking, and code generation. Changes to grammars take effect immediately; grammars are interpreted which makes the system flexible and allows the addition of new constructs.

The two main interface principles are direct manipulation and context visualization, through hierarchic windows. In the use of graphics, the positioning of objects can be vital for their meaning; moving objects in this context is similar to the edit operation on a program. Magnusson also points out the increase in power because of the object-oriented nature of the environment. Code can be generated in many object-oriented languages.

The system presented by Hart and Shilling [51] represents a set of classes or components of object-oriented documentation units which are presented in a "nonlinear" fashion using a syntax-directed editor. The design and implementation can be linked together through the placement of links between modules and documentation segments. The particular advantage of this method is in the documentation of code features; the word "feature" is used to indicate a noteworthy point, such as a subprogram's call within a separate unit or a dependency. Features can be extracted to provide facilities for code reuse or debugging. It is also possible to parameterize or add predefined code structures so that features are used in a generic way. The linkage between components and features are easily established using commands provided within the interface. The system is implemented using the Aloegen system of Gandalf [86]. Hart and Shilling comment on the use of features in both the maintenance and reuse fields of software development.

2.3.6. *Configuration, planning and management*

Together with the development of compatible tools and increase in interest in object-orientation, the late 1980s also saw the marked increase in management tools, particularly those for configuration management [27, 52, 72].

Lin and Levary [69] combine expert systems with empirical research to develop SLICS, the Software Life-Cycle Simulator, which is composed of staff, product, and budget subsystems and can be used for given software development environments. Calibration to fit the unique characteristics of the environment occurs during the requirements phase of the project life-cycle. SLICS can then be used on planning estimates to simulate the running of the project in the environment, giving projections for the entire project and its individual phases. Thus, it would be possible using heuristic data to construct a cost plan of a project under several different environments, to find the most appropriate environment for a given project.

The Conic environment [66] provides an early insight into graphical configuration programming and the use of process modeling. This environment works at two levels, the level of the individual task and configuring groups of tasks.

Gustavsson [48] in his 1990 thesis studies the maintenance of information within the Mjølner programming environment. He considers the situation from the perspective of the data modeling for mapping the structure of a software object, the implementation of a model (delta) to reduce disk space, and the relation between a data model and software configuration management. The storage model allows different components of the internal program to be retrieved as part of a tree structure. The model groups frequently accessed and highly related information chunks into data objects. The advantage of this model is that the tool builder can take the access characteristics of the tool into consideration when designing the mapping between the internal program structure and the data model. The solution to the configuration problem involved a classification of software objects, and thus some of the problems of file stores, can be resolved.

Several other papers in 1990, for example, [65, 73, 81, 88] consider the topic of configuration or consistency management in programming environments. Most of these center around the question:

> Get a box full of useful tools and some kind of glue to put in between the tools. Stick the tools together and put a smooth surface on top of the whole thing. This is the basic idea of the mechanism for constructing integrated software engineering environments, ... Does this really work? [72]

and come to the conclusion that although the concept is good, making the system work and workable requires a considerable amount of effort.

2.3.7. *CASE and IPSEs*

A standard terminology is used to categorize environments; this paper has not attempted any classification beyond that of orientation towards structure. It is useful to provide such a definition, so that these terms can be put in perspective. In current acronyms two main streams exist for describing the environments that are the subject of this article: Computer-Aided Software

Engineering (CASE)tools, see [20], and Integrated Project Support Environments (IPSEs).

CASE tools are used to support a particular method and are not readily extensible, for example, Software Through Pictures [111]. They are designed primarily for individual support. CASE tools are usually targeted at the support of standard methods and in "main stream" data processing activity [35].

The term IPSE has developed from the Ada Project Support Environment (APSE) coined in the Stoneman report [16]; it is used generically to describe a wide range of open, multimethod, multitool environments. IPSEs are usually targeted at working in large groups, they often include management and configuration facilities.

Both CASE and IPSE technologies have been the subject of major academic research, for example, the Eureka Software Factory project [41], and Eclipse [12]. Developments that have come from this collaboration between industry and academe have been centered around smaller software houses [18]. Recent announcements have herald comprehensive CASE product strategies by major vendors (IBM AD/cycle, H-P SoftBench), and an increase in standards for CASE [37].

Current trends, together with movements towards CASE tool integration [17], signal a coming of age in CASE. There has been an emergence of CASE meta-tools, or CASE shells, for example, IPSYS's Tool Builders Kit, CADware's Foundry, and Systematica's Virtual Software Factory.

The integration in an IPSE has been primarily concerned with integration at three levels: data, interface, and control. The Portable Common Tool Environment (PCTE) [1] is an example of a public tool interface which provides the basis for integration.

CASE tools require a higher degree of integration [109] so that the benefits of each tool can be achieved. "IPSE infrastructures like PCTE are, at best, at the syntactic level of integration .... To get a higher level than syntactic integration, you must must encode either semantic or method knowledge into the tools." [14].

The mainstream acceptance of CASE, together with integration and standardization, will result in the convergence of CASE and IPSE technologies [70].[a] The emergent technology will involve a higher degree of integration, and a more robust environment.

[a]For example, Atherton Technology's Software BackPlane is described as both CASE and IPSE [17, pp. 18 and 27].

2.4. *Internal representation*

This short section concentrates on the internal representation of the structured data to be manipulated within the environment. Initially internal representation used was based on compiler technology; in order to handle the increased complexity of structure the representation used needed to become more appropriate, both for the change in the underlying structure and the increase in the amount of information which it must contain. The change monitored in this section is from an abstract syntax tree, to an enhanced abstract syntax tree and then the introduction of directed graph techniques.

Early editors such as the Cornell Program Synthesizer [105] used an abstract syntax tree for internal representation. Early targetable editors also used a syntax tree, but additional features and descriptive methods were used to enhance this tree. The Syned editor [58] used a textual representation, an abstract syntax tree, and a translation description; a translation is a dataflow containing a string of interpretable commands. A user could then edit or represent a structure in either a textual or transaction medium; the editor itself could represent a structure in textual, transaction, and syntax tree styles.

The Synthesizer Generator [93], a descendent of the CPS, was a targetable environment using both the abstract and concrete syntax of the language. The abstract syntax consists of a collection of phyla and operators (similar to Medina Mora [76]) instead of the more usual but less powerful terminal/nonterminal productions. An abstract-tree is formed under edit, with attributes decorating the phyla, which are typed objects in a unified domain. Reps and Teitelbaum [93] contend that abstract syntax trees often contain a convenient representation of a semantic value needed for computation.

The Aloe family of editors generated by Gandalf also uses a tree structure; Notkin [86] believes that it is important that a user is not forced to use a textual view, but that a tree structure can be directly created.

Garlan *et al.* [44] are concerned with software invalidation as a result of a new release of an environment. They point out that time is lost while conversion takes place, often in an ad hoc manner, for example, programs are altered and recompiled, whilst old data versions are painstakingly transformed. Garlan *et al.* concern themselves with tree to tree transformation; they say that most conversion takes place as an unparsing of the tree, followed by textual transformation and reparsing into the new structure. TransformerGen is part of the Gandalf project [86] and transforms directly from the old tree structure to that required by the new version.

Ballance *et al.* [7] consider the use of parser technology, as it relates to representation in language-based editors. They contend that the parser technology used in editors dictates the abstract syntax used and that an alternative would be some form of representation where the abstract and concrete syntax could be related. From this the grammar could be separated from the internal representation and the parser becomes more independent. Grammatical abstractions, as practiced by Ballance, are the formation of a relationship between two context free grammars. A mapping between the two syntaxes must be formed. Ballance goes on to describe the methods of weak and strong grammatical abstraction. A problem exists in that because of the differences between the two syntaxes used, it is not possible to build the same tree in a bottom-up tree construction as that which would be constructed in a top-down nonterminal expansion.

Many other projects at this time (the mid-1980s) were also considering the underlying representation used, whether it was possible to extend attribute grammars and syntax trees, or perhaps move to other representations. Kaiser [63] demonstrates that it is possible to extend attribute grammars to specify dynamic semantics in addition to static semantics, thus reducing the dependence on separate user written checking actions, which are external to the editor. He comments on the extended use of these grammars for the generation of interpreters and debuggers within, or complementary to, an environment. The debate between those who use an attributed syntax tree and those who prefer a graph structure is also entered by Alpern *et al.* [3]. He suggests that not all problems are characterized by an underlying tree structure. Alpern *et al.* suggest using attributed graph specifications instead of attributed trees. These would not necessarily support a graphical representation, but would present a uniform paradigm for expressing the desired relations among many and varied chunks of information.

Engels *et al.* [39] describe the procedure for the development of an arbitrary structure-oriented editor based on graph technology. They express the increasing dissatisfaction within the field with the ability of attributed and decorated syntax trees to represent program structure. A typical distinction is drawn between simple and complex user increments. In a structure-oriented style, simple increments are entered as text, and complex ones by command. A particular interest is taken in the relationship between graphic and user increments.

Meyers and Reiss [77] describe the use of semantic program graphs, showing how they can act as a foundation for multiparadigm software development environments. Semantic program graphs also facilitate communication between paradigms, as changes in one view can be reflected in the other views. Meyers and Reiss start by examining the possible reasons for multiple views in program environments and continue to look at the problems that existed in the multiple view environment, Garden [92], in that the creator must write a two-way translator for each pair of views which are to be kept consistent. They contend that a preferable arrangement is to have a single canonical representation of program semantics, then additional views need only to map to this central program repository.

Arefi *et al.* [5] comment on the problems of earlier editors and decide to use a deterministic, labeled-directed graph as the basis of a generic, syntax-directed editor. The project is at present a conceptual framework from which a system could be built. The system essentially has four components: the rule base, the graph, the user interface, and the supervisor. Essentially, Arefi *et al.* submit that any programming language can be generalized into a graph that can be "deterministically" transformed into any other graph that is possible within that language. Therefore, starting from a simple graph, a skeleton, one can expand or transform to a completed program structure. A set of graph transformation rules is necessary to indicate the transformation from one set of graphs to a further set of graphs. The system must have a set of transformation rules and a starting graph. To change from one graph to another, a rule is used to identify those components (nodes and edges) that are used in two graphs and those that are either added to or deleted from the graph, **a**, to achieve **a'**. The supervisor acts as an intermediary layer between the graph and the user. Acting upon information in the database, the supervisor maintains a view of the internal graph and applicable operations that can be invoked upon user request. The instantiator is warned by the system of potential ambiguity in the rules, by the supervisor. Arefi *et al.* describe this notation as a "new approach for the description of programming languages ... [which] ... concentrates on how instances of the language will be created and modified in a language-sensitive editor". In this way the editor can be seen to start writing the grammar (at least) of an editor in a way that is directed to the editor, rather than designing a tool that uses a standard notation. This is part of a general trend or feeling that grammars and languages dedicated to parsing technology are no longer a necessity as the basis of programming environments.

The movement in internal representation has been caused by the need for information within the underlying data structure. The increase in complexity first led to the attribution of syntax trees and later the movement to graph structures. The movement to multiple view architectures is also instrumental in this change; the need for parser-based technology in representation declined in importance with the increasing use of graphics and the associated change in structural data stored.

2.5. *Textual manipulation*

The large proportion of early editors worked on a textually-based notation, the themes and trends of interaction with textually-based bit structure-orientated editors are examined in this section. After a description of the editing structures of the CPS [105], the section will continue with a look at the variation between completely structure-oriented and text-dominated interaction, the advantages that each of these provides, the solutions at each extreme, and those created by hybridization.

In the CPS, syntax-directed editing is used for high-level statements; at a lower level, such as expressions and assignment constructs, this become tedious and uneconomic because the user has to make a complex selection from menus. The CPS presents an early hybrid solution where a program is built by top-down insertions of syntax units and all operations are syntax drivers. Within the CPS certain enhancements to the hybrid system are available, these include syntactic elision,[b] the use of syntactic templates, and a clip buffer.

The elison mechanism allows a programmer to compress displayed representation of a syntax unit; this increases the percentage of a program that is visible "on screen". The clip buffer is used for temporary storage and manipulation of a syntactic unit.

The template metaphor is used to provide "an immutable program framework" [105], it consists of unalterable keywords and syntactic sugar with embedded placeholders, at which a nonterminal derivation or insertion can occur. Teitelbaum comments on the problems that occur because of the different treatment of high- and low-level statements: "the immutability of templates" precludes textual change from one template to another, whilst retaining the applicable internal structure. This also gives rise to the problem of movement of syntactically correct objects, such as low-level conditions, to a situation

[b]This mechanism is attributed by Allison [2] to Hansen [50] in his "holophrasting" work.

in which they are not correct semantically, because of the underlying type structure.

The CPS is termed a syntax-directed editor as its action is determined by the language syntax. Morris and Schwartz [84] consider a language-directed editor as combining "the text manipulation functions of a general purpose editor with the syntax checking functions of a compiler". This type of editor is referred to as syntax-oriented as the editor checks the input with reference to the syntax rather than functioning with respect to the syntax. Morris and Schwartz identify two problems with these editors: the profligate amount of resources which are consumed, to which no solution is proffered, and the problem of transforming between language constructs. They suggest the use of "a new model", shortest route incremental parsing solution, as an alternative to the template. Some of the time saving advantage of the template is offset by Morris and Schwartz with the use of a keyword completion system, upon sufficient structural disambiguation. The approaches suggested are in many ways less ambitious than the CPS and seem to intend that editors move back towards the enhanced text editor [116]. This debate is further advanced by Waters [114] and Shani [98].

The SED [2] editor for Pascal was developed at the University of Western Australia. Allison contends that simplicity, minimal layout interference, and the ability to edit incomplete programs are important. He concludes that "Editors should edit"; other functions such as pretty printing and type checking can be performed optionally or externally. The elision mechanism used in SED has an integer parameter to give several preset elision levels. Allison rejects on screen formatting as highly subjective. However, many commercial organizations are working towards standardization and Allison's statement seems shortsighted. SED has a solution to the problem of transformation between constructs; text like substitutions are allowed between statements so that constructs may be substituted without loss of the lower levels of the hierarchy; for example, an "If" construct can be transformed to a loop statement, with the body of the loop composed of the body of the "If" statement.

A completely structured approach to interaction is used in the Gandalf editors [86]. The differences between those advocating the structural approach and those preferring free-form input continued as most measures of "instability" were seen as subjective by [30]. Studies, such as [67], showed that those who had not used text editors quickly picked up the structural approach and that the majority of recalcitrance existed among experienced programmers used to the edit-compile cycle.

Many editors developed with hybrid vigor and new techniques. Among these were the inclusion of parser technology to check structure, or parse text, into an underlying structure.

The Support [119] environment could handle projects of up to twenty thousand lines of source code and contained editors for both program design and programming languages. Nonterminal expansion was used to the statement level (to form templates), beyond which free-form text/code (subsequently parsed) could be entered. The environment included a multiwindow capability allowing simultaneous views on code; a "hybrid top-down, bottom-up parser" allowed construction to occur at any stage, either textually or from a menu. A text edit window superseded the CPS clip buffer allowing text modifications which were subsequently parsed back into the structure.

Degano [29] is also concerned with parsing; he draws the distinction between the two separate structure editing groups, those that use a top-down generated technique (generative), e.g., Mentor and Gandalf, and those which perform bottom-up construction by parsing (analytic). He comments that those hybrid editors that do exist produce "monolithic" environments, and that this can be improved by improving the efficiency of LR parsing techniques; this would also enable editors to be used together more efficiently. This is achieved by splitting parsing tables into several parsing subtables, each of which analyzes consistent program fragments.

Syned [58], one of the first language independent editors, included a multiple-entry parser; multiple-entry meant that parsing could continue from any nonterminal, and thus the user could choose at any point to use either structured or textual input.

Poe (Pascal-Oriented Editor) [42] was another early targetable editor with more recent ongoing implementation for VAL [75], a data flow language, and ABE [64]. Fischer *et al.*, unlike Allison (SED above), take the view that " 'pretty printing' is automatic (and inescapable) when programs are displayed". Poe also contains an automatic syntactic error corrector which takes input and displays a full structure as soon as an appropriate disambiguation occurs. An undo mechanism is available if the the correct production does not appear. Elision is supported over the smallest syntactic structure containing the cursor. A placeholder-like marker is then displayed; Poe tries to include valuable parts of the elided structure, such as the condition of an "If" statement, whilst keeping the on screen representation as small as possible.

The Tioga editor, part of the leader project [106], is a language-based editor and documentation system. EMACS-like extensions, are available with a "Do What I Mean" system which corrects spelling in a similar style to Interlisp [107].

The structured environment community appears to have reached a subjective stalemate between the camps of free-form text editors, which are subsequently checked, and structured editors. The rule of thumb for these editors is that those with little structuring have few semantic checks, while structured editors are more likely to have semantic checking.

An established hybridization has occurred where structured commands are used at a high-level and free-form text at a lower level. Solutions to the problems of transformation between language contract have been proposed, ranging from text-like substitution to tree pruning and rebuilding, for example, the work of Dykes and Cameron [36]. Dykes and Cameron divide the manipulations on structures into patterns of similar operations. These can then be embedded within a command structure so as to reduce the potential number of manipulations to a reasonable level. These operations can be used for optimization of structure as some knowledge-based elements are included. The implicit knowledge of structure necessary precludes a language independent generalization at this stage.

The range of hybridization and application precludes any statement that the problems of these editors have been solved by a single solution. Solutions are very much domain- and technique-oriented. Many editors adopt an extensibility in the EMACS genre. For example, Pan [8] can operate on documents in both a textual and structured domain as well as being used for unstructured text. Systems are tailorable not only to local, but also individual work practices. This is achieved through a mixture of declarative and imperative commands.

2.6. *Conceptual programming*

In contrast to the previous section, where environments were targeted at structures represented textually, this section highlights some of the developments that have sought to maximize the technology available to them. That is, to allow the user of the environment more freedom over the representation, or to provide assistance, in some knowledge-based fashion, in its manipulation. The term "conceptual programming" first attained prominence through the work of Reiss [92]; however, the ideas behind the concept can be traced to earlier work [86, 105].

> Programs are not text; they are hierarchical compositions of computational structures and should be edited, executed and debugged in an environment that consistently acknowledges and reinforces this viewpoint. [105]

The CPS then gives a structured manipulation of the textual objects. Programming languages were developed in tandem with compiler technology; compilers use parsing as a fundamental operation and parsing is based upon grammar rules. The languages that develop in this way are designed to be parsed. The structured environment is based on technology inherited from parsers, but is not necessary for the manipulation of the structure. The point, which is a major theme, is that rather than using the power of the environment, the environment is used to support a familiar paradigm.

The first real conceptual project was MAGPIE [30], a project which attempted to create an environment which requires no "mental context switching" by its users. In this way it can be seen as a fore-runner of many of the later developments in cognitive mapping of program structure.

> The goal of integrating a programming environment is more than simply building tools that share a common data base and provide a consistent user interface. Ideally the programming environment appears to the programmer as a single tool. [30]

Delisle and Schwartz consider that menus in similar systems to MAGPIE contain too much information and that the usability of any system is too subjective to quantify. Magpie uses a browser (editor) window system for code as well as daemon and heap views of code structures. Within the code browser the user is notified about any errors, but not forced to correct them; a think-time throw-away compilation allows immediate execution of code fragments. Magpie facilities include assert statements for debugging which become part of the code, first seen in [76], and the ability to test individual code modules.

Integral C [96] continues in the MAGPIE genre; Ross highlights the main aim of Integral C as similar to that of MAGPIE. To implement an environment in a manner which is faithful to the language definition, he cites MAGPIE as one of the few editors to achieve this.

Reiss is also concerned with the representation of the program: PECAN [91] was an instantiable development system for multiple program views. Among the goals of PECAN was to support multiple and concurrent views of the system; this would allow experimentation with new views in a modular environment; thus new views or even new languages could be tested without a complete system rewrite. Reiss also comments on the goal of developing a graphical program interface, to replace or complement the textual interface presently used. This would allow the user to choose the most appropriate view, the internal representation being a product of whichever view was currently edited. This is one of the first papers within the structured environment community that attempts to use the advantages of the tool to solve the underlying problem. Other environments attempt to fit a tool that can be built, to a paradigm that is a known solution. PECAN also supports a semantic representation which allows multiple views of arbitrary data structures.

In "Programming in the Garden conceptual programming environment" [92], Reiss sets out the case for designing a software environment. He comments that the programmer could use a variety of methods, which could be tailored to a particular problem. Rather than an environment which the programmer has to adapt to, the environment should conform to the programmer; for example, it should contain many different design paradigms. The eventual goal would be a system in which a design could be edited and maintained at the design rather than the code level, with code automatically produced from a design. Garden [92] is designed to support a concurrent use of languages supporting different paradigms. A conceptual model is the model of the system that the designer has in his head. Garden seeks to capture this model and then turn it into a program; the building blocks for this are the multiple view paradigm and provision of an appropriate environment. Reiss champions the cause of object-orientation, with hierarchical inheritance for prototyping, encouraging reusability, and data abstraction. The object basis gives scope for the syntax to be defined textually, or graphically, or both (developed by Ratcliffe *et al.* in Dora [89]); the representation is not important. Reiss comments that this represents a step forward from his work on Pecan [91], which only had one language but several graphics views. This step is achieved by reducing the dependence on the syntax. Reiss mentions that further work will be in the area of layout heuristics. At present, the automatic screen representation is not satisfactory; this is due to the lack of suitable structure in the underlying objects.

The Lilac [13] system also uses a conceptual approach. The edit-compile cycle of document preparation systems is broken by a multiview representation of both source code and associated WYSIWYG preview. The user may interact with either representation and an automatic update appears in the alternative representation. Lilac presents a good example of an application of both the multiview and conceptual concepts. The user is able to interact with the structure in the most appropriate form.

The ideas of conceptual programming are initially appealing. However, the increased emphasis in the industrial market place for toolsets based on one or the other standard method (e.g., HOOD in Europe) would indicate that the lack of uniformity it represents is not desired (at present). In the industrial situation more limited cases, such as those within Lilac for structure manipulation, will perhaps be supported; these will then have to be "upgraded" to some organizational or international standard.

Many environments embody "knowledge", either implicitly or explicitly, about program structure. A few try to capture the knowledge of the programmer and utilize it. Among these is the Programmer's Apprentice [94], which seeks to add techniques of artificial intelligence to the environment arena.

> The long-term goal of the Programmer's Apprentice project is to develop a theory of how expert programmers analyze, synthesise, modify, explain, specify, verify and document programs. [94]

Rich [94] describes the Programmer's Apprentice as an intersection of the artificial intelligence and software engineering worlds, to automate the programing process. This he hopes will provide intelligent assistance in all phases of the programing task. Rich maintains that human programmers think in terms of primitive elements or building blocks when structuring program segments; Rich calls these elements "clichés" which consist of roles and constraints. Roles are the part of the clichéd segment which change in use. The programmer can choose between the various clichéd paradigms to implement his cognitive program map. As well as the Programmer's Apprentice, several other environments with a strong knowledge-based component appeared in the literature in 1988 [40, 97, 110].

With the increase in understanding of knowledge-based techniques and the software engineering discipline, a gradual increase in the replacement of human by machine effort is assured. The time scale of these developments is likely to be dominated by the design effort put into them, rather than any technical or technological constraints.

2.7. *Environment evaluation*

The final topic for exploration in this tour of environment trends is that of environment evaluation. This area has not received the attention in the literature that could be expected. There are several reasons for this: the lack of widespread use of tools and thus a consensus on which to base any evaluation; self-evaluation and pier evaluation in an informalised manner; the lack of standard tests; the diversity of environment facilities and resulting difficulty in comparison; the subjectivity of many requirements such as usability.

In this section three papers are highlighted, that of Weiderman on a standard evaluation; Lang on syntax editors; and a more recent publication by Minör on interacting with structure-oriented editors.

Weiderman [115] attempts to establish an outline for the evaluation of environments. He argues the case for a standard method that is comprehensive, repeatable, user-oriented, and partially environment dependent. "The purpose of defining a methodology is to add a degree of rigour and a standardization to the process of evaluating an environment." The paper however fails to deliver a comprehensive method, producing instead a general description of procedures.

In his paper, Lang [67] also attempts some form of evaluation of the interaction with these environments. This is related from experience of using MENTOR "on the usefulness of syntax-directed editors". Lang feels that for simple, semantics-free editing commands and tools, little advantage (worthy of the conceptual and implementation cost) is gained over text-oriented, or off-line, use of the same tools. Lang also stresses the importance of extensibility in the toolset for tailoring to fit both individuals and projects. He emphasizes the use of syntax editors for maintenance activities, for example, the transport of programs between dialects, or for repetitive functions. MENTOR initially had an interface similar to a line-based editor; in 1981, a full screen editor was added, with parser-driven tree (syntax) editor commands. This was developed to the stage of a bit-mapped, mouse-interfaced, menu-driven system in 1984. The benefit for novice users occurred in the use of menus, which (Lang mentions) were rarely used by experts. Lang concludes that for maintenance activities the advantage of syntax-directed tools outweighs the user friendliness of full screen editing. He contends that the single greatest factor especially for the novice user is the design of the user interface, "bridging the conceptual gap of the syntax-directed paradigm, and by simply looking nicer". He considers syntax direction as irreplaceable for maintenance, but the user must always "play the game" and stay within the confines of the tool rather than reverting to textual forms.

Minör [78] comments on the problems encountered when interacting with structure-oriented editors, suggesting possible solutions where they have occurred and admitting the shortcomings of these editors. The paper concentrates on the differences in interaction between structured editors and text editors. Minör uses Norman's [85] model to present the user activities in the two editing types; he continues to comment on the hybrid editor, which seeks to overcome the problems by combining both textual and structured facilities. This paper also contains a discussion of the conceptual models for these various editor types and a suggestion of an interaction model based on direct manipulation is discussed. The direct manipulation paradigm is to supply a user interface which physically models the real or imagined world, rather than using an intermediate interface such as a menu or command language. The display of program language structures is textual but presented in semi-graphical boxes so that it is clear which syntactic units constitute a structure. Minör tries to calibrate the measure of directness under two criteria:

1. engagement: the users' feeling of being involved,
2. distance: the distance between the users' intentions and the requirements of the system.

The trend in this limited field is to evaluate environments with regard to the user. Intangible and subjective measures are often used. If any development is to be made in the environment evaluation, some form of quantification of these features could be attempted. The diversity of environment applications, structures, and architecture would imply that standard benchmarking and methodological evaluations are both impractical and inconclusive. The increase in standards and reference models, such as [37], will give the industry a set of criteria; rather than an independent set of tests, an increasing, objective comparison will be made with reference to these standards.

3. Summary and Conclusion

The decade of structure editing which this chapter focuses on has produced a growth and flowering of the field. There are several themes and trends which run through this period, and these are highlighted by the examples within this paper.

The early 1980s produced editors that could basically be classified into two camps: those that were syntax-directed and those that were syntax-oriented, generative and analytic respectively. With the realization that neither of these two held a complete and workable solution, many editors contained a hybridization; these consisted of macros in analytic editors, to produce, for example, code skeletons, and in the case of generative environments, lower level statements such as expressions which often utilized parsed text. These editors were language specific, typically single window, and extensions would be made by altering the source code of the editor.

With the advance in window technology it became possible to present simultaneously more than one representation of the underlying structure. This was used particularly for graphical views of textually represented entities, and allowed the representation of further information such as semantic data associated with the target structure. With the increase in power and ease of use, the target of these editors became extended from the original language structures to more complex domains. With the Stoneman report and concepts of the APSE and IPSE, the single editor developed into a suite of tools which together could comprise a total environment for project development. These environments often included, for example, compiling and debugging tools as well as many diverging representations in both textual and graphic form, commonly using a decorated underlying syntax tree as a base.

The mid 1980s saw a shift towards a nondedicated environment, an expansion in the size, target, and complexity of the dedicated environment and the production of tools that could be linked to such an environment, in particular, tools for semantic evaluation and incremental compilation. These early nondedicated or targetable environments usually comprised a central kernel, which was combined with a target (language) description to form the environment. The kernel would contain the facilities common to all applications such as window and user interface management control, as well as language independent tree or database manipulation commands. The environment description, usually containing an abstract and concrete syntax and often some code modules for increased functionality, was usually preprocessed before being bound to the kernel at instantiation. The end of this period also saw the extension of graphics capabilities (particularly by Reiss) and the increased emphasis on multiuser environments with the associated data management, configuration, and control problems.

One of the major problems in providing structured editors for programming languages was the transformation between one language construct and another, which was textually a little different. This was a problem common to both generative and analytic editors. Early solutions included a temporary suspension of checking whilst the program being edited moved through an incorrect program state. Later generative editor grammars contained code modules to map between the various constructs; this system was advanced and generalized, together with an enhanced understanding of grammars, to achieve a more general mapping to groups of similar structures, perhaps engendered by the increased awareness of object orientation. Meanwhile, the comparable solution in analytic editors was the demarcation, both visually and internally, of the temporarily incorrect structure. These remained in the overall representation but were highlighted for further future modification.

The latter part of the 1980s saw environments develop in what can be seen as three major overlapping thrusts. The basic problem that each tried to solve was that tool sets could be seen as either extensible or well integrated but not both. Each tried to develop a method of producing a well-integrated but extensible environment. The process modeling school sought to define the relation between the tools in the environment; the communication between the components would be defined in a central process description formalism. A similar but more rule-based school contained many of the influences of artificial intelligence; a particular early example of this was the Darwin environment. The third school of thought was concerned with the communication between cooperating agents. At first this developed as control between individual agents, which became further defined into two systems. In one, an intelligent "mail box" intercepted the relevant broadcasts from central or individual sources, and in the other, the central "sorting office" forwarded the relevant communication to the appropriate agents.

The increasing complexity of the environments meant that many projects developed on multiple sites, and that tools were produced as a product of, or to be included within, more major projects such as Gandalf, Arcadia, PCTE and Mjølner.

Some of the more innovative research centered on the cognitive mapping of programs, which was enhanced by the emergence of representations as an alternative to the abstract syntax tree. The abstract syntax tree became less necessary [46] as parser-based technology was replaced by systems that interactively interrogated the database. The increase in size and complexity of the support which these environments give has lead to further interest in configuration and version management, particularly systems that use an underlying database.

The increasing size of the environments and the technical knowledge necessary to instantiate them has meant that the cost to many commercial organizations may seem considerably less than a purpose-built tool kit. However, the instantiated environment will take a considerable effort in terms of both internal and possibly consultant manpower as the languages and concepts used within these environments tend to have a long and steep learning curve. The development of the structured environment can be seen as the first attempt by software engineers, since the development of compilers, to produce a tool for "their own use". This is a direct result of the increasing size and complexity of the tasks with which they are involved. The structured environment has passed from its heady days of an early emergent technology to the status of a necessary and efficient tool. Although development in many of its concepts continues, the financial effort needed to build a state-of-the-art environment has precluded this development from an academic arena; the exception is a small number of funded, large and often collaborative (between industrial and academic partners) projects, from which many smaller developments "spin off", although these are more likely to develop more commercially viable case tools. This commercialism in turn depends on the applicability of the research to the market. We will continue to see developments in the targets of these environments, and in the tools which they incorporate. Having attained expertise in this field, the majority of effort will now switch to implementing those techniques and methods which are in current favor in the most user friendly way with an emphasis on ease of learning and extensibility. The process modeling area will be particularly important as a future influence for the development of extensible environments. However, the process model lacks the maturity and stability, at this stage, to provide either a basis for environment architecture or project environment standards.

Acknowledgements

The authors would like to express their appreciation to Dr. Peter Robinson for his constructive comment on this paper.

References

1. *PCTE: A Basis for a Portable Common Tool Environment*, Commission of the European Communities, DG XIII/Esprit, 45, Av. Auderghem, Brussels, Functional Specification, 1.5 edition (1989).
2. L. Allison, "Syntax-directed program editing", *Software — Practice and Experience* **13**, 5 (1983) 453–465.
3. B. Alpern, A. Carle, B. Rosen, and P. Sweeney, "Graph attribution as a specification paradigm", in [53], (1988) 121–129.
4. R. Altmann, A. Hawke, and C. Marlin, "An integrated programming environment based on multiple concurrent views", *The Australian Computer J.* **20**, 2 (1988) 25–34.
5. F. Arefi, C. Hughes, and D. Workman, "Automatically generating visual syntax-directed editors", *Computing Practices* **33**, 3 (1990) 449–460.
6. R. Bahlke and G. Snelting, "The PSG — Programming System Generator", *SIGPLAN Notices* **20**, 7 (1985) 28–33.
7. R. Ballance, "Grammatical abstraction and incremental syntax analysis in a language-based editor", *SIGPLAN '88 Conf. Programming Language Design and Implementation* (1988).
8. R. Ballance, S. Graham, and M. VanDe Vanter, "The PAN language-based editing system for integrated development environments", in [102], (1990) 77–93.
9. D. Bjørner and C. Jones, *Formal Specification and Software Development* (Prentice-Hall International, 1982).
10. D. Bjørner and C. Jones, "The Vienna Development Method: the meta-language", *Lecture Notes in Computer Science* **61** (1978).
11. P. Borras, D. Clèment, Th. Despeyroux, J. Incerpi, G. Kahn, B. Lang, and V. Pascal, "CENTAUR: the system", in [53], (1988) 14–24.
12. M. F. Bott, ed., *Elipse — An Integrated Project Support Environment* (Peter Pereginus, 1989).
13. K. Brooks, "Lilac: a two-view document editor", *Computer* **24**, 6 (1991) 7–19.
14. A. Brown and J. McDermid, "Learning from IPSE's mistakes", *IEEE Softw.* **9**, 2 (1992) 23–28.
15. R. Buhr, G. Karam, C. Hayes, and C. Woodside, "Software CAD: a revolutionary approach", *IEEE Trans. Softw. Eng.* **15**, 3 (1989) 235–249.
16. J. N. Buxton, *STONEMAN: Requirements for Ada Programming Support Environments*, United States Department of Defense, WAshington, USA (1980).
17. C. Chang, ed., "Special issue: integrated CASE," *IEEE Softw.* **9**, 2 (1992).
18. M. Chen and R. Norman, "A framework for integrated CASE", *Softw.* **9**, 2 (1992) 18–22.
19. M. Chesi, E. Dameri, M. Franceschi, M. Gatti, and C. Simonelli, "ISDE: an interactive software development environment", in [54], (1984) 81–88.
20. E. Chikofsky, ed., "Special issue: CASE", *IEEE Softw.* **5**, 2 (1988).

21. C. Childs and F. Vokolos, "AWB-ADE: an application development environment for interactive, integrated systems", in [55], (1986) 111–120.
22. L. Clarke, D. Richardson, and S. Zeil, "TEAM: a support environment for testing, evaluation, and analysis", in [53], (1988) 153–162.
23. D. Clément, "A distributed architecture for programming environments", in [102], (1990) 11–21.
24. G. Clemm, "The Workshop system — a practical knowledge-based software environment", in [53], (1988) 45–54.
25. E. Cohen, D. Soni, R. Gluecker, W. Hasling, R. Schwanke, and M. Wagner, "Version management in Gypsy", in [53], (1988) 201–215.
26. R. Cook and R. Auletta, "StarLite: a visual simulation package for software prototyping", in [55], (1986) 102–110.
27. K. Cooper, K. Kennedy, and L. Torczon, "Editing and compiling whole programs", in [55], (1986) 92–101.
28. R. Dannenberg, "A structure for efficient update, incremental redisplay and undo in graphical editors", *Software — Practice and Experience* **20**, 2 (1990) 109–132.
29. P. Degano, S. Mannucci, and B. Mojana, "Efficient incremental LR parsing for syntax-directed editors", *ACM Trans. Programming Languages and Systems* **10**, 3 (1988) 345–373.
30. N. Delisle, D. Menicosy, and M. Schwartz, "Viewing a programming environment as a single tool", in [54], (1984) 49–56.
31. N. Delisle and M. Schwartz, "A programming environment for CSP", in [55], (1986) 34–41.
32. P. Dewan and M. Solomon, "Dost: an environment to support automatic generation of user interfaces", in [55], (1986) 150–159.
33. V. Donzea-Gouge, G. Huet, G. Kahn, and B. Lang, "The Mentor program manipulation system", Technical Report, IRIA-Laboria (August 1979).
34. M. Dowson, "ISTAR — an integrated project support environment", in [55], (1986) 27–33.
35. DTI, *The STARTS Guide*, 2nd ed. (NCC Publishing, 1987).
36. L. Dykes and R. Cameron, "Towards high-level editing in syntax-based editors", *IEE BCS Softw. Eng. J.* **5**, 4 (1990) 237–244.
37. ECMA, "A reference model for frameworks of computer-assisted software engineering environments", Technical Report, Report No. TR/55, 2nd ed., European Computer Manufacturers Association, 114 Rue du Rhone — CH-1204 Geneva, Switzerland (December 1991).
38. M. Edel, "The Tinkertoy graphical programming environment", *IEEE Trans. Softw. Eng.* **14**, 8 (1988) 1110–1115.
39. G. Engels, M. Nagl, and W. Schaefer, "On the structure of structure-oriented editors for different applications", in [55], (1986) 190–198.
40. L. Erman, J. Lark, and F. Hayes-Roth, "ABE: an environment for engineering intelligent systems", *IEEE Trans. Softw. Eng.* **14**, 12 (1988) 1758–1770.

41. C. Fernström, "The Eureka Software Factory: concepts and accomplishments", *Proc. 3rd European Software Engineering Conf.* (Springer-Verlag, 1991).
42. C. Fisher, A. Pal, D. Stock, G. Johnson, and J. Mauney, "The POE language-based editor project", in [54], (1984) 21–29.
43. D. Garlan and E. Illias, "Low-cost, adaptable tool integration policies for integrated environments", in [102], (1990) 1–10.
44. D. Garlan, C. Krueger, and B. Staudt, "A structural approach to the maintenance of structure-oriented environments", in [55], (1986) 160–170.
45. D. Garlan and P. Miller, "GNOME: an introductory programming environment based on a family of structure editors", in [54], (1984) 65–72.
46. R. Gautier, "Structure-oriented environments", Technical Report, Computer Science Department, University of Wales, Aberystwyth, UK (1990).
47. A. Goldberg and D. Robson, *Smalltalk 80: The Language and its Implementation* (Addison-Wesley, 1983).
48. A. Gustavsson, "Software configuration management in an integrated environment", Ph.D. Thesis, Lund University, Sweden (1990).
49. W. J. Hansen, "Creation of hierarchic text with a computer display", Ph.D. Thesis, Stanford University, USA (1971).
50. W. J. Hansen, "User engineering principles for interactive systems", *AFIP FJCC* **39** (1971) 523–532.
51. C. Hart and J. Shilling, "An environment for documenting software features", in [102], (1990) 120–132.
52. D. Heimbinger and S. Krane, "A graph transform model for configuration management environments", in [53], (1988) 216–226.
53. P. Henderson, ed., *Proc. ACM SIGSOFT/SIGPLAN, Software Engineering Symp. Practical Software Development Environments 1988.* ACM published as *SIGPLAN Notices* **24**, 2 (1989), *SIGSOFT Softw. Eng. Notes* **13**, 5 (1988).
54. P. Henderson, ed., *Proc. ACM SIGSOFT/SIGPLAN, Software Engineering Symp. Practical Software Development Environments.* ACM published as *SIGPLAN* **19**, 5, *Softw. Eng. Notes* **9**, 5 *SIGPLAN Notices* **19**, 5 (1984).
55. P. Henderson, ed. *Proc. SIGSOFT/SIGPLAN, Software Engineering Symp. Practical Software Development Environments 1986.* ACM published as *SIGPLAN* **22**, 1 (1987).
56. W. Henhapl and G. Snelting, "Context relations — a concept for incremental context analysis in program fragments", in *GI — Fachtagung Programmiersprachen und Programmentwicklung Informatik Fachberichte 77* (Springer Verlag, 1984).
57. C. Hoare, "Communicating sequential processes", *Commun. ACM* **21**, 8 (1978) 666–677.
58. J. R. Horgan and D. J. Moore, Techniques for improving language-based editors", in [54], (1984) 7–14.
59. K. Huff and V. Lesser, "A plan-based intelligent assistant that supports the software development process", in [53], (1988) 97–106.

60. E. Hvannberg and M. Krishamoorthy, "An object-based parallel programming assistant", *SIGPLAN Notices* **24**, 4 (1989) 200–202.
61. E. Ipser, D. Wile, and D. Jacobs, "A multi-formalism specification environment", in [102], (1990) 94–106.
62. G. Kahn, B. Lang, and B. Mélèse, "METAL: a formalism to specify formalisms", *Science of Computer Programming* **3** (1983) 35–42.
63. G. Kaiser, "Incremental dynamic semantics for language-based programming environments", *Trans. Programming Languages and Systems* **11**, 2 (1989) 161–193.
64. A. A. Klug, "A query language for constructing aggregates by-example", *Workshop on Statistical Database Management* (1981).
65. H. Kobialka, "Configuration editing, generating and test within working contexts", in [102], (1990) 173–182.
66. J. Kramer, J. Magee, and K. Ng, "Graphical configuration programming: the structural description, construction, and evolution of software systems using graphics", *Computer* **20**, 5 (1989) 53–65.
67. B. Lang, "On the usefulness of syntax-directed editors", in *Proc. IFIP WG2.4 Int. Workshop on Advanced Programming Environments* (1986).
68. C. Lewerentz, "Extended programming in the large in a software development environment", in [53], (1988) 173–181.
69. C. Lin and R. Levary, "Computer-aided software development process design", *IEEE Trans. Softw. Eng.* **15**, 9 (1989) 1025–1037.
70. F. Long, ed., *Software Engineering Environments*, Vol. 3 (Ellis Horwood, 1991).
71. B. Magnusson, "The Mjølner/ORM environment: incremental language and software development", Technical Report, Department of Computer Science, Lund University, Sweden (February 1990).
72. A. Mahler and A. Lampen, "An integrated toolset for engineering software configurations", in [53], (1988) 191–200.
73. A. Mahler and A. Lampen, "Integrating configuration management into a generic environment", in [102], (1990) 229–237.
74. K. Marzullo and D. Weibe, "Jasmine: a software system modeling facility", in [55], (1986) 121–129.
75. J. R. McGraw, "The VAL language: description and analysis", *Trans. Programming Languages and Systems* **4**, 1 (1982) 44–82.
76. R. Medina-Mora and P. Feiler, "An incremental programming environment", *IEEE Trans. Softw. Eng.* **7**, 5 (1981) 472–481.
77. S. Meyers and S. Reiss, "Representing programs in multiparadigm software development", *13th Annual Int. Computer Software and Applications Conf.*, Orlando, Florida, USA (September 1989).
78. S. Minör, "Interacting with structure-oriented editors", Technical Report, Department of Computer Science Lund University, Sweden (January 1991).
79. S. Minör, "On structure editing", Ph.D. Thesis, Lund University, Sweden (1990).

80. N. Minsky and A. Borgida, "The Darwin software-evolution environment", in [54], (1984) 89–95.
81. N. Minsky and D. Rozenshtein, "Configuration management by consensus: an application of law-governed systems", in [102], (1990) 44–55.
82. N. Minsky and D. Rozenshtein, "A software development environment for law-governed systems", in [53], (1988) 55–64.
83. E. Morcos-Chounet and A. Conchon, "PPML, a general formalism for pretty-printing", *Int. Federation for Information Processing Congress* (Springer Verlag, 1986).
84. J. M. Morris and M. D. Schwartz, "The design of a language-directed editor for block structured languages", *SIGPLAN Notices* **16**, 6 (1981) 28–33.
85. D. Norman, "Cognitive engineering", in *User Centered System Design* (Lawrence Erlbaum Associates Inc., 1986) pp. 31–61.
86. D. Notkin, "The Gandalf Project", *J. Syst. Softw.* **5**, 2 (1985) 91–105.
87. L. Osterweil, "Software processes are software too", *9th Int. Conf. Software Engineering* (March–April 1987).
88. X. Qian, R. Jullig, and M. Daum, "Consistency management in a project management assistant", in [102], (1990) 34–43.
89. M. Ratcliffe, C. Wang, R. Gautier, and B. Whittle, "Dora — a structure-oriented environment generator", *IEE BCS Softw. Eng. J.* **7**, 3 (1992) 84–190.
90. S. Reiss, "Connecting tools using message passing in the Field environment", *IEEE Softw.* **7**, 4 (July 1990).
91. S. Reiss, "PECAN: program development systems that support multiple views", *IEEE Trans. Softw. Eng.* **11**, 3 (1985) 276–284.
92. S. Reiss, "Working in the garden environment for conceptual programming", *IEEE Softw.* **4**, 6 (1987).
93. T. Reps and T. Teitelbaum, "The Synthesizer Generator", in [54], (1984) 42–48.
94. C. Rich and R. Waters, "The Programmer's Apprentice", *IEEE Comput.* **21**, 11 (1988) 11–25.
95. T. Rodden, P. Sawyer, and I. Sommerville, "Interacting with an active, integrated environment", in [53], (1988) 76–84.
96. G. Ross, "Integral C — a practical environment for C programming", in [55], (1986) 42–48.
97. E. Schoen, R. Smith, and B. Buchanan, "Design of knowledge-based systems with a knowledge-based assistant", *IEEE Trans. Softw. Eng.* **14**, 12 (1988) 1771–1779.
98. U. Shani, "Should program editors not abandon text-oriented commands?", *SIGPLAN Notices* **18**, 1 (1983) 35–41.
99. D. Socha, M. Bailey, and D. Notkin, "VOYEUR: graphical views of parallel programs", *SIGPLAN Notices* **24**, 1 (1989) 206–215.
100. T. Strelich, "The Software Life-Cycle Support Environment: a computer-based framework for developing software systems", in [53], (1988) 35–44.
101. K. Sullivan and D. Notkin, "Reconciling environment integration and component independence", in [102], (1990) 22–33.

102. R. Taylor, ed., *Proc. 4th ACM SIGSOFT, Software Engineering Symp. Software Development Environment.* ACM published as *SIGSOFT Softw. Eng. Notes* **15**, 6 (1990).
103. R. Taylor, W. Selby, M. Young, F. Belz, L. Clarke, J. Wileden, L. Osterweil, and A. Wolf, "Foundations for the Arcadia environment architecture", in [53], (1988) 1–13.
104. R. Taylor and T. Standish, "Steps to an advanced Ada programming environment", *IEEE Trans. Softw. Eng.* **11**, 3 (1985) 302–313.
105. T. Teitelbaum, "The Cornell Program Syntheiser: a syntax-directed programming environment", *Commun. ACM* **24**, 9 (1981) 563–573.
106. W. Teitelman, "A tour through CEDAR", *IEEE Trans. Softw. Eng.* **11**, 3 (1985) 285–301.
107. W. Teitelman and L. Masinter, "The Interlisp programming environment", *Computer* **14**, 4 (1981) 25–34.
108. T. Tenma, H. Tsubonati, M. Tanaka, and T. Ichikawa, "A system for generating language-oriented editors", *IEEE Trans. Softw. Eng.* **14**, 8 (1988) 1089–1109.
109. I. Thomas and B. Nejmeh, "Definitions of tool integration for environments", *IEEE Softw.* **9**, 2 (1992) 29–35.
110. B. Wah, "Special issue on artificial intelligence in software applications", *IEEE Trans. Softw. Eng.* **14**, 12 (1988).
111. A. Wasserman and P. Pircher, "A graphical, extensible integrated environment for software development", in [55], (1986) 131–142.
112. A. Wasserman, P. Pircher, and R. Muller, "An object-oriented structured design method for code generation", *Softw. Eng. Notes* **14**, 1 (1989) 32–55.
113. A. Wasserman, P. Pircher, and R. Muller, "The object-oriented structured design method for software design representation", *Computer* **23**, 3 (1990) 50–63.
114. R. C. Waters,"Program editors should not abandon text-oriented commands", *SIGPLAN Notices* **17**, 7 (1982) 39–46.
115. N. Weiderman, A. Haberman, M. Borger, and M. Klein, "A methodology for evaluating environments", in [55], (1986) 199–207.
116. D. Weinreb and D. Moon, "Lisp machine manual", Technical Report, MIT AI Lab (March 1981).
117. A. Wolf, L. Clarke, and J. Wileden, "The AdaPIC tool set: supporting interface control and analysis throughout the software development process", *IEEE Trans. Softw. Eng.* **15**, 3 (1989) 250–263.
118. M. Young, R. Taylor, K. Forester, and D. Brodbeck, "Integrated concurrency analysis in a software development environment", *Softw. Eng. Notes: Proc. ACM SIGSOFT 3rd Symp. Software Testing, Analysis, and Verification* **14**, 8 (1989).
119. M. V. Zelkowitz, "A small contribution to editing wiht a syntax-directed editor", *SIGPLAN Notices* **19**, 1 (1984) 1–6.

TECHNIQUES AND TOOLS FOR KNOWLEDGE-BASED REQUIREMENTS ENGINEERING

DAVID BOLTON and DAVID TILL

Department of Computer Science, City University, Northampton Square, London EC1V 0HB, UK

STEWART GREEN

Department of Computer Science, University of the West of England, Coldharbour Lane, Frenchay, Bristol BS16 1QY, UK

SARA JONES

School of Information Sciences, University of Hertfordshire, Hatfield, Herts AL10 9AB, UK

Approaches to providing knowledge-based support for the process of requirements engineering are discussed. The kinds of knowledge commonly used in providing such support are placed within a taxonomy and the definition and representation of each kind is considered. There is a brief review of the ways in which knowledge is used in providing support for commonly recognized stages in the requirements engineering process. It is concluded that knowledge-based techniques are capable of providing significant support requirements engineering, but that much more remains to be done before the full potential of these techniques can be realized.

1. Introduction

1.1. *Overview*

The term **requirements engineering** is used to refer to the early stages of the software engineering process during which requirements for a system to be developed are gathered and documented before being passed on to the system designer. A number of different kinds of requirement are commonly collected. The term **functional requirements** is used to describe the services which the system should provide. **Nonfunctional requirements** describe the constraints under which the system will have to operate, and also constraints on the process by which it is to be developed. More detailed descriptions of the kinds of requirements which might be collected can be found in, for example, [72] or [78].

In recent years, a considerable amount of research into the process of requirements engineering has been initiated. Efforts to provide computer-based support for this process, which has been found to be both difficult and time-consuming, have increased. Particular emphasis is beginning to be placed on the provision of knowledge-based support. Requirements engineering is a knowledge intensive activity: according to Curtis [18], "knowledge application is the key to effective software development". The incorporation of facilities providing intelligent or knowledge-based support in the current generation of computer-based tools for requirements engineering is therefore likely to increase the efficiency with which such a process can be carried out to a considerable degree.

There is some agreement that the techniques of artificial intelligence (AI) might be exploited in software engineering. According to Ramamoorthy *et al.*, "AI has matured enough to provide useful ideas, techniques and systems to SE" [66]. Harandi too claims that "by using the knowledge representation and manipulation techniques which are standard in AI today, we could greatly improve the quality of the specification process with relatively low effort" [41]. There is, however, less of a consensus as to the ideas and techniques which might at present most readily provide support for the process of requirements engineering. It is hoped that the provision of a framework within which existing work in this field can be compared, considered, and contrasted might facilitate decisions regarding the direction of future work.

1.2. *Terms and definitions*

There is some confusion over the precise meanings of terms used to refer to various stages in the process of requirements engineering. We consider the process as consisting of three stages referred to as:

- requirements elicitation,
- requirements analysis,
- requirements validation.

The term **requirements elicitation** is used analogously to "knowledge elicitation" and refers to activities directed towards facilitating the articulation of requirements for a system to be developed. The goal of this stage is to gather a full set of requirements from various sources including the purchasers, the developers, and, of course, the intended users of the system.

The use of the term **requirements analysis** is again analogous to that of "knowledge analysis" and refers to the process of placing the elicited requirements in appropriate formal structures and eliminating, where possible, undesirable features such as redundancy, ambiguity, inconsistency, and incompleteness.

Requirements validation is the process of checking with stakeholders that the system described by the requirements collected is actually the one which is wanted. The term is again used analogously to those of "knowledge" and "system validation".

The use of a knowledge-based approach means that knowledge about the domain in which a system is to be developed must often be collected before any of the processes described above are initiated. A preliminary stage, taken to precede those listed, termed **domain knowledge acquisition** is therefore also considered. The term domain knowledge acquisition is used to refer to the process of acquiring the knowledge about a domain which is later to be used in supporting the process of capturing the requirements for a particular system in that domain. Such knowledge might typically be acquired by performing an analysis of the domain (**domain analysis**) and constructing a model of relevant characteristics. There are some differences in opinion as to exactly which characteristics of a domain should be captured in a model which is intended to support the process of requirements engineering. The views of those working on a number of different projects in this area are discussed in Subsec. 2.2.

The concept of a **generic domain abstraction** should be mentioned at this point. An example of a generic domain might be resource allocation: There are things which can be said about all domains in which resources of some kind are allocated to, hired by, consumed by users or consumers of such resources. Given a body of knowledge about such generic domains, domain knowledge for a more concrete domain such as theatre ticket reservation, could at least partly be synthesized by instantiation and specialization. Generic domain abstractions may therefore range over several concrete domains.

It should be noted that a considerable amount of iteration is to be expected both between and, to some extent, within the stages listed. The discovery of ambiguity, inconsistency, or incompleteness at the stage of requirements analysis creates a need for further elicitation. If, during validation, it is found that the system described by the requirements collected is not what the client wants, then further elicitation and analysis are required as well as validation of the new set of requirements. Furthermore, the activities of domain analysis and domain model construction which are part of domain knowledge acquisition might not take place strictly in sequence. Finally, while it is expected that the domain knowledge gathered should support the development of a number of systems, it may be found that the domain model itself must be evolved in order to incorporate new information discovered during the later stages of requirements engineering.

The requirements engineering process therefore uses several kinds of knowledge as follows:

- domain knowledge,
- meta-knowledge,
- application-specific knowledge.

The term **domain knowledge** describes knowledge which is specific to one domain of activity and which is applicable to many possible applications in the domain; domain knowledge may include instantiations of generic domain abstractions. The term **meta-knowledge** is used to describe knowledge which relates to all domains and describes the structures of domains and of individual requirements in a way which is helpful to the requirements engineer. The formally represented requirements for a specific system or application to be developed are termed **application-specific knowledge**.

Two other kinds of knowledge may be also used in providing support for the process of requirements engineering. These are referred to as:

- method knowledge,
- analyst skills knowledge.

We use the term **method knowledge** to refer to knowledge about particular methodologies for requirements capture such as, for example, CORE [61]. **Analyst skills knowledge** is defined as the kind of knowledge developed by an expert requirements analyst, which may not relate specifically to any single methodology.

Each of these kinds of knowledge are described in Sec. 2. The way in which such knowledge is used in providing support for the stages of requirements engineering is discussed in Sec. 3.

1.3. *Aims and scope*

Our aim is to provide a framework within which existing work on the provision of knowledge-based support for requirements engineering can be examined, compared, and contrasted.

The scope of the work is restricted in two ways. First, the focus in Sec. 3 is mainly on approaches to the definition and representation of knowledge about the domain. Second, the emphasis in Sec. 4 is on the process of requirements acquisition (again by analogy with knowledge engineering, we may use this term to describe the activities of elicitation, analysis, and validation) rather than those of domain knowledge acquisition or requirements verification. This choice of emphasis reflects partly our perception of the emphasis of work currently in progress in the field, and partly our own interests [10].

In Sec. 2, we discuss the kinds of knowledge used in requirements engineering, and briefly describe the approaches taken by a number of projects to defining and representing knowledge of each kind. Section 3 describes some of the ways in which such knowledge has been used in providing support for the various stages of requirements engineering. Section 4 presents some overall conclusions and discusses promising avenues for further work.

2. A Taxonomy of Knowledge Types

2.1. *Introduction*

A number of different views have been expressed regarding the nature of each type of knowledge used in requirements engineering. The diversity of these views is due, in part, to variations in focus on the kinds of systems to be developed and the kinds of requirements to be captured, also to differences in opinion regarding the kind of support which might be provided by knowledge-based techniques. These differences in definition lead to differences in the approach adopted to the representation of relevant knowledge and also of the requirements themselves. Such differences then tend to reinforce any emphasis on providing particular kinds of support, possibly at the expense of others.

This section describes a number of different views on the definitions of each kind of knowledge used and outlines different approaches to representation. The corresponding differences in the kinds of support provided at each stage in the requirements engineering process are described in Sec. 3.

2.2. *Domain knowledge*

2.2.1. *Definition*

This section deals with domain knowledge, that is, knowledge which can be said to relate specifically to one domain. According to Giddings [36], most data processing software is domain dependent. Harandi too notes how "an enormous amount of domain-specific knowledge ... is brought to bear on the process [of software specification]" [41]. The use of an explicit representation of domain knowledge might therefore be expected to facilitate the process of requirements engineering to a considerable degree.

There is some difference of opinion in the literature about whether the term "domain" should be used to refer to that part of the real world which needs to be considered for some particular application, or whether it refers to something which is essentially wider than any single application and is in fact a part of reality within which many applications are possible. Such a group of applications may share a common theme, but may differ considerably in detail or indeed may focus on smaller fields within the wider area of concern. In this discussion, we adopt the second view.

Domain knowledge is typically acquired through a process of domain analysis. Domain analysis is a process by which an analyst discovers what is important or significant about some field of human endeavour where it is felt that hardware/software systems could provide useful assistance. The analyst wants to discover what are the objects, relationships, processes, causes, effects and goals of that domain; he or she wants to know what kinds of things happen in the domain, what are the agents and objects of the events which occur and why those events occur. It is usually prudent to attempt domain analysis only in domains in which there is already a good deal of human expertise, perhaps even an already existing theory for that domain which is adequate for most purposes.

There are some differences in opinion as to exactly which characteristics of a domain should be described within a model intended for use in requirements engineering. Barstow [8] defines a domain model as "a collection of concepts, attributes and relationships which organize the entities of some coherent set of natural or computational phenomena". According to Arango and Freeman [4], we might expect a domain model to capture knowledge specific to a particular domain which can act as a reusable framework enabling the user or analyst to think in a focussed manner about particular problems in the domain. The

Requirements Apprentice [69] holds definitions of generic concepts which model fragments of domain knowledge by describing aspects of the environment or external behaviors and constraints which a system will have to deal with, needs perceived by users of systems within the domain, and functional descriptions of systems which might satisfy both the constraints of the environment and the needs of the users. KBRA [19] stores "components for physical laws, abstract descriptions of systems, requirements building blocks, typical data and domain specific formulas" as part of the domain model it uses to provide knowledge-based support.

Several recent projects used, or intend to use, particular forms of domain knowledge in providing support for various stages in the requirements engineering process. Ramesh and Dhar's prototype, built to support the REMAP (REpresentation and MAintenance of Process knowledge) model of the requirements engineering process, supports the user in specifying knowledge about the domain in such a way that requirements defined within that domain can later be reasoned about [67, 68]. Kaindl's RETH (Requirements Engineering Through Hypertext) tool [47] also provides simple structures, including hypertext nodes and links, within which knowledge about the attributes and services of objects in the domain of interest can be stored. The ARIES project, a part of Rome Laboratory's KBSA programme (which also produced the KBRA tool), is currently experimenting with modeling domain knowledge in order that it can be reused in developments of several systems needed within the same domain [46]. Finally, the F-cube (From Fuzzy to Formal) [56] and TEMPORA [51] projects are also planning to use domain knowledge to support various aspects of the requirements engineering process.

2.2.2. *Generic domain abstractions*

Resource allocation is mentioned in Subsec. 1.2 as an example of a generic domain, and it is suggested that knowledge for more concrete domains, for example, theatre ticket reservation, could be partially synthesized by instantiating generic domain abstractions. It seems quite possible that a small number of such very general domains might serve as a spanning set which more specialized domains could draw upon, perhaps using more than one such domain for different aspects. This would seem to be in line with work on analogical reuse of domain abstractions [58]. However, whereas that work suggests that requirements for a new system could be constructed by discovering analogies with previous systems (not necessarily in the same domain, in our sense of the word) or by specializing more abstract domains, in the GMARC [10] project the suggestion is that such reuse of high level abstractions should be done by specialist domain knowledge engineers so that the client with a desired new system in mind chooses fragments from domain knowledge already specialized to the domain within which the new system falls. One of the inspirations for this idea is a very elegant paper in which a formal specification for a facilities booking system known as CAVIAR [34] is developed.

There is other work which also employs generic abstractions or generic models. Feather [27] describes how two related generic models at different levels of abstraction may be used to investigate the relationship between the two models, and also the completeness and consistency of the models. The F-cube project [56] is planning to use knowledge about enterprises and environments which applies across a number of domains. The tools developed by the ARIES project include a knowledge-base of common requirements which can be specialized or adapted for use in developing multiple systems [46].

2.2.3. *Approaches to representation*

The Taxis project [38] was involved from a relatively early stage in the development of a language suitable for use in representing domain models. The language developed was called RML (Requirements Modeling Language) and reflects a belief in the use of "natural" abstractions (that is, abstractions which people find easy and expedient to use in organizing their view of the world) as the basis for structuring requirements specifications.

The following is an abstract from an RML description of the domain of hospital information systems:

```
PATIENT
    parts
        name:  PERSON_NAMES
        address:  ADDRESSES
        hasPhysician:  DOCTOR
        hasDiagnosis:  DISEASE
ADMIT
    participants
        newPatient:  PERSON
        toWard:  WARD
        admitter:  DOCTOR
    parts
```

```
        document:  GET_INFO
            (from - newPatient)
        checkIn:  ASSIGN_BED
            (toWhom - newPatient,
            onWard - toWard)
    precondition
        canAdmit?:  HAS_AUTHORITY
            (who - admitter,
            where - toWard)
```

This example illustrates the way in which RML permits description of significant entities and actions in the domain. Here, the PATIENT entity is characterized by its parts or attributes, and the action ADMIT by its participants (objects and agents), attributes, and preconditions. A full specification would contain many such descriptions, further structure being imposed by the use of class hierarchies. A full description of RML can be found in [37].

The Telos language, which was developed during the course of the LOKI and DAIDA projects [63], and continues to be developed within the NATURE project [43, 45] extends the ideas of RML. In Telos, it is possible to define the structure of domain knowledge (or knowledge about the "subject world" as it is called by the designers of Telos) within the language itself. The language is object-oriented, in the sense that it permits hierarchies of classes, but also admits meta-classes, meta-meta-classes and so on. Thus, for example, the nature of a classification scheme for expressing domain knowledge can be specified by defining the appropriate meta-classes. Ramesh and Dhar's REMAP tool is based on ConceptBase, an implementation of Telos developed at the University of Passau [44].

In IDeA [53, 54], domain knowledge is represented in terms of abstract design schemata describing domain-specific functional specifications. This knowledge may be used and reused whenever IDeA is used in defining a new application but support for the development or evolution of the knowledge itself is not apparently provided.

KBRA's domain knowledge is represented in terms of the system's own programming language which merges frame-, object-, and constraint-based programming components and supports automated inference, inheritance, default reasoning, and procedural attachment [19]. Components of domain knowledge which are suitable for reuse are identified on the basis of "key discriminators" which are either entered by the knowledge engineer when the domain model is initially created or derived automatically.

In KATE [31], the domain model takes the form of a set of domain-specific policies or potential specification goals described using KATE's augmented version of the Petri net formalism. Before using this knowledge in the development of a new specification, the user must input a utility value for each of the policies in the domain of interest in order to describe the particular needs of the new application.

Users of the Requirements Apprentice [69] are allowed to provide an informal input description of ideas in the domain of interest in terms of a command language which allows declaration of the existence of objects, classification of objects in terms of existing definitions, and the specification of attribute values, relations, and constraints. Domain knowledge specified in this way is stored in terms of "clichés": These are frame-like structures consisting of a body and a set of attributes or "roles" whose values may be constrained by statements held in the body. Domain knowledge specified in this way may be used and reused in the development of new requirements specifications.

Domain knowledge or "background knowledge" is expressed in KAOS in the same language as the requirements model (see Subsec. 2.4) in a structure which reflects that of the conceptual meta-model (see Subsec. 2.3). Background knowledge is also categorized according to the type of task with which it is concerned, and can therefore be described as being expressed in terms of "domain/task specific instances of the domain/task-independent components of [the] meta-model" [80]. In the work of Maiden and Sutcliffe [59, 60, 76], domain knowledge is organized in a hierarchy of domain abstractions whose structure is based upon a meta-schema like that of KAOS.

Draco's view of domain knowledge is unusual in its emphasis on the development of a "domain language." This view is explained by Neighbors [64] as follows: "The basis of the Draco work is the use of domain analysis to produce domain languages which may be transformed for optimization purposes and implemented by software components, each of which contains multiple refinements which make implementation decisions by restating the problem in other domain languages." Thus, the initial effort of domain analysis is regarded as a "once and for all" process which provides the basis for numerous subsequent specifications to be transformed into executable code. Meta-compiler techniques are provided to support the initial definition of the domain language and reuse of the languages and software components is supported, both within and between domains.

At this point, it may be noted that the provision of knowledge-based support of the kind envisaged relies on knowledge both about the domain and about individual requirements within the domain being expressed in terms of a suitable formal representation language. Many of the tools described express domain knowledge using representations closely related to those used in AI such as logic, frames, or object-oriented paradigms. Sometimes, however, the conventional AI representation has been augmented in some way to suit the particular use to which the relevant domain knowledge was to be put. The same kinds of representations are often used in the expression of individual application-specific requirements (see Subsec. 2.4).

2.3. *Meta-knowledge*

2.3.1. *Definition*

At least five different kinds of meta-knowledge are potentially of relevance in the development of knowledge-based tools for requirements capture which are intended to be used in a number of domains. These kinds of knowledge are closely inter-related, but the important differences in emphasis may be characterized as follows. Meta-knowledge may take the form of:

- knowledge about the conceptual structure of a number of domains,
- knowledge about the entities or activities in those domains and their characteristics,
- knowledge about the requirements which will always be placed on those entities or activities,
- knowledge about the kinds of requirements which may be expressed in any domain,
- knowledge about the structure of requirements of any or all of those kinds.

Approaches to providing knowledge-based support for requirements engineering vary according to the extent to which knowledge of any of these kinds is explicitly represented and the generality with which it can be applied across domains. A number of projects make at least implicit reference to meta-knowledge as follows.

At one end of the spectrum are systems which make only an implicit acknowledgement of the fact that certain structures and entities can be seen to be common to a number of domains. Work on Draco [35, 64] and the Requirements Apprentice [69, 70] has emphasized the provision of a common framework for the characterization of domain-specific frameworks. In both cases, the possibility of reuse of existing constructs across domains is admitted.

Systems such as Analyst-Assist [2], RUBRIC [5], and IDeA [53, 55] represent domain knowledge within the context of a hierarchy of knowledge about a number of domains and subdomains of varying levels of generality, thereby providing more explicit support for the transfer (at least by inheritance) of knowledge between domains and subdomains. The SIBST (Software Information Base — Selection Tool) [16] supports the use of classification, generalization, and aggregation hierarchies to classify information about software components (such as requirements), and also provides correspondence links which permit the definition of families of related components. Such systems embody implicit assumptions about the nature of structures common to all (or at least some) domains, and about the characteristics or dimensions which form a suitable basis on which to place domains within this kind of hierarchy.

Other approaches make slightly more explicit use of some kind of meta-knowledge. The RUBRIC system aims to capture meta-knowledge of the third kind (i.e., knowledge about requirements which apply within all domains) by providing an explicit representation of business policy and constraints. Meta-knowledge incorporated in KBRA [19] reflects a view on the concerns of requirements capture in general, and on the types of requirement likely to be encountered. This knowledge is, however, very rudimentary and consists mainly of a list of keywords (such as "update", "generate", "transfer", "evaluate", "perform", and "associate") which can be located in informal input and linked with existing reusable items in its library.

A stronger idea of an underlying meta-model can be found in work related to the Taxis project and the development of the language RML. Greenspan *et al.* [38] explain how this work has been based on the premise that the world can be viewed in terms of objects, relations, and activities and that there is a small set of abstraction mechanisms which can be used to structure all specifications in any domain. This premise rests on implicit meta-knowledge of the first of the five kinds described above.

Further developments have led to the design of the language Telos [63] as described in the previous section. This language is intended to have the power to express various kinds of knowledge about information systems, which is to say that it adopts a database-oriented approach to software systems. It allows for classes, meta-classes, meta-meta-classes and so on, so that it is itself capable of expressing a meta-model. The necessity to commit to a fixed meta-model is thus removed. TELOS forms the basis for the knowledge-base management system ConceptBase which is currently in use in the NATURE project.

The TEMPORA project [51] proposes the use of three separate meta-models. TEMPORA is concerned specifically with the use in requirements engineering of corporate knowledge, i.e., knowledge about that part of the domain in which a system is required which relates to business strategies, concepts, rules, and constraints. An Entity-Relationship-Time Model is used to capture structural knowledge about aspects of an office domain; Process Interaction Diagrams capture behavioral or dynamic aspects of the domain; and the Conceptual Rule Language can be used to specify declarative knowledge about business rules which govern both the structural and dynamic knowledge.

2.3.2. *Approaches to representation*

Of all the projects considered, one which makes a particularly strong and most explicit reference to meta-knowledge is KAOS [20, 80]. The KAOS project has defined a comprehensive conceptual meta-model which has formed the basis for the development of both a methodology for requirements capture and a tool to support it (the Acquisition Assistant). The KAOS meta-model focuses on the ideas of concepts, relations, attributes (of either concepts or relations), and constraints (on any of the former) with goals playing a central role. Domain and requirements or application models consist of instances of components of the meta-model and the language in which they are expressed also reflects this structure (see Subsec. 2.4).

The following is an example of a structured representation of part of the KAOS meta-model which can be used as a basis for the expression of domain or background knowledge or of individual requirements:

```
meta-concept_name <concept_name>
    {meta-relation_role_name {<target_concept_name>
        with {meta-attribute_name <value>}*}*
        where {relation_feature<feature_value>}*}*
    {meta-attribute_name [<value>]
        where {attribute_feature<feature_value>}*}*
end <concept_name>
```

where {...}* stands for "zero, one or more of" and [...] for "optional."

A similar meta-schema to the one which KAOS uses is also employed in the work of Sutcliffe and Maiden [59, 60, 76] as the basis for the description of a hierarchy of domain abstractions.

Two simpler meta models are described in [27]. These models determine the structure of (in Feather's terms) domain models and domain instance models respectively. The domain meta model comprises just two entities: goal and policy. The domain instance meta model includes in addition an instance entity. The four relationships in the domain meta model include "policy support goal" and "goal is sub-goal of goal".

2.4. *Application-specific knowledge*

2.4.1. *Definition*

Formally represented requirements may be seen as knowledge about a specific system or application to be developed. The provision of comprehensive knowledge-based support for requirements engineering relies on the existence of a suitable scheme for the formal representation of application-specific knowledge or requirements. "In advanced paradigms [for requirements engineering]", explain Czuchry and Harris [19], "formal representations for requirements serve as a basis for proving specification properties". It is, of course, especially important that it should be possible to prove that such properties as completeness and consistency hold for specifications of safety critical applications such as air traffic control [19] or railway signaling systems [6].

If the representation used in the expression of individual requirements or knowledge about particular applications is the same as that used in the representation of knowledge about the domain, then still further properties of the requirements specification with respect to the domain may be proved [4].

2.4.2. *Approaches to representation*

Numerous schemes for the representation of requirements have been proposed (see, for example, [72]) and many authors have specified criteria which any new scheme might ideally fulfill (for example, [7, 13, 38, 40, 72, 79]). A number of authors have proposed the use of formalisms based on representation schemes commonly used in AI such as logic, frames, or conceptual graphs (see, for example, [7, 41]). Such representations are obviously well suited to use in tools providing knowledge-based support for the acquisition of such requirements. This section provides a small number of examples of representations of this kind.

Logic. First, we consider a formalism used by the FOREST project [57] which is based on a number of extensions to first order logic. Modal Action Logic

(MAL) is a "layered logic" designed to be able to express the properties of agents that can perform actions. Atkinson and Cunningham [6] provide the following description of its components:

- a standard classical first-order predicate logic with sorts in which the static properties of data and other objects can be described,
- a modal logic of actions, in which the effects of performing actions are expressed,
- a deontic logic which specifies the circumstances under which an action is legitimate,
- combinators on actions for describing complex actions in terms of simpler ones,
- a temporal component for expressing time constraints in terms of intervals of time.

The action logic uses axioms of the form:

$$\mathit{precondition} \implies [\mathit{action}, \mathit{agent}]\ \mathit{postcondition}$$

In the context of a system specification, this says that if the precondition holds and the agent performs the action, the postcondition will hold. For example, the specification of a single-item buffer might read as follows:

$$\mathit{is\_empty} \implies [\mathit{put}, \mathit{producer}]\ \neg \mathit{is\_empty}$$

Note that the precondition and postcondition can be any MAL formula, so that this mechanism may be used for describing any observable sequential behavior.

The deontic logic describes when an action is legitimate by using the operators *per* and *obl* which take actions as parameters. Expressions using these operators are constructed as follows (see also [48]):

- $\mathit{obl}(\mathit{action}, \mathit{agent})$ means that the agent has an obligation to perform the action and must perform it next,
- $\mathit{per}(\mathit{action}, \mathit{agent})$ means that the agent has permission to perform the action: It may carry out the action, but it need not.

Requirements may be expressed using combinations of actions and obligations as for example in:

$$[\mathit{put}, \mathit{producer}]\ \mathit{obl}(\mathit{get}, \mathit{consumer})$$

which means that after the producer has put an item in the buffer, the consumer is obliged to get it, or:

$$per(put, producer) \Leftrightarrow is\_empty$$

which means that the action of putting an item in the buffer is only legitimate if the buffer is empty.

Structured MAL [75] introduces agent composition, with collections of agents viewed as a single agent incorporating the behaviors of individuals. Agents interact by sharing attributes and actions, with interaction precisely controlled by locality axioms. Structuring into agent composition hierarchies overcomes the frame problem, and fits well with object-oriented specification — each agent models private attributes and public procedures for manipulation. A formalism (Ordered Theory Presentations) can be used for representing defaults in specifications, statements which are true unless some specified stronger statement overrides them [73].

Notations inspired by the ERAE language [23, 24, 25] have been used to represent application specific constraints in the requirements engineering research undertaken in the Critter [30] and KAOS [21] projects. ERAE supports essentially the same features as MAL, and also has a mechanism for structuring specifications, like Structured MAL. However, in addition, it is also able to support both partial functions and real time requirements, and it has a graphical syntax which is equivalent to its textual syntax. Support for partial functions enables expressions denoting objects with currently undefined internal objects to be specified. Support for real time requirements makes it possible to constrain not just the order of possible states but also the "temporal distance" between states. The graphical syntax enables diagrams which are equivalent to textual specifications to be created; such diagrams are often more readily understood than their textual counterparts.

Jackson and Zave [42] describe ongoing work aimed at allowing composition of requirements specifications and descriptions written in different formal notations by adoption of first-order untyped predicate logic with equality and recursion as a base language to which other representations may be translated.

Frames. A frame-like representation scheme is used in the Requirements Apprentice. Here, requirements or fragments of application-specific knowledge (as well as domain knowledge) are expressed in terms of "clichés" or "cliché-frames". The following description of clichés is taken from Reubenstein's thesis [69].

Cliché-frames represent three kinds of information:

- definitional — definitional information is asserted to be true of each instance of the cliché-frame,
- computational — computational information assists in performing a task. For example, canned text assists in the production of text to be included in a summary document,
- predictive — predictive information provides an index into the facts that will become true if an object is asserted to be an instance of the cliché frame. It is used to help resolve ambiguities.

A cliché-frame consists of a set of roles (slots) and a set of constraints that relates the roles. An example of a cliché-frame definition of a bicycle is as follows:

```
(Def-Cliche Bicycle (Vehicle)
    (Def-Roles
        (Front-Gearing Gearing)
        (Rear-Gearing Gearing)
        (Number-of-Gears Integer))
    :Preconditions
        (Low-Gear ?Front-Gearing ?Rear-Gearing)
    :Consequents
        (< ?Maximum-Speed 60mph)
    :Default-Consequents
        (> ?Number-of-Gears 10))
```

In this definition, the cliché-frame `Bicycle` is defined as inheriting the semantics of `Vehicle`, its parent cliché-frame. Roles are defined in the `Def-Roles` section and role values are referenced in constraints using an expression of the form `?role-name`. Note that there are three types of constraints describing `Preconditions`, constraints necessary for an object to be an instance of a cliché-frame; `Consequents`, which are asserted to be true of each instance of the cliché-frame; and `Default-Consequents` which are identical to consequents except that they are supported by a default premise.

A further frame-like representation scheme is used by the KAOS project [80]. Here, the units of description are referred to as "sections". Two sections taken from the specification of a telephone system are as follows:

```
relation CONNECTIONS
    links PHONE with role Caller, card 0:1,
        PHONE with role Callee, card 0:1,
            where inheritance mode full_inheritable
end CONNECTIONS
```

```
action Disconnect
    applies_to CONNECTIONS with arg connections,
        HANG_UP_REQUEST with arg hang_req,
    yields CONNECTIONS with res new_connections,
    performed_by LINE_ALLOCATOR
    pre-condition:
        <Caller:hang_req.phone1, Callee:hang_req.phone2>
            in connections
        or <Caller:hang_req.phone2, Callee:hang_req.phone1>
            in connections
        where inheritance mode concept_inheritable
    post-condition:
        not (<Caller:hang_req.phone1, Callee:hang_req.phone2>
            in new_connections
        or <Caller:hang_req.phone2, Callee:hang_req.phone1>
            in new_connections)
        where inheritance mode concept_inheritable
    situation internal
end Disconnect
```

Note that these examples are instances of the general form for a meta-concept shown in Subsec. 2.3.2.

Conceptual graphs. Conceptual graphs can be used to represent both requirements and domain knowledge. Individual requirements may be expressed using individual graphs as in the following example in the notation of Analyst-Assist [14] (see [74] for an alternative but similar representation). Here, a description of the fact that customers borrow tools is represented as:

$$
\begin{array}{llll}
[BORROW] - & & & \\
\rightarrow & (AGENT) & \rightarrow & [CUSTOMER] \\
\rightarrow & (OBJECT) & \rightarrow & [TOOL]
\end{array}
$$

This graph may be read as "a borrowing of a tool by a customer" or more naturally as "a customer borrows a tool".

The use of conceptual graphs in the representation of both domain knowledge and individual requirements means that support for a particular approach to requirements elicitation and analysis can be provided as described in Subsec. 3.3.

2.5. *Method knowledge*

2.5.1. *Definition*

The term "method knowledge" is used here to refer to knowledge about well-known methodologies for requirements engineering.

Early work in the Taxis project [38] reported a need for computer-based support for the use of well-defined methodologies for requirements engineering and corresponding languages (such as RML). It was also suggested that the translation of requirements or application models into specification notations such as SADT should be supported.

Kramer *et al.* [49] introduced the notion of "Active Guidance". Methods were defined as systems of recommended procedures, and it was suggested that providing guidance on using those methods might involve providing advice on normal use, "remediation" (when the normal pattern of use has broken down), and advice on preferences between alternative courses of action (for example, "Do remedial action before continuing normal action!").

Moving towards the idea of expert requirements analysis, Loucopoulos and Champion [52] define method knowledge as being the means by which an analyst might attempt to derive representational models and apply transformations to those models. Examples of this kind of method knowledge include knowledge about the construction of conceptual data models and the way in which they may be transformed into logical schema designs. Such knowledge might form the basis for a mechanism for guiding the process of requirements engineering according to the "theoretical" ideas supported by the chosen methodology. According to this view, knowledge relating to any particular methodology would include descriptions of the model formalisms employed and specifications of possible transformations which might take place in mapping from one formalism to another.

Lefering [50] describes a generic framework for integrating tools supporting different requirements modeling methods (and software design methods). The generic architecture includes an integration document which documents the links between different forms of requirements representation, and a rule base which expresses allowed linkages and consistency checks to relate different representations during incremental development of a requirements specification (and also on to design). Implemented methods include Structured Analysis and Entity Relationships.

The CARD environment [65] supports requirements description, analysis, and verification under their Requirements Frame method (see Subsec. 3.5).

2.5.2. *Approaches to representation*

The tool described by Kramer *et al.* [49] supports the CORE methodology and uses the SD Analyst CORE support tool as its basis. The SD Analyst tool supports CORE description and diagramming, and here, is augmented with the active guidance system. The active guidance system maintains an internal model of the method, with dynamic priority lists of actions to be done by the analyst. The normative model is defined by Prolog clauses, in CORE-specific form. According to [49], the remediation model seems to be a set of general comments, implemented ad hoc. The desirability of using the same formalism for representing normative, remediative, and descriptive components of the method knowledge is emphasized.

In the NATURE process model [39, 43, 71] what is in effect a meta-model for process is used; of course the specialization to an instance intended to support a particular set of possible decisions, actions, arguments and so on, would be related to the (meta-)structure of the domain knowledge used and that of the requirements specification to be produced as the output of the process.

One of the conclusions reached by Kramer *et al.* is that the work described in [49] is too method-specific (in this case CORE-specific) and that strategies more concerned with the semantics of the chosen method rather than the syntax of notations would be more effective. For even more general semantics, method models must be used in conjunction with domain models.

2.6. *Analyst skills knowledge*

2.6.1. *Definition*

The term "analyst skills knowledge" is used to refer to the skills or knowledge developed by an experienced requirements analyst. Whereas method knowledge has been defined as detailed knowledge about particular methodologies for requirements engineering, "analyst skills knowledge" may be defined as knowledge of the strategies adopted, and behaviors evinced, by analysts while engaged on analysis and design tasks independent of any methodology.

Fickas [28] has investigated the systems analysis process using two kinds of experiments. One series of experiments involved observing the analysis process as exemplified in software projects undertaken by students on a "Senior Project" course over a period of four years. The results of these experiments indicated that the best analysts set up hypothetical situations or scenarios relevant to a problem domain which the user may then work through in order to find an adequate level of representation of a problem. Fickas noted that "the more scenarios that can be generated showing the system in use, the better the chance of finding the events and states that must be represented".

A second series of experiments was performed using analysts with between five and fifteen years' experience. These experiments involved capturing the requirements for a library automation system and an information management system. The results indicated that experienced analysts used their knowledge of the problem domain in interactions with users in order to "zero in on key questions" and to generate and present "hypothetical examples as both an explanation device and an acquisition device". In addition analysts' domain knowledge included the pros and cons associated with omitting and including certain requirements information, and they were able to impart this knowledge to the users. Finally, experienced analysts tended to summarize requirements information for users. Fickas suggests that such summaries were "an attempt to verify that all the items had been considered and that there really was complete understanding between analyst and client".

In an earlier experiment carried out by Vitalari and Dickson, the performance of groups of high- and low-rated analysts on a requirements acquisition task was measured and analyzed [82]. The main results indicated that high-rated analysts reject more of their hypotheses than low-rated ones, that they modify their strategies in the light of new information more frequently, and that they have a greater tendency to search for "triggers" in user requirement information and to use the results of such searches to determine their subsequent behavior.

Adelson and Soloway [1] investigated the role of domain experience in software by conducting experiments which investigated the performance of both expert and novice designers in three types of design task context. The three contexts involved:

- an unfamiliar application in an unfamiliar domain,

- an unfamiliar application in a familiar domain,
- a familiar application in a familiar domain.

In each context, six salient behaviors were evinced by the analysts. These were the following:

- forming mental models,
- simulating (running) the models,
- systematically expanding (refining and elaborating) the models,
- asserting facts about, and deriving inferences from the given requirements, these facts and inferences then acting as constraints on the mental models,
- retrieving named plans of action from memory,
- making notes about potential design issues to be dealt with later.

As might be predicted, the degree to which each behavior was shown differed both between the novice and the expert designers, and across the three design task contexts. In particular, whatever the context, the novice designers' performance was inferior to that of the experts. For example, the novices' mental models tended to be created using "pseudocode" and were not, in contrast to the experts' models, capable of simulation.

The following observations were made concerning the variation in contexts. For an experienced analyst designing a familiar object in a familiar domain, the overall task could be characterized as being dominated by the retrieval of previously stored knowledge. In such a situation the analyst tended to be able to retrieve from memory a very abstract, highly appropriate preformed mental model; the analyst also tended to be able to retrieve implementation plans for each familiar subsystem in the mental model. This may be contrasted with an analyst designing an unfamiliar object in an unfamiliar domain. In such a situation, without the help of previous experience (i.e., without appropriate knowledge of the domain) the analyst is forced to go through the iterative process of creating, simulating, and expanding mental models until an appropriate one has been generated. There is also a tendency to note down many concerns: this can be contrasted with the situation in which the domain is familiar where there is no need for note-taking since concerns are already dealt with in successful plans.

Both F-cube and the REMAP model are also based on results from task and protocol analyses of requirements engineers working in the field. Ramesh and Dhar have developed a conceptual model or meta-model of analyst skills knowledge [67]. It shows relationships seen between key concepts in requirements engineering such as Requirements, Issues, Arguments, Assumptions, Decisions, Constraints, and Design Objects.

2.6.2. *Approaches to representation*

The results of the experiment carried out by Vitalari and Dickson have influenced the architecture of a number of systems for requirements engineering such as KATE [28] and Analyst-Assist [2]. Others of the skills outlined have been captured in the Requirements Apprentice [70].

KATE can exhibit analogical reasoning in as much as it can automatically compare elicited requirements to a domain model stored on a computer and then report on application components which do not match the domain model, and on components in the domain model which are absent from the application requirements. KATE can also summarize information it has either obtained or deduced and present it back to users. The Requirements Apprentice and Analyst-Assist have similar capabilities.

The REMAP prototype has been built using ConceptBase and Telos. It uses relationships between the key requirements concepts to support simple reasoning about the evolution of requirements for particular systems. For example, If a Decision is recorded as "resolving" an Issue, which was "generated by" a particular Requirement, then that Requirement can be said to "lead to" the Decision.

In NATURE [43] domain abstractions are formed into a hierarchy, the levels of which correspond to different kinds of discriminatory properties. Requirements elicitation is effected by matching the features of a new application against the abstractions in the hierarchy in order to find that one which constitutes the closest analogue.

2.7. *Summary*

This section has introduced definitions and example representations for different kinds of knowledge thought to be relevant to the provision of knowledge-based support for requirements engineering. The ideas of a number of projects regarding the nature of domain knowledge, meta-knowledge, application-specific knowledge, method knowledge and finally analyst skills knowledge have been presented, and some examples of the approaches taken by various projects to the representation of each of these kinds of knowledge have been given.

3. Knowledge-Based Approaches to Support

3.1. *Introduction*

The previous section concentrated mainly on the definition and representation of different kinds of knowledge. This section provides a brief review of the ways in which these various kinds of knowledge are used in providing support at each stage in the process of requirements engineering.

3.2. *Domain knowledge acquisition*

The use of a knowledge-based approach to providing support for the process of requirements engineering means that the elicitation, analysis, and validation of requirements must be preceded by a process of domain knowledge acquisition. During this process the domain in which new systems are to be developed is analyzed and a suitable model of that domain is constructed.

Most tools embody an assumption that domain knowledge will be entered into the system's knowledge base by a human expert who is able to structure the knowledge and represent it in an appropriate way with little in the way of computer-based support. For example, Czuchry and Harris suggest that "knowledge engineers" should "manually encode" new domain models for use in KBRA [19]. IDeA [55], Analyst-Assist [2], KATE [28, 31], RETH [47], and REMAP [67] all embody a similar assumption that domain knowledge can be encoded by a domain expert and stored in the system's knowledge base in order to support a subsequent activity of requirements acquisition.

Some support for the definition of real-world concepts and constraints in a new domain is provided by RML's strong conceptual meta-model and corresponding methodology. The Requirements Apprentice provides more concrete support for the acquisition of domain knowledge. Users of the Requirements Apprentice are allowed to provide an informal input description of ideas in the domain of interest in terms of a command language which allows declaration of the existence of named objects, classification of objects in terms of existing definitions, and the specification of attribute values, relations, and constraints.

As suggested in Subsec. 2.3, the idea of using meta-knowledge about the conceptual structure of models of a range of domains is apparently gaining popularity. Both KAOS [20] and Telos [63] embody an assumption that one or more meta-models can be constructed and used as a basis on which to build models of a number of domains. The explicit representation of such meta-models in relatively formal terms makes it considerably easier to provide automated support for the development of domain models [77, 80]. KAOS, for example, can automatically update domain or "background" knowledge using explanation-based learning techniques. The KAOS meta-model has also been used as the underlying model for a natural language-based approach to domain model acquisition using domain independent heuristics to derive a conceptual model from a domain-specific lexicon [22]. The provision of a structure within which the common features of a number of domain models can be related also promotes reusability and reduces the effort required from skilled personnel in defining new domains.

Ideas of a similar kind have been investigated in other fields. For example, Barr *et al.* [7] provide a brief description of Ozym, a so-called "meta-generation system" which provides intelligent support for the creation of domain-specific application program generators on the basis of "an object-oriented model ... that provides a conceptual structure for the types of domain knowledge required". In the field of expert systems, the idea of providing a domain-independent "expert system shell" for the creation of expert systems in particular fields was first introduced by the authors of EMYCIN [81]. More recent work in the field of knowledge acquisition has investigated the possibility of using intelligent domain-independent tools or shells for the elicitation of knowledge in a variety of domains [62]. The identification of commonalities between work in different fields remains, however, a topic of research.

3.3. *Requirements elicitation*

The activities involved in requirements elicitation are directed towards facilitating the articulation of requirements for a system to be developed by all interested parties. Each of the different kinds of knowledge described in the previous section may be used to provide support for these activities. The following paragraphs present some examples of ways in which this is done.

Some components of knowledge about the domain may be presented to the user as modifiable templates which prompt consideration of relevant issues which concern the particular application to be developed and provide an appropriate framework within which to define new requirements. For example, the Requirements Apprentice [69] stores fragments of knowledge about the domain as cliché bodies which are expected to be used in the development of a number of different specifications of applications within the same domain. Values of items or roles held in the slots may then be varied within the constraints described. Domain knowledge can be used to provide support for effective, domain-specific communication including the provision of user guidance and explanations [7]. This is especially useful for clients who are unfamiliar with the domain.

Domain knowledge can also be used in providing support for early analytical activities which can be commenced while elicitation is still in progress. KATE [31], Analyst-Assist [2] and the Requirements Apprentice [70] can, for example, automatically compare elicited requirements to a domain model and then report any mismatches between the developing model of the application and that of the domain. The lack of components in the application model corresponding to certain parts of the domain model can also be detected and reported. Thus, the use of domain knowledge supports early checking for both consistency and completeness.

The analogical matching used in NATURE is discussed in Subsec. 2.6.2. Champion and Loucopoulos [14] describe how Analyst-Assist uses domain knowledge to support a form of analogical reasoning which can enhance the process of requirements elicitation. In Analyst-Assist, both domain and application-specific knowledge are represented in terms of conceptual graphs. Newly elicited requirements may thus be matched against components of the existing domain knowledge in order to discover further possibilities for investigation. This process is illustrated by the following example.

Consider the following fragment of domain knowledge:

[BORROW] –			
→	*(AGENT)*	→	*[PERSON]*
→	*(OBJECT)*	→	*[PHYSICAL_OBJECT]*
→	*(START)*	→	*[LOAN]*

This may be seen as a definition of the concept "borrow" and may be read as "a loan is a start of a borrowing of a physical object by a person".

Now consider the following application requirement elicited from a user:

[BORROW] –			
→	*(AGENT)*	→	*[CUSTOMER]*
→	*(OBJECT)*	→	*[TOOL]*

This describes the fact that customers borrow tools and may be read as "a borrowing of a tool by a customer" or more naturally as "a customer borrows a tool".

When these two graphs are merged, the effect is to introduce the concept of "loan" into the application model. Now, "the information on *LOAN* in the domain knowledge base, such as the concepts *RETURN*, *LOAN-PERIOD*, and *OVERDUE* can be suggested as appropriate avenues for further investigation of the concepts involved in the modeled application".

The ReqColl tool [74] also uses conceptual graphs to represent domain concepts and attempts to recognize new concepts through the use of a matching facility, and may also store software structures described using JSD notation so as to support the early stages of design.

Of course, the kinds of support described in the previous paragraphs can only be provided if both domain and application-specific knowledge are represented in a formal, structured manner. The implementation of such facilities is likely to be easiest if both kinds of knowledge are represented using the same formalism, as is the case in Analyst-Assist which uses conceptual graphs in each case [2]. Often, formal representations which permit automatic manipulation are unsuitable for presentation to naive users such as those who may need to be involved in requirements elicitation. It is often claimed that conceptual graphs are easy for such users to understand and use, as well as being suitable for machine processing. Some projects have, however, provided different representations for the user: for example, the Requirements Assistant [9, 19] attempts to deal with the informal nature of the requirements elicitation process through support for user manipulation of requirements expressed in the "Wide Spectrum Language". Meta-knowledge may also be useful in providing well-structured support for requirements elicitation although there are apparently few examples of this in the literature. Dardenne *et al.* [20] suggest that meta-knowledge of the kind held in KAOS is intended to play an important part in the acquisition of new requirements models. The Assistant's meta-knowledge can be used during requirements elicitation to spot incompleteness or inconsistencies in a way similar to that described in relation to domain knowledge: when the meta-concept associated with a concept to be acquired is known, the system can detect the absence (in the new concept) of characteristics described at the meta-level. It can also spot violations of constraints specified at the meta-level.

A number of tools for knowledge acquisition provide users with hypertext facilities that enable them to highlight parts of an electronic document and then produce formal representations of relations between highlighted concepts in terms of conceptual graphs or semantic nets [12]. Further support for this process might be provided by a system which used its domain knowledge to recognize such key concepts and highlight them automatically. Suggestions might also be made regarding the relation of new concepts to existing domain knowledge or to other requirements already made.

3.4. *Requirements analysis*

The analysis of requirements involves placing statements collected during elicitation in appropriate formal structures and eliminating, where possible, undesirable features such as redundancy, ambiguity, inconsistency, and incompleteness.

A certain amount of analysis can be done during the course of elicitation. The consistency of the developing model of the application and completeness of particular components of that model can be checked on an ongoing basis. Ambiguity is eliminated by the development of formal representations of elicited requirements as application-specific knowledge [6]. This in turn means that a certain amount of redundancy may be identified and eliminated automatically. Software tools can be produced which automatically detect the addition to an emerging specification — expressed in a logic — of a requirement which creates an inconsistency. For example, the Requirements Apprentice contains a component which automatically detects contradictions [70].

Further checks must, however, also be performed on completion of the first round of elicitation. Some properties (such as those which have implications for safety) may need to be shown to hold for a specification as a whole. The TEMPORA project uses meta-models of the three aspects of a domain described in Subsec. 2.3.1 to check the correctness of requirements specifications. Completeness of the application knowledge with respect to the domain knowledge may also be checked at this stage provided both are formally represented.

Method knowledge has been successfully used to support requirements analysis in a number of cases. The tool described by Kramer *et al.* [49] supports the CORE methodology using the SD Analyst CORE support tool as its basis. Facilities supporting the use of CORE description and diagramming are provided and augmented with an active guidance system. The active guidance system maintains an internal model of the method, with dynamic priority lists of actions to be done by the analyst.

In IC-DC and its successors [32, 33] a requirements specification is developed as a tool-supported dialog between viewpoints, in which the viewpoints negotiate to establish commitments and responsibilities. This method is supported by monitoring for illegality in dialogs, with dialogs explained and rolled back to the legal state. The suggestion is that different representational styles must be supported to allow expression of different sorts of requirements, so tools are to be provided for a repertoire of defined methodologies [33]. Examples should include those used in SSADM and JSD.

The problem of representation of alternative, conflicting viewpoints in a single requirements model is tackled in a framework described by Easterbrook [26]. The framework is based on the development of hierarchies of viewpoint descriptions, where lower levels of the hierarchies contain the conflicts. These hierarchies can be viewed in a number of ways, so that conflict resolution is assisted.

Method knowledge is also incorporated into Analyst-Assist in the form of the JSD "Method Adviser" [2] which contains primitives supporting JSD model primitives, different abstraction primitives, and heuristic rules which guide the selection and classification of appropriate primitives during analysis.

Generic knowledge has been reused in three recent goal-oriented approaches [15, 27, 30]. The Critter approach [30] introduces a strategy for creating formal specifications: it first identifies behaviors of an initial specification that violate global goals (requirements), and then applies design operators to overcome those deficiencies. Each design operator embodies generic knowledge of a composite system design strategy. By matching an operator to a design state characterized by a deficient combination of goals and specification, a less deficient combination may be generated. The process ends with a specification that satisfies the (possibly modified) global goals.

An approach developed at Toronto University [15] enables global nonfunctional requirements to be iteratively decomposed into subgoals through the use of "goal decomposition methods". Such methods embody generic knowledge. For example, one method embodies the knowledge that a requirement or goal for a class of objects will be achieved if the goal is achieved for all the specializations of that class. In addition, it is intended that a formal decomposition hierarchy produced in this way may be inspected both manually and with tool assistance in order that inconsistencies implicit in the global nonfunctional requirements may be detected.

Feather [27] describes how two related generic models — a resource management system model and a wilderness permit system model — can be explored both to determine the relationship between the two models, and to detect inconsistency and incompleteness in both models. Both kinds of models have a formal structure and have been implemented in an extended version of Common Lisp. It is possible to pose the following kinds of queries to the implementation: "Which of the resource management system goals are supported by the wilderness permit system's policies?", "which resource management system goals are mutually conflicting?" (inconsistency), and "which resource management system goals have no supporting policies?" (inconsistency). For each query the implementation is able to automatically return the correct answers.

Analyst skills knowledge is exploited by Champion and Loucopoulos [14] who encourage the development of informal models supported by facilities which closely match the behavior of a systems analyst. Behaviors supported include the use of analogy, construction of concept hierarchies, formulation of hypotheses, and use of domain knowledge. The ARIES project provides knowledge-based support for creating formal specifications from informal requirements by exploiting knowledge of the evolutionary steps commonly taken on route from requirements to specification. As described in Subsec. 2.6.2, REMAP also uses knowledge of the form typically employed by skilled analysts to support simple reasoning about a specification.

3.5. *Requirements validation*

Requirements validation is the process of checking with stakeholders that the system described by the elicited requirements embodies all of the desired properties.

Formal representations of application-specific knowledge are extremely useful at this stage. The fact that requirements are formally represented eliminates ambiguity. It also enables inferences and deductions which follow from the requirements collected to be made automatically and presented to the user for checking as, for example, in KATE [31].

In some cases, the formal representations of requirements are themselves suitable for presentation to the user. Conceptual graphs are often claimed to have a close affinity to natural language and are therefore thought to be relatively comprehensible to a majority of users.

The designers of the REMAP tool also envisage that their formal representations of what they call process knowledge (i.e., knowledge about the history of design decisions taken during the development of a requirements specification) could be used by "end users interested in understanding exactly how the design-deliberation process addresses their requirements".

In other cases, such formal representations may be transformed into other representations more suitable for user consumption. Champion and Loucopoulos suggest that conceptual graphs could be translated into natural language statements for user validation of the requirements they represent [14]. The ARIES tools support the use of a range of notations including state transition diagrams, information flow diagrams, decomposition hierarchies, and formal specification languages and, by mapping information expressed in such notations onto a common internal representation, provides translations of certain forms of specification into others which are easier to use in validation of requirements.

In the Requirements Frame model [65], objects, object types, operations among objects, and the roles of these operations (agents and goals, for example) are described using various textual and graphical formal languages, which are validated by conversion to user-oriented forms (logical assertions, relational views, control, and data flows, for example) and also by symbolic execution of a derived prototype.

Work on the FOREST project describes how a theorem generator (the reverse of a theorem prover) is used to generate a stream of the consequences which follow from a set of formally represented requirements. These can then be given a suitable representation in application domain terms and presented to the users. An example of this can be found in Cunningham *et al.* [17]. Here, three consequences, among many others, of a "blocks world" theory were the theorems $on(a,a)$, $on(b,b)$, and $on(c,c)$. A picture of a table with block a stacked upon block a clearly indicated that something was not quite right. TEMPORA's meta-models are intended to be used in a similar way to generate scenarios for checking by the end user of a required system. In the OPIE tool [3], client objectives (situations to be either supported or prevented) are input to a process which produces a specification of an "artifact" from which scenarios can be generated. These scenarios comprise sequences of possible actions for the specified system, and are subject to user validation.

3.6. *Summary*

This section has described a number of approaches to using the kinds of knowledge identified to provide support at various stages in the process of requirements engineering. Each kind of knowledge has been used at a number of stages. The greatest emphasis has, however, been on the use of domain knowledge and the formal representation of application-specific knowledge in providing support for requirements analysis.

4. Conclusions

The work described in the preceding sections illustrates a trend towards increased use of knowledge-based techniques in providing support for the process of requirements engineering. This is in line with observations made by Ramamoorthy *et al.* [66] and Harandi [41] regarding the increased applicability of AI techniques to the problems of software engineering. It might also be seen as indicative of a general trend towards an increase in the use of formal techniques at every stage in the software engineering process. The need for formality in a system specification generates a need for formality in the process of creating that specification. The fulfillment of this need by the development of a formal framework within which requirements engineering can take place in turn enables the use of AI techniques and hence the possibility for improved computer-based support. The existence of such a formal framework means that it becomes theoretically possible to develop powerful tools which might provide automated support for much of the process of requirements engineering.

There is as yet little consensus regarding the way in which AI techniques might most readily be exploited in providing support for requirements engineering. Many such techniques are not yet used to any great extent, often because they are not yet sufficiently powerful to be applied to problems of any scale or domains of realistic size. Techniques for machine learning and natural language processing, while at first sight are highly applicable, are at present only suitable for use on relatively small problems or in well-known, restricted domains.

We have focussed on the use of various kinds of knowledge and the approaches taken to exploit and reason with that knowledge. A number of projects are now investigating the use of formal representations of requirements (application-specific knowledge). Knowledge about the domain which encapsulates generalizations thought to hold for a range of applications within that domain is increasingly used in providing support at various stages. The main emphasis in this work has until now been on supporting analytical activities by providing a basis on which analogical reasoning can be performed, and completeness and consistency of requirements for new applications can be checked. There is some evidence for a move towards even greater generality in the use of meta-knowledge expected to apply across a number of domains. Work on the use of this kind of knowledge is, however, at a relatively early stage.

The use of knowledge-based techniques of the kind described is likely to improve both the efficiency of the process by which requirements are gathered and documented and the quality of the specification which results from that process. The time and effort expended by a skilled requirements analyst in the production of a requirements specification is likely to be reduced and the specification itself is likely to contain fewer instances of redundancy, ambiguity, inconsistency, or incompleteness.

The full potential of such techniques has, however, not yet been exploited. Further work is needed in order to investigate new ways in which domain knowledge might be used to support activities such as requirements elicitation. Work on the benefits of using meta-knowledge of the kind envisaged is also needed. Further development of techniques making use of method knowledge will be needed as more methodologies for requirements engineering become well-defined, and representations of analyst skills knowledge may need to be updated as understanding of the process of requirements engineering evolves.

Such work might usefully draw on research in related fields. Techniques for the acquisition of domain knowledge suitable for use in requirements engineering might be based on those developed for knowledge engineers. The development of new techniques for requirements elicitation might draw on those for knowledge elicitation. Finally, the problem of finding representations for requirements with a well-defined semantics which have sufficient expressive power and are comprehensible to the majority of users might be tackled by considering work in the field of formal methods and human-computer interaction.

In summary, it may be stated that the development of a framework within which to consider existing work on the provision of knowledge-based support for requirements engineering has led to a number of interesting insights regarding the nature of the support which is currently provided and the way in which this support might in future be enhanced. While it is clear that knowledge-based techniques are at present capable of providing significant support for the requirements engineer, it is also clear that a considerable amount of work has still to be done before the potential of these techniques can be fully realized.

Acknowledgements

This article is an updated and expanded version of an earlier article [11] which resulted from work on the GMARC project [10]. Besides the present authors,

David Furber, then of King's College London, also contributed to that earlier article.

References

1. B. Adelson and E. Soloway, "The role of domain experience in software design", *IEEE Trans. Softw. Eng.* **11**, 11 (1985) 1351–1360.
2. E. Adhami, R. Pyburn, and R. Champion, "A knowledge-based approach to requirements engineering", in *Software Engineering Environments: Research and Practice*, ed. K. Bennett (Ellis Horwood, 1989) Chpt. 12, pp. 187–202.
3. J. S. Anderson and Brian Durney, "Using scenarios in deficiency-driven requirements engineering domains", in [29].
4. G. Arango and P. Freeman, "Modeling knowledge for software development", *Proc. 3rd Int. Workshop Software Specification and Design* (IEEE Computer Society Press, 1985) pp. 63–66.
5. F. Van Assche, P. Layzell, P. Loucopoulos, and R. Venken, "Rule-based specifications of information systems", in *Software Engineering Environments*, ed. P. Brereton (Ellis Horwood, 1988) Chpt. 15.
6. W. Atkinson and J. Cunningham, "Proving properties of a safety-critical system", *Softw. Eng. J.* **6**, 2 (1991) 41–50.
7. A. Barr, P. Cohen, and E. Feigenbaum, *The Handbook of Artificial Intelligence*, Vol. 4 (Pitman, 1981).
8. D. Barstow, "Should we specify systems or domains?", in [29].
9. K. Benner, "Knowledge-based software assistant", *Knowledge-Based Sys.* **1**, 4 (1988) 221–226.
10. D. Bolton, S. Jones, D. Till, D. Furber, and S. Green, "Using domain knowledge in requirements capture and formal specification construction", in *Requirements Engineering: Social and Technological Issues*, eds. M. Jirotka and J. Goguen (Academic Press, 1994).
11. D. Bolton, S. V. Jones, D. Till, D. Furber, and S. Green, "Knowledge-based support for requirements engineering", *Int. J. Softw. Eng. Knowl. Eng.* **2**, 2 (1992) 293–319.
12. J. H. Boose, "A survey of knowledge acquisition techniques and tools", *Knowl. Acquisition* **1**, 1 (1989) 3–37.
13. A. Borgida, S. Greenspan, and J. Mylopoulos, "Knowledge representation as the basis for requirements specifications", in *Readings in Artificial Intelligence and Software Engineering*, eds. C. Rich and R. C. Waters (Morgan Kaufmann, 1986) pp. 561–569.
14. R. E. M. Champion and P. Loucopoulos, "Concept acquisition and analysis for requirements specification", *Softw. Eng. J.* **5**, 2 (1990) 116–124.
15. L. Chung, "Representation and utilization of non-functional requirements for information system design", *Proc. 3rd Int. Conf. CAiSE '91*, eds. R. Anderson, J. A. Bubenko and A. Solvberg (Springer-Verlag, 1991) pp. 5–30.

16. P. Constantopoulos and E. Pataki, "A browser for software reuse", in *Advanced Information Systems Engineering*, ed. P. Loucopoulos (Springer-Verlag, 1992). Also in *Proc. 4th Int. Conf., CAiSE'94*, Manchester, UK, 12–15 May (1992) pp. 304–326.
17. R. J. Cunningham, M. Costa, and J. Booth, "Logical animation", *Proc. 12th Int. Conf. Software Engineering* (IEEE Computer Society Press, 1990) pp. 144–149.
18. B. Curtis, "Panel session", *Proc. 9th Int. Conf. Software Engineering* (1987).
19. A. J. Czuchry and D. R. Harris, "KBRA: a new paradigm for requirements engineering", *IEEE Expert* **3**, 4 (1988) 21–35.
20. A. Dardenne, S. Fickas, and A. van Lamsweerde, "Goal-directed concept acquisition in requirements elicitation", Technical Report CIS-TR-91-08, Department of Computer and Information Science, University of Oregon, Eugene, Oregon 97403 (1991).
21. A. Dardenne and A. van Lamsweerde, "Goal-directed requirements acquisition", *Science of Computer Programming* **20**, 1–2 (1993) 3–50.
22. J. C. S. do Prado Leite and A. P. M. Franco, "A strategy for conceptual model acquisition", in [29].
23. E. Dubois, "A formal language for the requirements engineering of computer systems", in *Introducing a Logic-Based Approach to AI*, Vol. 3, ed. A. Thayse (John Wiley, 1991) pp. 357–433.
24. E. Dubois, Use of deontic logic in the requirements engineering of composite systems, in *Deontic Logic in Computer Science: Normative System Specification*, eds. J. Meyer and R. Wieringa (John Wiley, 1993) pp. 125–139.
25. E. Dubois and J. Hagelstein, "A logic of action for goal-oriented elaboration of requirements", *Proc. 5th Int. Workshop Software Specification and Design*, Vol. 14 (1989) pp. 160–168.
26. S. Easterbrook, "Domain modelling with hierarchies of alternative viewpoints", in [29].
27. M. Feather, "Requirements reconnoitering at the juncture of domain and instance", in *IEEE Int. Symp. Requirements Engineering* (IEEE Computer Society Press, 1993).
28. S. Fickas, "Automating the analysis process", *Proc. 4th Int. Workshop Software Specification and Design* (IEEE Computer Society Press, 1987).
29. S. Fickas and A.C.W. Finkelstein, eds., *Proc. IEEE Int. Symp. Requirements Engineering* (IEEE Computer Society Press, 1993).
30. S. Fickas and R. Helm, "Knowledge representation and reasoning in the design of composite systems", *IEEE Trans. Softw. Eng.* **18**, 6 (1992) 470–482.
31. S. Fickas and P. Nagarajan, "Critiquing software specifications", *IEEE Softw.* **5**, 11 (1988) 37–47.
32. A. Finkelstein and H. Fuks, "Multi-party specification", *Proc. 5th Int. Workshop Software Specification and Design* (IEEE Computer Society Press, 1989).

33. A. Finkelstein, J. Kramer, and M. Goedicke, "ViewPoint-oriented software development", *Proc. 3rd Int. Workshop Software Engineering and its Applications*, Vol. 1 (SIGREF EC2, 1990) pp. 337–351.
34. B. Flinn and I. Sorenson, "CAVIAR: a case study in specification", in *Specification Case Studies, Prentice Hall International Series in Computer Science*, ed. I. Hayes (Prentice Hall, 1987).
35. P. Freeman, "A conceptual analysis of the Draco approach to constructing software systems", *IEEE Trans. Softw. Eng.* **13**, 7 (1987) 830–844.
36. R. Giddings, "Accommodating uncertainty in software design", *Commun. ACM* **27**, 5 (1984) 428–434.
37. S. Greenspan, "Requirements modelling: a knowledge representation approach to software requirements definition", Ph.D. Thesis, University of Toronto, Computer Systems Research Group (1984). Also in Technical Report CSRG-155.
38. S. Greenspan, J. Mylopoulos, and A. Borgida, "Principles for requirements and design languages: the Taxis project", in *Requirements Engineering Environments*, ed. Y. Ohno (North-Holland, 1982).
39. S. Grosz and C. Rolland, "Using artificial intelligence techniques to formalize the information system design process", *Proc. Int. Conf. Databases and Expert Systems* (1990) pp. 374–380.
40. J. Hagelstein, "Declarative approach to information systems requirements", *Knowledge-Based Sys.* **1**, 4 (1988) 211–219.
41. M. Harandi, "Report on the fourth international workshop on software specification and design", *Softw. Eng. Notes* **13**, 1 (1988) 29–38.
42. M. Jackson and P. Zave, "Domain descriptions", in [29].
43. M. Jarke, J. Bubenko, C. Rolland, A. G. Sutcliffe, and Y. Vassiliou, "Theories underlying requirements engineering: an overview of NATURE at genesis", *Proc. IEEE Symp. Requirements Engineering, RE93*, San Diego, California, 4–6 January 1993 (IEEE Computer Society Press, 1993) pp. 19–31.
44. M. Jarke, M. Jeusfeld, and T. Rose, A software process model for knowledge engineering in information systems, *Info. Sys.* **15**, 1 (1990) 85–116.
45. M. Jarke, K. Pohl, S. Jacobs, J. Bubenko, P. Assenova, P. Holm, B. Wangler, C. Rolland, V. Plihon, J. Schmitt, A. G. Sutcliffe, S. Jones, N. A. M. Maiden, D. Till, Y. Vassiliou, P. Constantopoulos, and G. Spanoudakis, "Requirements engineering: an integrated view of representation", in *Proc. 4th European Software Engineering Conf.*, Garmesh-Partenkirchen, 1993. Also in *Lecture Notes in Computer Science 717*, eds. I. Sommerville and P. Manfred (Springer-Verlag, 1993) pp. 100–114.
46. W. L. Johnson, M. S. Feather, and D. R. Harris, "Applying domain knowledge to requirements engineering", *SIGOIS Bulletin* **13**, 2 (1992) 48–57.
47. H. Kaindl, "The missing link in requirements engineering", *Softw. Eng. Notes* **18**, 2 (1993) 30–39.
48. S. J. H. Kent, T. S. E. Maibaum, and W. J. Quirk, "Formally specifying temporal constraints and error recovery", in [29].

49. J. Kramer, K. Ng, C. Potts, and K. Whitehead, "Tool support for requirements analysis", *Softw. Eng. J.* **3**, 2 (1988) 86–96.
50. M. Lefering, "An incremental integration tool between requirements engineering and programming in the large", in [29].
51. P. Loucopoulos and E. Katsouli, "Modelling business rules in an office environment", *SIGOIS Bulletin* **13**, 2 (1992) 28–37.
52. P. Loucopoulos and R. Champion, "Knowledge-based approach to requirements engineering using method and domain knowledge", *Knowledge-Based Sys.* **1**, 3 (1988) 179–187.
53. M. D. Lubars, "Domain analysis and domain engineering in IDeA", Technical Report, Microelectronics and Computer Technology Corporation, USA (1988).
54. M. D. Lubars, "A domain modelling representation", Technical Report, Microelectronics and Computer Technology Corporation, USA (1988).
55. M. D. Lubars and M. T. Harandi, "The knowledge based refinement paradigm and IDeA: concepts, limitations and future directions", Technical Report, Microelectronics and Computer Technology Corporation, USA (1988).
56. C. Macnee, S. Lambert, and G. Ringland, "Application domain knowledge acquisition and use in requirements engineering computerized systems", in *AI (Artificial Intelligence) in Enterprise Modelling*, IEE Digest No. 1993/078 (1993) (Proceedings of a one day colloquium, 7th April 1993).
57. T. S. E. Maibaum, "A logic for the formal requirements specification of real-time embedded systems", Technical Report, FOREST Project, Department of Computing, Imperial College of Science, Technology and Medicine, London, UK (1986).
58. N. A. Maiden and A. G. Sutcliffe, "Exploiting reusable specifications through analogy", *Commun. ACM* **35**, 4 (1992) 55–64.
59. N. A. Maiden and A. G. Sutcliffe, "Analogical matching for specification retrieval", in *Proc. 6th Knowledge-Based Software Engineering Conf.* (IEEE Computer Society Press, 1991) pp. 108–116.
60. N. A. Maiden and A. G. Sutcliffe, "Requirements critiquing using domain abstraction", in *Proc. 1st Int. Conf. Requirements Engineering* (IEEE Computer Society Press, 1994) pp. 184–193.
61. G. P. Mullery, "CORE — a method for controlled requirement specification", *Proc. 4th Int. Conf. on Software Engineering* (September 1979).
62. M. Musen, "Conceptual models of interactive knowledge acquisition tools", *Knowledge Acquisition* **1**, 1 (1989) 73–88.
63. J. Mylopoulos, A. Borgida, M. Jarke, and M. Koubarakis, "TELOS: a language for representing knowledge about information systems", Technical Report, MIP-9011, Fakultät für Mathematik und Informatik, Universität Passau, Germany (September 1990).
64. J. M. Neighbors, "The Draco approach to constructing software from reusable components", *IEEE Trans. Softw. Eng.* **10**, 5 (1984) 564–574.
65. A. Ohnishi and K. Agusa, "CARD: a software requirements definition environment", in [29].

66. C. V. Ramamoorthy, L. Miguel, and Y.-C. Shim, "On issues in software engineering and artificial intelligence", *Int. J. Softw. Eng. Knowl. Eng.* **1**, 1 (1991) 9–20.
67. B. Ramesh and V. Dhar, "Supporting systems development by capturing deliberations during requirements engineering", *IEEE Trans. Softw. Eng.* **18**, 6 (1992) 498–510.
68. B. Ramesh and Luqi, "Process knowledge-based rapid prototyping for requirements engineering", in [29].
69. H. B. Reubenstein, "Automated acquisition of evolving informal descriptions", Ph.D. Thesis, MIT AI Laboratory, Cambridge, MA 02139, USA (1990).
70. C. Rich, R. Waters, and H. Reubenstein, "Toward a Requirements Apprentice", *Proc. 4th Int. Workshop Software Specification and Design* (IEEE Computer Society Press, 1987).
71. C. Rolland, "Modelling the evolution of artefacts", *Proc. 1st Int. Conf. Requirements Engineering* (IEEE Computer Society Press, 1994) pp. 216–219.
72. G. Roman, "A taxonomy of current issues in requirements engineering", *IEEE Comput.* (April 1985) 14–22.
73. K. Ryan, "Defaults in Specifications", in [29].
74. K. Ryan and B. Mathews, "Matching conceptual graphs as an aid to requirements reuse", in [29].
75. M. D. Ryan, J. Fiadeiro, and T. Maibaum, "Sharing actions and attributes in modal action logic", in *Theoretical Aspects of Computer Software, Lecture Notes in Computer Science 526*, eds. T. Ito and A. Meyer (Springer-Verlag, 1991) pp. 569–593.
76. A. G. Sutcliffe and N. A. Maiden, "How specification reuse can support requirements analysis", *Proc. Software Engineering 90 Conference*, ed. Pat Hall (Cambridge University Press, 1991) pp. 489–509.
77. V. Tseng and M. Mannino, "A method for database requirements collection", *J. Management Info. Sys.* **6**, 2 (1989) 51–75.
78. UK Department of Trade and Industry and National Computing Centre, *The STARTS Guide*, 2nd ed. (NCC Publications, 1987).
79. N. van Diepen and H. Partsch, "Some aspects of formalizing informal requirements", in *Proc. 2nd Meteor Workshop on Methods for Formal Specification* (Springer-Verlag, 1989).
80. A. van Lamsweerde, A. Dardenne, and F. Dubisy, "KAOS knowledge representations as initial support for formal specification processes", Technical Report 15, KAOS Project, Facultes Universitaires de Namur, Belgium (1990).
81. W. van Melle, A. Scott, J. Bennett, and M. Peairs, "The EMYCIN manual", Technical Report, Stanford University Heuristic Programming Project, USA (1981).
82. N. P. Vitalari and G. W. Dickson, "Problem solving for effective systems analysis: an experimental exploration", *Commun. ACM* **26**, 11 (1983) 948–956.

SAFETY-CRITICAL SOFTWARE: A RESEARCH AGENDA

ALFS T. BERZTISS

Department of Computer Science, University of Pittsburgh,
Pittsburgh, PA 15260, USA
E-mail: alpha@cs.pitt.edu
and
SYSLAB, University of Stockholm, Sweden

A system is safety-critical if failure of the system would result in loss of human life, personal injury, or significant material loss. Software that supports or supplants human control of safety-critical systems has to be highly reliable, but much research remains to be done before all the reliability-related issues of safety-critical software are fully understood. We discuss a research agenda under the following headings: completeness of requirements, readability of specifications, validation tools, validation of responsiveness, verification of implementations, software robustness, common-cause failures, reuse of reliable software, the software process, and ethical issues.

1. Introduction

Under a narrow definition, a system is *safety-critical* if failure of the system could result in loss of human life or in personal injury. Broadening the definition, we also include cases in which failure can result in material loss serious enough to affect the health of an organization. Software of very high reliability has to support or supplant human control of safety-critical systems in the following situations:

1. human reaction times are too slow,
2. human error is likely, and
3. the environment in which the system operates is inhospitable to humans.

The construction of safety-critical software has been surveyed by Nancy Leveson [1, 2] and by Abbott [3]. However, the analysis of the failures of just one device, the Therac-25, shows that much remains to be done [4]. The purpose of this paper is to discuss several research topics relevant to the improvement of the reliability of safety-critical systems.

We shall use the following terminology, which is becoming fairly standard [5]. An observed deviation of a software system from its specification is a *failure*; a *fault* is a defect in the software system that is capable of causing a failure; an action by a software developer that introduces a fault is an *error*.

2. What Can Go Wrong

Nearly all safety-critical software systems are real-time systems embedded in hosts that they control. The typical development of such a system starts with requirements formulation and the allocation of system components to humans, hardware, and software. In an ideal situation, the software requirements are next converted into a formal specification. The specification is converted into an implementation. We thus have three interfaces:

1. between sponsor and developer in the initial capture of requirements;
2. between requirements and specification;
3. between specification and implementation of the system.

The biggest problems arise with (1) and (2), and are primarily due to incompatibility of representations. The requirements, as supplied by the sponsor who will use the software, are expressed in an informal language; the specification and implementation are in languages with formal syntax and semantics. Therefore, although formal techniques can be used to show that an implementation is functionally consistent with a specification, no formal consistency check of a specification against requirements can exist. This creates a dilemma: because initial requirements are informal, writers of specifications may misinterpret the requirements; because formal specifications are often difficult to read, sponsors of the system cannot clear up the misinterpretations. Furthermore, although formal proofs can be used to show that an implementation is consistent with its functional specification, responsiveness requirements are not as easy to deal with.

The next group of problems relates to the completeness of requirements. Clients may omit to state crucial requirements because they

(a) assume such requirements to be part of everyone's general knowledge;
(b) forget to state them;
(c) omit them because they cannot find the right formulation for expressing them;
(d) are unaware that a particular safety hazard could arise and hence do not provide for the hazard in the requirements.

Although technical reviews [6, 7], particularly in the form of a JAD-type workshop [8], could be used to reduce incompleteness, it cannot be eliminated completely. Therefore, it is essential to realize that control systems will contain faults, and that failures will arise.

A scientific or engineering discipline is based on measurements. If failures cannot be avoided, at least the probability of their occurrence should be determined. This can be done by means of the reliability theory applied to test results. In hardware design, the reliability of a system can be made arbitrarily high by use of redundancy in building up a system with components of known reliability. Unfortunately, software is subject to common-cause failures, and this means that component redundancy is of not much help in improving the overall reliability of a software system. However, if multiple copies of a software system have been used over an extended period of time, the failure data collected for this system can be used to provide an accurate estimate of the reliability of the system. If the host of such a system is to be replaced by a new model, the embedded control software should be transformed to suit the new model in a correctness-preserving manner. This suggests that the process by which a safety-critical system is being developed can have considerable effect on the reliability of the system.

This brief overview leads us to the identification of a number of research topics. We now list these topics, which will be discussed in some detail in the rest of the paper:

- Completeness of requirements.
- Readable representation languages for specifications.
- Tools for the validation of specifications.
- Validation of the responsiveness of a system.
- Verification of an implementation.
- Robustness of control software.
- Effect of common-cause failures.
- Reuse of reliable software.
- The development process for safety-critical software.
- Ethical issues.

The last topic relates to risks — what reliability values are appropriate for safety-critical software?

3. Completeness of Requirements

In Sec. 2, we gave four reasons why requirements as given by the sponsor of a software system to developers of the system are often incomplete. The incompleteness will show up during technical reviews of the requirements only if representatives of sponsors of the software become aware of the incompleteness and point out what is missing. To help detect the incompleteness in the requirements, three devices can be used:

i. a checklist of what the requirements should contain;
ii. a fault tree, which is constructed by listing as many safety-critical failures as possible that come to mind, and building a tree in which a failure can be traced back to a missing software requirement;
iii. a state table, which is similar in purpose to a fault tree.

Much attention should be given to the construction and updating of checklists. Of particular importance are checklists that capture the safety concerns of domain experts. The safety concerns should be classified, and the classification used to suggest how the safety concerns collected with respect to one domain could be adapted in setting up a checklist for another domain.

In an early article on safety, Leveson and Harvey [9] distinguish correctness and safety. Their example is an aircraft that is on a *correct* flight path, but must temporarily deviate from this flight path to avoid collision with another aircraft. The aircraft thus makes a transition from a correct and unsafe state to an incorrect and safe state. In our view, this is too narrow an interpretation of correctness. We prefer to think of the aircraft as a reactive system that regularly monitors its environment, and that is required to alter its flight path when it finds itself in danger of collision, i.e., the altered flight path is still to be regarded as correct. The rationale for separating safety from the rest of the specifications is that this highlights safety, and that more attention will then be given to safety aspects. This was a worthwhile objective in 1983, but we hope that most system developers today are conscious of safety demands. Indeed, the Therac-25 article [4] shows that, if anything, safety concerns need to become fully integrated into every aspect of system development. Hence, we share the view, expressed by Parnas *et al.* [10], that safety is not to be regarded as a separate issue.

We also disagree with the statement that correctness specifications should indicate what is to happen, while safety specifications should indicate what is not to happen. Hence, although a very simple way of dealing with safety requirements would be to produce a list of possible safety-critical failures and to state that the system is not to let these failures arise, we maintain that safety-critical requirements should always indicate explicitly what a system is to do. The requirements must define the most effective way to avoid failure, e.g., how to avoid aircraft collision with minimal course deviations, and the specialized knowledge of domain experts is needed for this. Domain experts can use the fault tree to detect safety hazards in a systematic way [9, 11]. Another tool to investigate this task is the causal map [12].

Suppose a system is made up of k components, each of which may be in one of several states. Then a state table can be drawn up in which each combination of states is identified as indicating a *safe* or *unsafe* system state, or it is found that the combination of states cannot arise [13]. Even with each component having just 2 states, the table has 2^k entries, but the table can usually be compressed using techniques that have been developed for the construction of limited-entry decision tables (see, e.g., [14]). The research task is to develop tools that will assist domain experts in constructing fault trees, causal maps, and limited-entry state tables. Keep in mind that in building a safety-critical system, it is not a question of which tool to use in preference over another. Every possible method for improving the requirements must be put to use, and the greater the number of tools that highlight different views of the system, the safer will we be.

4. Readable Specifications

Specifications must be precise and unambiguous, and they should be readable. These are conflicting requirements in that a quest for precision and unambiguity tends to result in representations that are difficult to understand. The main thrust of research on specifications should aim at resolving this conflict. There can be three lines of attack. First, improve the readability of specifications. Second, provide the specifications with informal explanations. Third, improve the literacy level of readers of specifications.

If specifications are to be precise and unambiguous, they have to be formal, i.e., written in a language with fully defined syntax and semantics. In [15], a formal specification of a text formatter is given in terms of predicates. It is unreadable. Two different specifications in Z (see, e.g., [16]) for this problem, which were provided to the author by Andrew Parle (Australian Atomic Energy Commission) and Ian Hayes (University of Queensland), respectively, have somewhat better readability properties, but in this instance, the clearest specification appears to be the program itself [15, pp. 64–65]. It is commonly accepted that specifications should state *what* is to be done, and implementations should tell *how* to do it. The rationale for the *what-how* split is that a specification should allow implementation freedom. However, in many instances, a *how* is the only clear way of stating the *what.* One instance of this is the text formatter. We saw another instance in the discussion of how to avoid aircraft collision with minimal flight-path disruption. Here, the *how* has to come from domain experts, and the domain experts have to supply this knowledge during requirements gathering. In these cases, implementation freedom has to be sacrificed in the interests of obtaining a software product that corresponds to what the sponsor of the software product actually wants. The research task is to develop classifications of safety-critical software and specification styles, and to match each class of software with an appropriate specification style.

Specifications written in Z are expected to be annotated [16]. Even with specification languages that are comparatively easy to read, such as Gist [17] and SF [18], annotation will help the reader. Unfortunately, writers of specifications can misstate their intentions in the specifications, but get them right in the annotations. Automatic generation of annotations from specifications has therefore been investigated for Gist [19] and for data base schemas expressed as entity-relationship diagrams [20]. This work needs to be greatly expanded.

People understand that it takes considerable time to learn a new programming language, yet expect to be able to read a specification without much preparation. This attitude has to change, and teaching materials have to be developed for specification languages that are of the same quality as teaching materials for programming languages. So far, the only language for which this has been attempted is Z [16, 21]. For Z, this is an absolute necessity because Z is intrinsically very difficult to read.

5. Validation of Functional Specifications

A functional specification is to capture precisely and unambiguously the use to which the sponsor of a software system wants to put the system. Validation is a systematic determination that this has happened. Functional specifications can be validated in two ways. If a specification has been executable from the beginning, or it has been turned into executable code by correctness-preserving transformations, or the code has been proven "correct", then any faults discovered during testing can be attributed to the specification. In these instances, the specification and the code are consistent, but neither meets the expectations of the sponsor of the system. The other validation mode is by inspection of specifications, for which a checklist similar to that discussed in Sec. 3 would be used. We shall not discuss the checklist-based mode further.

Validation by testing of safety-critical software raises three major problems. One relates to reliability. Software reliability is expressed as the probability of a software system not failing over a given time period, and the reliability of a system at the time of its release is established by testing it before its release, where the test data are to represent the operational profile for the software. However, reliability in this technical sense is not a good indicator of the dependability of safety-critical software [22]. A new measure has to be established for safety-critical software. As an initial suggestion for this research, one approach would be to give weights to failures in proportion to the safety effects of the failures. Suppose the reliability of a system is to be r. To measure reliability in the conventional sense, all weights are set to 1.0, and testing proceeds until the value r is reached. With heavy weights assigned to safety-critical failures, much more testing would have to be undertaken to achieve the same reliability target. This increases the probability that a safety-critical fault is exercised during testing. In [22], it is recommended that in the construction of the operational profile, larger weights should be given to inputs that lead into safety-critical regions. This appears to be a better approach, but then we no longer have random black-box testing, and the development of a theory of reliability for testing that which is not black-box appears to be a difficult research topic. The whole issue of how to determine an accurate operational profile, on which statistical validation depends, has been discussed by Musa [23], but much additional work still needs to be done on the development of a dependable general methodology for this task. Recently, a new technique was developed for arriving at operational profiles by Markov analysis [24]. This work opens up an interesting new research area.

The second problem deals with all systems requiring ultrahigh reliability. If a single version of a system is used, experimental determination of the reliability is a physical impossibility [25]; if n independently-developed versions of the software are used in parallel, common cause failures complicate reliability calculations. The topic of n-version programming and common cause failures will be taken up again in Sec. 9.

Finally, the assumptions made in the development of software reliability theory do not always apply to reactive software. For programs that transform an input into an output by means of a lengthy computation, the important parameter is execution time – the probability of failure is related to the time for which a program executes. While programs that transform data are generally exercised as smoothly executed long sequences of operations, reactive software, and much of safety-critical software is in this category, reacts to sporadically occurring external events, and executions sequences are short in general. The failures of data transformers are mostly due to fairly minor coding errors; those of reactive software are mostly due to major errors in the formulation of conceptual models of application domains. This does not mean that conventional reliability theory is inapplicable to reactive systems in all cases. For example, it has been successfully applied to computer operating systems, which are more reactive than transformative. In many cases, though, a theory based on what has been called discrete time analysis [26, 27] is more appropriate, and has in fact been used in the analysis of failure data of n-version programs. Research should be undertaken on the ranges of applicability of execution time and discrete time reliability analyses.

Once a fault has been discovered in a specification, it has to be removed – we speak of diagnosis and correction. A technique for fault diagnosis and correction developed by Shapiro in his Ph.D. dissertation [28], called algorithmic debugging, has led to numerous extensions. One such extension is the application of the algorithmic debugging concept to specifications of safety-critical systems. This extension is due to Jeffrey Tsai *et al.* and is reported in this issue [29]. Tsai *et al.* express a specification in FRORL (Frame and Rule Oriented Requirements Language). A useful continuation of their work would be to adapt its techniques to other specifications languages.

6. Validation of Responsiveness

Responsiveness is the measure of the time it takes for software to respond to a stimulus. For example, software performance requirements for a control system may state that the software is to complete a corrective action at most 0.01 seconds after a transition of the system into an unsafe state. The 0.01 seconds is an absolute value that the software must satisfy. Adequate responsiveness depends on design decisions that are made in very early stages of software development; experimental determination, that the design actually does support the responsiveness requirement comes only after implementation, and by this time, design changes are costly and may prolong project completion beyond an acceptable limit.

This means that a prototyping language should allow the responsiveness properties of the released software to be deduced from the responsiveness of the prototype, as has been recommended by Luqi [30]. Then, if the prototype shows that the released software will not meet its responsiveness requirements, design changes are made in the prototype. For safety-critical software, time constraints on the following three activities are particularly important:

(a) the determination that the system it controls is in an unsafe state;
(b) looking up the information needed to determine what corrective action to take;
(c) the carrying out of the corrective action.

Further research is needed on software and hardware architectures that will allow these time constraints to be satisfied. The difference in execution times between prototype and the released software should be negligible for tasks (a) and (c), but could be appreciable for (b). For a general survey of software performance estimation, see [31].

7. Verification of an Implementation

To paraphrase Barry Boehm, validation determines whether the system being built is the right one; verification determines whether it is being built the right way. Put another way, validation establishes whether specification and requirements are consistent, verification does the same for implementation and specification. Verification can be logical, mathematical, or statistical. Under *logical* verification, the specification is a set of axioms, the implementation is a theorem to be proven from the axioms, and each step of the proof is the application of one of the rules of inference that define this particular system of logic. The verifier can be assisted by a set of powerful tools. In addition, tools can be used to check the consistency of the axioms. This can work very well for some programs that are specified in terms of input-output relations, i.e., systems that transform data. Logical verification becomes more problematic with reactive systems, i.e., systems that respond to a query or a stimulus, and safety-critical systems tend to fall into this category. Although the answer to a query could be regarded as a transformation of the query, and the control response as the transformation of a stimulus received from the system that is being controlled, this is not a natural way in which to regard reactive systems.

Moreover, just as disciplines such as numerical analysis and hydrodynamics are too far removed from the foundations of mathematics for theorems in these disciplines to be proven in terms of set theory and formal logic, so too are the application domains of safety-critical software. This suggests that informal *mathematical* verification should be used in place of strictly formal logical verification. Informality does not mean lack of rigor, but mathematical "proofs" sometimes turn out to be invalid. The most common cause for this is failure to consider all cases that could arise.

Large physical systems, such as gas molecules moving in a closed container, are composed of too many constituents to allow exact prediction of their behavior. Statistical techniques have been developed for the analysis of such systems. Similarly, in the realization that large software systems will rarely be completely free of faults, software reliability theory is used to make predictions about future failures of large software systems. This we call *statistical* verification.

Logical verification is already a very active research area of computer science. It is also so highly specialized that a general survey is not the right place for making suggestions regarding future research in this area. We direct the reader to Ostroff's outstanding survey of the formal methods as they relate to real-time safety-critical systems [32]. The use of formal methods in four safety-critical applications is discussed in [33, 34]. Statistical verification will be taken up again in Sec. 9. Here, we point out the need for a methodology of mathematical verification that enforces consideration of all cases. In [15], we give some instances of mathematical verification in which such enforcement was attempted, but this is only a beginning.

8. Robustness of Control Software

Robustness is a term that covers fault- and failure-tolerance. A software system is *fault-tolerant* if the effect of exercising a fault is masked; it is *failure-tolerant* if the consequences of a software failure are small. In particular, a failure-tolerant system is *fail-safe* if a failure of the system does not create a safety hazard; it is *fail-soft* if there is no actual interruption of operation of the system, merely a graceful degradation of its performance or a loss of some noncritical capabilities. Software that controls a safety-critical system should be fault-tolerant and fail-safe. Research on fault-tolerant computing to 1986 is surveyed in [35]; references to later work can be found in [36] (written in German — most of the 295 items in the bibliography are annotated, and the annotations are in English).

In a discussion of fault-tolerant and fail-safe computing there are actually four components to consider: the software system, the hardware on which the software executes, a communication network linking components when the system is distributed, and an interface to human operators. The human-machine interface can be separated into its software and hardware components, and each component considered with the rest of the software or hardware, respectively. The hardware-software system is considered under a composite designation of X-ware in [27]. Most research on fault-tolerance has targeted distributed systems. Valuable surveys of the issues to be considered in this context under a client-server model are provided by Schneider [37] and Cristian [38]. A later survey [39] addresses the problem of establishing a consensus between processors; an inclusion relation between seven fault classes is particularly interesting (shown as Fig. 5 in [39]).

Software fault-tolerance is implemented by means of recovery-block or n-version strategies. In both cases, n different versions of the software unit under consideration have to be provided. Under the recovery-block strategy, the first version is executed. An oracle determines whether it has succeeded or failed. If the latter, the second version is executed for the same input, the oracle again consulted, and so forth, until a version succeeds or all versions have failed. Under n-version programming, all n versions are executed in parallel and, for k-out-of-n acceptance, if at least k versions produce the same result, the result is accepted. One problem is that the oracle or the k-out-of-n counter has to be assumed to have perfect reliability. Another is that all k can produce the same false result. In an extremely well-documented experiment involving independent versions developed in England, Finland, and Norway [40], all seven residual faults detected after software acceptance by the sponsor were due to ambiguous or incorrect specifications, which demonstrates that coding errors can be quite effectively identified by a 3-version strategy. Unfortunately, the experiment also showed that two of the residual faults were common to two of the versions.

The k-out-of-n counter can be a standard reusable piece of software. As regards the oracle, a software classification should be undertaken to identify cases in which a result can be verified by a computation that is much simpler than the computation of the result. Instances in which this is possible include the solution of simultaneous equations. Another research area to be investigated is the use of expert systems to rank the results obtained by n-version software in order of feasibility.

Still another research undertaking would be to use source-to-source transformations that would attempt to transform one program version into another. The transformation problem is in general unsolvable because program equivalence is in general unsolvable (see, e.g., [41]). However, whenever the transformation system would succeed in giving the two versions similar form, the differences between them would highlight faults, which could then be removed.

When failure does occur, we should minimize its effect by making the system fail-safe or fail-soft, with preference given to fail-soft operation. Of course, every system needs to be treated differently, but we can set up general check lists of what to look for in technical inspections of safety-critical software designs and code so as to minimize the effects of failure.

9. Common-Cause Failures

When n versions of a program are produced from the same requirements by n development teams working independently, we would want to assume that no two versions would fail for the same input. If this were so, we would need no more than three versions: if two of the versions produced one result, and the third another, we would know that the third version had failed. Unfortunately, the assumption is invalid. There are two cases. First, under *coincident* failure, two or more versions can fail for the same input (and even in the same way) due to totally unrelated causes. Second, under *common-cause* failure, two versions can contain essentially the same fault, and if this were their only fault, they would always either both fail or both survive.

Several experiments have demonstrated that common-cause failures cannot be avoided. We have already referred to the England-Finland-Norway experiment of [40]. The results of an experiment carried out at Irvine in California and Charlottesville in Virginia with 27 versions are reported and analyzed in [42–44]. In another experiment, four sites were used to develop 20 versions of an aerospace application program [45]; a 3-version experiment is discussed in [46]. All these experiments have demonstrated that improperly understood requirements contribute most of the common-cause faults. Indeed, a field study [47] has found that software developers realize that a lack of understanding of application domains is a major contributing factor to the ills associated with the software development process.

The construction of a mathematical model for the analysis of coincidental failures in n-version software was begun by Eckhardt and Lee [48]. They demonstrated that independently-developed versions do not fail independently. Littlewood and Miller [49] have continued this work. In particular, they have carefully investigated the meaning of terms such as independence and variability in this context. They point out that lack of failure independence in independently-developed versions is due to a variability of the "difficulty" particular inputs represent for the software. Their work shows that methodological diversity is an important fault reduction strategy. Nicola and Goyal [50] investigate the appropriateness of a particular probability density function for correlated failures.

The "difficulty" of particular inputs could be related to the execution time between the input of test data and the failure occasioned by these data. Therefore, reliability estimation in terms of execution times, as advocated in, for example, [51] and [52] should be extended to n-version software that exhibits common-cause failures. Execution time has been shown to be a natural limiting case for discrete time in [26] and [27]. Another interesting research topic is the incorporation of fault-failure causality considerations in reliability models. Both are difficult topics.

10. Reuse of Reliable Software

For the most part, software reuse has been advocated as a way of reducing development costs. We consider the increase of reliability of a software system over time to be an even more important reason for increased reuse. For example, given an operating system that has been run at 5000 sites for 24 hours a day for three and a half years, analysis of failures observed over this time suggested that the expected number of failures would be just 0.9 for the next 1000 years of operation of one such operating system [51, p. 205]. Moreover, if the operating system were to support safety-critical software, and the operating system were to fail, the failure would not necessarily have safety-critical consequences. For the estimation of the reliability of software installed at multiple sites, and undergoing field service at these sites, an appropriate model of the effects of the field service is essential – one such model is studied in [53].

Given a highly reliable software system, the best course of action is not to replace the system at all. Thus, when a new host system is being built to replace the host that an embedded software system was controlling, the interface between controller and host should not be changed. When this is not possible, as much of the existing software as possible should be retained unchanged. If there is a mandated language change from, say, Fortran to Ada, an automated code translation system should carry out the code translation. This suggests that whenever new safety-critical software is being written, the development process should ensure that reuse of the software at a later time would be easy. Most of the research on reusability has concentrated on indexing that would allow appropriate software to be retrieved for reuse when needed. In our context, this is not a critical concern. For us, reuse is actually thorough maintenance. The study of the relationship between maintenance and reuse has begun [54]; research on this relationship should be continued with emphasis on preservation of reliability.

Sometimes, however, existing code has become so badly patched over time that any attempt to change it is likely to introduce new faults. This danger is always present. For example, during the removal of the seven residual faults in the England-Finland-Norway experiment of [40], two new faults were introduced. In a case like this, the best approach would be to automatically derive a formal specification from the code by reverse engineering. In this issue, Gannod and Cheng [55] show how to use the properties of block-structured languages to arrive at high-level specifications of programs written in such languages. Then, either the appropriate modification can be introduced in the specification and code generated from the modified specification, or well-structured code can be generated from the unmodified specification and the code then modified. In the latter case, the unmodified specification serves merely as an intermediate form. As was discussed in Sec. 4, code may be easier to read. On the other hand, a theorem prover can be used with a formal specification to demonstrate that any program defined by the specification would have certain properties. Hence, a maintenance task could proceed as follows: construct a specification from original code by reverse engineering, transform the specification into code, modify the code, construct new specification from new code by reverse engineering, reason about the new specification. The development of the methodology and tools to support these tasks is an important research challenge.

11. The Software Process and Safety

The quality of a product depends on the quality of the process by which it is produced. It is particularly important to develop process models that ensure sufficiently high reliability of safety-critical systems. Development of process models has two aspects, managerial and technical. Management responsibility is primarily the identification and analysis of development risks, which relate to losses that arise when the development process fails. Such failures are observed as cost and schedule overruns. Most activities that are strictly managerial have little effect on software safety, but, if management neglects to arrange for a close interaction between software developers and application domain experts, the developers may easily settle on improper controller responses that can create unsafe conditions for the host. Also, unrealistic initial cost and schedule estimates may create a panic mode when the due date for the project approaches, and the usual result of the panic is the release of an inadequately validated system. Unsafe conditions can again arise.

Operational risks relate to losses due to failure of the system after its release. By our definition of safety-critical systems, as given in Sec. 1, we are to avoid failures that result in loss of life, personal injury, or significant material loss. As we saw above, operational risks are sometimes a consequence of management decisions, but for the most part they relate to the technical aspects of process models. The managerial aspects of software development are the main concern of the software process maturity model of the Software Engineering Institute [56]. We have been discussing the technical aspects throughout this paper.

Although a software development *process* should differ little from the processes that are its *products*, there is a fundamental difference. Initially, the software process was entirely manual. With the arrival of CASE tools, it was hoped that much of the software process could be mechanized, but this has not happened, primarily because we lack a proper understanding of the software process. Indeed, just as a software product differs to a greater or lesser extent from other software products, so the process that is to produce one product is also likely to differ from the process that is to produce another. Thirteen software process languages are surveyed in [57], and one would hope that all this activity is leading toward a unified approach to process and product. This does not seem to be the case. However, our concern here is not with process languages. We are interested in seeing that safety-consciousness is built into software process models. Since it is not at all clear how this is to be accomplished, much research remains to be done on the software process in general, and on how it relates to safety in particular.

12. Ethical Issues

If risks were to be totally avoided, we would not undergo surgical procedures, would not permit the mining of coal, and would never again get into an automobile. But we do have surgical wards, coal mines, and automobiles on the road. We have learnt to weigh risks against benefits. In a recent paper [58], a general theory of justice as developed by Rawls [59] has been adapted for the software process. The theory is based on three principles – the least advantaged principle, the risking harm principle, and the publicity test principle. Let us look at the three principles in turn.

The least advantaged principle requires that the introduction of a new system does not increase harm to the least advantaged, e.g., the general population of an area surrounding a nuclear power plant. The determination of the least advantaged category is not always straightforward. In the case of the Therac-25 accidents [4], the patients who underwent radiation treatment supplied by the machine were not least advantaged – they expected advantage from the treatment. The question is what the overall situation would have been had there not been a Therac-25 at all.

The risking harm principle tries to answer this question. The principle requires that a system is to avoid increasing harm in environments that are already risky. This is a fairly straightforward principle, but not without problems. The principle is easily applied to the Therac-25: evaluate the machine on the basis of the expected gain in the total number of years of life attributable to the use of the machine against the expected years of life lost as a result of accidents. Such a calculation, should it come out in favor of the machine, does not, of course, justify ignoring safety hazards that could be easily eliminated.

Difficulties arise when there is no easy basis for comparison. Arthritis is not regarded as a life-threatening disease, but sufferers from arthritis experience considerable discomfort. Suppose a drug were developed that eliminates much of the discomfort, but has side-effects that in some very rare instances can be fatal. A way to determine the effectiveness of the drug would be by quantitative comparison

without considering the intangible "quality of life" factor, we would weigh the economic value of increased productivity by takers of the drug against the value of lost lives.

Such a comparison, however, could have a hard time finding acceptance under Rawls' publicity test principle. It requires that, in balancing the benefit to one constituency against the harm to another, constituency measures be used, which, if made public, would not outrage most members of the public. Suppose human life is valued at $2,400,000 (an estimate for a human life cut short by murder, as given in [60]). This figure, or any figure at all, could well outrage the public as demonstrating a cynical attitude towards human life.

Still, we need to start somewhere. Suppose that the reliability of a software system at a particular instant in time is found to be 0.9 for 100 hours of operation, i.e., the probability that the system will not fail in the next 100 hours of operation is 0.9. Suppose further that one in ten thousand failures would result in the loss of a human life. Then, taking the figure of $2,400,000, the human-life risk over ten years of operation of the system would not be much higher than $200,000. Suppose that a further $1,000,000 spent on additional testing would improve the reliability to 0.95 for 100 hours. If the human-life risk were the only factor to consider, would the software developers be acting responsibly in performing the additional tests? Keep in mind that the new reliability value still translates into a ten-year human-life risk of $100,000.

In Sec. 5, we suggested that weights be assigned to failures in proportion to the safety effects of the failures. Then a weighted reliability value could be estimated. Such weights would be assigned after the failure by examination of the effects of the failure. In such a context we need to find ways of estimating the effect of a failure in a simulated test setting, and of estimating the cost of future failures. This would lead to a methodology that is to determine when to stop testing. In particular, comparison to the risks we face from natural disasters and everyday accidents may show that the reliability requirements on some software systems tend to be set at unreasonably high levels.

References

1. N. G. Leveson, "Software safety: what, why, and how", *ACM Comp. Surv.* **18**, 2 (1986) 125–163.
2. N. G. Leveson, "Software safety in embedded computer systems", *Comm. ACM* **34**, 2 (1991) 34–46.
3. R. J. Abbott, "Resourceful systems for fault tolerance, reliability, and safety", *ACM Comp. Surv.* **22**, 1 (1990) 35–68.
4. N. G. Leveson and C. S. Turner, "An investigation of the Therac-25 accidents", *Computer* **26**, 7 (1993) 18–41.
5. IEEE/ANSI Standard 982.1–1988, "IEEE standard dictionary of measures to produce reliable software".
6. D. P. Freedman and G. M. Weinberg, *Handbook of Walkthroughs, Inspections, and Technical Reviews*, 3rd ed. (Little Brown, 1982) (Reprinted: Dorset House, 1990).
7. C. P. Hollocker, *Software Reviews and Audits Handbook* (Wiley, 1990).
8. J. H. August, *Joint Application Design* (Yourdon Press, 1991).
9. N. G. Leveson and P. R. Harvey, "Analyzing software safety", *IEEE Trans. Softw. Eng.* **SE-9**, 5 (1983) 569–579.

10. D. L. Parnas, A. J. van Schouwen, and S. P. Kwan, "Evaluation of safety-critical software", *Comm. ACM* **33**, 6 (1990) 636–648.
11. N. G. Leveson, S. S. Cha, and T. J. Shimeall, "Safety verification of Ada programs using software fault trees", *IEEE Softw.* **8**, 4 (1991) 48–59.
12. G. Burgess, T. Clark, R. Hauser, and R. Zmud, "The use of causal maps as a requirements analysis tool: a case assessment of research propositions", in *Human Factors in Information Systems Analysis and Design*, eds. A. Finkelstein, M. J. Tauber, and R. Traunmuller (North-Holland, 1990) pp. 187–207.
13. A. T. Berztiss, "Catastrophe prevention in safety-critical systems", *Proc. 5th Int. Conf. Softw. Eng. Knowl. Eng.* (1993) pp. 102–108.
14. S. L. Pollack, H. T. Hicks, and W. J. Harrison, *Decision Tables: Theory and Practice* (Wiley, 1971).
15. A. Berztiss, *Programming with Generators* (Ellis Horwood, 1990).
16. B. Potter, J. Sinclair, and D. Till, *An Introduction to Formal Specification and Z* (Prentice Hall, 1991).
17. R. Balzer, N. M. Goldman, and D. S. Wile, "Operational specification as the basis for rapid prototyping", *ACM SIGSOFT Softw. Eng. Notes* **7**, 5 (1982) 3–16. Also in W. W. Agesti, ed., *New Paradigms for Software Development* (IEEE Computer Science Press, 1986) pp. 116–132.
18. A. Berztiss, "Formal specification methods and visualization", in *Principles of Visual Programming Systems*, ed. S.-K. Chang (Prentice-Hall, 1990) pp. 231–290.
19. W. Swartout, "GIST English generator" *Proc. AAAI Natl. Conf.* (1982) pp. 404–409.
20. H. Dalianis, "A method for validating a conceptual model by natural language discourse generation", in *Advanced Information Systems Engineering*, ed. P. Loucopoulos (Springer-Verlag, 1992) pp. 425–444.
21. M. McMorran and S. Powell, *Z Guide for Beginners* (Blackwell Scientific, 1993).
22. K. K. Aggarwal, M. P. Kumar, V. Santurkar, and R. Ratnaparkhi, "Towards weighted operational profile", *ACM SIGSOFT Softw. Eng. Notes* **18**, 1 (1993) 52–53.
23. J. D. Musa, "Operational profiles in software-reliability engineering", *IEEE Softw.* **10**, 2 (1993) 14–32.
24. J. H. Whittaker and J. H. Poore, "Markov analysis of software specifications", *ACM Trans. Softw. Eng. Methodology* **2**, 1(1993) 93–106.
25. R. W. Butler and G. B. Finelli, "The infeasibility of experimental quantification of life-critical software reliability", *Proc. ACM SIGSOFT '91 Conf. Softw. for Critical Systems* (1991). Also in *ACM SIGSOFT Softw. Eng. Notes* **16**, 5 (1991) and *IEEE Trans. Softw. Eng.* **19**, 1 (1993) 3–12.
26. F.-W. Scholz, "Software reliability modeling and analysis", *IEEE Trans. Softw. Eng.* **SE-12**, 1 (1986) 25–31.
27. J.-C. Laprie and K. Kanoun, "X-ware reliability and availability modeling", *IEEE Trans. Softw. Eng.* **18**, 2 (1992) 130–147.

28. E. Y. Shapiro, *Algorithmic Program Debugging* (MIT Press, 1983).
29. J. J. P. Tsai, A. Liu, and K. Nair, "Debugging logic-based requirements specifications for safety-critical systems — a FRORL approach", *Int. J. Softw. Eng. Knowl. Eng.* **4**, 1 (1994) 205–227.
30. Luqi, "The role of prototyping languages in CASE", *Int. J. Softw. Eng. Knowl. Eng.* **1**, 2 (1991) 131–149.
31. C. U. Smith, *Performance Engineering of Software Systems* (Addison-Wesley, 1990).
32. J. S. Ostroff, "Formal methods for the specification and design of real-time safety-critical systems", *J. Sys. Softw.* **18**, 1 (1992) 33–60.
33. S. Gerhart, D. Craigen, and T. Ralston, "Experience with formal methods in critical systems", *IEEE Softw.* **11**, 1 (1994) 21–28.
34. S. Gerhart, D. Craigen, and T. Ralston, "Regulatory case studies", *IEEE Softw.* **11**, 1 (1994) 30–39.
35. A. Avizienis, H. Kopetz, and J. C. Laprie, eds., *The Evolution of Fault-Tolerant Computing* (Springer-Verlag, 1987).
36. U. Voges, *Software-Diversitaet und ihre Modellierung* (Informatik-Fachberichte No. 224) (Springer-Verlag, 1989).
37. F. B. Schneider, "Implementing fault-tolerant services using a state machine approach: a tutorial", *ACM Comput. Surv.* **22**, 4 (1990) 299–319.
38. F. Cristian, "Understanding fault-tolerant distributed systems", *Comm. ACM* **34**, 2 (1991) 56–78.
39. M. Barborak, M. Malek, and A. Dahbura, "The consensus problem in fault-tolerant computing", *ACM Comput. Surv.* **25**, 2 (1993) 171–220.
40. P. G. Bishop *et al.*, "PODS – a project on diverse software", *IEEE Trans. Softw. Eng.* **SE-12**, 9 (1986) 929–940.
41. D. Tsichritzis, "The equivalence problem of simple programs", *J. ACM* **17**, 4 (1970) 729–738.
42. J. C. Knight and N. G. Leveson, "An experimental evaluation of the assumption of independence in multiversion programming", *IEEE Trans. Softw. Eng.* **SE-12**, 1 (1986) 96–109.
43. S. S. Brilliant, J. C. Knight, and N. G. Leveson, "The consistent comparison problem in N-version software", *IEEE Trans. Softw. Eng.* **15**, 11 (1989) 1481–1485.
44. S. S. Brilliant, J. C. Knight, and N. G. Leveson, "Analysis of faults in an N-version software experiment", *IEEE Trans. Softw. Eng.* **16**, 2 (1990) 238–247.
45. D. E. Eckhardt *et al.*, "An experimental evaluation of software redundancy as a strategy for improving reliability", *IEEE Trans. Softw. Eng.* **17**, 7 (1991) 692–702.
46. J. R. Dunham, "Experiments in software reliability: life-critical applications", *IEEE Trans. Softw. Eng.* **SE-12**, 1 (1986) 110–123.
47. B. Curtis, H. Krasner, and N. Iscoe, "A field study of the software design process for large systems", *Comm. ACM* **31**, 11 (1988) 1268–1287.

48. D. E. Eckhardt and L. D. Lee, "A theoretical basis for the analysis of multiversion software subject to coincident errors", *IEEE Trans. Softw. Eng.* **SE-11**, 12 (1985)
1511–1517.
49. B. Littlewood and D. R. Miller, "Conceptual modeling of coincident failures in multiversion software", *IEEE Trans. Softw. Eng.* **15**, 12 (1989) 1596–1614.
50. V. F. Nicola and A. Goyal, "Modeling of correlated failures and community error recovery in multiversion software", *IEEE Trans. Softw. Eng.* **16**, 3 (1990) 350–359.
51. J. D. Musa, A. Iannino, and K. Okumoto, *Software Reliability — Measurement, Prediction, Application* (McGraw-Hill, 1987).
52. M. Dyer, *The Cleanroom Approach to Quality Software Development* (Wiley, 1992).
53. C. T. Baker, "Effects of field service on software reliability", *IEEE Trans. Softw. Eng.* **14**, 2 (1988) 254–258.
54. V. R. Basili, "Viewing maintenance as reuse-oriented software development", *IEEE Softw.* **7**, 1 (1990) 19–35.
55. G. C. Gannod and B. H. C. Cheng, "Facilitating the maintenance of safety-critical systems", *Int. J. Softw. Eng. Knowl. Eng.* **4**, 1 (1994) 183–204.
56. W. S. Humphrey, *Managing the Software Process* (Addison-Wesley, 1989).
57. P. Armenise, S. Bandinelli, C. Ghezzi, and A. Morzenti, "A survey and assessment of software process representation formalisms", *Int. J. Softw. Eng. Knowl. Eng.* **3**, 3 (1993) 401–426.
58. W. R. Collins, K. W. Miller, B. J. Spielman, and P. Wherry, "How good is good enough? An ethical analysis of software construction and use", *Comm. ACM* **37**, 1 (1994) 81–91.
59. J. Rawls, *A Theory of Justice* (Harvard University Press, 1971).
60. "The economics of crime", *Business Week* (December 13, 1993).

RECENT TRENDS IN FORMAL SPECIFICATION OF REAL-TIME SYSTEMS

L. M. PATNAIK
Microprocessor Applications Laboratory, Indian Institute of Science, Bangalore 560 012, India
E-mail: lalit@micro.iisc.ernet.in

R. MALL
Dept. of Computer Science and Engineering, Indian Institute of Technology, Kharagpur 721 302, INDIA
E-mail: rajib@cse.iitkgp.ernet.in

Inspite of numerous advancements made in recent years in the area of formal techniques, specification of real-time systems is still proving to be a very challenging and difficult problem. In this context, this work critically examines state-of-the-art specification techniques for real-time systems and analyzes the emerging trends.

1. Introduction

The dramatic fall in hardware prices in recent years has made it possible to use computers in many applications that were previously considered to be too costly or too complex to automate. This scenario of increasing automation has given rise to rapid growth in the use of computers in real-time applications. Currently, real-time systems are being extensively used in the areas of industrial process control, aircraft and aerospace systems, traffic control, telephony, nuclear power plant control, medical life-support systems, robotics, etc. Most of these applications are highly safety-critical, and therefore, require extremely reliable system operation. An example of such a stringent reliability requirement is the NASA guideline of less than 10^{-10} safety-critical failures per hour of operation of aircraft flight control systems. This requirement works out to be roughly equal to one failure per million years of flight [1].

As far as hardware failures are concerned, it is possible to achieve extremely low failure rates by using ultra-reliable components together with redundancy and majority voting. This leaves software as the most potent cause of system failures. The main factors contributing towards software failure are the unavailability of suitable techniques for developing error-free software, and the fact that, while most of the complex functions of a system are implemented in software, relatively simple functions are realized through hardware. It is no wonder then that development of reliable software for real-time applications is proving to be a very difficult and challenging problem.

The commonly used techniques to increase software reliability are testing and software fault-tolerance. Several innovative test techniques have been proposed by researchers [36, 45]. While these test techniques have been reported to be successful in detecting many errors in system implementations, exhaustive testing to detect *all* faults is almost impossible to carry out even in simple real-time systems, due to large test domains [36]. In other words, test techniques can only reveal the presence of errors but cannot guarantee the absence of errors. Nevertheless, test techniques have been extensively used. For flight control systems, it is estimated that by using the available test techniques, one can at best reduce failure rates to about 10^{-4} failures per hour of operation [1].

Two important software fault-tolerance techniques are *n-version programming* [35] and *recovery blocks* [33]. These techniques have been extensively used to increase system reliability. However, these fault-tolerance techniques suffer from several handicaps, especially when used in complex applications. A major shortcoming of the n-version programming technique is its inability to tolerate statistical correlation of faults in different versions of a program. Careful experiments have revealed that, for complex applications, very often all versions of a program fail together, rendering the n-version programming technique ineffective (more discussions on this point can be found in [2]).

Furthermore, it has been shown that testing and software fault-tolerance techniques are effective only in cases of relatively simple faults, and are not satisfactory for insidious program errors like timing bugs. It is estimated in [1] that by using software fault-tolerance together with the available testing techniques one can achieve a reliability figure of about 10^{-5} faults per hour of operation for flight-control systems. However, this figure still falls far short of NASA's requirement of 10^{-10} faults per hour of operation.

In this context, formal methods seem to be a promising technique to meet the challenge of high reliability requirements. Formal techniques provide mathematically sound frameworks to specify and verify systems. Unfortunately, formal methods have not yet achieved the required maturity to be commercially viable, and therefore, are not extensively used. In this regard, the objectives of this paper are to examine some of the promising formal techniques for real-time applications and to discuss the emerging trends.

This paper is organized into sections as follows. In Sec. 2, we discuss some basic concepts in formal methods. In Sec. 3, we discuss some of the special characteristic features of real-time systems, and assess their impact on the development of appropriate formal techniques. In Sec. 4, we look into logic-based, process-algebraic, Petri net-based, and trace-theoretic techniques for ensuring real-time safety. In Sec. 5, we discuss temporal and modal logic-based techniques, including some of our own work. Section 6 concludes this paper.

2. Formal System Development Techniques

In recent years, formal techniques have emerged as a central issue in software engineering. This is not accidental; the importance of precise specification, modeling, and verification is recognized in most engineering disciplines. Formal methods provide us with tools to precisely describe a system and show that a system is correctly implemented. We say a system is correctly implemented when it satisfies its given specification. The specification of a system can be given either as a list of its desirable properties (property-oriented approach) or as an abstract model of the system (model-oriented approach). These two approaches will be discussed in more detail in Subsec. 2.2. We start this section by briefly highlighting some of the important concepts in formal methods, subsequently we examine the merits and demerits of using formal techniques.

2.1. *What is a formal technique?*

A formal technique is a mathematical method to specify a hardware and/or software system, verify whether a specification is realizable, verify that an implementation satisfies its specification, prove properties of a system without necessarily running the system, etc. The mathematical basis of a formal method is provided by its specification language. More precisely, a formal specification language consists of two sets *syn* and *sem*, and a relation *sat* between them [40]. The set *syn* is called the *syntactic domain*, the set *sem* is called the *semantic domain*, and the relation *sat* is called the *satisfaction relation.* For a given specification *syn*, and model of the system *sem*, if *sat (syn, sem)*, then *syn* is said to be the *specification of sem*, and *sem* is said to be the *specificand of syn.*

The generally accepted paradigm for system development is through a hierarchy of abstractions. Each stage in this hierarchy is an implementation of its preceding stage and a specification of the succeeding stage. The different stages in this system development activity are requirements specification, functional design, architectural design, detailed design, coding, implementation, etc. In general, formal techniques can be used at every stage of the system development activity. For a more detailed discussion on the use of formal techniques at different stages of system development, the reader may refer to [40].

2.1.1. *Syntactic domains*

The syntactic domain of a formal specification language consists of an alphabet of symbols and a set of formation rules to construct well-formed formulas from the alphabet. The well-formed formulas are used to specify a system.

2.1.2. *Semantic domains*

Formal techniques can have considerably different semantic domains [40]. Abstract data type specification languages are used to specify algebras, theories, and programs. Programming languages are used to specify functions from input to output values. Concurrent and distributed system specification languages are used to specify state sequences, event sequences, state-transition sequences, synchronization trees, partial orders, state machines, etc. In this paper, we will be mostly interested in the last type of semantic domains since we are primarily interested in the specification of real-time systems (the question of appropriate semantic domains for real-time systems will be further elaborated in Sec. 3).

2.1.3. *Satisfaction relation*

Given the model of a system, it is important to determine whether an element of the semantic domain satisfies the specifications. This satisfaction is determined by using a homomorphism known as *semantic abstraction function* [40]. The semantic abstraction function maps the elements of the semantic domain into equivalent classes. There can be different specifications describing different aspects of a system model, possibly using different specification languages [40]. Some of these specifications describe the system's behavior and the others describe the system's structure. Consequently, two broad classes of semantic abstraction functions are defined: those that *preserve* a system's behavior and those that *preserve* a system's structure [40]. In this paper, we will mostly be interested in the first kind of abstraction function, since we are interested in specifying the real-time behavior of systems.

2.2. *Model versus property-oriented methods*

Formal methods are usually classified into two broad categories, the so-called model-oriented and property-oriented approaches [40]. In a model-oriented style, one defines a system's behavior directly by constructing a model of the system in terms of mathematical structures such as tuples, relations, functions, sets, sequences, etc. In the property-oriented style, the system's behavior is defined indirectly by stating its properties, usually in the form of a set of axioms that the system must satisfy. Let us consider a simple producer/consumer example. In a property-oriented style, we would probably start by listing the properties of the system like: the consumer can start consuming only after the producer has produced an item, the producer starts to produce an item only after the consumer has consumed the last item, etc. However, in a model-oriented approach, we would start by defining the basic operations, p (produce) and c (consume). Then we can state that $S \Leftarrow S1 + a$, $S1 \Leftarrow s + b$. Thus, the model-oriented approaches essentially specify a program by writing another, presumably simpler program.

It is alleged that property-oriented approaches are more suitable for *requirements specification*, and that the model-oriented approaches are more suited to *system specification* [22]. The reason for this distinction is the fact that property-oriented approaches specify a system behavior not by what they say of the system but by what they do not say of the system. Thus, property-oriented specifications permit a large number of possible implementations. Furthermore, property-oriented approaches specify a system by a conjunction of axioms, thereby making it easier to alter/augment specifications at a later stage. On the other hand, model-oriented methods do not support logical conjunctions and disjunctions, and thus, even minor changes to a specification may lead to overhauling an entire specification.

2.3. *Operational semantics*

Informally, the operational semantics of a formal method is the way it represents computations. There are different types of operational semantics according to what is meant by a *single run* of the system and how the runs are grouped together to describe the *behavior* of the system. In the following, we discuss some of the commonly used operational semantics and examine their suitability to describe the behavior of real-time systems.

Linear semantics. In this approach [26, 39], a run of a system is described by a sequence (possibly infinite) of events or states. The concurrent activities of the system are represented by nondeterministic interleavings of the atomic actions. For example, a concurrent activity $a||b$ is represented by the set of sequential activities a;b and b;a. This is a simple but rather unnatural representation of concurrency. The behavior of a system in this model consists of the set of all its runs. To make this model more realistic, *justice* and *fairness* restrictions are usually imposed on computations to exclude the unwanted interleavings. Although such models have been successfully used to reason about the nonreal-time properties of systems, the assumption of total ordering of all the events occurring in a system is often counter-intuitive and makes it difficult to reason about the system's real-time behavior. Besides, the difficulties in implementing global clocks in distributed systems (which could otherwise be used to map their behavior to totally ordered sequences), make the interleaving model unattractive for reasoning about the real-time behavior of distributed systems.

Branching semantics. In this approach, the behavior of a system is represented by a directed graph. The nodes of the graph represent the possible states in the evolution of a system. The descendants of each node of the graph represent the states which can be generated by any of the atomic actions enabled at that state. Although this semantic model distinguishes the branching points in a computation, still it represents concurrency by interleaving, and consequently suffers from the drawbacks of an interleaving model, as far as analysis of real-time behavior of distributed systems is concerned.

Maximally parallel semantics. In this approach, all the concurrent actions enabled at any state are assumed to be taken together. This is again not a natural model of concurrency since it implicitly assumes the availability of all the required computational resources. On the other hand, real-time systems usually have limited computational resources with each node running a set of processes. Consequently, this approach is also not satisfactory for modeling and reasoning about the real-time behavior of systems.

Partial order semantics. Under this view [20–23, 28–30], the semantics ascribed to a system is a *structure of states* satisfying a partial order relation among the states (events). The partial order represents a *precedence ordering* among events, and constrains some events to occur only after some other events have occurred; while the occurrence of other events (*concurrent events*) is considered to be incomparable. This fact identifies concurrency as a phenomenon not translatable to any interleaved representation.

Since most real-time systems are distributed in nature (the reasons for the distributed nature of real-time systems is discussed in Sec. 3), it appears that partial order operational semantics can provide a natural model of real-timed concurrency.

2.4. *Merits and limitations of formal methods*

In addition to facilitating precise formulation of specifications, formal methods possess several positive features, some of which are discussed below.

- Formal specifications encourage rigour. Often, the very process of construction of a rigorous specification is more important than the formal specification itself. The construction of a rigorous specification clarifies several aspects of system behavior that are not obvious in an informal specification. It is widely acknowledged that it is cost-effective to spend more efforts at the specification stage. Otherwise, many flaws would go unnoticed only to be detected at the later stages of software development that would cause iterative changes to occur in the development life-cycle. According to an estimate, for large and complex systems like distributed real-time systems, 80% of project costs and most of the cost overruns result from the iterative changes required in a system development process due to inappropriate requirements specification. Thus, the additional effort required to construct a rigorous specification is well worth the trouble.
- Formal methods usually have a well-founded mathematical basis. Thus, formal specifications are not only more precise, but formal techniques can be used to mathematically reason about the properties of a specification and to rigorously prove that an implementation satisfies its specifications. Informal specifications may be useful in understanding a system and its documentation, but they cannot serve as a basis of verification. Even carefully written specifications are prone to error, and experience has shown that unverified specifications are comparable in reliability to unverified programs [1].
- Formal methods have well-defined semantics. Therefore, ambiguity in specifications is automatically avoided when one formally specifies a system.
- In case of real-time systems, quantitative reasoning about time is important.

Formal techniques facilitate expression of the quantitative timing properties due to their underlying mathematical nature.

- The mathematical basis of the formal methods leaves scope for automating the analysis of specifications. For example, a tableau-based technique has been used to automatically check the consistency of specifications [31]. Also, automatic theorem-proving techniques can be used to verify that an implementation satisfies its specifications. The possibility of automatic verification is one of the most important advantages of formal methods.
- Formal specifications can be executed to obtain immediate feedback on the features of the specified system [29]. This concept of executable specifications is related to rapid prototyping. Informally, a prototype is a "toy" working model of a system that can provide immediate feedback on the behavior of the specified system, and is especially useful in checking the completeness of specifications [34].

It is clear that formal methods provide mathematically sound frameworks within which large, complex systems can be specified, developed, and verified in a systematic rather than in an ad hoc manner. However, formal methods suffer from several shortcomings, some of which are the following.

- Formal methods are difficult to learn and use.
- The basic incompleteness results of first-order logic suggest that it is impossible to check *absolute* correctness of systems using theorem proving techniques.
- Formal techniques are not able to handle complex problems. This shortcoming results from the fact that, even moderately complicated problems increase the complexity of formal specifications and their analysis. Also, a large, unstructured set of mathematical formulas is difficult to comprehend.

It has been pointed out by several researchers that formal specifications neither replace nor make the informal descriptions obsolete but complement them. In fact, the comprehensibility of formal specifications is greatly enhanced when the specifications are accompanied by an informal description. What is suggested is the use of formal techniques as a broad guideline for the use of the informal techniques [22]. An interesting example of such an approach is reported in [38]. In this approach, the use of a formal method identifies the necessary verification steps that need to be carried out, but it is legitimate to apply informal reasoning in presentation of correctness arguments and transformations [38]. Any doubt or query relating to an informal argument is resolved by formal proofs.

3. Real-Time Systems

A real-time system is usually a concurrent system whose processes work in conjunction with a set of (external) processes of the real-world (called its environment). In other words, most of the real-time systems interactively control some ongoing physical process(es). A real-time system is embedded if it is physically enclosed in its environment, for example, a guidance and control system onboard an aircraft is an embedded system. Real-time systems usually have a basic feedback structure that is divided between a "controller" and the outside environment (see Fig. 1). The controller accepts input data from the "sensors", performs the necessary computations, and uses the computational results to move the "actuators". The consequences of the actuator movement are fed back to the controller through the "sensors" which sense the response of the physical environment. For example, an autopilot accepts inertial position and velocity parameters, computes the current position, and moves the control surfaces appropriately to achieve the desired aircraft state (e.g., constant altitude). The control surface movement affects the subsequent readings of speed, altitude, and/or position sensors.

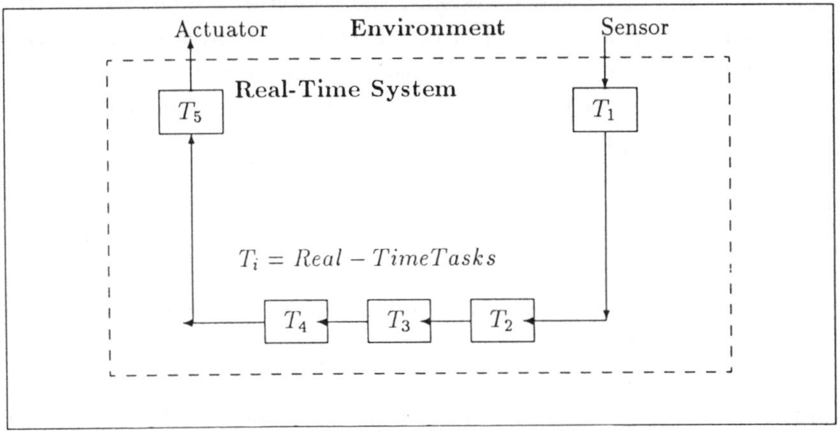

Fig. 1. A typical real-time system.

Real-time systems possess several characteristic features which make them very difficult to specify. We examine several such characteristic features of real-time systems, and assess the constraints imposed by these features on the specifications.

- Real-time systems usually have most of their functionalities constrained by time. Thus, the computed results must not only be functionally correct but must also be produced on time. The correctness of nonreal-time sequential programs do not depend on the speed of computation (performance). Nonreal-time concurrent programs can always be designed (using semaphores, etc.) such that the speeds of the individual components do not affect the final result. Thus, performance and correctness are independent notions for nonreal-time systems systems. Real-time systems are a sharp contrast on this count and the issues of performance and correctness of real-time systems are intricately related. This aspect indicates that it is necessary to have an integrated framework for specification of real-time systems in which it would be possible to verify both functional and timing correctness.
- Real-time systems are usually classified as *reactive* systems. A reactive system is expected to maintain continuous interaction with its environment, rather than producing a final result. Therefore, reactive systems cannot be described by the *transformational view* [22]. The transformational view describes a system as a function/relation from an input domain to an output range of values. In reactive systems, the notion of a final state is either undefined or is identified with error. Therefore, reactive systems have to be described by their behavior. Although *transformational description* is much simpler than *behavioral description*, for reactive systems *behavioral description* is unavoidable.
- Due to the asynchronous nature of the actions of the environment, the demands on the system for responses may occur in parallel rather than in strict sequence. This is one of the major reasons for real-time software to be almost always implemented using a number of concurrent processes.
- Many real-time systems are inherently distributed. This distributed nature of real-time systems arises due to the fact that the sensors and the actuators often need to be positioned wide apart. Consequently, it is necessary to process the data in a distributed fashion to reduce communication overheads. In such a distributed implementation, each processor (node) of the system controls a set of interacting real-world processes. The distribution

of the structure of a real-time system necessitates a partial order approach to formally describe these systems as system-wide clocks which are very difficult to implement in distributed systems, and hence, global states are not reasonably obtained in distributed systems [22].

- The environment of a real-time system usually generates a number of events (usually known as the external events). In the general case, only some of these events may be safety-critical and impose hard real-time constraints on a system. The external events may repeat at regular intervals or may be sporadic. Thus, real-time processes are either cyclic when the deadlines fall at regular intervals, or event-driven when the deadlines fall at a specified time after the occurrence of some external event(s). A cyclic process initiates a new cycle of actions following an internal timer interrupt and an event-driven process initiates a cycle of actions following an interruption generated by a sensor hardware. For example, the speed sensor of an aircraft may sense and transmit speed readings to the computer system periodically or only when the speed changes beyond a certain tolerance value. An appropriate specification formalism should allow representation of these aspects.
- One of the most important feature of real-time systems is the necessity of quantitative representation of time. Typically, in response to the reactions of the environment, a real-time system initiates (or completes) the necessary action(s) within a predetermined time limit. For this purpose, it is necessary for a real-time system to explicitly refer to a physical clock. However, system-wide clocks are difficult to implement in distributed systems. Therefore, formal methods should use the local clocks of individual nodes to assign time values to events and actions occurring at a node.
- A real-time system evolves according to its own logic and is not under the control of the programmer. Such a behavior adds to the complexity of specification, testing, and verification of real-time systems.
- The basic feedback structure of real-time control systems suggests that the controller subsystem can be implemented as a pipeline of software modules through which information flows unidirectionally. Typically, real-time processing is done by 10–100 pipelined software modules that operate concurrently. Such a system can give rise to end-to-end timing errors. More discussions on this point can be found in [29].
- A vast majority of real-time systems find application in safety-critical areas where the effect of system failures can be highly disastrous. Therefore, real-time systems need to be extremely reliable. This fact becomes more sig-

nificant considering the fact that most of these (embedded) systems function without any human operator, who can intervene when exceptions arise.

4. Formal Techniques for Real-Time Systems

In the previous section, it was pointed out that real-time systems possess several characteristic features that are fundamentally different from the nonreal-time ones. Such fundamental differences suggest that the development of an appropriate formal technique for real-time systems needs novel approaches rather than simple extensions of the techniques that have already been developed for nonreal-time applications. This fact has been emphasized by Schneider in [37], where he points out that adding semantic band-aids to the existing methods is not the best way to devise suitable methods for real-time systems. Completely ignoring the existing methods is also not prudent. New methods should be built upon and the old ones generalized. Thus, when the time dimension is ignored, the new methods should degenerate into old ones, allowing exploitation of the strength of the old ones without being subject to their weaknesses. Although such a technique is yet to be devised, several novel approaches have been reported in the literature (e.g., [21, 28]). In this section, we briefly discuss some important specification methods, namely, the logic-based, process-algebraic, Petri net-based, and trace-theoretic techniques. This survey is not a comprehensive one, as a comprehensive survey of this area is extremely difficult not only because of the large number of papers published in this area but also due to the diverse mathematical tools and theories that have been used.

4.1. *Logic-based methods*

Several first-order logic-based methods have been reported in the literature [3, 24, 25, 27, 42]. A notable formalism in this category is RTL (Real-Time Logic) [25, 42]. RTL was developed as part of the SARTOR project, which was to provide a unified environment for the development and verification of real-time programs. The syntax and semantics of RTL was reported in [42]. More recently, RTL has been used by Barbacci and Wing for separating timing constraints from the functional specification of abstract data types [3]. RTL was extended by MacEwen to a second order language for specification of hardware [24]. The main components of the RTL language are events, actions, state attributes, and an occurrence predicate (@). The occurrence predicate ascribes time values to event occurrences. In RTL, the start and stop events of an action A are denoted by $\uparrow A$ and $\downarrow A$ respectively. The notion of occurrence relation is central to RTL. In particular, the timing behavior of a system is specified as restrictions on the occurrence relation and its arguments. An important advantage of using an occurrence relation rather than an occurrence function is that the occurrence relation does not require that all occurrences of an event must happen, and allows an event to occur a finite number of times or even not at all. RTL provides constructs to conveniently represent open and closed intervals of time. The safety of a real-time system is proven by showing that the negation of the safety property is not satisfiable. An example of RTL specification [13] is the following.

Certain information is to be displayed on demand from an external stimulus. When the external stimulus ($\Omega STIMULUS$) occurs, an action SAMPLE is to be completed within 30 time units. The computation time of the action SAMPLE requires at most 20 time units. The following formulas partially describe the system:

$$\forall i,\, \forall t(\Omega STIMULUS,\, i,\, t) \rightarrow \exists x,\, y@(\uparrow SAMPLE,\, i,\, x)$$
$$\wedge @(\downarrow SAMPLE,\, i,\, y) \wedge (t \leq x \wedge y \leq t + 30)$$
$$\forall i,\, \forall x,\, y@(\uparrow SAMPLE,\, i,\, x) \wedge @(\downarrow SAMPLE,\, i,\, y) \rightarrow x + 20 \leq y\,.$$

A decision procedure for RTL was developed in [25]. This decision procedure can be used to automatically determine whether a safety assertion is consistent with its specifications. This decision procedure is based on Pressburger arithmetic [25]. Informally, Pressburger formulas are those that can be constructed from integer constants, integer variables, the addition function, and the set of predicates ($<, \leq, >, \geq, =$). In [25], all the existentially quantified variables are replaced by the corresponding Skolem constants or functions, and a resolution-based procedure is adopted for proving theorems about specifications.

The classical logic-based approach presented in [13, 25] has the advantages of simplicity and tool support for automatic verification of the consistency of the specifications. However, several important concepts like fairness [29] and eventuality [21, 22, 29] are not expressible in this approach. Further, it is not easy to describe and reason about the properties of a system with respect to its architectural configuration, though such reasoning with respect to an architectural configuration is important for system specification.

4.2. *Process-algebraic approaches*

Process algebras are usually the denomination of systematic exploration of (families of) algebraic calculi. During the last decade, several of them have been proposed, such as CCS (Calculus of Communicating Systems) [15, 16], CSP (Communicating Sequential Processes) [17, 18], and ACP (Algebra of Communicating Processes) [19]. Usually, these process algebras consist of a set of combinators for constructing new systems from the existing ones together with a mechanism for recursive definitions. For example, if a, b, c, ... are the actions of a given alphabet A, then a system S defined by $S \Leftarrow (c;\ S)+(a;\ b;\ S)$ describes a reactive system which can perform a c-action and proceed as before or perform an a-action followed by a b-action and proceed as before.

Timing models for process algebras have been studied by several researchers (e.g., [4–9]). Some of these models are based on a dense time domain, whereas others employ a discrete time domain. In some of these models (e.g., [4, 9]), the atomic actions are considered to take no time. As a consequence, it is possible to specify systems that perform an infinite amount of actions in no time. In [6], a small delay is associated with each action, and thus, only a finite number of actions can take place in any finite time. The algebraic model of CSP with wait t, developed by Gerth and Boucher, is based on untimed failures model of CSP [6]. The time domain considered in this work is any total order with a least element. A failure of a process is a pair $(s,\ X)$ where s is a trace and X is a failure set — the set of events in which the process will refuse to participate after engaging in s. The timed semantic model of Gerth and Boucher uses relations between times so that if a process refuses to participate in an event, the time of that refusal is known. The semantics is fully abstract and all the process operators and the semantic operation of hiding are continuous.

The work reported in [43] assumes that actions are instantaneous, i.e., no time is associated with actions. Time passes when no action is possible (idling) or when a delay is explicitly specified. A discrete time domain is used, and time is viewed as a sequence of ticks. This work also models time-out of actions. Time is introduced through a special time-out operator Δ. Intuitively, $N_1 \Delta_i N_2$ denotes that a process becomes N_2 after i time units, unless N_1 performs any action prior to that. If N_1 can perform an action (within i time units) and becomes N_1', then $N_1 \Delta_i N_2$ can perform the same action and become N_1'. Although timed versions of process algebra formalisms are elegant and useful for system specification, they are cumbersome for requirements specification where many iterative changes usually occur.

4.3. *Petri net-based approaches*

Petri nets have drawn considerable attention from researchers as a specification tool [47]. Petri nets are directed graphs consisting of places and transitions. To describe real-time computations Petri nets have been augmented by assigning time values to the places in the net. The places in the net represent processing (actions), and the instantaneous transitions represent the start and stop actions of a process. A place may also represent a condition. In this case, the time assigned to the place is zero. After residing at a place for an assigned time, a token enables the output transition of the place it occupies, causing it to fire immediately. If more than one transition is enabled, then a nondeterministic selection takes place. Once a model is constructed, real-time safety of the system can be proved by using the standard analysis techniques available [10]. However, a major shortcoming of the Petri net formalism is the state-space explosion of the models when the complexity of a system increases. The other shortcomings of Petri nets include their unsuitability to represent data-related properties and their inability to express liveness properties. While Petri net models are an effective and versatile tool, useful extensions for hard real-time applications are still required [41].

Petri nets are well-suited for specifying and modeling dynamic properties of systems [41]. Some of the important characteristics of Petri nets that make them especially suitable for specification, modeling, and verification of systems are the following.

- Petri nets support explicit representation of causal dependencies. Actions of a system are represented by a partial order. In Sec. 3, we have already argued for the need of a partial order model for real-time applications.
- Petri net models allow description of systems at different levels of abstractions, which is valuable for hierarchical system development. Petri nets are graphical formalisms, therefore, the models of a system behavior are easily understood.

4.4. *Expressing timing assumptions using trace theory*

In [11, 12], Dill describes a technique based on trace theory for verifying speed-independent circuits. In the developed theory, a trace is a string of symbols. Each symbol is the name of the circuit being modeled. A trace represents a possible behavior of a circuit. The presence of a symbol in the trace represents a transition on the corresponding wire. All the possible behaviors of a circuit can be represented by a set of traces. Dill's technique differs from other trace theoretic techniques by having a trace structure that contains two sets — a success set and a failure set, instead of just one. Trace structures are used to represent both circuits and their specifications. Various timing parameters, such as the minimum and maximum delay of a gate, can be modeled using the theory. This extended theory is called trace theory with discrete time [13]. This extended theory allows traces to contain additional symbols not corresponding to physical wires. The presence of such symbols in a trace represents a lapse of time quanta. Thus, a trace text represents a single behavior in which a transition on a wire x occurs at time $T0 + 2t$, where $T0$ is the time at which the behavior described by the trace begins. An automatic verifier based on this theory has also been developed [13]. This verifier is linear in the number of states in the circuit; thus, it is exponential in the number of components in the circuit.

4.5. *Timed event structures*

The notion of an event structure was introduced and studied in [23]. An event structure describes the behavior of a distributed system by means of a set of partially ordered event occurrences. Timed versions of an event structure appear to be especially suited to describing and reasoning about the timing behavior of distributed systems as the timing aspects are naturally and conveniently associated with event occurrences. Timed versions of event structures have been proposed in [20, 32]. An event structure (ES) is a triple $(E, <_c, \sharp)$, where

1. E is a set of events;
2. $<_c \subseteq E \times E$ is a partial order, called the causality relation;
3. $\sharp \subseteq E \times E$ is an irreflexive, symmetric relation, called the conflict relation;
4. for any e, e', $e'' \in E$, $e \sharp e' <_c e''$ implies $e \sharp e''$.

The last clause denotes *conflict preservation*, implying that an event cannot be in conflict with any of the events in its past. The event structure formalism was extended to a timed one by timing event occurrences and by associating a timing component with the causality relation. Under this partial order relation, the timings of only the causally-related events can be compared. It is assumed that events denote instants of time and that the event occurrences assume time values from a *temporal domain* T which can be either dense (e.g., positive real or rational numbers) or discrete (e.g., the set of positive integers). The *timed event structure* (TES) proposed in [32] is a quadruple $(E, T, <_t, \sharp_t)$, where

1. E is a set of events;
2. T is a temporal domain;
3. $<_t \subseteq ((E\times T)\times(E\times T)\times T\times T)$ is a quaternary relation, called the *temporal causal relation*, $<_t$ satisfies the conditions:
   (a) for all $(e, t), (e, t') \in (E \times T)$ and $t_1, t_2 \in T$,
   $<_t ((e, t), (e', t'), t_1, t_2))$ iff $e <_c e'$, $t < t'$, and $t_1 \leq t' - t \leq t_2$,
   (b) $<_t ((e, t), (e, t), t_1, t_2)$ for all $(e, t) \in E \times T$, and $t_1, t_2 \in T$, $t_1 \leq t_2$,
   (c) for all $(e, t), (e', t'), (e", t") \in (E \times T)$, and $t_1, t_2, t_3, t_4 \in T$ $<_t$ $((e, t), (e', t'), t_1, t_2)$, and $<_t ((e', t'), (e", t"), t_3, t_4)$ implies $<_t ((e, t), (e", t"), t_1 + t_3, t_2 + t_4)$;
4. $\sharp_t \subseteq ((E \times T) \times (E \times T))$ is an irreflexive, symmetric relation, called the conflict relation, and is such that $(e, t)\sharp_t(e', t')$ iff $e\sharp e'$;
5. for any $(e, t)(e', t'), (e",t") \in E \times T$, and $t_1, t_2 \in T$, $(e, t)\sharp_t(e', t')$, and $<_t ((e', t'), (e", t"), t_1, t_2)$ implies $(e, t)\sharp_t(e", t")$.

Intuitively, the relation $<_t ((e, t), (e', t'), t_1, t_2)$ denotes that the occurrence of the event e somehow causes e' to occur after t_1 and before t_2 time units. The parameters t_1 and t_2 correspond roughly to the delay and deadline on an event occurrence.

There has not been much research work for specification of real-time systems using timed versions of event structures. The partial order operational semantics is useful for specifying the real-time behavior of distributed systems. An important criticism against timed event structures is its inherent undecidabilty. However, the formalism can be made decidable by restricting the time domains to be finite. Probably a modal logic patterned after a timed version of event structures can be an elegant formalism for specification of real-time systems.

5. Temporal Logic of Real-Time Systems

Temporal logic has been widely acknowledged as a useful tool to specify, model, and verify programs [21, 22, 26, 28–30]. However, classical temporal logic does not allow quantitative treatment of time. Several extensions to the classical temporal logics have been proposed to quantitatively deal with time. In the following, we first briefly discuss a few important concepts in classical temporal logic. Subsequently, we examine some of the proposed extensions to the theory of classical temporal logic to deal with real-time, including some of our own work.

5.1. *Classical temporal logic*

Temporal logic is derived from modal logic. Temporal logic describes the evolution of a system as a sequence of states. Intuitively, the states are snapshots of a program execution. In a first-order temporal logic, classical first-order logic formulas are used to describe any particular state. The temporal operators are used to describe the dynamic behavior of the system. Thus, whereas classical logic formulas are interpreted at a single state, formulas containing temporal operators are interpreted over a number of states. The standard temporal operators are: F (Eventually), G (Always), X (Nexttime). A formula of the form F(A) means that the formula A eventually holds at some state in the future, G(A) means that henceforth A holds at all states in the future, and X(A) means that A holds at the next state.

5.1.1. *Linear versus branching time temporal logic*

In linear temporal logic, a system is described in terms of a set of (linear) state sequences. Concurrent activities of a system are described by the non-deterministic interleaving of the atomic actions. While a state in the linear temporal logic has only one future, a state in branching time temporal logic has several futures depending on the alternate continuations possible from that state. In other words, in the branching time approach, a system is described by a tree structure. Each node of the tree represents a state, and the descendants of a node describe the new states obtainable from that state. Although the branching time temporal logic can distinguish branching points in a computation, they still represent concurrent activities by totally ordered sequences (i.e., by interleaving).

5.2. *Real-time extensions to temporal logic*

Numerous extensions to classical temporal logics proposed by researchers to reason about real-time computations have been classified into GCTL (Global Clock Temporal Logic) and QTL (Quantized Temporal Logic) by Pnueli *et al.* [39]. GCTL represents a global clock by a global variable (T). The value of this variable at any state denotes the clock reading at that state. In QTL, a timing component is associated with each of the temporal operators. Thus, the range of states over which a temporal formula is interpreted is bounded by the timing component of the corresponding temporal operator. In the following, we study two sample extensions proposed to temporal logic to handle real-time.

5.2.1. *TRIO*

TRIO [21] is a first-order logic language, augmented with temporal modalities. TRIO allows specification of time-dependent properties of a system, and provides constructs to precisely specify the timing of events. The basic temporal operators, $\mathrm{Futr}(\mathrm{A}, t)$ and $\mathrm{Past}(\mathrm{A}, t)$, have a timing component associated with them. The formula $\mathrm{Futr}(\mathrm{A}, t)$ means that the formula A holds at an instant that is t time units in the future, $\mathrm{Past}(\mathrm{A}, t)$ is the corresponding past operator. To facilitate expression of time-related properties, several derived temporal operators have been provided. Those derived operators are expressible in terms of the basic temporal operators, $\mathrm{Futr}(\mathrm{A}, t)$ and $\mathrm{Past}(\mathrm{A}, t)$. As an example, the requirement that messages input to a transmission line must be output at the other end after 10 time units can be expressed by the following TRIO formula:

$$\forall m(in(m) \rightarrow Futr(out(m),\, 10))\,.$$

A system can be specified as a conjunction of closed TRIO formulas. A tableau-based decision procedure has been developed to automatically check the satisfiability (consistency) of specifications [21].

5.2.2. *Distributed logic*

To specify and reason about the real-time behavior of distributed systems, a modal logic called Distributed Logic (DL) was proposed in [28, 44]. In this work, the authors argue for the need of a partial-order framework for specification and verification of the real-time behavior of distributed systems. They examine the roots of temporal logic (i.e., modal logic) for developing a suitable partial order framework, and decide to use spatial modal operators in addition to the temporal operators. DL models a distributed real-time system by defining a partial order among the states of a set of totally ordered state sequences. Another important feature of DL is that it allows specification of and reasoning about a distributed system with respect to an underlying configuration. The authors demonstrate that DL can accurately model the real-time behavior of distributed systems and can naturally represent *local knowledge* of nodes in a distributed environment. They have reported the development of several tools to reason about the specifications [31]. A specification language [30] based on DL, and an automatic decision procedure for a restricted class of this logic have been reported [31].

6. Conclusions

Formal techniques hold the promise of assuring reliable operation of real-time systems in safety-critical applications. However, inspite of several research advancements made in this area, several problems still need to be overcome before formal techniques can be put to practical use. We have briefly surveyed some of the promising formal techniques reported in the literature, and have highlighted the relative merits and limitations of each of these approaches. It is difficult to project any particular formal technique as the best one. On the other hand, it appears that for specific problems at hand, one should choose an appropriate method from the available techniques to suit the problem. For example, a partial order operational semantics may be necessary to specify the real-time behavior of distributed systems, a property-oriented method may be necessary for requirements specification, and so on.

References

1. L. E. Moser and P. M. Melliar-Smith, "Formal verification of safety-critical systems", *Software Practice and Experience* **20**, 8 (1990) 799–821.
2. N. G. Leveson, "Software fault-tolerance in safety-critical applications", *Proc. 3rd Int. Conf. Fault-Tolerant Systems* (September 1987).
3. M. Barbacci and J. Wing, "Specifying functional and timing behavior for real-time applications", *Lecture Notes in Computer Science*, Vol. 259 (Springer-Verlag, 1987) pp. 124–140.
4. J. C. M. Baeten and J. A. Bergstra, "Real-time process algebra", Technical Report P8916, University of Amsterdam, Programming Research Group, The Netherlands (1989).
5. M. Hennessey and T. Regan, "A temporal process algebra", Technical Report 2, Department of Computer Science, University of Sussex, UK (1990).
6. R. Gerth and A. Boucher, "A timed failure model for communicating processes", *Proc. 14th ICALP, Lecture Notes in Computer Science*, Vol. 267 (Springer-Verlag, 1987) pp. 95–114.
7. I. Lee and A. Zwarico, "Timed acceptances: a model of time dependent processes", *Lecture Notes in Computer Science*, Vol. 331 (1989).
8. X. Nicollin, J. Richier, J. Sifakis, and J. Voirer, "ATP: an algebra for timed processes", Technical Report RT C-16, IMAG, Grenoble, France (1990).

9. W. Yi, "Real-time behavior of asynchronous agents", *Lecture Notes in Computer Science*, Vol. 458 (Springer-Verlag, 1990) pp. 502–520.
10. J. Coolahan and N. Roussopoulous, "Timing requirements for time-driven systems using augmented Petri nets", *IEEE Trans. Softw. Eng.* **SE-9** (1986) 603–616.
11. D. L. Dill, "Trace theory for automatic hierarchical verification of speed-independent circuits", Ph.D. Thesis, Department of Computer Science, Carnegie Mellon University, USA (1988).
12. D. L. Dill, "Trace theory for automatic hierarchical verification of speed-independent circuits", *Advanced Research in VLSI: Proc. 5th MIT Conf.* (1988).
13. J. R. Burch, "Modeling timing assumptions with trace theory", *Proc. Int. Conf. Computer Design* (1989).
14. G. H. MacEwen, "Using higher order logic for modular specification of real-time distributed systems", CS Lab, SRI International, Menlo Park, CA, USA (1987).
15. R. Milner, "A calculus of communicating systems", *Lecture Notes in Computer Science*, Vol. 92 (Springer-Verlag, 1980).
16. R. Milner, *Communication and Concurrency, Prentice Hall International Series in Computer Science* (Prentice Hall, 1989).
17. C. A. R. Hoare, "Communicating sequential processes", *Comm. ACM* **21** (1978).
18. C. A. R. Hoare, *Communicating Sequential Processes* (Prentice Hall, 1985).
19. J. A. Bergstra and J. W. Klop, "Process algebra for synchronous communication", *Information and Control* **60** (1984).
20. D. Murphy, "Approaching a real-timed concurrency theory", *Proc. Int. Workshop Computing Theory,* Leicester (July 1990) pp. 295–310.
21. C. Ghezzi, D. Mandrioli, and A. Morzenti, "TRIO: a logic language for executable specification of real-time systems", *J. Systems and Software* **12** (1990) 107–123.
22. J. Castro, "Distributed system specification using a temporal-causal approach", Ph.D. Dissertation, Imperial College, London, UK (October 1990).
23. G. Winskel, "An introduction to event structures", in *Linear Time, Branching Time and Partial Order in Logics and Models of Concurrency,* eds. J. de Bakker, E. de Roever, and G. Rozenberg, *Lecture Notes in Computer Science*, Vol. 354 (Springer-Verlag, 1989).
24. G. H. MacEwen and T.A. Montgomery, "Expressing requirements for distributed real-time systems", in *Proc. IEEE Computer Society Workshop Real-Time Operating Systems*, Cambridge, Massachussetts, USA (1987) pp. 125–128.
25. F. Jahanian and A. Mok, "Safety analysis of timing properties of real-time systems", *IEEE Trans. Softw. Eng.* **SE-12**, 9 (1986) 890–904.
26. J. S. Ostroff, "Real-time computer control of discrete event systems modeled by extended state machines: a temporal logic approach", Ph.D. Thesis, University of Toronto, Canada (January 1987).

27. R. Mall and L. M. Patnaik, "Specification and verification of timing properties of distributed real-time systems", *Proc. IEEE TENCON*, Hong Kong (September 1990) pp. 274–278.
28. R. Mall and L. M. Patnaik, "A temporal logic over partial orders for verification of timing properties of distributed systems", *Proc. IEEE TENCON*, New Delhi, India (September 1991) pp. 335–339.
29. L. M. Patnaik and R. Mall, "Critical issues in real-time software development", *Proc. National Workshop Computers in Real-Time Applications*, Indore, India (February 1991).
30. R. Mall and L. M. Patnaik, "A new approach to specify the real-time behavior of distributed systems", *Proc. IEEE Pacific RIM Conf. Fault-Tolerant Systems*, Tokyo, Japan (September 1991).
31. R. Mall and L. M. Patnaik, "A specification environment for distributed real-time systems", *Proc. Int. Conf. Software Engineering* (October 1991) pp. 85–92.
32. R. Mall and L. M. Patnaik, "A logic for timed event structures" (submitted for publication).
33. N. G. Leveson, "Software safety: why, what, and how", *ACM Comput. Surv.* **18**, 2 (1986) 125–163.
34. Luqi and V. Berzins, "Rapidly prototyping real-time systems", *IEEE Softw.* (1988) 25–36.
35. L. Chen and A. Avizienis, "N-version programming: a fault-tolerance approach to reliability of software operation", *Proc. 8th Symp. Fault-Tolerant Computing*, Toulouse, France (June 1978) pp. 3–9.
36. R. L. Glass, "Real-time: the lost world of software debugging and testing", *Comm. ACM* **23**, 5 (1980) 264–271.
37. F. B. Schneider, "Critical of issues in real-time systems", Technical Report TR-88-914, Department of Computer Science, Cornell University (May 1988).
38. C. B. Jones, "Software development — A rigorous approach", Prentice Hall International (1980).
39. A. Pnueli and E. Harel, "Application of temporal logics to the specification of real-time systems", in *Lecture Notes in Computer Science*, Vol. 331 (Springer-Verlag, 1989) pp. 84–98.
40. J. M. Wing, "What is a formal method?", Technical Report CMU-CS-89-200, Carnegie-Mellon University, USA (November 1989).
41. S. T. Levi and A. K. Agrawala, *Real-Time System Design* (McGraw Hill Publishing, 1990).
42. F. Jahanian, A. K. Mok, and D. A. Stuart, "Formal specification of real-time systems", Technical Report TR-88-25, Department of Computer Science, University of Texas at Austin, USA (1988).
43. J. R. Burch, "Modeling timing assumptions with trace theory", *Proc. Int. Conf. Computer Design* (1989).
44. R. Mall and L. M. Patnaik, "Formal timing analysis of distributed systems", *Int. J. Parallel Programming*, **20**, 2 (1992) 75–94.

45. W. J. Quirk, *Verification and Validation of Real-time Software* (Springer-Verlag, 1985).
46. R. Mall, "A specification environement for distributed real-time systems", Ph.D. Thesis, Department of Computer Science and Automation, Indian Institute of Science, Bangalore, India (April 1992).
47. C. Ghezzi and D. Mandrioli, "On ecleticism in specificartions: a case study centered around Petri nets", *Proc. 4th IEEE Int. Workshop Software Specification and Design*, Monterey, USA (1987).
48. J. Voas, L. Morrel, and K. Miller, "Predicting where faults can hide from testing", *IEEE Softw.* **3** (1991) 41–48.
49. M. J. Harrold and M. L. Soffa, "Selecting and using data for integration testing", *IEEE Softw.* **3** (1991) 58–65.

RECENT EFFORTS IN INTERNET REPOSITORY SERVICES*

DAVID EICHMANN

Repository-Based Software Engineering Project,
Research Institute for Computing and Information Science,
University of Houston, Clear Lake, Box 13, 2700 Bay Area Boulevard, USA

Recent network information retrieval systems are compared for their expressiveness and usefulness — first, in the general context of information retrieval, and then as prospective software reuse repositories. While the representational capabilities of some of these systems are limited, they provide a useful foundation for future repository efforts, particularly from the perspective of repository distribution and coherent user interface design.

1. Introduction

As information becomes an increasingly important sector of the global economy, the way in which we access that information — and thereby the way in which we access and structure *knowledge* — becomes a critical concern. The engineering of knowledge is quickly becoming an area of research in its own right, independent of its parent disciplines of artificial intelligence, database systems, and information retrieval. Wegner recognized the value of knowledge engineering in his landmark article on the role of capital in software development:

> "Knowledge engineering is a body of techniques for managing the complexity of knowledge... it is capital-intensive in the sense that reusability is a primary consideration in the development of books, expert systems, and other structures for the management and use of knowledge." [18, p. 33]

*This work was supported in part by NASA as part of the Repository-Based Software Engineering project, cooperative agreement NCC-9-16, project no. RICIS RB.02.

Just as Wegner observed that the products of software engineering are capital, so are the products of knowledge engineering a form of capital. Identification, structure, and locatability are critical to the enabling of this knowledge capital. Innovation in this area is driven from two diverse perspectives, the traditional perspective of researchers and a not-so-traditional perspective of what might be referred to as an information underground.

The goal of this information underground is not necessarily an extension of the state of the art, but a rather more pragmatic development of an informational infrastructure [12]. The prototypes resulting from this type of work propagate quickly over the Internet, immediately generating large numbers of users. Even while still experimental, systems that provide distinct benefit frequently need to limit access in order to maintain reasonable system performance for other users of the underlying platforms.

My reference to this community as an underground is calculated, for even within the computer science community (let alone the academic or commercial communities as a whole), only a small percentage of individuals have historically been aware of such information systems. Recent emphasis in the United States on the National Information Infrastructure have broadened general awareness of some of this technology. This article was spurred by my interest in software repositories, a number of recent conversations, and the benefit I think that can be gained by widening the forum for such systems to a larger audience.

In particular, it is interesting to evaluate these systems as an enabling technology for software reuse repositories. Repositories and, by implication, information retrieval mechanisms, play a critical role in successful reuse. This statement disagrees with the conventional wisdom [17] that reuse is a social and managerial issue, and not a technical one. A closer examination of the "conventional wisdom" leads to a recognition that without a repository with substantial representational capability many of the social and managerial requirements cannot be supported.

This paper surveys a number of interesting information server projects, with an eye towards enabling technologies. It concludes with remarks on the potential of future systems.

2. Archie

The archie system is "an on-line resource directory service for an internetworked environment" [11]. While archie is not truly a repository *per se*, since it does not actually contain the artifacts that it classifies, when treated as a whole with the diverse anonymous File Transport Protocol (FTP) sites that it references, it does fit into our discussion. Archie grew out of the efforts of Emtage and Deutsch to automate the creation and referencing of an index of the anonymous FTP sites many organizations support. A demon periodically sweeps through a list of known FTP sites, creating a list of artifacts accessible at each of them. This list of artifacts is then indexed for access by clients throughout the Internet seeking a site for some particular item.

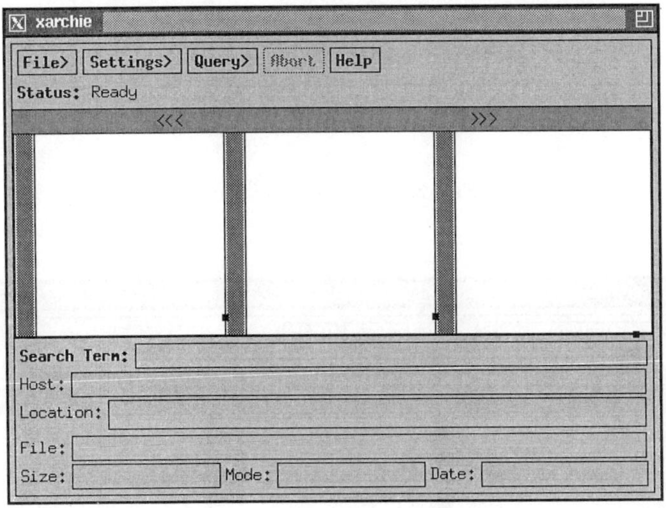

Fig. 1. Archie entry screen.

The interface described here is that of xarchie, developed by Ferguson for the X-windows system from the ASCII interface developed by Kehoe and the Prospero system developed by Neuman [13,14]. Figure 1 shows xarchie's screen at entry. The series of buttons across the top of the window control the activity of the user's xarchie client and its interaction with an archie server and the FTP sites which the server indexes. Figure 2 shows the xarchie settings panel, including in particular the mode of search (exact, substring, regular expression, etc.), the order that hits are presented (sorted by name, modification date, etc.), and the archie server host to interrogate, in this case archie.sura.net.

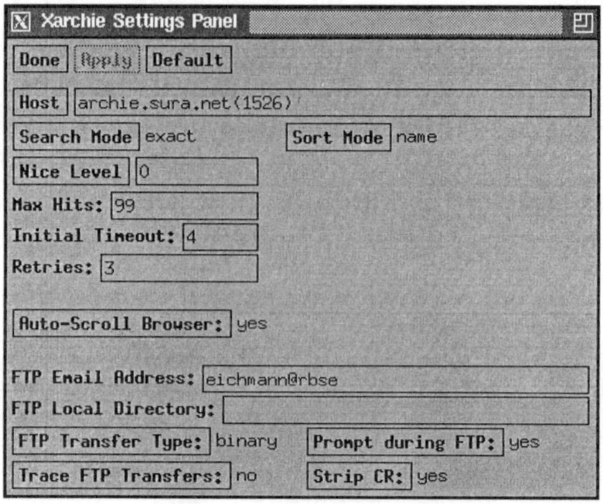

Fig. 2. Archie settings panel.

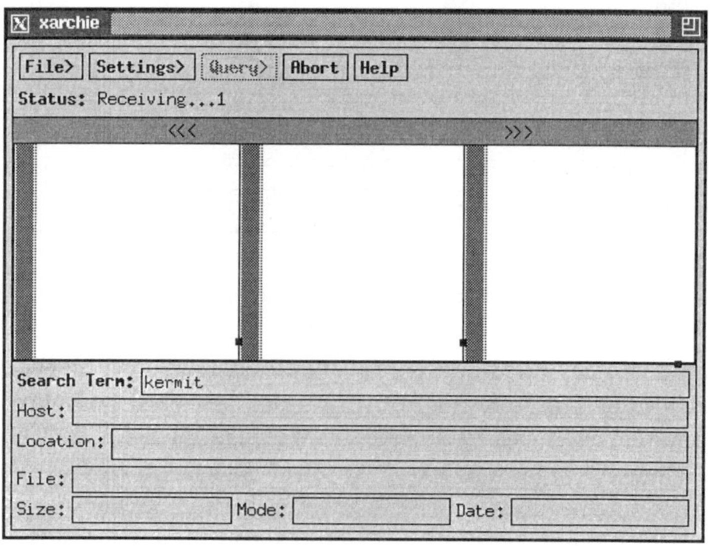

Fig. 3. Initiating an Archie search.

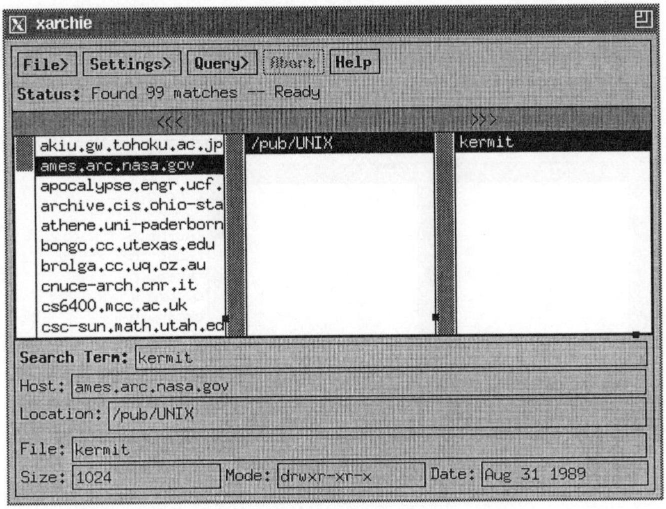

Fig. 4. Archie search results.

Entering a search term for an artifact, say Kermit (a communications package), and clicking the query button initiates the search, as shown in Fig. 3. As the search progresses, xarchie updates the status line, indicating establishment of connection, progress, and completion.

Figure 4 shows the results of the search as a list of sites in the left scrolling region in the middle of the window. Selecting a particular site by clicking on it results in Fig. 5, with the location, size, and so on for this artifact at this site. A single instance of a match at the selected site automatically selects the middle scrolling region(s) (corresponding to the directories) and the right scrolling region (corresponding to the files). Multiple matches (typical with inexact matches) require the selection of both a directory and a file for the lower fields to be filled in. Selecting the Retrieve option from the File menu establishes an anonymous FTP session to the archive site and retrieves a selected artifact into the local directory shown in the settings panel (shown in Fig. 2 as ‘ ’, the current directory).

Figure 6 shows the contents of a specific file, retrieved through the “Open” option in the File menu on the initial screen. Opening a file initiates an FTP session with the particular host using the user information specified in the settings panel.

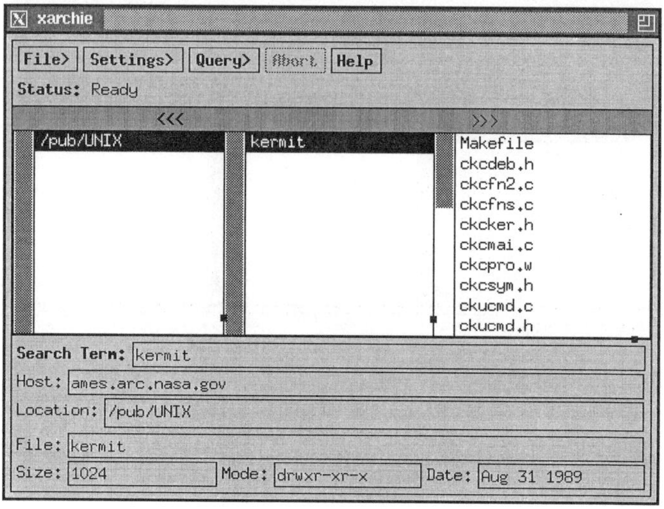

Fig. 5. Further examination of results.

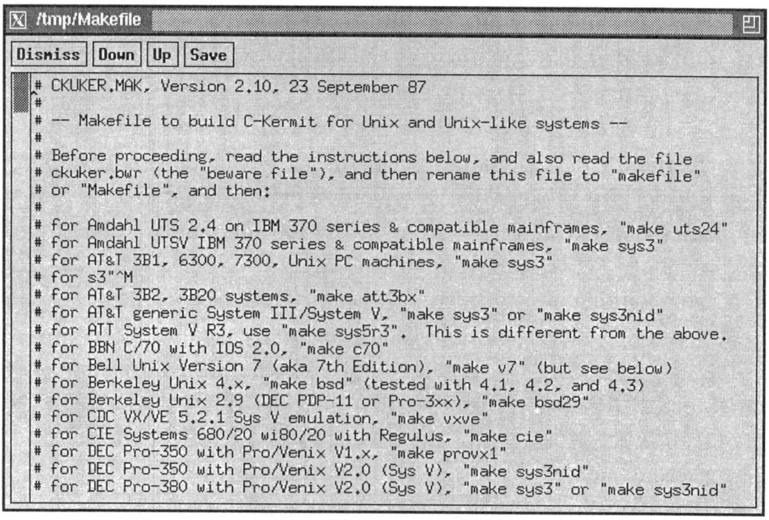

Fig. 6. Contents of a specific file.

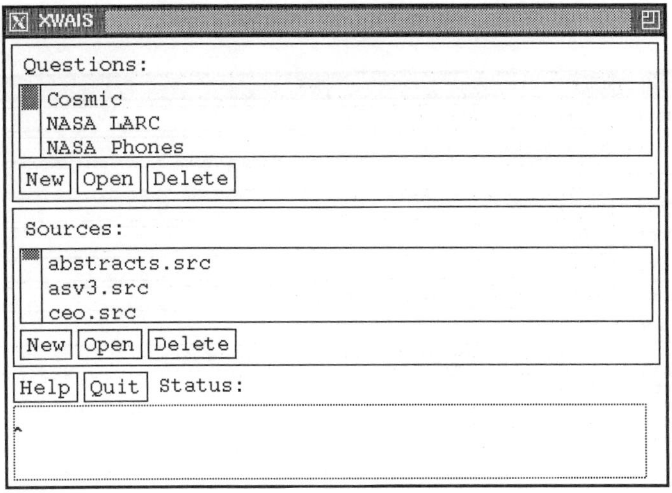

Fig. 7. XWAIS initial screen.

3. WAIS

The Wide Area Information Service (WAIS) started as an experiment in text-based distributed information systems by Thinking Machines and a number of collaborators [12]. (A commercial venture has subsequently been formed.) WAIS supports the notion of multiple servers; a user selects one or more servers to respond to a question, phrased as a string of words which are deemed relevant to the question. Figure 7 shows the main window, containing a list of existing questions and a list of already known sources. Opening a source displays a window containing information concerning the nature and location of that source, as shown in Fig. 8, for the software archive that the COSMIC group maintains for NASA. This information includes the internet address and service port that the server listens to, as well as unit and cost fields (as yet unused), and a textual description of the source. A single server can support multiple sources, each separately indexed and independently accessible. A distinguished source server, maintained by Thinking Machines, acts as a directory to other servers by indexing source definitions such as the one shown in Fig. 8. These source definitions are retrievable using the same question mechanism

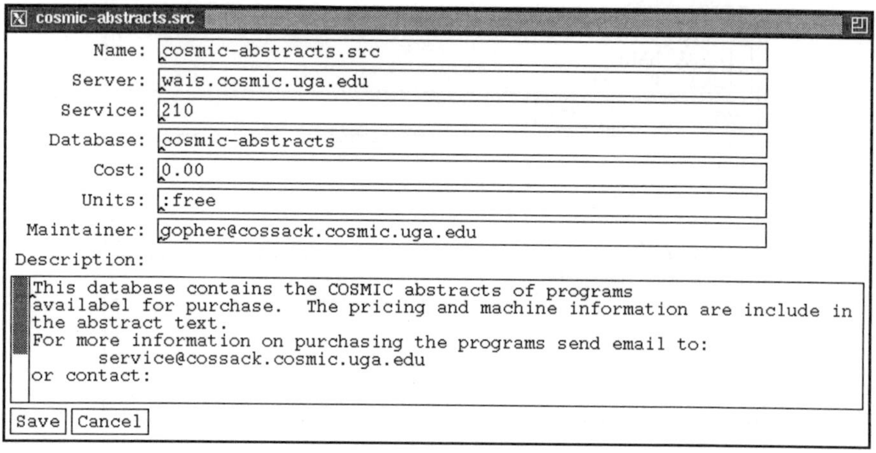

Fig. 8. XWAIS server definition.

employed for other questions. The sole distinction is in the saving of results; saving a source definition places it in the directory containing the user's known sources, making it accessible for subsequent questioning.

Figure 9 shows the question window following a successful search of the COSMIC source. Users select one or more already known sources to be consulted for this question by clicking the add source button and selecting from the resulting display of sources. The "Tell me about:" field accepts a collection of words to be used as a specification of the question. WAIS uses relevance feedback as its search mechanism; documents which match one or more of the words contained in the "Tell me about:" field are added to the collection of matching documents, and then presented to the user in the "Resulting Documents:" field ranked by a relevance metric, an indication of the fit to the words occurring in the query string. Relevance feedback has been shown to be more effective than boolean expression as a search mechanism for textual information (a report of one such study appears in [15]).

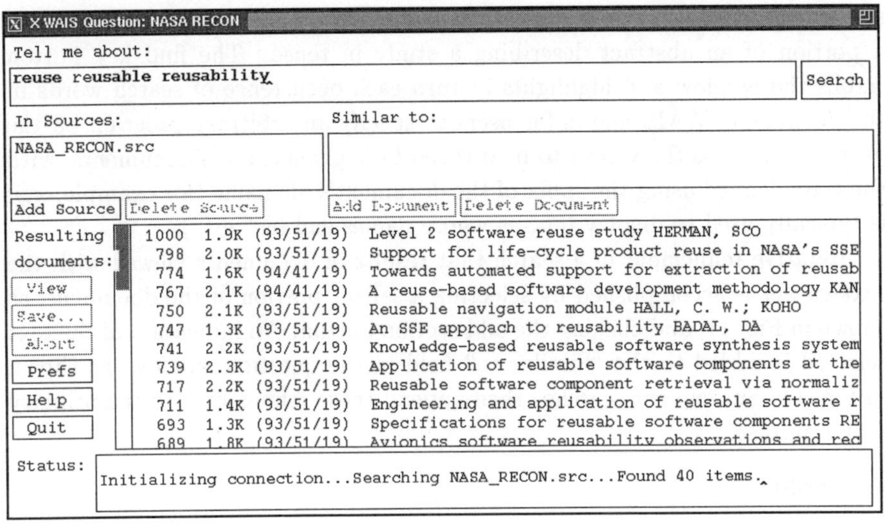

Fig. 9. XWAIS question and results.

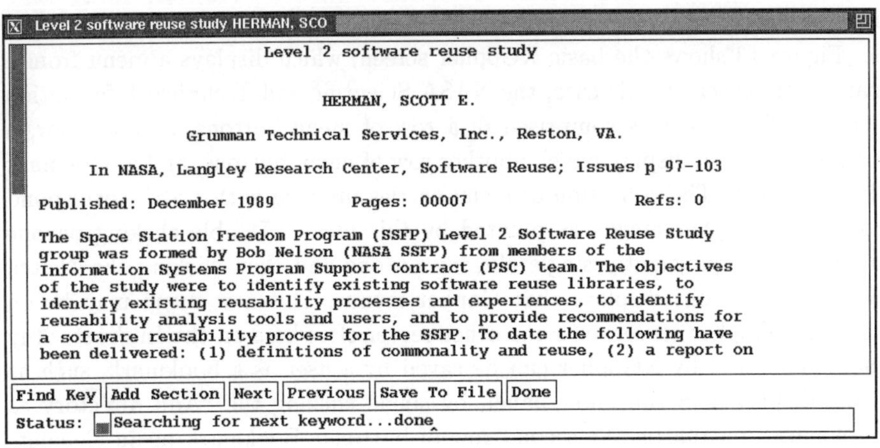

Fig. 10. XWAIS document screen.

Selecting a result document for viewing retrieves the document from its server and displays it in a window such as that shown in Fig. 10, which contains a portion of an abstract describing a study in reuse. The find key button scrolls the window and highlights in turn each occurrence of search words in the document. WAIS allows for users to specify an arbitrary program on the user's machine as the viewer to be invoked for a given class of documents, with the class defined using the suffix of the document's file name (for example, xgif is typically used to display images whose names end in "_gif").

Iterative refinement of a search that results in documents viewed with the text viewer is accomplished by selecting a salient portion of the document, as shown in Fig. 11, and clicking the add section button. An indication of the text selected is added to the "Similar to" field in the question window, as shown in Fig. 12. Subsequent searches then append these refinements to the primary search phrase.

4. Gopher

Gopher originated at the University of Minnesota[a] as a delivery system for campus-wide information. It subsequently expanded to a distributed client/ server system spanning hundreds of servers. Gopher is a menu-based system, targeting simple terminals as well as more advanced systems. This section presents XGopher, a Gopher client based on X-Windows, developed by Tuchman at the University of Illinois at Urbana-Champaign.

Figure 13 shows the basic XGopher screen, which displays a menu from a particular server, in this case, the NASA Scientific and Technical Information service. The screen is comprised of a row of menu buttons, a status bar, a title bar, a menu display panel, another row of menu buttons, and a bookmark display panel. The collection of menu entries prefixed with ">>" correspond to further Gopher menus as pointed by this menu. Double clicking on one of these (or equivalently single clicking on one and then clicking the "Fetch Selection" button) displays that Gopher menu. This new menu may be on the same Gopher server, or some other server elsewhere on the Internet. Any menu displayed by XGopher can be saved by a user as a bookmark, such as those displayed in the lower panel, by single clicking the "Add directory as bookmark" button on the second row of buttons. Bookmark menu elements have similar action semantics to the elements of the main menu.

[a]The gopher, a small, squirrel-like mammal indigenous to North America, is the university mascot.

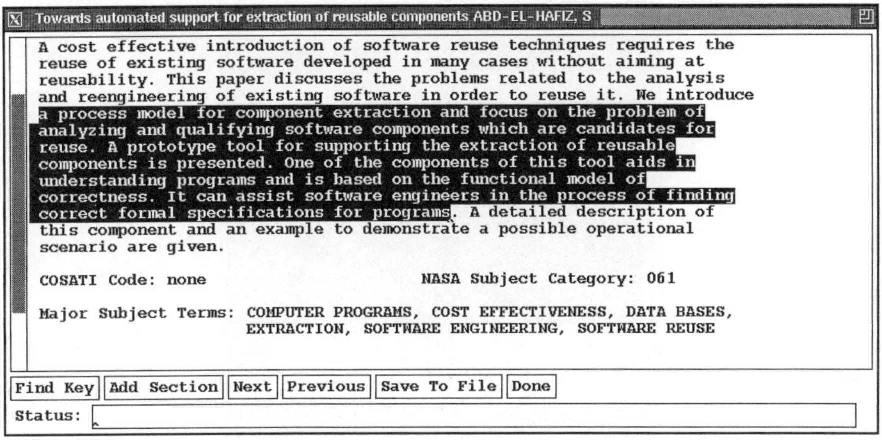

Fig. 11. Selection of additional search criteria.

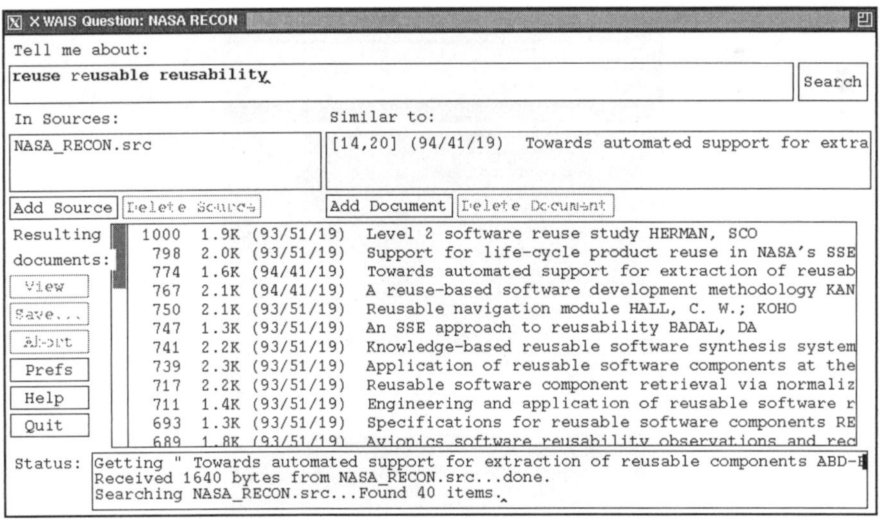

Fig. 12. Refined search results.

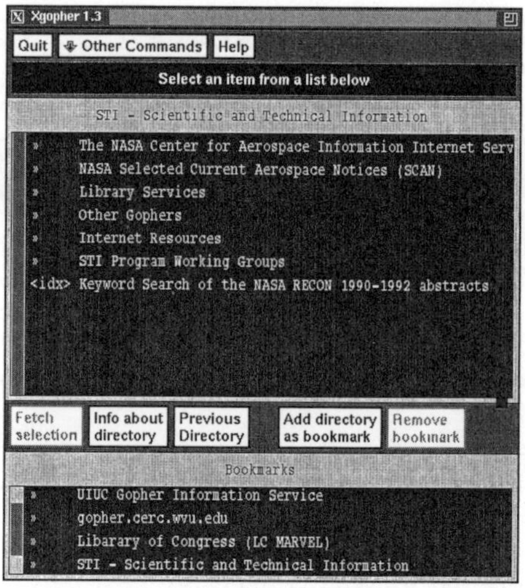

Fig. 13. XGopher initial screen.

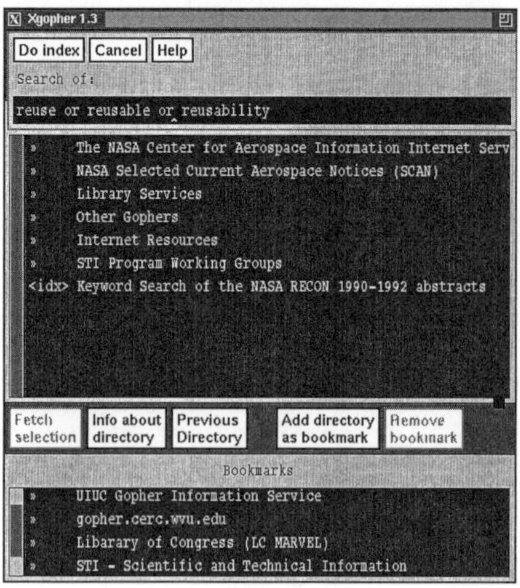

Fig. 14. Specifying a XGopher search.

The menu entry prefixed with "<IDX>" corresponds to a searchable index available from this Gopher server. Double clicking on this entry results in a pop-up entry form, as shown in Fig. 14. Entering a search expression and clicking on "Do index" submits the expression to the Gopher server for evaluation, resulting in a menu such as that shown in Fig. 15. Each of these menu entries are simple documents, indicated by the lack of a prefix in the menu. Double clicking any of these creates a document display screen, as shown in Fig. 16.

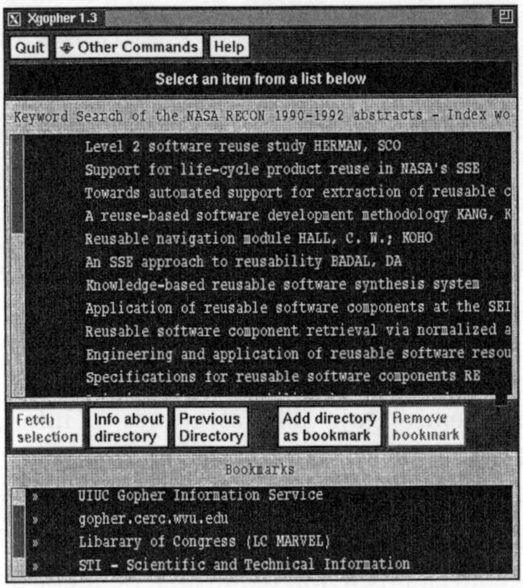

Fig. 15. Results of the search.

While Gopher originated as a distribution and display mechanism for text, recent experimental enhancements to both servers and clients support a variety of "document" types, including sound and images. Each of these are handled by captive application programs, spawned from the client process after retrieval from the server.

5. NELS

The NASA Electronic Library System (NELS), a follow-on system to autoLib [1, 9], is a monolithic application supported by a commercial relational database system (comprising the meta-information) and a UNIX file system (com-

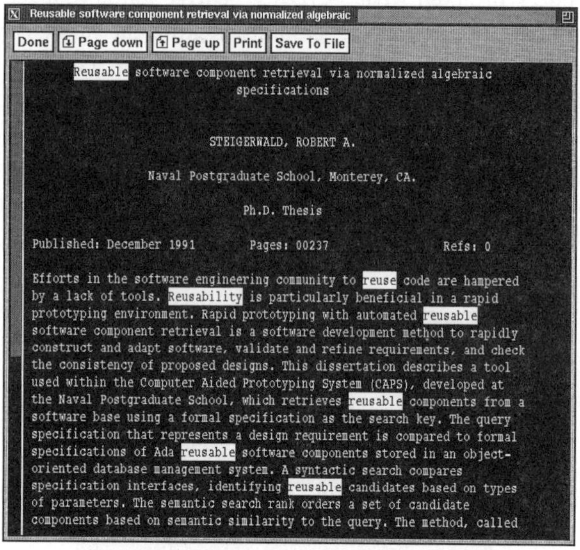

Fig. 16. Document display screen.

prising the artifacts themselves). The structure of information provided by archie and WAIS is flat in the sense that there is little structure provided other that an indexing mechanism. Gopher is comprised of a hierarchy of menus and indices. NELS, on the other hand supports both a flexible single inheritance class mechanism for definition of meta-information, and the definition of heterogeneous collections of instances of classes drawn from the inheritance scheme. Individual meta-data records are instances of a single class and members of a single collection.

The class mechanism is rooted in a predefined superclass, comprised of an object identifier, title, the class and collection identifiers, its status in the repository (developmental, production, etc.), its format (ASCII, PostScript, etc.), and a UNIX pathname to the artifact itself. Repository librarians have a complete interface within NELS to extend both the class and collection structures as needed. NELS automatically generates the necessary database information.

Figure 17 shows the main window for NELS, including the top-most collection and its immediate subcollections. (The particular instance of NELS presented in this section is the public repository operated by the Repository-Based Software Engineering project.) Clicking on an entry in the list moves

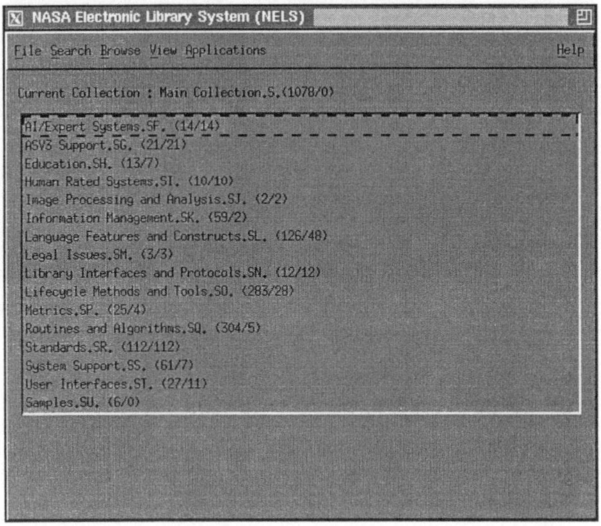

Fig. 17. NELS initial screen.

the user down the hierarchy of collections to the corresponding subcollection, and that collection's subcollections are then displayed. The menu items at the top of the window allow the user to invoke a variety of search mechanisms, browsers, and viewers, and to navigate the collection hierarchy. The collection hierarchy can be presented in a number of ways, as shown in Fig. 18. The hierarchical view presents a single collection at a time (as in Fig. 17), showing only the immediate subcollections. The outline view and the alphabetic views present the entire set of collections as an indented list or alphabetically by name, respectively.

Clicking on a specific collection from the display and selecting the "Browse objects" option from the browse menu displays the "Object Browser" screen shown in Fig. 19, which lists the objects that are members of that collection. Selecting "Meta-data" from the view menu of the "Object Browser" in turn displays the "Meta-data" screen shown in Fig. 20. The fields displayed in the "Meta-data" screen are determined dynamically based on the class structures defined by the librarians. Browsing mechanisms similar to that just described for collections are also available for the class hierarchy.

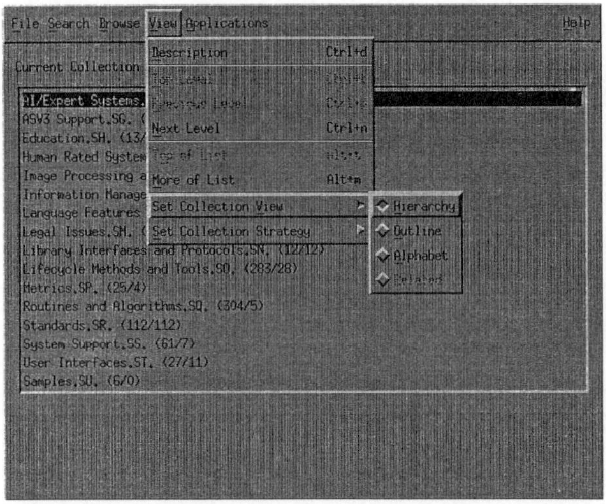

Fig. 18. NELS view menu.

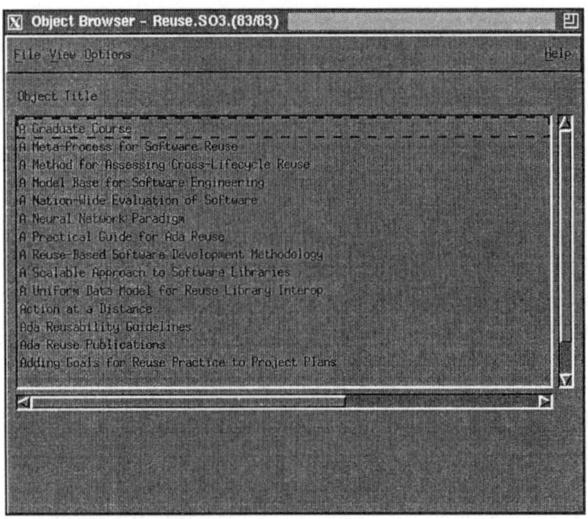

Fig. 19. NELS object browser.

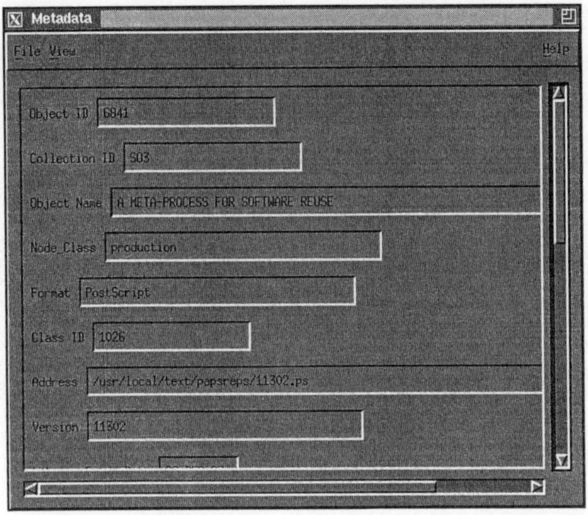

Fig. 20. A NELS meta-data screen.

In addition to the browsing mechanisms described here, NELS supports traditional boolean expression retrieval and a form of relevance feedback. Each object class has associated with it a tool, which is used to view actual instances of the class, as opposed to the meta-data characterizing that object, i.e., the fields presented in the object view window. Unlike WAIS, where tool execution occurs on the user workstation, tool execution in NELS occurs on the NELS server — the user workstation merely acts as an X-windows display.

6. World Wide Web

The World-Wide Web (known also as WWW or just "the Web") [2, 3] is a distributed collection of clients and browsers, connected through the HyperText Transport Protocol (HTTP) [4] and using the Hypertext Markup Language (HTML) [5]. Clients refer to specific servers and specific artifacts on those servers through Universal Resource Locators (URLs), of the form:

`<service>://<hostname>/<pathname>`

where services include not only HTTP, but also Gopher, WAIS, FTP, news, and Telnet. The hostname is a traditional Internet domain name (e.g.,

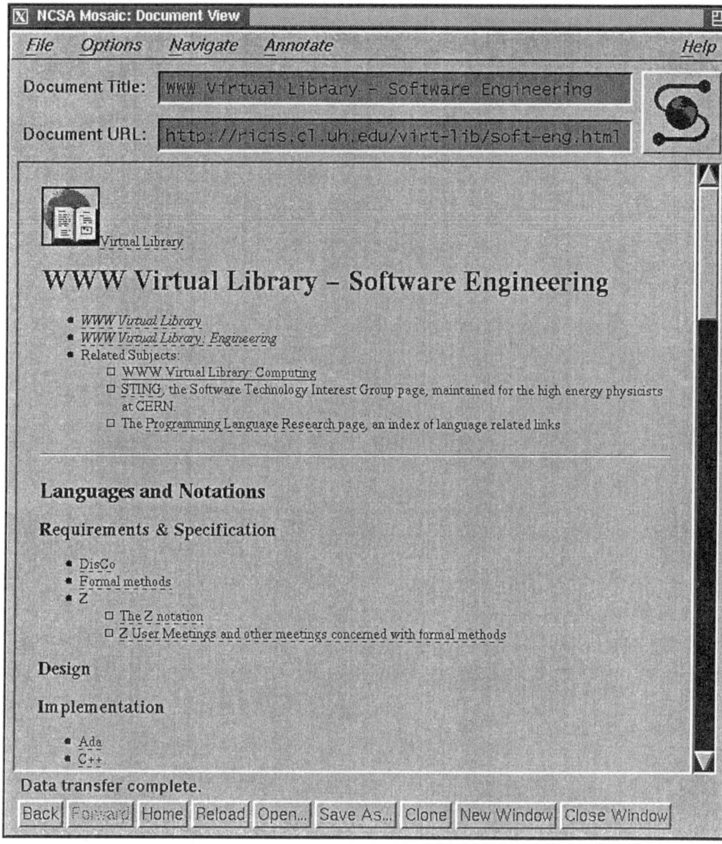

Fig. 21. Mosaic display of an HTML page.

rbse.jsc.nasa.gov), and pathname refers to a particular artifact in the server's file space. Web clients requesting a specific URL receive an artifact prefixed with a MIME header [6], indicating the artifact's type, creation/last modified dates, etc. Artifacts are displayed either by the client itself (in the case of HTML documents or Gopher menus, for example) or by a helper application (in the case of GIF images or PostScript documents, for example). HTML contains support for a client-independent definition of formatted text, including a variety of headers, and other usual text markup features. Figure 21 shows one such document, the "Software Engineering" page for the WWW

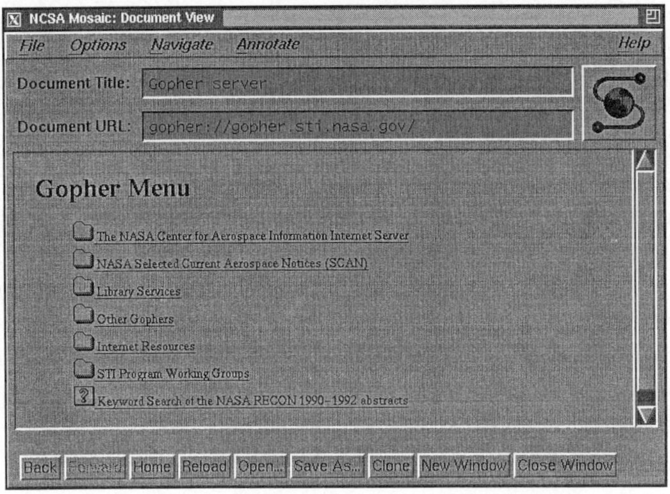

Fig. 22. Mosaic display of a Gopher menu.

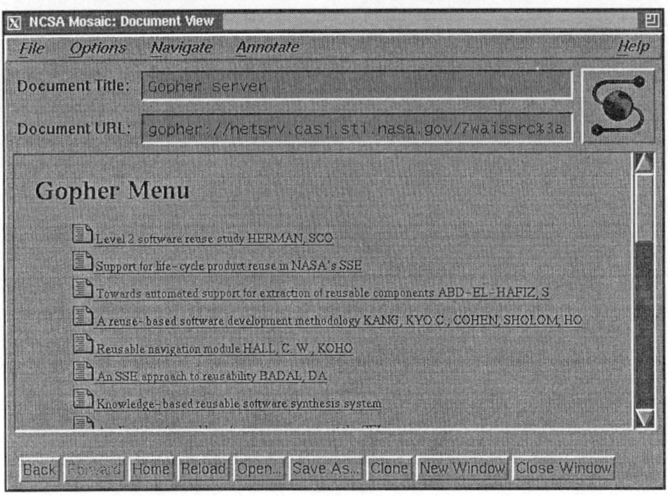

Fig. 23. Mosaic display of results of Gopher research.

Virtual Library, using one of the most popular clients, Mosaic, developed by the National Center for Supercomputer applications (NCSA) at the University of Illinois. Note the embedded graphic — Web clients support a limited set of image types (GIF and X bitmap) for in-line presentation. Solid underlining in the document indicates hyperlinks to other artifacts, in the case of a link to another artifact on the same or another server, or another reference point within the same document. Mosaic logs all access to URLs and logs and uses dashed underlining to indicate hyperlinks that have already been visited.

Figure 22 shows Mosaic presenting a Gopher menu, as indicated by the Document URL field. Note that the interface is quite similar to the central panel of XGopher, discussed in Sec. 4. In this case, each menu item is prefixed with an icon indicating its type and the menu item is marked-up as a hyperlink. Figure 23 shows the results of a search of a Gopher index.

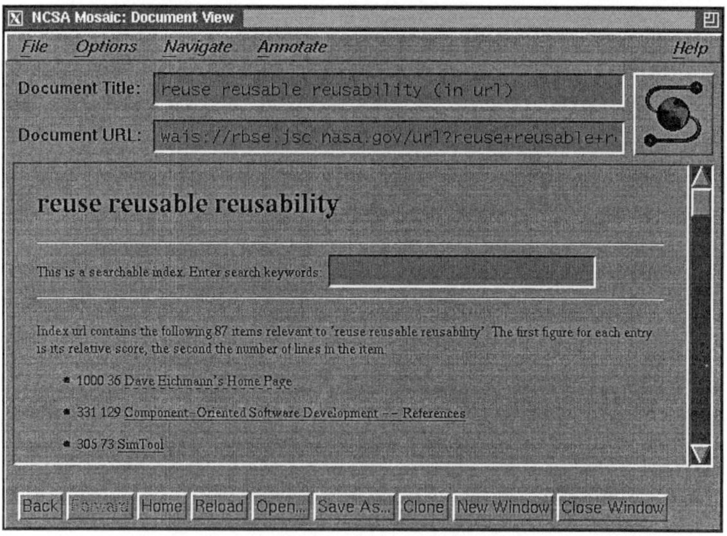

Fig. 24. Mosaic display of WAIS index and results.

WAIS indices are accessible in a similar manner. Figure 24 shows the results of searching a WAIS index: The search terms appear at the top of the document, followed by an index search block (allowing additional searches directly from this page), and the results themselves, each marked-up as a hyperlink. Note the dashed underlining of the first result, indicating that the user has visited this URL before. Clicking on any of these items results in the retrieval and display of the associated artifact, as shown in Fig. 25. In this case, the artifact was a document directly displayable by Mosaic. Other document types can, as mentioned above, result in the invocation of a helper application to present the artifact.

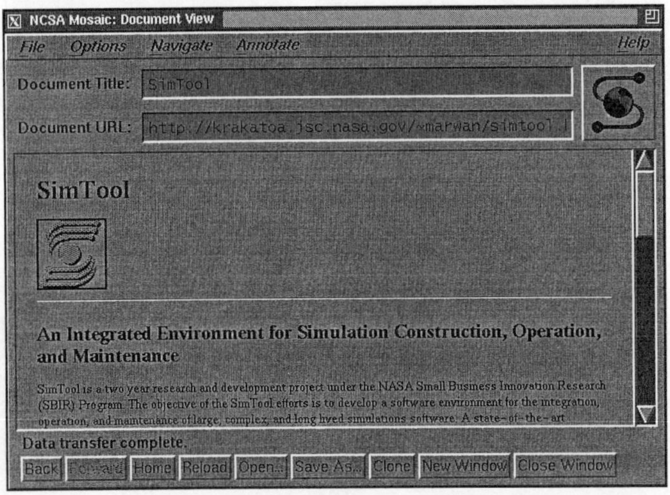

Fig. 25. Mosaic display of WAIS document.

7. MORE

The Multimedia-Oriented Repository Environment (MORE) [10] was designed as a set of application programs (more specifically a set of CGI executables[b]) that operate in conjunction with a stock HTTP server to provide access to a relational database of meta-data similar to that for NELS (Sec. 5). Each MORE facility is generated by a distinct program, resulting is a very modular

[b]Common Gateway Interface (CGI) executables are programs intended to be driven by requests to servers for information not directly available as artifacts in the server's file space. The Gopher and WAIS index search results are similar, none exist as a static file, but rather are generated on demand as a stream of HTML formatted text.

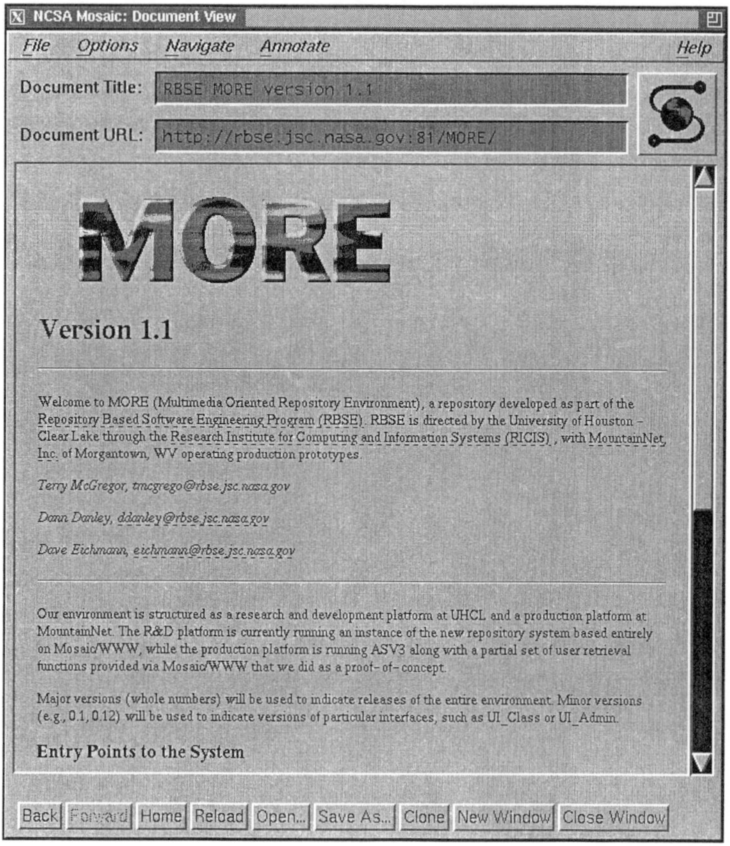

Fig. 26. MORE home page.

and hence adaptable system architecture. The entire MORE interface, client browsing and search, repository definition, data entry and other administrative functions, is provided through stock Web clients. MORE provides separate hierarchies of meta-classes and collections and support for controlled access to proprietary collections through the definition of user groups. With the single exception of the system front page (shown in Fig. 26), the entire user interface is accomplished as dynamically generated HTML.

MORE is a meta-data based repository — the information stored in its underlying database is not the artifacts themselves, but rather information concerning the artifact, which is stored using other mechanisms (the file system, another database, or another software package such as a configuration management tool or CASE environment). The two distinct representation mechanisms allow a mix of homogeneous (through the class definition hierarchy) and heterogeneous information (through the collection hierarchy).

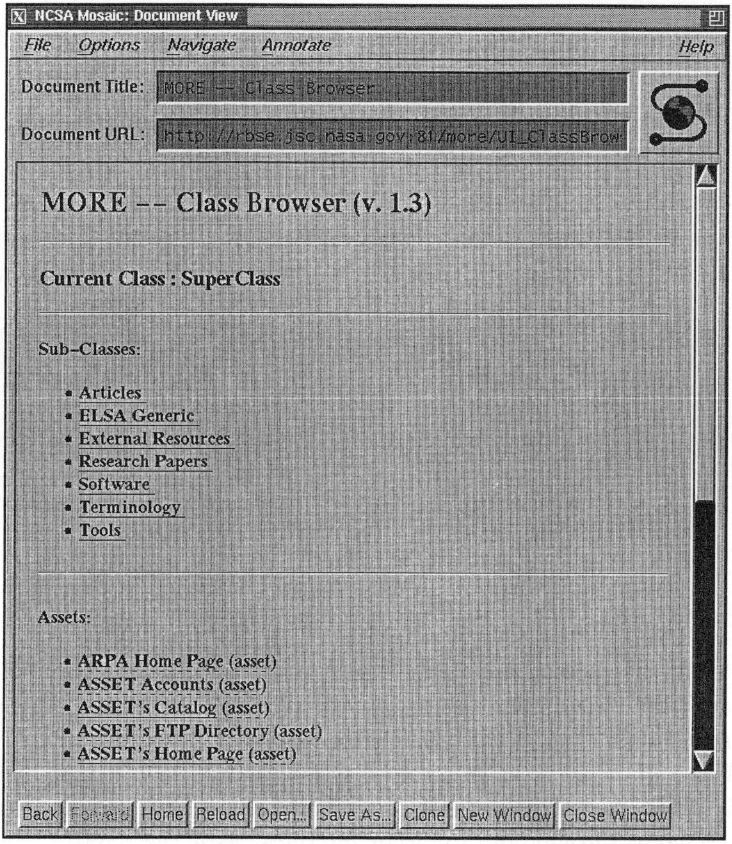

Fig. 27. MORE class browser.

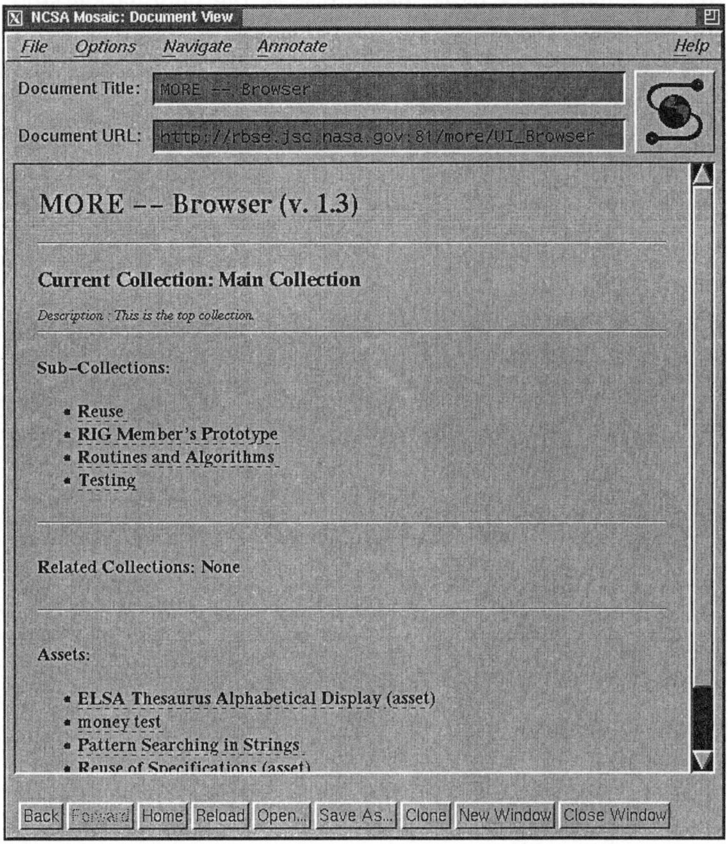

Fig. 28. MORE collection browser.

The class definition hierarchy is single inheritance, with a base class that is customizable at installation time through the database definition scripts (no software changes are required). The semantics of the system require that the base class contains at least an asset id, title and node type — with additional fields added as required. Further definition of the class hierarchy is then carried out completely through the librarian interface, with the database interface generating the calls to the DBMS to dynamically create and destroy classes and their corresponding relations as necessary. Figure 27 shows the MORE class browser.

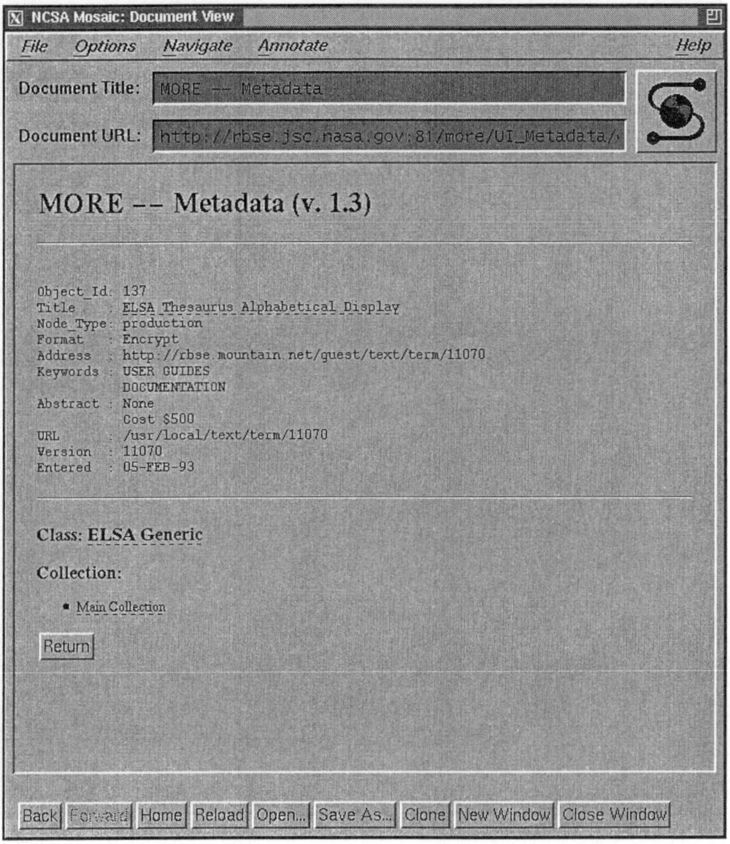

Fig. 29. MORE meta-data browser.

The collection hierarchy supports the aggregation of assets without respect to their defining class. Any given collection can contain a set of assets drawn from any number of classes, as well as sets of subcollections and related collections. The MORE collection browser is shown in Fig. 28. Any asset will always be a member of at least one collection in the hierarchy, but can be a member of as many collections as is appropriate, at any level in the hierarchy. Furthermore, each collection can have associated with it one or more groups which are authorized to access the assets and subcollections making up the

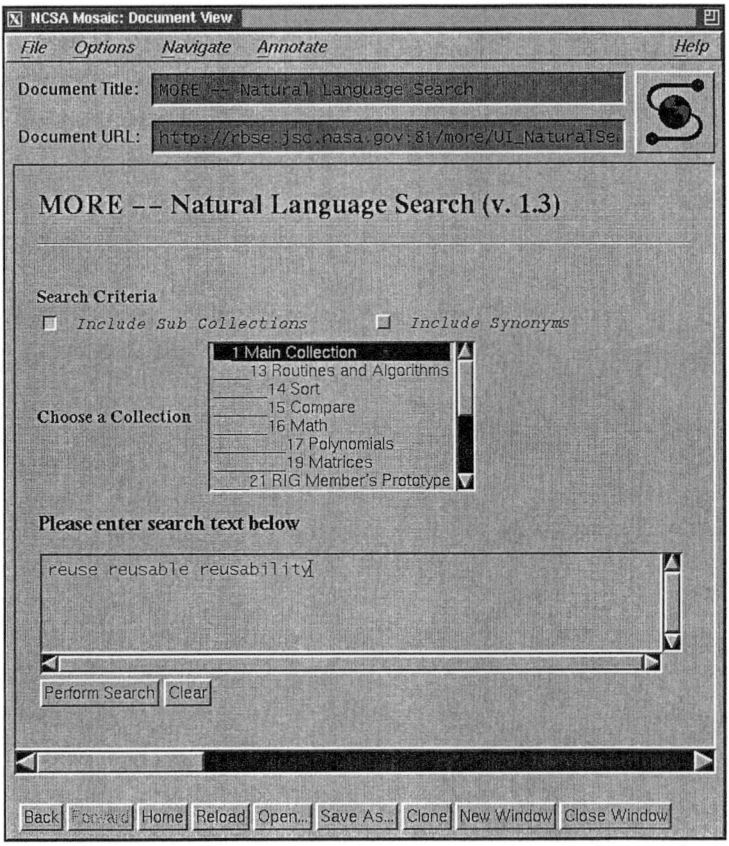

Fig. 30. MORE natural language search form.

collection. Groups in turn are made up of sets of users and other groups — all defined through the librarian interface. Users not transitively a member of a designated group for a given collection will never see the collection (or its contents) through any of the browser or search mechanisms.

The related collection mechanism is unary, a given collection can refer to another collection without the referenced collection being required to reciprocate. This allows work groups to reference more public collections without revealing the contents (or existence) of their own collections to the organization or public at large.

Assets, as mentioned earlier, are characterized by their meta-data, which includes an address (normally a URL) that provides a clickable path to the asset by marking-up the title field, as shown in Fig. 29. A special case involves assets that are composites — made up of a number of distinct artifacts. We organize these into directories in a server file space (usually the same server that MORE uses), one asset per directory and one asset artifact per file. The URL is then a path from the server root directory to the asset's directory. This results in a list of files marked up as links.

In addition to the browsers, MORE supports both relevance-feedback search and search by field value. Relevance-based search is provided by the Natural Language Search facility, shown in Fig. 30. Users select a collection to start the search with, indicate whether the search should be limited to just that collection or include its subcollections, whether to expand the search to include synonyms for search terms, and enter the search terms themselves. Results, as shown in Fig. 31, are returned as a ranked list of hyperlinks to the corresponding meta-data (and a direct link to the artifact itself if it is accessible), as shown in Fig. 31). The search results span the class and collection hierarchies, constrained by the user's access to proprietry collections, matching text that appears in the meta-data for that artifact (artifacts themselves are not searched).

Pattern Search initiates, as shown in Fig. 32, with the user indicating a starting class and collection, whether the search should include subclasses and subcollections, and whether case should be taken into account. Submitting this form results in the display of a second form, as shown in Fig. 33, containing the fields associated with the selected class. Values (including wildcard characters) entered in these fields generate a conjunctive constraint used in querying each of the classes involved in the search. Only matching artifacts that are also members of some collection contained by the selected collection(s) are presented in the results, displayed in a manner similar to those in Fig. 31 (but without the relevance weightings).

8. A Brief Comparison

Viewing these systems as potential software repositories is interesting, and at the same time somewhat unfair to their designers, as only two (NELS and MORE) were created with that purpose in mind. However, systems such as these are frequently called into service in such contexts, and the flexibility and adaptability exhibited provides interesting concepts and features for inclusion

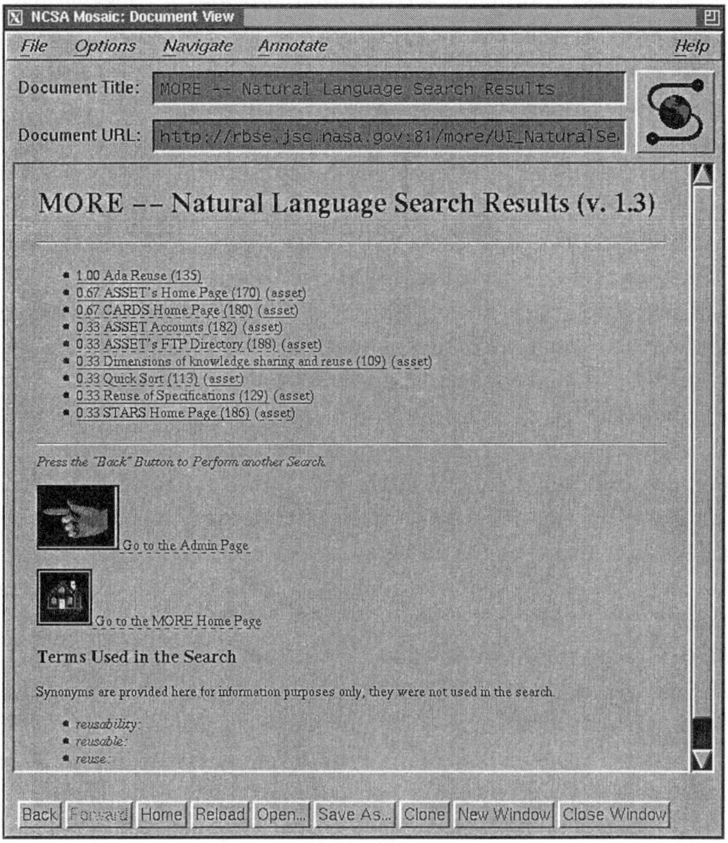

Fig. 31. MORE natural language search results.

into systems specifically intended as repositories. Table 1 summarizes major aspects of the three systems.

The popularity of archie stems not from its rich representation scheme or novel search mechanisms, but rather on the low levels of effort required on the part of archive administrators and users to employ the system. It is an excellent example of how a limited-purpose system implemented by volunteers can provide a valuable resource. Referring to archie as a software repository, however, stretches the definition of repository perhaps a little too far. Consi-

Table 1. Systems synopsis.

	archie	WAIS	Gopher	NELS	WWW	MORE
Architecture	Client/server	Client/server	Client/server	Monolithic	Client/server	Client/server
# server sites	~10	~100	~1400	1	~6000	~5
Interfaces	X-Windows, ASCII	X-Windows, ASCII	X-Windows, ASCII	X-Windows (and limited ASCII)	X-Windows, ASCII	X-Windows, ASCII
Retrieval mechanisms	Pattern-matching (on name only)	Relevance feedback	Keyword	Browsing, boolean expression, relevance (on abstract only, not full text)	Keyword	Browsing, patterns, relevance feedback
Information domain	Material available by anonymous FTP	Text, some images, and other formats	Text, some images, and other formats	Text, some images, and other formats	Text, images, sound, movies	Text, images, sound, movies
Information stored	Name, location, file attributes	Word occurrence, headline, full text	Menu definitions	Full text/image, index terms, meta-data (administrator-defined)	Artifact files (including HTML documents)	Meta-data (administrator-defined)
Archiving responsibility	Decentralized	Decentralized	Centralized	Centralized	Decentralized	Centralized
Indexing responsibility	Centralized	Decentralized	Centralized	Centralized	Decentralized	Centralized
Support required (archive site)	None	Moderate	High	Moderate	Moderate	Moderate
Support required (indexing site)	Moderate	Low	Moderate	High	Moderate	Moderate
Promise as a repository	Poor	Limited	Limited	Good	Good	Very good
Availability	Public	Public	Public	Private	Public	Public

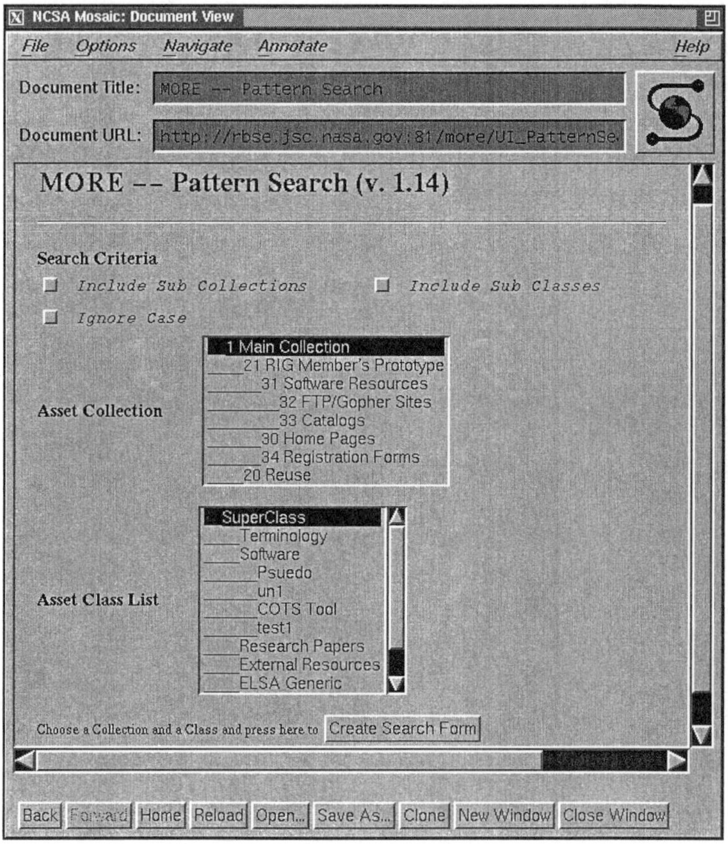

Fig. 32. MORE pattern search initial page.

deration of an artifact at a site as a candidate component requires that the user knows both the name and the purpose of the artifact, and the retrieval of the complete artifact (irrespective of the total size) before further consideration can be made.

The display facilities of WAIS alleviate the limitations of archie by presenting the user with a flexible means of query specification (without requiring classification by the archivist) and the opportunity to select from a variety of candidates and view portions of them prior to retrieving the complete text of

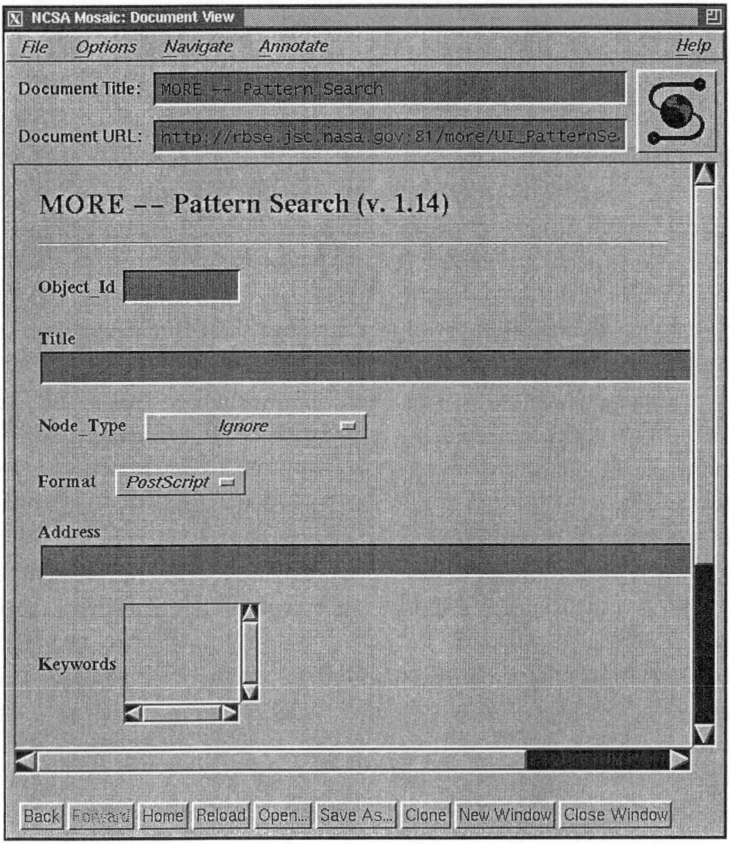

Fig. 33. MORE pattern search form.

the final selection. WAIS further increases flexibility in the nature of repositories by supporting interrogation of multiple sources for a given query and the generation of both public and private sources. (Note, however, that there is no technical impediment in doing this with archie as well — the archie designers simply chose global indexing rather than regional or local indexing.) The principal virtue of WAIS, its treatment of all material as text to be indexed, is also its principal failing from our perspective — there is no discrimination between code, supporting documents, and so forth — resulting in slightly more cumbersome search behavior.

Gopher has been very successful as a campus-wide information system, due in part to the low entry requirements for access (a simple ASCII terminal). Its utility as a sophisticated information repository is limited, however, due to its focus on a single dimension of hierarchical menus.

The use of an adminstrator-defined set of collection and class definitions provides NELS a great deal of flexibility in organizing the information. In addition to the ability to organize the global structure of the information base, this definitional facility supports meta-descriptions of artifacts, a useful feature in our chosen context.

The Web is experiencing dramatic growth, the server count of 6000 included in Table 1 is based on estimates from a number of Web-traversing programs in June 1994 — up from approximately 1500 as recently as February 1994! HTML offers a rich and flexible means of generating information that can be served to the general Internet community, but scaling up to a large body of information, such as our focus of a software repository, creates a large maintenance load on the librarians, as all information structures are static and hand-constructed.

The structuring, classification, and retrieval mechanisms of MORE are by far the richest of all the systems compared here, extending the facilities of NELS with access from any Web client as well as the ability for a given artifact to be a member of multiple collections. Much of this power obviously stems from the fact that NELS is a proprietory system, whereas archie is a volunteer effort and WAIS is a research project. However, NELS' look and feel suffers dramatically in our sample context. Unlike archie and WAIS, which use a client/server paradigm, NELS executes solely on the server platform. In wide-area domains like the one in which our programmer operates, this results in slow display and update of windows, and an inability for a user to select alternative viewing tools without the intervention of the repository administrator. MORE was created, in part, to move beyond these limitations.

9. Conclusions

This paper reviewed six example information retrieval systems currently in use by a broad diversity of users. It focussed on computer-supported repositories for software artifacts (i.e., components, documents, test suites, executable images, etc.) rather than addressing the more broadly scoped notion of an information repository, which could easily encompass entities such as public libraries. The surveys of Danzig *et al.* [8] and Schwartz *et al.* [16] provide more general characterizations of network information discovery and retrieval mechanisms.

While these systems were not explicitly designed as software repositories, they do each provide some aspects of repository requirements. Each is a legitimate step forward in utility from earlier techniques for wide distribution of software. This analysis leads to the following proposal for perceiving the current state of software repository efforts from the standpoint of information systems.

Generation 1 — Program libraries. This includes not only traditional compiler libraries, but also more distributed mechanisms such as the Ada Software Repository [7] and the various archives for news groups such as comp.sources.unix.

Generation 2 — Information servers. Examples of this generation include the systems described here. The emphasis here is on the indexing and retrieval mechanisms, rather than upon deep representation.

Generation 3 — Component bases. Fine-grain characterization of components and interrelationships distinguishes this generation. The nature of reuse in this generation is compositional, and is typified by the Department of Defense STAR's efforts and the Japanese Software Factory projects.

Generation 4 — Software knowledge bases. This generation provides deep knowledge about representation, generation, and composition of components and design schemes and the process of software development.

The separation criteria for repository generations involves the nature and accessibility of the knowledge of each artifact that comprises the repository. Generations one and two provide wide access to artifacts, but little supporting infrastructure (although it might be argued that NELS and MORE could, through the proper configuration efforts of a repository administrator, be turned into rudimentary generation 3 systems). Generations three and four provide increasingly rich information concerning the nature of the artifacts contained within them. However, with this richness comes increasing specialization of domain, and increasing difficulty in supporting interoperability between repositories. The component base services of today and the software knowledge base services of tomorrow should not lose sight of the design goals of today's successful information servers.

References

1. Barrios Technology, *autoLib Automated Online Library Version 3 Product Overview* (March 1990).
2. T. J. Berners-Lee, R. Cailliau, J.-F. Groff, and B. Pollermann, "Worldwide Web: the information universe", *Electronic Networking: Research, Applications and Policy* (Spring, 1992) 52–58.
3. T. Berners-Lee, R. Cailiau, A. Loutonen, H. F. Nielsen, and A. Secret, "The Worldwide web", *Commun. ACM* **137**, 8 (1994) 76–82.
4. T. Berners-Lee, "Hypertext transport protocol", CERN, ftp://info.cern.ch/pub/www/doc/http-spec.ps, txt.
5. T. Berners-Lee and D. Connoly, "Hypertext markup language protocol", CERN, ftp://info.cern.ch/pub/www/doc/html-spec.ps, txt.
6. N. Borenstein and N. Freed, "MIME (Multipurpose Internet Mail Extensions): mechanisms for specifying and describing the format of internet message bodies", Internet RFC 1341 (June 1992).
7. R. Conn, "The Ada software repository and software reusability", *Proc. 5th Annual Joint Conf. Ada Technology and Washington Ada Symp.* (1987) pp. 45–53. Also appears in *Tutorial: Software Reuse: Emerging Technology*, ed. W. Tracz (IEEE Press, 1988) pp. 238–246.
8. P. Danzig, K. Obraczka, and S.-H. Li, "Internet resource discovery services", *IEEE Comp.* **26**, 9 (1993) 8–22.
9. D. Eichmann, "Assessing repository technology — where do we go from here?", *Int. J. Softw. Eng. Knowl. Eng.* **2**, 3 (1992) 467–481.
10. D. Eichmann, T. McGregor, and D. Danley, "Integrating structured databases into the Web: the MORE system", *Proc. 1st Int. Conf. World Wide Web*, 25–27 May, Geneva, Switzerland (1994) pp. 369–378.
11. A. Emtage and P. Deutsch, "Archie — an electronic directory service for the Internet", *Proc. USENIX*, San Francisco, CA (January 1992) pp. 93–110.
12. B. Kahle, *Wide Area Information Server Concepts* (Thinking Machines Inc., 1989).
13. C. Neuman, "The virtual system model for large distributed operating systems", Technical Report UW-CSE-89-01-07, The University of Washington (1989).
14. B. C. Neuman, "Prospero: a tool for organizing Internet resources", *Electronic Networking: Research, Applications and Policy* (Spring 1992) pp. 30–37.
15. S. E. Robertson and K. Sparck Jones, "Relevance weighting of search terms", *J. American Society for Information Science* **27** (1976) 129–146.
16. M. F. Schwartz, A. Emtage, B. Kahle, and B. C. Neuman, "A comparison of Internet resource discovery approaches", *Comput. Sys.* **5**, 4 (1992) 461–493.
17. W. Tracz, "Software reuse myths", *ACM SIGSOFT Softw. Eng. Notes* **13**, 1 (1988) 17–21.
18. P. Wegner, "Capital-intensive software technology", *IEEE Softw.* **1**, 3 (1984) 7–45.

MEASUREMENT SUPPORT IN SOFTWARE ENGINEERING ENVIRONMENTS

CHRISTOPHER M. LOTT*
Software Technology Transfer Initiative Kaiserslautern,
Gebäude 57, Universität Kaiserslautern,
67653 Kaiserslautern, Germany
E-mail: lott@informatik.uni-kl.de

ABSTRACT

The use of empirical data to understand and improve software products and software engineering processes is gaining ever increasing attention. Empirical data from products and processes izs needed to help an organization understand and improve its way of doing business in the software domain. Additional motivation for collecting and using data is provided by the need to conform to guidelines and standards which mandate measurement, specifically the SEI's Capability Maturity Model and ISO 9000-3. Some software engineering environments (SEEs) offer automated support for collecting and, in a few cases, using empirical data. Measurement will clearly play a significant role in future SEEs. The paper surveys the trend towards supporting measurement in SEEs and gives details about several existing research and commercial software systems.

Keywords: Software metrics, process modeling, empirical data collection, measurement-based project guidance, MVP Project.

1. Introduction

The current trend towards process improvement and maturity (see *IEEE Softw.* **1**, 4 (1993)) reveals organizations focusing on gaining intellectual control over their software projects. Intellectual control is an all-encompassing expression for gaining skill in predicting project costs and duration, developing products that meet quality standards, capturing organizational knowledge, and

*Funding for the Software Technology Transfer Initiative Kaiserslautern was provided in part by the Ministry of Commerce and Transport (BMWV) of the State of the Rheinland-Palatinate, Germany.

improving work processes. A significant assumption is that the improved process will yield higher quality products at a manageable cost. The major factor in understanding processes, testing predictions, gauging product quality, and judging whether improvement has occurred is measuring the processes, products, and resources. Understanding is not solid and improvements cannot be recognized until the understanding, changes, costs, and benefits are quantified using empirical data. Current motivation for measurement efforts consists of both a carrot, the possibility of improving how a software organization works, and a stick, the requirement to conform with guidelines.

The first motivational factor in measurement, the carrot, is improving how a software organization works. Organizations measure their work in order to characterize, understand, and improve it. Measurement is used for these purposes in the Quality Improvement Paradigm (QIP) [1]. The QIP approach involves defining goals, collecting empirical data from the processes and products, and analyzing the data. Once goals such as characterizing the process, attaining the next maturity level, improving the reliability of a product, or achieving ISO conformance are defined, a significant step towards judging whether the goals have been met is collecting empirical data and analyzing it in light of the goals. The importance of starting with goals is vital, because goal-directed data collection skirts the pitfall of gathering large amounts of data that are never used [3].

Conformance with guidelines, such as the Software Engineering Institute's Capability Maturity Model (CMM) [16, 31] and the International Organization for Standardization's ISO 9000-3 [14], is the other major motivational factor, the stick driving organizations to measure their work. This factor can arguably be viewed as a threat because of its use in awarding competitive contracts [38]. Empirical data collection and use are described in detail in the CMM and also mentioned in 9000-3. However, only the CMM appropriately identifies the vital connection between work processes and data collection. Not until a reasonable understanding of those work processes has been gained can the data collectors be confident that they are collecting data from what is actually happening, not from some fantasy processes.

This paper surveys research into future SEEs and focuses on their support for collecting and using empirical data. This support can be found in at least two types of software engineering environments, namely, computer-aided software engineering (CASE) systems and computer-aided process enactment (CAPE) systems. Feiler introduced the term CAPE in [10], and I feel that it captures both the similarities and differences between the two types of systems. A CASE system offers construction tools for evolving software artifacts (documents, designs, code, etc.) in a single life-cycle phase or across multiple phases. An example of a CASE system is the "Integrated Structured Environment", which provides editors for structured analysis and structured design diagrams [9]. In contrast, a CAPE system uses some formal representation of a process to guide people through enaction of that process. An example of a CAPE system is Process Weaver, which provides a system for defining a process using a network formalism and enacting the process using the network [11].

Due to the great diversity of existing CASE and CAPE systems, it is often difficult to draw the dividing line between them precisely and unambiguously. Two primary differences are used in this paper. The first is the system's awareness of a process or life-cycle. A CASE system is either totally unaware of an overarching process or supports one fixed process; the tool generally supports one or two activities that can be part of any development life-cycle process or an activity that is part of one particular process. In contrast, a CAPE system does not assume any fixed work process but can be used to model a process and guide people while they enact that process. The second difference involves construction tools. A CASE system invariably provides construction tools for software artifacts, while a CAPE system generally offers access to an existing set of tools and provides no new tools of its own.

A theme touched upon in previous surveys [22, 36], namely, support for measurement in SEEs, is explored in more detail in this paper. Here, the trend towards collecting and using empirical data in CASE and CAPE systems is surveyed, and details about several software systems are given. The reader can expect to gain an understanding of the motivation for measurement, with emphasis on guidelines and standards, and an overview of some recent work on implementing support for collecting and using empirical data. Section 2 gives some background information on measurement, including guidelines, cost-benefit analyses, and goal-directed measurement. Section 3 gives examples of CASE and CAPE systems, including both research prototypes and commercial products. Section 4 summarizes aspects of the systems surveyed here and offers some conclusions.

2. Background

The appearance of the Software Engineering Institute's Capability Maturity Model (CMM) [31] and its subsequent widespread use in awarding contracts [38] is a huge factor motivating software process improvement as well as measurement efforts. Put briefly, the CMM establishes an ordinal scale with five process maturity levels, assuming that organizations which have attained higher levels will perform more predictably and reliably than organizations at lower levels. Organizations are certified as having attained specific maturity levels based on their responses to a detailed questionnaire and the findings of an assessment team which visits the organization. The CMM presents an approach in which the collection and use of empirical data is legislated at the higher levels. Furthermore, the issue of measurement is deeply integrated into the whole maturity model, meaning that the CMM discusses measuring processes, measuring products, establishing a collection of historical data, and using that data in all activities at maturity levels three, four, and five.

A second guideline that has received much attention is the ISO 9000 series [12, 13, 14]. ISO conformance is rapidly becoming the prerequisite for conducting business in the European Union.[a] Part 3 of ISO 9000 (ISO 9000-3) applies the policies set forth in ISO 9001 for the software domain and is most directly comparable in terms of its goals to the CMM (see also [30] for a detailed comparison). In the 9000-3 guidelines, measurement is split into product and process measurement for the purposes of control and improvement. Empirical data collection and use is not as thoroughly integrated into 9000-3 as in the CMM.

Despite the convincing argument of conformance with guidelines that will help win contracts, an organization must still consider the costs and benefits of process improvement, of which collecting and using empirical data is a vital part. These activities can be quite expensive, but there is strong evidence that organizations have found the effort worthwhile. Dion reports on process improvement at Raytheon, where measurement is an integral part of their efforts [8]. They claim to have measured a return of US$7.70 for every US$1 spent and to have evolved to CMM level three. McGarry reports on empirical data collection and use in NASA's Goddard Space Flight Center and states that measurement is "not cost prohibitive" [27]. He further mentions

[a]The European Community officially changed its name to the European Union on 1 January 1994.

that although collecting data may cost extremely little, processing and analyzing the collected data can add 10–15% to development costs on a single project. These analysis costs are arguably unavoidable because data that is collected but never analyzed almost certainly should never have been collected at all. McGarry concludes by noting that the benefits, which include improved manageability, improved productivity, reduced fault rates, and improved reuse rates, far outweigh the costs.

Any cost-benefit analysis must take into account two separate process-improvement cycles. One is the intra-project cycle, in which a single project improves its work processes during the course of a single project. The other is the inter-project (or intra-organization) cycle, in which an organization learns from projects and uses the captured knowledge to improve the performance of future projects. Data is collected and used in both cycles but the cost-benefit analyses and decisions about what data to collect may be very different.

One of the most difficult problems in empirical data collection is deciding what to measure. It is easy to begin collecting inexpensive-to-collect data such as lines of code or time-sheet information, but an unfocused effort wastes people's time because the data will rarely yield anything useful when analyzed. The exact answer about what data to collect cannot be found here or copied verbatim from any guideline, standard, or success story that does not address the specific goals of the organization. In addition to goals, the second important aspect in deciding what data to collect and when to collect it is an explicit, formal description (a model) of the organization's work processes. By creating, reviewing, and iteratively enhancing a model of the work processes, opportunities for measurement can be identified, people will clearly understand what will be measured, and the responsibility for data collection can be assigned appropriately. Furthermore, by integrating the data collection with the process model, measurement-based feedback and guidance can be offered to the people who perform the processes [7, 23, 33].

A goal-directed approach towards deciding what to measure and how to interpret the results of measurement is embodied in the Goal/Question/Metric (G/Q/M) paradigm [3, 4]. Building a data collection plan by using a goal-directed method such as G/Q/M is not a guarantee for success (see also [2, 6, 41]) but will encourage goal definition and assist in interpreting the collected data in the context of those goals. In the G/Q/M method, organizational goals are defined first. The goals are then refined into subgoals and questions while preserving traceability from the goals to the questions. Finally, metrics are chosen that will answer each question. The result is not a pure tree but a graph, because questions may refine a number of goals and similarly a single metric may answer a number of questions. A closely related method is ami, a European refinement of the G/Q/M paradigm, which offers a twelve-step approach towards implementing a data collection program in an organization [20]. Ami is similarly directed by goals but offers additional help for deriving metrics, implementing a measurement plan, and exploiting the collected data.

3. Measurement in SEEs

The systems discussed in this section are motivated by the approaches from the previous section. SEEs may implement various aspects of data collection and use. The benefits of automating data collection and other measurement activities are expected to include reducing the cost of collecting and using the data as well as increasing the validity of the collected data.

Many of the CASE and CAPE systems surveyed here work towards the ideal of integrating process definition, document construction, and measurement capabilities into a single system that can guide developers in their work activities. Figure 1 shows project work activities at three different abstraction levels, ranging from the coarse-grained activity of conducting a project to the fine-grained activity of invoking a tool on a computer. Guidance may be provided for activities at any of these abstraction levels. An ideal CAPE system might guide software developers in their choice of methods based on a process model or might give developers feedback about their work based on empirical data (the middle abstraction level in Fig. 1). It may be possible to mediate access to documents and tools stored in a computer through a process model and the use of empirical data, and much activity has focused on using an SEE to guide developers in their activities on the computer (the lowest abstraction level in Fig. 1). All of these long-range goals are highly subjective, but they will help the reader understand the approaches surveyed here.

I offer a simple scenario of how such an ideal system might be used. Assume that a project has completed a portion of a software design document, and in response, a design inspection must be conducted. Assume further that the ideal SEE has a representation of the project's work processes, the project's different design inspection methods, the criteria for applying each inspection method, and automatic data collection capability for the design document. The SEE could conceivably collect data from the design document automatically and,

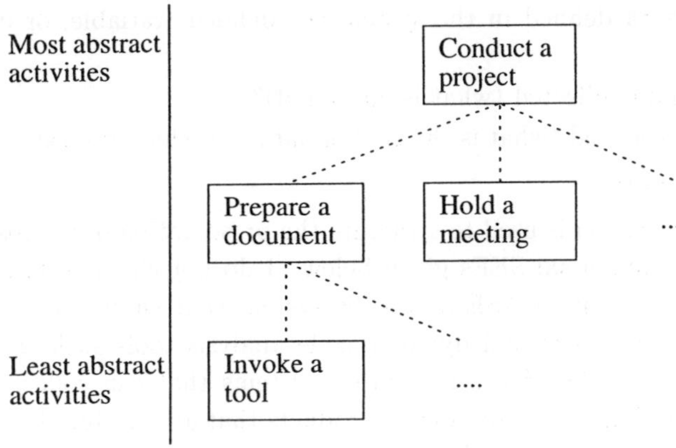

Fig. 1. Abstraction levels of work activities.

using that data, advise all persons responsible for conducting the inspection about the most applicable method for conducting it.

Next, I present an explanation of this survey's purpose, structured in the form of a goal, a set of questions, and a set of metrics [3, 4].

Goal. To survey CASE and CAPE systems for the purpose of characterizing them, with respect to their support for collection and use of measurement data, from the point of view of the researcher.

Questions. The following questions refine the goal.

1. What role does the SEE play in the software evolution process?
2. How sensitive is the system to work processes?
3. What role does measurement play in the system?

Metrics. Each of the previous questions is further refined into three metrics. These concrete items are not software metrics in the classical sense but help characterize the systems surveyed here.

1.1. Who is the target user of the system?
1.2. What software evolution activities are supported?
1.3. What construction tools does the system provide?
2.1. Are work processes assumed (implicit), fixed, or variably definable?
2.2. How are work processes modeled (what is the underlying enaction model)?

2.3. How are work process models used (understand, guide)?
3.1. How is data defined in the system (predefined, variable, or depends on tools)?
3.2. How is data collected (what is measured)?
3.3. How is data used (what is the goal of data use: characterization, feedback or planning)?

This G/Q/M schema is used to structure the presentation of the research prototypes and commercial SEEs given below. I do not claim to have surveyed every process-sensitive CASE or CAPE system that supports measurement, and do not cover static and dynamic code analysis tools such as code complexity analyzers. The focus here is on systems that can collect data from processes as well as collect data from products that are produced earlier in the software development life-cycle, such as requirements and design documents. The systems are presented in rough chronological order of publication.

Ginger. The Ginger system consists of a set of monitoring and feedback tools designed to record and improve programmer productivity during coding activities [21, 24, 25, 26]. In Ginger, the focus is on measurement of on-line activities, and data is collected from these activities unobtrusively and automatically. The data thus collected is evaluated and stored in a database, and real-time feedback is provided to the system's users.

Ginger assumes that users repeatedly perform a process consisting of editing the source code, saving the file, compiling the code into an object file, and running the object file to test the program. The data collected include calendar time, terminal time, number of command executions, and CPU time consumed. Additionally, the source-code file is sampled at five-minute intervals to capture the number of changes made since the last sample. The system treats changes as error removals, assuming that repeatedly editing the same file will result in a final, error-free version. Programmers who use the system can ask it to compare the data gathered from their work to historical baselines for their organization and thereby obtain immediate feedback about their work.

Despite Ginger's inability to define process models at will, the absence of a workbench-like capability forces its classification as a CAPE system. It was developed based on the UNIX operating system. Ginger's target user is the programmer (metric 1.1), only the coding activity is supported (1.2), and it provides only access to construction tools (1.3). The system assumes a fixed edit-compile-test process (2.1), is unable to model work processes (2.2), and does not use a model of work processes for any purpose (2.3). Data definitions are fixed in the system (3.1), data is automatically collected by watching the programmer's code file and commands (3.2), and Ginger uses the collected data to evaluate the process and give feedback based on predefined baseline models (3.3).

Teamwork/SD. The Teamwork/SD system[b] supports the Yourdon/Constantine software design process with editors for structure charts and module specifications. This system differs from most commercial CASE tools in that it collects values for a limited set of metrics to help designers evaluate the complexity and quality of their designs. Beyond module call-trees and many types of cross references, the system collects data for the following metrics: fan-out, tramp data couples, and tramp control couples.

Some of the advantages of design measurement that were discussed in [15, 37] are repeated here briefly. Based on the assumption that software structure and complexity affect the maintainability of the software, appropriate choices made in the design phase can have a large influence on later phases. Data values for structure and complexity metrics can easily be gathered from on-line design documents, such as the ones produced using the Teamwork/SD tool. One goal is to conduct redesign efforts promptly, in response to data gathered from the design, instead of much later when experience from the coding phase forces both the design and code to be rewritten.

The Teamwork/SD system is classified here as a CASE tool because it is unaware of any work processes and because of its construction tools. It is available both for personal computers and UNIX workstations. The target user is the software designer (metric 1.1), only the design process is supported (1.2), and the system offers a construction tool (an editor) for software designs (1.3). Teamwork/SD assumes a fixed design process (2.1), is unable to define work process models (2.2), and consequently does not use process models (2.3). Data definitions are fixed in the system (3.1), only the diagrams can be measured (3.2), and the data is only collected; use and interpretation of all data is left to the user (3.3).

Amadeus. The Amadeus system[c] is best characterized as a subcomponent of a CAPE system [39, 40]. The objectives of the Amadeus system include

[b]Available from Cadre Technologies Inc., 222 Richmond St., Providence RI 02903, USA.

[c]A commercial version is available from Amadeus Software Research Inc., 12 Owen Court, Irvine, CA 92715, USA. E-mail: amadeus-info@amadeus.com.

integrating measurement with process enactment by presenting an abstract interface for data collection, data analysis, and feedback. This abstract interface attempts to isolate the primitives needed for using empirical data in a CAPE system. As originally developed, Amadeus made extensive use of classification trees as its basis for data analysis and feedback capabilities [32].

The objective of presenting an interface which consists solely of functions for data collection and use means that the Amadeus system has no process modeling component, nor does it serve as a means to evolve any work product. Instead, by working in cooperation with a CAPE system, Amadeus can augment that CAPE system with sophisticated data collection and analysis capabilities. The CAPE system is required to deliver notifications of process events to Amadeus. Depending on the event and its internal status, the Amadeus system reacts to the events by triggering data collection, analysis, and feedback agents. The interpretation of each event must be specified by the system's users. Because of the system's independence, Amadeus is not restricted to any life-cycle phase, product, or process, and its data collection and use capabilities are fully configurable.

Internally, the Amadeus system is controlled by scripts. Each script consists of an event, a guard, and an agent. Briefly, when the event occurs, the guard is checked and the agent may be triggered. Events are defined in conjunction with the cooperating CAPE system, but are expected to include process events, product events, and clock events. A guard is simply any boolean expression defined using attributes of the events. The agent is any software tool or program that can be invoked on the host system.

Amadeus provides no construction tools of its own and does not support defining a process, so it is characterized here (albeit loosely) as a CAPE system. The target user of the system is the SEE builder (metric 1.1), any software evolution activity can be supported (1.2), and the system provides no construction tools (1.3). Work processes are assumed to be defined by the companion CAPE system (metrics 2.1, 2.2, and 2.3). The system can accept any data definition (3.1), collect any data that can be collected using on-line tools (3.2), and the data use is entirely up to the person who writes the scripts that control the system (3.3).

ES-TAME. The ES-TAME system is a prototype of an expert system to support the design process for real-time software [28, 29]. ES-TAME supports the design process in that the work processes to be performed can be represented in the system, the quality models for the products can also be represented, and these two sets of models can be integrated such that they function together. These models are linked based on metrics defined at each model's lowest refinement level. In addition, both products and processes can be measured. Although the prototype's knowledge is focused on real-time design methodologies, no design-related CASE tools are part of the system.

A sophisticated, highly structured framework supporting the Goal/Question/Metric paradigm ([3], also discussed earlier) is built into ES-TAME. The user can build a measurement plan in the form of a set of goals, questions, and metrics by using templates to write goals and then either selecting from a predefined set of questions and metrics or writing new questions and metrics. Reasoning on the part of the expert system is used primarily when constructing the measurement plans that are expressed as G/Q/M's. A rule-driven G/Q/M generator uses forward chaining to guess elements of the G/Q/M measurement plan under construction. The system is intelligent enough to ask the user for data and to look in existing quality models to obtain those data when possible.

Not only does the G/Q/M guide the representation of quality models in ES-TAME but the G/Q/M is also used to answer questions and interpret data collected from work products. When the user wants to evaluate a measurement plan, the system can automatically supply the user with data for those metrics where data exists. The system will further assist the user in answering the questions based on the metric values and interpreting the results in terms of the goals. Although work processes are modeled in this CAPE system, it is unclear how the system is made aware of progress made on the work represented therein.

The ES-TAME system is characterized here as a CAPE system because of its ability to model any process and the environment that the user works in to develop G/Q/M plans. It was developed principally on a personal computer. The system's target user is the real-time software designer (metric 1.1), the software design activity is the primary supported activity in the prototype (1.2), and although it provides no software construction tools (1.3), the system does provide an editor for writing G/Q/M plans. ES-TAME supports the variable definition of processes (2.1), work processes are defined using an object-oriented knowledge representation (2.2), and the process definitions are used to guide the user during work processes (2.3). Although the prototype system focuses on the design activity, it is completely flexible about defining data (3.1) and collecting data from on-line artifacts (3.2). In addition to using the data for feedback and improvement, metric capabilities in the system, especially the G/Q/M construction support, may be used for planning purposes (3.3).

JoYCASE. The JoYCASE system consists of editors for structured analysis and entity relationship diagrams, as well as tools that calculate values from those diagrams for Albrecht's function point metric, DeMarco's function bang metric, and Symon's Mark II function point metric [34, 35]. The assumption in JoYCASE is that these metrics correlate well with finished system size and therefore can be used to predict the resources needed to develop that system. A major objective of JoYCASE is to measure the size of various requirements documents objectively in the hope of estimating the effort and time needed to develop the software described by the requirements.

Values for the predefined set of three functional metrics are computed automatically from the structured analysis diagrams drawn using the JoYCASE system. The function point metric is computed using external input and output types, external inquiry types, and logical internal and interface file types. The function bang metric is also defined for structured analysis diagrams. Values for it are computed based on the complexity of data flows and the types of functions that process the data flows. The Mark II function point metric is a derivative of Albrecht's metric. Mark II treats the system as a collection of transactions, where each transaction is a combination of inputs, processes, and outputs, and emphasizes how data is used in those transactions. Figure 2 shows an excerpt from a report generated by the JoYCASE system for a diagram's function bang metric value.

There are several advantages to be gained by automating the calculation of values for the function point and function bang metrics. First, the cost of collecting the values is zero because the system does all the work. Second, traditional function point analysis is known to depend highly on the personnel performing the analysis, so automating these counts for a certain class of systems will yield reproducible and wholly objective data. Finally, these metrics are defined on work products which appear extremely early in the life-cycle. Because requirements documents are regularly noted to be the most influential as well as problem-causing documents in the software life-cycle, collecting objective data about them can be expected to be extremely useful for characterizing the requirements and improving an organization's processes of requirements definition; this is measurement for understanding rather than for prediction. The obvious caveat is that the connection between the requirements metrics predefined in the JoYCASE system and actual system size may

```
--------------------------------------------------------------------
DeMARCO'S FUNCTION BANG
--------------------------------------------------------------------
Spec: A:\EXAMPLES\YOURD-1
Date: 09.03.1994 Wed
Page: 1
--------------------------------------------------------------------
PRIMITIVE NUMBER AND NAME              SIZE       CORRECTED SIZE
          dataflow and size
--------------------------------------------------------------------
1     ENROLL CUSTOMER IN AGENCY         41          109.83
          initial-order            17
          agency-plan-respons       1
          dummy-31                  2
          dummy-1                  19
2     SEND INVOICES                     35           89.76
          dummy-2                  18
          INVOICES (unlabeled      17
....

3.5   ENTER ORDER                       67          203.21
          CUSTOMERS (unlabele       7
          INVOICES (unlabeled      17
          ORDERS (unlabeled)       14
--------------------------------------------------------------------
DeMARCO'S FUNCTION BANG =                           926.49
```

Fig. 2. Excerpt of a JoYCASE metrics report.

not be as strong as potential users of the system would like. These data will almost certainly require careful calibration for each new environment.

The JoYCASE prototype was developed for a personal computer and it is characterized here as a CASE system. The target user is the requirements engineer (metric 1.1), only the requirements analysis activity is supported (1.2), and the diagram editor is the construction tool provided by the system (1.3). The JoYCASE system is unaware of a life-cycle process (2.1) and can neither define nor use a process model (2.2, 2.3). The metrics are predefined (3.1), the data is collected from the diagrams upon request from the user (3.2), and the collected data is only given to the user; no evaluation or feedback is done in the system (3.3).

Provence. Provence is a system for monitoring and visualizing software development processes and uses advanced hooks into the file system of its host computer to do so [19]. Provence demonstrates how a number of special-purpose tools can be integrated with a process-sensitive system to form a CAPE system. Their process-sensitive system is Marvel, a rule-driven system for process representation and enaction [17]. Processes are monitored and enacted based on their representation as Marvel rules, and any work activity performed on the computer can be supported.

Provence focuses on visualizing process data. These data include process status and progress as well as process and product metric values. A special aspect of this system is the component called the 3D file system, which lets it monitor all accesses on certain files or in file system directories. This capability allows the system to collect data unobtrusively as well as to collect data from all tools that use the standard file system. From this capability, the Provence system derives a genuine openness and flexibility for collecting and using data from any on-line products.

The Provence system is characterized here as a CAPE system because it supports definition of a process and also because the system offers its users an environment in which they can work. It was developed for UNIX workstations. The target user is any software developer or manager (1.1), any software evolution activities can be supported (1.2), and it provides no construction tools nor access to tools (1.3). Provence allows a process to be variably defined (2.1), uses the Marvel strategy language to describe and enact processes (2.2), and uses process models to facilitate data visualization (2.3). Because the Provence system offers no support for defining metrics, the definition, collection, and use of data is left to the tools which it invokes (3.1, 3.2, 3.3).

Ceilidh. The Ceilidh system[d] is a quality control system for teaching students how to develop programs according to specifications and to quality standards [5]. Ceilidh (pronounced "cay-lee") offers measurement-based guidance for coding activities. Like all systems for measurement-based guidance, it is critically dependent on the models used as the baseline for comparison with the collected data. In the Ceilidh system, the baseline is based on a sample solution to the problem.

Students use Ceilidh to write, test, get feedback upon, and eventually submit their coding assignments to the instructor. The system automatically provides the students with feedback by compiling and testing the submitted assignment and by comparing the submitted source code and test results to established quality standards. Quality standards are set out in Ceilidh in terms of correctness (determined by testing), run-time efficiency of the program, and structure, complexity, and style of the source code. Figure 3 shows an example

[d]Available for anonymous ftp from host marian.cs.nott.ac.uk in directory/pub/ceilidh.

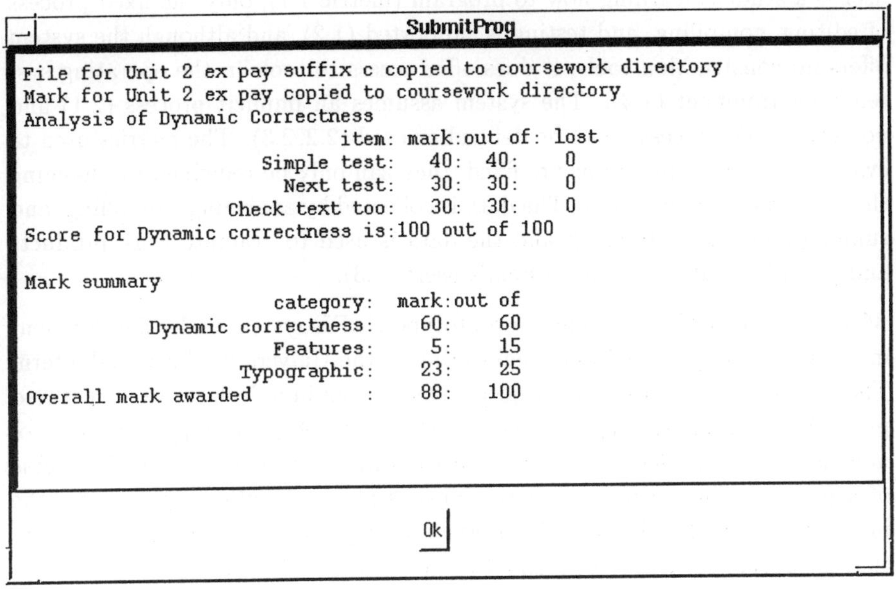

Fig. 3. Feedback provided by Xceilidh.

of the feedback provided by the system to students after they submit a solved exercise. Ceilidh additionally provides students with course notes, examples, program requirements, and access to editors, compilers, and test support.

Ceilidh's automatic assessment facility is responsible for grading the student's assignments. A necessary part of the assessment facility is a test oracle that determines whether output from student programs meets the specification or not. Regular expressions play a large role in matching the test results with the expected output, thereby lifting any requirements of specifying program output with the precision of what text must appear in what column. Test coverage tools are used to detect useless code in a student's program, static source code analyzers check complexity, and the UNIX tool *lint* is used to detect structural weaknesses.

Based on the system's lack of workbench-like tools, Ceilidh, like Ginger, is characterized here as a CAPE system for coding activities. But unlike Ginger, Ceilidh installations can define their own grading criteria. Ceilidh was developed for UNIX workstations and uses the X Window System. The target user is a student learning how to program (metric 1.1), only the fixed process of editing, compiling, and testing is supported (1.2), and although the system offers no construction tools, it does offer access to tools in the operating system's environment (1.3). The system assumes an implicit process (2.1) and no other work processes can be defined or used (2.2, 2.3). The metrics used to evaluate student's programs are fixed; they can only be redefined by changing the assessment engine (3.1). The data is collected by analyzing, compiling, and running code artifacts (3.2), and the data is used to evaluate work products and provide feedback to the system's users (3.3).

MVP-S. The MVP-S system is a prototype CAPE system under development in the work group for software engineering at the University of Kaiserslautern. The system executes explicit project plans written in a declarative, structured process modeling language named MVP-L [18]. A project plan consists of models of the products, processes, and roles that people assume in the course of a project. The system currently consists of an execution machine for the project plans and a developer's interface that presents a view of the project that is specific to the roles assumed by the software developers.

The difference between our system and many other CAPE systems is its focus on the use of measurement data to guide the enaction of processes. Using the modeling language, entry and exit criteria can be specified in terms of data collected from the processes and products in the environment. MVP-S also places special attention on the problems of collecting data by interacting with humans, a very different problem than collecting data from on-line products, such as diagrams or source code.

I characterize MVP-S as a CAPE system because of its awareness of processes and lack of tools. It was developed for UNIX workstations. The target user is any developer involved in evolving software products (metric 1.1), any software evolution activities may be supported (1.2), and the system provides no construction tools (1.3). MVP-S allows processes to be defined at will (2.1) using the MVP-L modeling language (2.2), and process models are used to plan and guide projects (2.3). Data can be defined variably (3.1), data may be collected both from on-line products and by querying users (3.2), and the data is used both to plan a project, by incorporating the values in the models, and to guide a project, by providing measurement-based guidance during enaction (3.3).

Table 1. Summary of system features.

	Metr. 1.1 Target user	1.2 Evol. act'y	1.3 Const. tools	2.1 Work proc.	2.2 Proc. def.	2.3 Proc. used	3.1 Data def.	3.2 Data coll.	3.3 Data used
CASE Systems									
JoYCASE	req. eng.	req. an.	editor	unaware	n/a	n/a	fixed	dgms.	charac.
Teamwork/SD	designer	design	editor	fixed	n/a	n/a	fixed	dgms.	charac.
CAPE Systems									
Ceilidh	student	coding	access	fixed	n/a	n/a	fixed	code	f'back
Ginger	pgmr.	coding	access	fixed	n/a	n/a	fixed	code	f'back
Amadeus	SEE bldr.	any	none	CAPE	CAPE	CAPE	var.	var.	var.
ES-TAME	designer	design	none	var.	kwn. rep.	guide	var.	var.	plan
Provence	s/w dev.	any	none	var.	Marvel	visual.	tools	tools	tools
MVP-S	s/w dev.	any	access	var.	MVP-L	guide	var.	var.	plan

Table 1 presents a summary of the systems that were surveyed in the paper. The columns correspond to the metrics explained in Sec. 3.

4. Summary and Conclusions

Many of the CASE and CAPE systems surveyed here struggle with the problems of integrating software construction, process definition, and measurement capabilities into a single system. A classification scheme first presented in [36] is expanded and used to classify the integration of these three elements in the surveyed systems. Figure 4 graphs construction against measurement components in SEEs. Figure 5 shows process definition against measurement capabilities. Finally, Fig. 6 charts construction against process definition facilities.

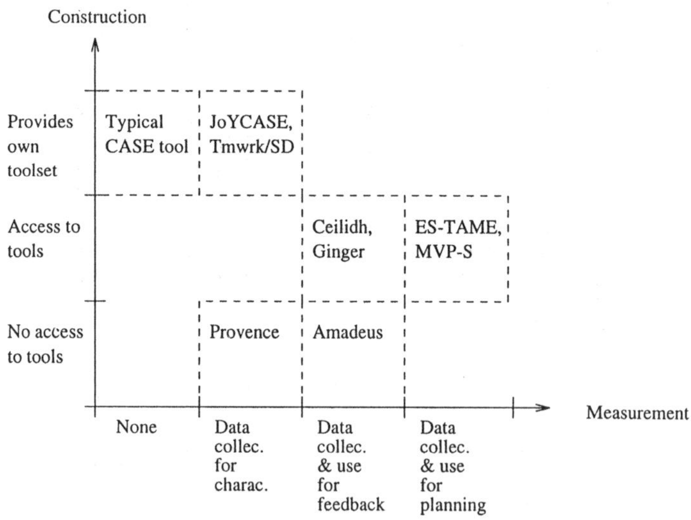

Fig. 4. SEE components: construction against measurement.

There is considerable progress towards the upper right regions in Figs. 4 and 5, meaning that systems will support both construction and measurement or both process definition and measurement, respectively. In Fig. 6, the upper right regions describe systems that provide their own tool sets and also support process definition. I believe that efforts to reach the upper right regions

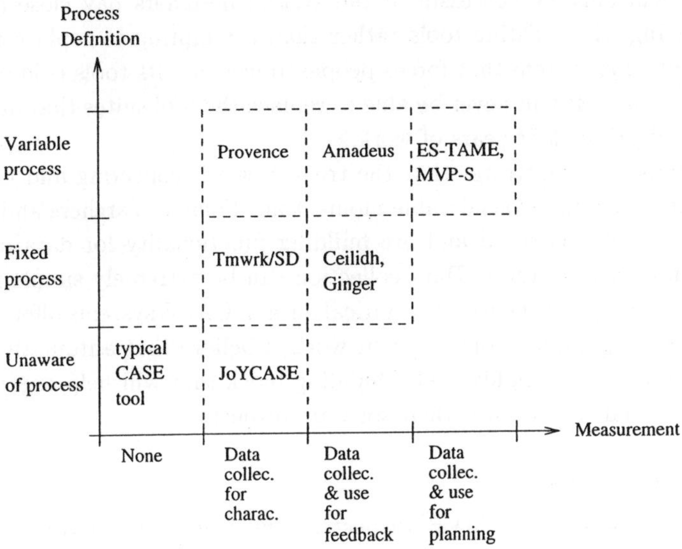

Fig. 5. SEE components: process definition against measurement.

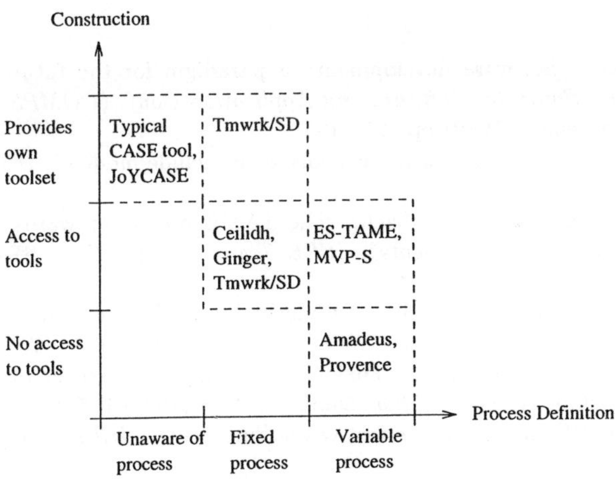

Fig. 6. SEE components: construction against process definition.

of Fig. 6 will only be successful if the system designers pay close attention to interfacing with existing tools rather than attempting to replace them. A process enaction system that forces people to use only its tools is highly questionable, because it will never be able to replace the tool suites that developers have assembled in their years of work.

This paper demonstrates that the trend towards collecting and using empirical data is gaining considerable momentum. Some researchers and vendors have recognized this trend and are building functionality for data collection and use into their systems. Data collection can be extremely simple for users of CASE systems and the use of empirical data in CAPE systems offer great opportunities for guiding people in their work. I believe that automatic support for measurement is a highly useful building block that will help organizations gain intellectual control over their software projects.

Acknowledgements

This work is part of the MVP Project at the University of Kaiserslautern, conducted under the direction of Professor H. Dieter Rombach. Discussions with Alfred Bröckers, Professor Rombach, and Martin Verlage improved the paper greatly.

References

1. V. R. Basili, "Software development: a paradigm for the future", *Proc. 13th Annual Int. Computer Software and Application Conf. (COMPSAC)*, Orlando, Florida (September 1989) pp. 471–485.
2. V. R. Basili, "GQM approach has evolved to include models", *IEEE Softw.* **11**, 1 (1994) 8.
3. V. R. Basili and H. D. Rombach, "The TAME project: towards improvement-oriented software environments", *IEEE Trans. Softw. Eng.* **SE-14**, 6 (1988) 758–773.
4. V. R. Basili and D. M. Weiss, "A methodology for collecting valid software engineering data", *IEEE Trans. Softw. Eng.* **SE-10**, 6 (1984) 728–738.
5. S. Benford, E. Burke, and E. Foxley," Learning to construct quality software with the Ceilidh system", *Softw. Quality J.* **2**, 3 (1993) 177–197.
6. D. N. Card, "What makes for effective measurement?", *IEEE Softw.* **10**, 6 (1993) 94–95.
7. B. Curtis, "Measurement and experimentation in software engineering", *Proc. IEEE* **68**, 9 (1980) 1144–1157.
8. R. Dion, "Process improvement and the corporate balance sheet", *IEEE Softw.* **10**, 4 (1993) 28–35.

9. Interactive Development Environments, *Software Through Pictures Integrated Structured Environment Release 4.2d*, 595 Market Street 10th Floor, San Francisco, CA 94105, USA (1992).
10. P. H. Feiler, "CASE and CAPE: conflict of interest", *Proc. 8th Int. Software Process Workshop*, ed. W. Schäfer (IEEE Computer Society Press, 1993) pp. 69–71.
11. C. Fernström, "Process WEAVER: adding process support to UNIX", *Proc. 2nd Int. Conf. Software Process* (IEEE Computer Society Press, 1993) pp. 12–26.
12. International Organization for Standardization, *ISO 9000: 1987 — Quality Management and Quality Assurance Standards — Guidelines for Selection and Use* (1987).
13. International Organization for Standardization, *ISO 9001: Quality Systems — Model for Quality Assurance in Design/Development, Production, Installation and Servicing* (1987).
14. International Organization for Standardization, *ISO 9000: Quality Management and Quality Assurance Standards, Part 3: Guidelines for the Application of ISO 9001 to the Development, Supply and Maintenance of Software* (1991).
15. S. Henry and C. Selig, "Predicting source-code complexity at the design stage", *IEEE Softw.* **7**, 2 (1990) 36–44.
16. W. S. Humphrey, *Managing the Software Process* (Addison-Wesley, 1989).
17. G. Kaiser, N. S. Barghouti, and M. H. Sokolsky, "Preliminary experience with process modeling in the MARVEL software development environment kernel", *Proc. 23rd Annual Hawaii Int. Conf. System Sciences*, Vol. II (IEEE Computer Society Press, 1990) pp. 131–140.
18. C. D. Klingler, M. Neviaser, A. Marmor-Squires, C. M. Lott, and H. D. Rombach, "A case study in process representation using MVP–L", *Proc. 7th Annual Conf. Computer Assurance (COMPASS 92)* (June 1992) pp. 137–146.
19. B. Krishnamurthy and N. S. Barghouti, "Provence: a process visualization and enactment environment", *Proc. 4th European Software Engineering Conf.*, eds. I. Sommerville and M. Paul. *Lecture Notes in Computer Science Nr. 717* (Springer-Verlag, 1993) pp. 451–465.
20. A. Kuntzmann-Combelles, "Quantitative approach to software management: the ami method", *Proc. 4th European Software Engineering Conf.*, eds. I. Sommerville and M. Paul. *Lecture Notes in Computer Science Nr. 717* (Springer-Verlag, 1993) pp. 238–250.
21. S. Kusumoto, K. Matsumoto, T. Kikuno, and K. Torii, "Ginger: data collection and analysis system", Technical Report SS 90–5, Osaka University, Toyonaka, Japan (1990).
22. C. M. Lott, "Process and measurement support in SEEs", *ACM SIGSOFT Softw. Eng. Notes* **18**, 4 (1993) 83–93.
23. C. M. Lott and H. D. Rombach, "Measurement-based guidance of software projects using explicit project plans", *Information and Software Technology* **35**, 6/7 (1993) 407–419.

24. K. Matsumoto, "A programmer performance model and its measurement environment", Ph.D. Thesis, Osaka University, Toyonaka, Japan (August 1990).
25. K. Matsumoto, K. Inoue, H. Kudo, Y. Sugiyama, and K. Torii, "Error life span and programmer performance", *Proc. 11th Annual Int. Computer Software and Application Conf.* (*COMPSAC*) (IEEE Computer Society Press, 1987) pp. 259–265.
26. K. Matsumoto, S. Kusumoto, T. Kikuno and K. Torii, "A new framework of measuring software development processes", *Proc. 1st Int. Software Metrics Symp.* (IEEE Computer Society Press, 1993) pp. 108–118.
27. F. E McGarry and R. Pajerski, "Towards understanding software — 15 years in the SEL", *Proc. 15th Annual Software Engineering Workshop*, NASA Goddard Space Flight Center, Greenbelt MD 20771 (November 1990).
28. M. Oivo, *Knowledge-Based Support for Embedded Computer Software Analysis and Design* (VTT Publication 68, 1990).
29. M. Oivo and V. R. Basili, "Representing software engineering models: the TAME goal-oriented approach", *IEEE Trans. Softw. Eng.* **18**, 10 (1992) 886–898.
30. M. C. Paulk, "Comparing ISO 9001 and the Capability Maturity Model for Software", *Softw. Quality J.* **2**, 4 (1993) 245–256.
31. M. C. Paulk, B. Curtis, M. Chrissis, and C. V. Weber, "Capability maturity model, Version 1.1", *IEEE Softw.* **10**, 4 (1993) 18–27.
32. A. A. Porter and R. W. Selby, "Empirically-guided software development using metric-based classification trees", *IEEE Softw.* **7**, 2 (1990) 46–54.
33. C. V. Ramamoorthy, W. T. Tsai, T. Yamaura, and A. Bhide, "Metrics-guided methodology", *Proc. 9th Annual Int. Computer Software and Application Conf.* (*COMPSAC*) (1985) pp. 111–120.
34. R. Rask, "Automating estimation of software size during the requirements specification phase", Ph.D. Thesis, University of Joensuu, Finland (November 1992).
35. R. Rask, P. Laamanen, and K. Lyytinen, "Simulation and comparison of Albrecht's function point and DeMarco's function bang metrics in a CASE environment", *IEEE Trans. Softw. Eng.* **19**, 7 (1993) 661–671.
36. H. D. Rombach, "The role of measurement in ISEEs", *Proc. 2nd European Software Engineering Conf.*, eds. C. Ghezzi and J. McDermid. *Lecture Notes in Computer Science Nr. 387* (Springer-Verlag, 1989) pp. 65–85.
37. H. D. Rombach, "Design measurement: some lessons learned", *IEEE Softw.* **7**, 2 (1990) 17–25.
38. D. Rugg, "Using a capability evaluation to select a contractor", *IEEE Softw.* **10**, 4 (1993) 36–45.
39. R. W. Selby, G. James, K. Madsen, J. Mahoney, A. A. Porter, and D. C. Schmidt, "Classification tree analysis using the Amadeus measurement and empirical analysis system", *Proc. 14th Annual Software Engineering Workshop*, NASA Goddard Space Flight Center, Greenbelt MD 20771 (1989).
40. R. W. Selby, A. A. Porter, D. C. Schmidt, and J. Berney, "Metric-driven analysis and feedback systems for enabling empirically-guided software development",

Proc. 13th Int. Conf. Software Engineering (IEEE Computer Society Press, 1991) pp. 288–298.

41. D. Weiss, "GQM plus heuristics better than brainstorming", *IEEE Softw.* **11**, 1 (1994) 8–9.

SYNTHESIZING METRICS IN SOFTWARE ENGINEERING AND KNOWLEDGE ENGINEERING

M. J. SHEPPERD
Department of Computing and Cognition, Bournemouth University, Talbot Campus, Fern Barrow, Poole, Dorset BH12 5BB, UK

D. C. INCE
Department of Computer Science, Open University, Walton Hall, Milton Keynes, MK7 6AA, UK

This paper examines the utility of much of the software metrics research that has been carried out in software engineering to problems in artificial intelligence. The paper first reviews the work that has been carried out and then makes a number of suggestions about how it could be transferred to the artificial intelligence arena — applying it in particular to expert system development. It concludes with a warning about using metrics in an off-the-shelf manner and describes one metric development method which can be used by workers in AI who wish to develop their own metrics.

1. Introduction

The last twenty-five years have seen a large increase in research into software metrics. This has taken place as a by-product of the elevation of software development into an engineering discipline. The major aim of software metrics researchers is to give software engineers the same level of predictive accuracy as, say, an automotive engineer or a civil engineer. For example, the automotive engineer, given the design of a car, is able to predict with accuracy the cost of manufacturing one car, given a particular batch run of cars. The analog of this in software engineering is to be able to predict the cost of a software project given metric values for factors such as the size of the product, the degree of tool support, the capability of the staff working on the project, and the application area for which the software is destined; or predict the development time of a module[a] given a metric which represents how complex it is. Before looking at the relationship between software engineering, artificial intelligence, and software metrication, a tutorial is first in order.

2. What is a Software Metric?

A software metric is a number. It is a number extracted from a process or product of a software project. Some examples of software metrics are:

- the number of decisions in a module;
- the number of executable lines of code in a system;
- the number of variables referenced in a module;
- the percentage of statements executed when a module is exercised with test data;
- the number of master files which are described in the system specification;
- the time taken to debug a module;
- the number of residual errors in a system after it has been released to customers;
- the cost of developing a system.

The ultimate aim of research in software metrics is to correlate one metric — known as a predictor metric — which can be extracted at a certain point in a project, with another metric that can be extracted later; this metric is known as a result metric.

Some examples of correlations in conventional projects are:

- the relationship between some measure of the functionality of a module, as expressed in its specification, and the amount of resource required to produce a correct version of the module,
- the relationship between the shape of the control flow of a module, and the amount of resource required to test that module. Some metrics such as the number of conditional branches may be a good numerical indicator of resource,
- the relationship between the complexity of the interface, in terms of calls on other modules, and the amount of resource required to understand and debug the module,

[a]In this paper the term *module* is used to represent a chunk of program code which can be called with control passing to the calling point after the module has completed its task. Typically, a module will be a subroutine, function, or procedure.

- the relationship between the number of global variables and their distribution and the amount of time required to understand the module,
- the relationship between the number of local variables in a module, and their pattern of access, to the amount of time required to understand a module,
- the relationship between the number of parameters in a module, and the amount of resource required to implement a correct version of the module.

Success in correlating metrics enables the project manager to exercise his or her monitoring and control functions [12]. To take a somewhat artificial example, the number of decisions in a module may be a major determinant of the amount of time that a programmer takes to understand the module: the larger the number of decisions the larger the number of processing paths, and hence the larger the amount of work that the module does and the more difficult it will be to understand. Given the number of decisions in a module the project manager can make decisions about the effort required for implementing the module and the amount of validation that should be applied.

Given this aim of predicting one metric from another, there are a number of uses of software metrics:

- To enable a project manager to predict vital data well in advance of receiving the actual values for the data. The classic example of this is project costing where, ideally, a project manager wants to know how much a software project will cost from a consideration of the system specification — or even an outline version of the system specification. Another less strategic example is the ability to predict the number of residual errors in a module based on a testing effectiveness metric measured as the percentage of branches executed by test data.
- To set numerical quality standards. For example, a common quality standard on many projects is to insist that a programmer tests a module to a particular percentage of structural coverage, usually 100% statement coverage and/or a high branch coverage — which could be as high as 95%.
- To judge competing software development methods and tools. Metrics could be used to judge the quality of software produced by differing techniques. For example, one could examine design metric values for modules generated by many of the structured methodologies that are currently available in order to select one for use within a company.
- To judge the performance of staff by examining the metric values of their work.

- To provide feedback on the quality of work to staff such as designers and programmers. For example, a CASE tool could be provided with a facility which displayed the metrics values of the designs produced by the user of the tool. These values would enable the user to pin-point those weak areas of a design which would lead to an abnormally high maintenance cost.

Because of the limited progress on software metrics that has been made a number of these uses are not yet feasible. For example, there is still not enough evidence that we can accurately predict one metric from another. However, we are at a stage where we can feel quite a high degree of confidence that certain high values of particular metrics drastically affect many activities on the software project. This means that the first use — prediction — really remains something for the future, although in the area of software costing there have been some advances [6], although it is still unclear for what categories of software and development costing these methods are effective [24]. However, our confidence in high levels of metric value leading to poor performance enables us to use metrics as a form of quality assurance standard.

The use of a metric to judge staff performance is not feasible for a number of reasons. First, metrics have not advanced sufficiently; thus, for both ethical and moral reasons it would be wrong to base judgements of staff performance on them. Second, even if we were more confident about software metrics, their use in judging performance would require, as a prerequisite, the staff who are being judged being told about what metrics are being used. It would be a relatively easy task for such staff to produce software with the sole aim of satisfying metrics limits, with other qualities such as correctness taking second place.

Employing metrics to judge methods and tools is potentially very useful. However, researchers have ignored this area in favor of basic research into causal relationships. However, once this research reaches maturity we would not be surprised to see metrics being used in this area.

This, then, is what a software metric is. The research that has been carried out in this area has, in the main, emanated from the United States. The bulk of this research has been concerned with product metrics: numerical values extracted from the products of a software project: requirements specifications, system designs and program code. However, there has also been a considerable amount of research into using metrics for software costing.

3. Product Metrics

Work has been carried out mainly on metrics which can be extracted from the products of the following activities: requirements specification, system design, detailed design and programming. Much of this work has examined program code; even those metrics which can be categorized as detailed design metrics or system design metrics have, in the past, been extracted from code written in languages such as JOVIAL, C, and Pascal. The reason for this concentration on programming code is purely pragmatic. Until comparatively recently, many software developers did not keep their designs in a computer-readable form. The only file-based product of a software project that was available for researchers was the program code. Consequently, even researchers who wanted to correlate features of system designs with other factors such as readability and maintainability, had to rely on program code in order to extract features such as the module calling hierarchy and the flow of information through modules.

3.1. *Code metrics*

The earliest research into software metrics was concerned with extracting numerical measures from program code. Indeed the majority of work carried out in the metrics arena can be lumped into this category. The metric family which has been most researched is that due to the American computer scientist Maurice Halstead [13, 14]. Halstead postulated that software obeyed natural laws in the same way that gasses obeyed natural laws, and that the existence of these laws enabled meaningful metrics to be extracted from program code.

Halstead's work has been used in predicting a wide variety of result metrics including residual bugs, readability and the effort required to produce a software module. Examples of this work can be found in [1, 9, 26, 27]. Unfortunately, this work has fallen into disrepute. There are a number of reasons for this. The original model used by Halstead was of small program development, primarily for early languages such as FORTRAN; it borrowed heavily on the controversial theories of the cognitive psychologist Stroud [35]; and the rules used for calculating the metric from counts of program features were not well-defined. Good accounts of the criticisms of the Halstead approach can be found in [8, 15].

However, what really makes code metrics, as a whole, not very useful is the fact that they can only be extracted late in a software project — well after a large amount of project resource has been expended, and when the project manager has very little scope for acting on the information given by these metrics.

3.2. *Detailed design metrics*

These metrics emerged during the mid-1970s and can be seen as a direct consequence of the rise of the structured programming movement. They measure the degree of unstructuredness of a module or a system — usually of a module. The most famous detailed design metric is cyclomatic complexity, invented by Thomas McCabe [29]. A number of subsequent metrics have been devised which attempt to overcome the problems with this original metric, for example, [30, 31]. These problems include the fact that a simple Boolean decision contributes as much to the metric value as a complex Boolean decision; and the fact that the metric ignores data aspects of a module, for example, it gives the same metric value irrespective of whether one variable is used in a module or 100 variables

In general, detailed design metrics have been proven to have some utility with regard to testing, for example, a high cyclomatic complexity value usually means that a module is rather difficult to test thoroughly. Because of the objections that researchers have made to cyclomatic complexity and other detailed design metrics a number of hybrid metrics have been developed. These metrics either give a single value based on an agglomeration of metric values for different features of a module or a program, or consist of a vector of values [16, 32].

There are major philosophical problems with these hybrid metrics. For example, assume we have a hybrid metric which has two components: one measuring control complexity and another measuring the complexity of the data accesses in a program or module. Given this metric what is one to make of a metric value of (12,88) for a module and one of (6,133) for another module? Obviously the first metric indicates that the first module has a higher control complexity, while the second indicates a higher data reference complexity— but which is the best module?

3.3. *System design metrics*

System design metrics are a comparatively recent phenomena. Their upsurge neatly corresponds to the massive increase in interest in both the United States and Europe in early software activities such as system design and requirements specification. Of all the categories of metrics outlined in this paper, system design metrics have the most utility.

A common theme running through system design metrics work is the measurement of a system design in terms of its coupling and cohesion. A good design being one which exhibits low coupling and high cohesion. Effectively, this means that a good system design will consist of modules which can be read in isolation, be changed without affecting very many other modules, can be easily tested in isolation, and can be integrated with few problems.

The classic work on system design metrics was carried out by Sallie Henry and Dennis Kafura. In effect, they measured the quality of a design in terms of the amount of information that flowed through modules in the design. This work is reported in [17, 18].

Another flavor of system design metric is due to Yau and Colofello who measured the quality of a design in terms of the ripple effect that occurs when a change is applied to the system corresponding to the design [38, 39]. A good design will result in change being localized, while a poor design will result in change rippling through a large number of the modules in a system.

Other notable work on system design metrics has used the shape of the module calling hierarchy to generate a metric value. Examples of this work can be found in [4, 40]. System design metrics are potentially of great use because they can be extracted at a relatively early stage in the software project — well before programming starts. They also have a huge potential for use during software maintenance where they can be used to measure the structural degradation that occurs when a system has been maintained for some time. The only prerequisite that is needed for system design metrics to be extracted is for an adequate system design notation to be available.

3.4. *Functional specification metrics*

Such metrics are extracted from the functional part of a system specification and are normally used for resource prediction or evaluating project productivity. Most of the metrics in this category are based on the work of Allen Albrecht at IBM [2], who devised a technique whereby the features of a system specification such as the number of master files and transaction files were used in an algebraic equation which gave the functional size of a system. This size, known as a function point count, was then used to predict resource utilization on a project by comparing it with past project resource utilization and function point counts. Albrecht's work was originally oriented toward information system projects, in particular, those which carried out batch processing. However, a number of recent improvements have been made to orient the metric towards transaction system development [36]. DeMarco has also developed a similar metric which can be used over a wide variety of projects [11].

3.5. *Metric trends*

There are a number of trends which can be discerned from the history of software metrics.

- Metrics that are available *early* in the software project offer the manager more leverage, thus, measures derived from specifications and designs are of particular value.
- *Structural* measures, for example, information flow between design units tend to be more powerful and widely applicable than metrics based upon highly detailed aspects of very specific development environments. For example, module interface metrics are usually of more utility than those that have as their major concern the column position of a semicolon.
- Metrics that are oriented to some properly articulated *measurement goal* are more successful than nebulous general complexity metrics that defy proper definition or validation due to the essentially metaphysical nature of terms such as *complexity*.
- It is clear that many research and industrial staff have used metrics in an off-the-shelf way, in that they have tended to use metrics without thinking about the purpose to which they are being put [23]. For example, a metric such as cyclomatic complexity has been used for readability, degree of testability, as a predictor of residual errors, and as a measure of maintainability.
- A more rigorous definition of an *underlying model* is another prerequisite for the successful application of a metric, for without a model it is unclear what a measurement means and whether a measurement value of, say, 129 is good, bad, or indifferent.
- The final point to emerge is that accurate prediction is difficult but that more modest goals may still yield useful results. For example, identification of anomalous components by means of the statistical technique of outlier analysis allows a project manger to effectively target scarce resources. Another type of application is to use metrics as triggers; so, for example, one

might subject modules with an information flow metric value that exceeds a certain predefined level to additional QA procedures which ensure the correctness of those modules. Another important measurement goal might be exploratory analysis where a particular process is poorly understood.

4. Software Engineering and A.I.

There has been recognition now for several years of the potential for a mutually beneficial relationship between knowledge-based system techniques and methods and more mainstream software engineering [33]. Of particular interest, however, to the main theme of this paper is the realization by KBS developers of their need for a more rigorous engineering approach; for example, Hickman [20] characterizes much of the present expert system development work as "prestructured development" where there is a need to borrow from the methods and tools of the more conventional software development community. In contrast, Kurbel [25] argues that given the highly iterative and evolutionary nature of KBS development, conventional engineering methods are not appropriate.

Arguably the truth lies some where between these two extremes — there are lessons that may be learnt from the software engineering community as there appear to be many parallels between current approaches to KBS development and software development of the 1960s — parallels such as little consideration of architectural issues and the future maintenance of the system and an overemphasis on implementational aspects. Possibly the point of contact between software engineering and artificial intelligence cultures comes in the area of prototyping.

The history of prototyping within software engineering has been an interesting one. In the 1960s prototyping was regarded as an undisciplined approach to software development, where the developer — for a number of possible reasons ranging from laziness to a genuine inability to capture user requirements — tended to produce a system with little, if any, specification and design documentation. Whatever the reason, early prototyping projects resembled many early expert system projects with their undisciplined use of the build-evaluate-modify paradigm.

The next stage in the development of prototyping was to employ the technique as an adjunct to requirements analysis [10]. This use of prototyping is almost certainly the most common. The main reason for this being the fact that it can be easily integrated into the conventional software engineering life-

life-cycle: as soon as prototyping is complete the developer can proceed with the activities of system specification, system design, and programming.

Prototyping in the late 1980s has been influenced by evolutionary development ideas such as those found in [22] and [41] and embodied in the classic work on evolutionary prototyping [7]. The proponents of evolutionary development point out that a software project very rarely fits the classic phase-oriented model but is more dynamic, with requirements changes impinging on a project almost up to the release date of the software.

Evolutionary prototyping involves the process of developing an initial prototype, and then using it as the basis for subsequent development. This subsequent development normally involves the optimization of the prototype with respect to response time, memory utilization, and file utilization [7]. This form of prototyping, which is dynamic and difficult to manage, has only really been made possible by the advent of fourth-generation programming languages and relational data base management systems. We feel that it is within the context of possible uses of metrics within an evolutionary prototyping paradigm that the greatest success in deriving metrics for expert system-based development lies.

It is worth stressing at this point that little work, if any, has been carried out on the application of software metrics in artificial intelligence-based software development. A major contribution in the area of expert systems methods is the KADS methodology [19] and its further development as CONCH [37]. The significant feature of these methods is their rejection of the *uncontrolled* prototyping approach and emphasis on modeling and documentation. Although design is recognized as a stage in these methods, the emphasis is principally upon problem solving and to a lesser extent performance issues. There is little emphasis of the relationship between architectural design decisions and future quality factors — numerical or otherwise — such as maintainability. Likewise, although there is discussion of quality assurance and the setting of QA objectives, this is not set up on a quantitative basis. Indeed, the only notable metrics work in the whole area is an attempt by Markusz and Kaposi to measure control flow complexity in Prolog programs [28]. Even so this work has not been subjected to rigorous validation, nor is it clear whether control flow is an entirely appropriate concept for nonprocedural software. Furthermore, it suffers from late availability, that is, you can only measure it once the software has been completed. Given this proviso, the remainder of this paper contains some suggestions for future use of metrics in artificial intelligence-based software projects.

5. Metrics and Costing

A major problem faced by both the developers of expert system software and developers who use evolutionary prototyping is that of resource estimation. In conventional software engineering projects where a system specification and outline design exist near the beginning of a project, staff charged with planning are able to identify the tasks of the project, assign a cost to each task, and total each task cost to produce a figure of developmental resources required.

Unfortunately, the luxury of having these documents is rarely granted to both the evolutionary prototype developer and the expert systems developer. In [7], a metrics-based technique is given for costing an evolutionary prototyping project. However, it suffers from two disadvantages. The first — which is relevant to expert system development — is that it requires some form of design notation. Second, in the early stages of the evolutionary prototyping project, it relies on an estimate of an estimate.

A better metrics-based approach to estimating may come from work carried out on the COCOMO cost model [5]. This technique is firmly rooted in the conventional software engineering culture. However, there is no reason why it cannot be adapted to artificial intelligence-based projects.

The user of COCOMO, typically a project manager, estimates a number of parameters for a future project. These parameters are then processed by a software tool which then produces a resource estimate which can be displayed on a phase-by-phase basis. The parameters that have to be provided are the estimated number of lines and the numerical values of factors called *cost drivers*. These cost drivers have been identified as major determinants of project cost and include the amount of tool support on a project, the degree of use of modern programming methods and the nature of a project, for example, whether it is a critical real-time project or a management information system project. COCOMO calculates a resource estimate for a future project by querying a database of past projects which contain the numerical values parameters and the real costs of the projects.

It is clear that COCOCMO cannot be applied directly to expert system projects; for example, it is not clear whether "lines of code" is a satisfactory input for such projects. However, the modifications to COCOMO would be relatively small as many of the cost drivers have analogs in expert system projects. The main problem lies with the lines of code parameter which could, for example, be replaced by the estimated number of production rules.

6. Structural Metrics

One of the potentially most useful families of metrics applicable to artificial intelligence software development are structural metrics. In order to illustrate this, consider a system built up from production rules. This is a simple example, but within it there are principles which can be transferred to other data structures.

One important facet that could be measured by metrics is the degree of interconnectivity in an expert system, that is, the extent to which the conditions of a production rules includes the conclusions of other production rules. There is an obvious relationship between metrics based on this idea and the performance of the program or shell which the rules drive. However, there is also a relationship between factors such as readability and maintainability and the density of rule references in a production system. In order to illustrate this, consider a production which contains conditions that are conclusions of other rules which also contain conditions that are, in turn, conclusions of other rules. The degree of effort required to understand the original rule is much higher than if it just contained atomic conditions. A metric based on the degree and depth of nesting of these conditions could be used in a number of ways.

- To pinpoint areas of the expert system that need to be restructured.
- To guide the programmer as to which, conflict resolution strategy to use.
- To direct the tester towards those areas of the expert system which require extensive testing. Obviously, production rules which contain atomic conditions on the left-hand side require little checking while a production rule which gives rise to a large degree of nesting will need to be demonstrated to an expert quite thoroughly.
- To provide further guidance on upgrades. Expert systems, like conventional systems are not static and require change as user requirements change. Thus, a developer with limited resources for an upgrade and two possible upgrade paths could determine which one should be taken by examining the metric values of the areas of the expert system to be changed. An upgrade which requires change to parts of the expert system that have low metric values, and hence, consume a small amount of resources would be applied, rather than an upgrade to an area with high values. Obviously this is just one factor

used by a project manager when deciding on an upgrade strategy, another is the importance of the reasons for a particular change. Nevertheless, metric information would be an important component to the information used by a manager who controls the upgrade process.

- To provide information about whether an expert system can be modified as it is, or whether a partial or full reimplementation is necessary. There comes a time when all software products — irrespective of whether they are conventional products or artificial intelligence-based products — when the structure of a product has degraded to the point where resources required for further modification may be prohibitively large. Metrics information about the complexity of the production rules would provide some quantitative evidence which would enable a project manager to determine whether a system should be scrapped and development started anew, or further modification carried out.

Many of these uses of metrics are those which could be applied to evolutionary prototyping projects. For example, the use of complexity metrics to pinpoint parts of a system which need to be restructured is needed on such projects because the prototyping process tends to concentrate on delivering the prototyped product quickly with considerations of architecture playing little, if any, in the development process.

7. Growth Metrics

A problem faced by staff who carry out evolutionary prototyping and those involved in expert system development concerns the process of monitoring the growth of a prototype. A manager in charge of a software project is rightly obsessed with progress on the project. The manager of a conventional software project has a number of devices which provide help in the monitoring process. For example, a project plan will specify a number of milestones which correspond to important events on a project such as the delivery of the system design or a user manual. The timing of the achievement of these milestones helps in judging the progress of a project. The manager of the expert systems or evolutionary prototyping project has very little information to aid the monitoring process. This is because much of the resources expended on such projects are consumed by the activities of building, modifying and evaluating an expert system or evolutionary prototype.

Hence, there is a need for some metric which enables the project manager to keep track of progress. Simple metrics such as the number of production rules currently extant would be inadequate, since an expert system could have changed quite drastically and yet the number of production rules could have remained the same. What is needed is some metric which provides a measure of the degree of difference in the code of an expert system. This would enable the project manager to:

- monitor whether the knowledge elicitation process was being carried out smoothly. For example, poor performance by a knowledge engineer might result in large metric values for the difference between the versions of an expert system which are generated in a project.
- track convergence towards a final system. A project manager faced with a trajectory of metric values which was decreasing would be able to predict with some confidence when the final version of an expert system would be ready.
- monitor whether particular parts of an expert system are modified frequently because that knowledge area is fuzzy or poorly defined. This enables the manager to make decisions concerned with allocating extra resources to the area.

The area relevant to change metrics is that of dynamic programming. This branch of mathematics is now exceptionally well researched and there are a number of documented algorithms in existence which are able to take two descriptions and provide a numeric value of the difference between them. Dynamic programming has been used in a wide variety of application areas such as molecular biology, geology, archeology, and the recognition of sounds, where the objects were molecules, mineral sites, artefacts, and sound recordings [34].

There has been a little work carried out in using dynamic programming methods in order to track the growth of a prototype produced in an evolutionary prototyping environment, primarily as an aid in determining whether the evaluation process was proceeding smoothly [21]. There is no reason why dynamic programming cannot be used to evaluate the difference between linear forms of representations of expert systems such as production rules or AND/OR graphs.

8. The Development of Metrics

One of the problems—alluded to previously in this paper—with the use of metrics is that industrial users tend to take an off-the-shelf attitude towards their use on a project. In effect, they pick one well-known metric and hope that it works. The aim of this section is to caution against this, and outline a more goal-oriented method for devising metrics for both a company and the software projects it undertakes. The method, which is suitable for artificial intelligence-based metrics is due to Victor Basili and his co-workers at the University of Maryland [3]. The method is known as the Goal Question Metric method (GQM).

The main starting point in GQM is a goal. Any metric extracted in a project must reflect some purpose, and the first thing that someone who wishes to use metrics has to do is to ask some questions about what the reason for gathering metrics is.

Once the goals have been decided the next stage is to ask a number of questions which clarify the goals (the Q part of GQM). Most goals tend to be expressed in nebulous terms and the questions enable staff to focus on some metrics. For example, a company may wish to employ a metric to satisfy the goal that their projects deliver better expert systems through more thorough validation with human experts. A number of questions suggest themselves from this:

- What sort of thoroughness is implied in the question?
- What is meant by the term "better"?
- Do the deficiencies that are left in a system through poor validation arise from poor performance on a particular activity?
- How can we identify deficiencies which remain in a system that have arisen from poor validation with the expert?

Once these questions have been answered the next stage is to identify the metrics which are important. Let us assume that the company, who has asked the above questions, has identified the fact that the vast majority of errors that emerge during operation are due to inadequate coverage of productions: that knowledge engineers have inadequately tested certain combinations of production rules. One metric which might be identified as helping to reduce such problems is the condition coverage achieved by a programmer: that if every production rule or some combination of production rule conditions that was exercised in a module was executed for its true and false values, then there would be a considerable reduction in the number of errors from validation.

The next stage is to identify a hypothesis or a set of hypotheses which can be tested in the developer's projects. Let us assume that a possible hypothesis is this.

> That by insisting on a certain percentage coverage we will reduce the number of errors due to inadequate validation by $x\%$.

Once the hypothesis has been derived the next stage is to plan the measurement process on some sample projects which attempt to validate the hypothesis. For example, this might involve for the testing example, activities such as writing a small software tool which tracked condition coverage, modifying test documentation to include details of condition coverage, introducing an extra procedure for those staff charged with fielding errors from customers, and providing resources to track down the source of the errors.

Once the measurement process has been planned, the next stage would be to collect the data. With the example used here this would mean collecting coverage percentages and defect data identified as being due to inadequate validation. Once this data is collected the next stage is to use statistics to validate it. The statistics would be used to check out the hypothesis. Sometimes the hypothesis has a high degree of truth in it, after all it is conjectured by experienced staff, but it may need some amendment.

Eventually, after trial and error, the developer will either validate the hypothesis or a variant. The final stage, then, is to apply the metric to all future projects. For example, knowledge engineers on future projects would be directed, via a standard, to provide evidence that their rule-based tests have covered $x\%$ of the true and false outcomes of the conditions in a production.

The stages in this process of metrics identification and eventual application in the GQM method are:

- the definition and clarification of goals,
- the posing of questions in order to make the goals clearer,
- the derivation of metrics,
- the identification of hypotheses which involve these metrics,
- the planning of the measurement process,
- the collection of data from the measurement process,
- the validation of the data,
- the analysis of the data,
- the application of the derived metrics on future projects.

It is worth stressing that this is rarely a strictly linear process. For example, the posing of questions often modifies the goal and the analysis of the data often results in the modification of the hypotheses. Nevertheless, it forms a useful way of developing metrics which can be adopted by developers of any type of system and which can lead to considerable process improvements.

9. Summary

This article has, of necessity, been somewhat speculative. The reason for this is that software metrics is a software engineering phenomenon which has only reached maturity after a large number of years of quality assurance experience on conventional software projects. Concern with the management and quality assurance aspects of expert systems technology is still very much a minuscule component of research and development in artificial intelligence. However, we hope that in this paper we have suggested some uses of software metrics that can be applied even in an expert system project which has few formal quality assurance mechanisms and little project management. It is important to point out that with the exception of the COCOMO technique the metrics which we present are analogous to program code metrics.

References

1. F. Akiyama, "An example of system software debugging", *Proc. IFIP Congress* (1971) pp. 353–358.
2. A. J. Albrecht and J. R. Gaffney, "Software function, source lines of code, and development effort prediction: a software science validation", *IEEE Trans. Softw. Eng.* **9**, 6 (1983) 639–648.
3. V. R. Basili and H. D. Rombach, "The TAME project: towards improvement-oriented software environments", *IEEE Trans. Softw. Eng.* **14**, 6 (1988) 758–773.
4. G. Benyon-Tinker, "Complexity models in an evolving large system", *Proc. ACM Workshop Quantitative Models* (1979) pp. 117–127.
5. B. Boehm, *Software Engineering Economics* (Prentice Hall, 1981).
6. B. Boehm, "Software engineering economics", *IEEE Trans. Softw. Eng.* **10**, 1 (1984) 4–21.
7. J. Connell and L. Brice Shaffer, *Structured Rapid Prototyping* (Yourdon Press, 1989).
8. N. S. Coulter, "Software science and cognitive psychology", *IEEE Trans. Softw. Eng.* **9**, 2 (1983) 166–171.
9. B. Curtis *et al.*, "Measuring the psychological complexity of software maintenance tasks with the Halstead and McCabe metrics", *IEEE Trans. Softw. Eng.* **5**, 2 (1979) 96–104.
10. P. Dearnley and P. Mayhew, "In favour of systems prototypes and their integration into the systems development cycle", *Comput. J.* **26**, 1 (1983) 36–42.

11. T. de Marco, *Structured Analysis and System Specification* (Yourdon Press, 1978).
12. T. de Marco, *Controlling Software Projects Management, Measurement and Estimation* (Yourdon Press, 1982).
13. M. H. Halstead, *Elements of Software Science* (Elsevier - North Holland, 1977).
14. M. H. Halstead, "Advances in software science", in *Advances in Computers*, ed. M. Yovits (Academic Press, 1979).
15. P. G. Hamer and G. D. Frewin, "M. H. Halstead's software science — a critical evaluation", *Proc. 6th Int. Conf. Software Engineering* (1982) pp. 197–206.
16. W. J. Hansen, "Measurement of program complexity by the pair (cyclomatic complexity, operator count)", *SIGPLAN Notices* **13**, 3 (1978) 29–33.
17. S. Henry, "Software metrics based on information flow", *IEEE Trans. Softw. Eng.* **7**, 5 (1981) 510–518.
18. S. Henry and D. Kafura, "The evaluation of systems' structure using quantitative metrics", *Software Practice and Experience* **14**, 6 (1984) 561–573.
19. F. Hickman *et al.*, *Analysis for Knowledge-based Systems* (Ellis-Horwood, 1989).
20. L. J. Hickman, "Towards a convergence in knowledge-based and conventional software engineering: tools, methods and techniques", *Proc. BCS/IEE Conf. Software Engineering: Software Engineering 90* (1990) pp. 161–181.
21. D. C. Ince, "Monitoring the growth of prototypes during software development", Technical Report 3, ESPRIT Project MUSE report (1989).
22. D. C. Ince and S. H. Hekmatpour, *Software Prototyping, Formal Methods and VDM* (Addison-Wesley, 1988).
23. D. C. Ince and M. J. Shepperd, *Derivation and Validation of Software Metrics* (Oxford University Press, 1993).
24. C. F. Kemerer, "An empirical validation of software cost estimation models", *Commun. ACM* **30**, 5 (1987) 416–429.
25. K. Kurbel, "An integrated approach to expert system development, project organization and project management", *Proc. BCS/IEE Conf. Software Engineering: Software Engineering 90* (1990) pp. 271–281.
26. L. T. Love, "An experimental investigation of the effect of program structure on program understanding", *SIGPLAN Notices* **12**, 3 (1977) 105–113.
27. L. T. Love and A. B. Bowman, "An independent test of the theory of software physics", *SIGPLAN Notices* **12**, 11 (1976) 42–49.
28. Z. Markusz and A. A. Kaposi, "Complexity control in logic-based programming", *Comput. J.* **28**, 5 (1985) 487–495.
29. T. J. McCabe, "A complexity measure", *IEEE Trans. Softw. Eng.* **2**, 4 (1976) 308–320.
30. G. J. Myers, "An extension to the the cyclomatic measure of program complexity", *SIGPLAN Notices* **12**, 10 (1977) 61–64.
31. G. Oulsnam, "Cyclomatic numbers do not measure complexity of unstructured programs", *Inf. Process. Lett.* (December 1979) pp. 207–211.
32. E. Oviedo, "Control flow, data flow and program complexity", *Proc. COMPSAC 80* (1980) pp. 146–152.

33. D. Partridge, "Artificial intelligence and software engineering. A survey of possibilities", in *The Software Life Cycle*, eds. D. Andrews and D. C. Ince (Butterworth Scientific, 1990) pp. 90–94.
34. D. Sankoff and J. B. Kruskal, eds., *Time Warps, String Edits, and Macromolecules: The Theory and Practice of Sequence Comparison* (Addison-Wesley, 1983).
35. J. M. Stroud, "The fine structure of psychological time", *Annals of the New York Academy of Sciences* (New York Academy of Sciences, 1966) pp. 623–631.
36. C. R. Symons, "Function point analysis: difficulties and improvements", *IEEE Trans. Softw. Eng.* **14**, 1 (1988) 2–11.
37. R. M. Taylor, "CONCH: a life-cycle model of knowledge-based systems development", *Proc. BCS/IEE Conf. Software Engineering: Software Engineering 90* (1990) pp. 282–301.
38. S. S. Yau and J. S. Collofello, "Some stability measures for software maintenance", *IEEE Trans. Softw. Eng.* **6**, 6 (1980) 545–552.
39. S. S. Yau, J. S. Collofello, and T. M. MacGregor, "Ripple effect analysis of software maintenance", *Proc. COMPSAC 78* (1978) pp. 60–65.
40. B. H. Yin and J. W. Winchester, "The establishment and use of measures to evaluate the quality of software designs", *Proc. ACM Software Quality Assurance Workshop* (1978) pp. 45–52.
41. P. Zave, "The operational versus the conventional approach to software development", *Commun. ACM* **27**, 2 (1984) 104–118.

UNDERSTANDING SOFTWARE PRODUCTIVITY

WALT SCACCHI

Information and Operations Management Department,
University of Southern California, Center for Software Engineering,
Los Angeles, CA 90089-1421, USA

What affects software productivity and how do we improve it? This report examines the current state of the art in software productivity measurement. In turn, it describes a framework for understanding software productivity, some fundamentals of measurement, surveys empirical studies of software productivity, and identifies challenges involved in measuring software productivity. A radical alternative to current approaches is suggested: to construct, evaluate, deploy, and evolve a knowledge-based "software productivity modeling and simulation system" using tools and techniques from the domain of software process engineering.

1. Overview

What affects software productivity and how do we improve it? This is a concern near and dear to those who are responsible for researching and developing large software systems. For example, Boehm [10] reports that by 1995, a 20% improvement in software productivity will be worth US$45 billion in the U.S. and US$90 billion worldwide. As such, this report examines the current state of the art in understanding software productivity. In turn, this report describes some fundamentals of measurement, presents a survey of studies of software productivity, identifies variables apparently affecting software productivity, and identifies alternative directions for research and practice in understanding what affects software productivity.

From the survey, it is apparent that existing software productivity measurement studies are fundamentally inadequate and potentially misleading. Depending on how and what indicators of software productivity are measured, it is possible to achieve results that show that modest changes in software development technologies lead to substantial productivity improvements (e.g., 300% in 5 years), while major changes to new technologies can lead to little productivity improvement. Different measurement strategies can show an opposite trend. In short, how and what you measure determines how much productivity improvement you see, whether or not productivity is actually improved.

This report advocates a radical alternative to current approaches to measuring and understanding what affects software productivity: to construct, evaluate, and deploy knowledge-based *software productivity modeling and simulation systems.* Accordingly, effort should be directed at developing a knowledge-based system that models and symbolically simulates how software production occurs in a given project setting. Such a modeling facility could be used to simulate software production under various product requirements, development processes, project settings, and computing resource conditions. It could also be used to incrementally capture information about the production dynamics of multiple software projects and thus improve the breadth of its coverage over time. As a result, this modeling technology could be used to articulate and update a computational knowledge-based "corporate memory" of software production practices.

The potential payoff of such technology is substantial. This technology provides a vehicle for delivering practical feedback that software developers and managers can use prior to and during a development project to help identify what might improve their productivity. Such a knowledge-based technology would enable project managers, developers, or analysts to query a model, conduct 'what if' analysis, diagnose project development anomalies, and generate explanations about how certain project conditions affect productivity. Such capabilities are not possible with current productivity measurement technologies.

Overall, this examination of software productivity primarily focuses on the development of large-scale software systems (LSS). LSS refers to delivered software systems developed by a team of developers, intended to be in sustained operation for a long time, and typically representing 50K–500K+ source code statements. The choice of LSS is motivated by economic and practical considerations. LSS are expensive to develop and maintain so that even modest software productivity improvements can lead to substantial savings. For example, it is reasonable to assume that 10,000 lines of code may cost a development organization US$100,000–250,000. For larger systems in the range of 50,000 to 250,000 lines of code, the cost may climb by as much as a factor of 4–25. In turn, it is reasonable to assume that software maintenance costs over the total life of the system dominate software development costs by a factor of 2–10. Small-scale programming productivity measurement often reveals more than *an order of magnitude variation* for different people, different programs, or both [18, 19], while large-scale programming efforts (with large staffs) can mitigate some of this variance.

An outline of the remainder of this report follows. Section 2 provides a brief exposition of the science of measurement. This section serves to identify some fundamental concerns in evaluating software productivity measures. Section 3 provides a select survey of studies that attempt to identify and measure what affects software productivity. The results of this survey are then summarized in Subsec. 3.14 as a list of software projects attributes that contribute to productivity improvement. These three sections set the stage for Sec. 4 which provides a discussion of the measurable variables that appear to affect software productivity. Section 5 follows with a new direction for research into identifying what affects software productivity, and how to improve it. We summarize our conclusions and the consequences that follow from this endeavor.

2. Notes on the Science of Measurement

Measurement is ultimately a quest for certainty and control: certainty in understanding the nature of some phenomenon so as to control, influence, or evaluate that phenomenon. In this paper, the phenomenon under study is *software production:* from system inception through delivery, operation, and support. Accordingly, we want to understand how software is produced, how to measure its production, and ultimately, how to positively influence or control the rate of its production. Curtis [18] provides an appropriate background on some fundamental principles involved in measuring software production characteristics, including measure validity and reliability, as well as instrumentation and modeling issues.

A desire to measure software production implies an encounter with the process of systematic or scientific inquiry. This implies the need to confront fundamental problems such as the role of measurement in theory development, hypothesis testing and verification, and performance evaluation. It also implies understanding the relationship between measurement and instrumentation — the artifacts employed to collect/measure data on the phenomenon under study. Instrumentation in turn raises questions on how to simplify or make trade-offs in:

- convenience of data collection versus cost of alternative instrumentation, collection, or sampling strategies;

- ease of rendering or displaying the results of data analysis for different audiences (e.g., internal management presentations versus journal publication);
- how to handle (or delete) anomalous data collected with survey instruments;
- use of collected data to monitor, evaluate, and intervene in the phenomenon under study;
- developing a narrative, diagrammatic, or operational abstraction of the phenomenon that is the source of the data collected.

Other fundamental concerns on the use of measurements include how to account for the influence of unmeasured units, the uniformity and consistency of measured units, how to rationalize the construction of composite measures, and how to rationalize measurement scales and normalizations. All of these concerns must be addressed in developing and sustaining an effort for measuring software production.

As such, what types of measures are appropriate for understanding software productivity? Productivity in most studies inside and out of the software world is usually expressed as a *ratio* of output units produced per unit of input effort. This simple relation carries some important considerations: for example, that productivity measures are comparable when counting the same kind of outputs (e.g., lines of source code) and inputs (person-months of time). Likewise, that a software development effort with productivity $2X$ is twice as productive as another effort whose productivity is X. Therefore, how outputs and inputs are defined are critical concerns if they are to be related as a ratio-type measure. As will become apparent through the survey that follows, other measure types — nominal, ordinal, and interval — are also appropriate indicators to characterize the variables that shape software productivity.

In the next section, a survey of studies of software productivity measurement shows there is often a substantial amount of difference with respect to the degree of rigor and the use of accepted analytical methods.

3. A Sample of Software Productivity Measurement Studies

A number of researchers have sought through empirical investigations to determine whether some software development attribute, tool, technique, or some combination of these has a significant impact on software production. These studies primarily focus on the development of LSS. Twelve major software productivity measurement studies are reviewed including those at IBM, TRW, NASA, and ITT, as well as at international sites. In addition, a number of other theoretical and empirical studies of programmer productivity, cost-benefit analysis, software cost estimation, and a software productivity improvement program are reviewed. Together, these studies provide a loosely-grounded basis for identifying a number of project characteristics that affect software productivity.

3.1. *IBM federal systems division*

Walston and Felix [56] conducted the classic study in this area. The authors state that a major difficulty arises in trying to identify and measure independent variables that can be used to estimate software development productivity, cost, and size. For example, they measured software productivity in terms of number of lines of code produced per person-hour. However, staff time was measured by the duration of the complete development project, rather than just the coding phase. Thus, we have no information as to the percentage of each measured project's effort that was dedicated to code production versus other necessary development activities. This omission tends to distort the results of their analysis.

3.2. *IBM DP services organization*

Albrecht [2, 3] developed the "function point" measure to compare the productivity in 24 projects that developed business applications. A function point is a composite measure of a number of program attributes including the number of inputs, outputs, function calls, file accesses, etc., that are multiplied by weighting factors then added together. These systems Albretch examined ranged in size from 3K to 318K lines of code written in either DMS, PL/1, or COBOL and developed over a five year period (1974–1978). Albrecht claims that over this period, software productivity, as measured with function points, increased 3 to 1. He finds that developers using DMS (a database management system language) are more productive than those writing in PL/1, who in turn were more productive than those writing COBOL. The application systems developed tended to be increasingly interactive (versus batch) overtime, accessing large data files/databases to produce reports. Also, during the five-year period, developers progressively began to practice structured coding, top-down implementation, and HIPO documentation. Such development techniques would seem to lead to more function points appearing in source code. That is, poorly structured code will tend to have fewer functions points than well-structured code conforming to the same specification. Thus, structured code can produce a higher function point measure, and therefore appear to be produced more productively.

But a number of confounding factors appear in Albrecht's results which undercut the validity of his reported productivity improvement claims. For example, his formula for computing function point values incorporate weighting multipliers which he reports produced reliable results. However, he does not discuss how these weights were determined, or how to determine them when other programming languages and software applications are to be measured. He also indicates that as department manager, he instructed his program supervisors to collect this function point data. To some extent then, his supervisors were encouraged to have their programs developed in ways that would lead to more function points produced per unit of effort. However, it is unclear whether the function point technique works equally well on nonbusiness application systems that do not rely on accessing large files, retrieving selected data, performing some computations on the data, and producing various reports. Thus, it is unclear whether the 3 to 1 productivity improvement that Albrecht claims is due to:

a. shifts in the choice of programming language to those that produce more favorable measures,
b. alternative program development techniques,
c. choice of multiplier weights,
d. management encouragement for collecting data that substantiates (and rewards) measured improvement.

3.3. *Equitable life organizations*

Behrens [5] also utilizes Albrecht's function point measures to compare software productivity in 25 application system projects developed in various life insurance companies from 1980 to 1981. His results are consistent with Albrecht's in supporting the contention that project size, development (computing) environment, and programming language impact software productivity. In particular, he finds that small project teams produce source code with more function points than large teams in a comparable amount of time. He also finds that developers working on-line are more productive than those working in a batched computing environment. We can also observe that in large projects, software runs tend to become more batch-like as their size grows, and the amount of computing resources they require grows.

3.4. *TRW defense systems group*

Boehm [9, 12] sought to identify avenues for improving software productivity based primarily on TRW's Software Cost Estimation Program (SCEP). This program served as an aid in developing cost estimates for competitive proposals on large government software projects. The program estimates the cost of a software project as a function of program size expressed in delivered source instructions and a number of other cost drivers. Experience with SCEP in turn gave rise to the development of the COCOMO software cost estimation model presented in [9]. Boehm recognized that software cost drivers are effectively the inverse of productivity (or "benefit") drivers. He found, for example, that personnel/team capability and product complexity had the greatest affect on driving software costs and productivity. Thus, high staff capability and low product complexity lead to high productivity/low cost software production. Conversely, low staff capability and high product complexity similarly imply low productivity/high cost software production. Through his experience with these cost estimation models, Boehm was able to develop quantitative support for the relative contribution of different software development characteristics that affect software cost and productivity.

3.5. *Australia-70 study*

Lawrence [39] conducted a study of 278 commercial applications developed in 23 medium-to-large organizations in Australia. The organizations and applications studies included those in government agencies, manufacturing and mining concerns, and banking and insurance firms. He performed a multivariate analysis of productivity variance using a combination of computing environment and organizational factors. His use of multivariate analysis of variance is in direct contrast to the preceding software productivity studies that employ only univariate analysis.

Lawrence observed that source lines of code, number of statements, number of procedure invocations, number of functional units, and number of transfers of control are all highly correlated. Other researchers have substantiated this as well. As such, he chose to employ the number of procedural lines of code divided by the total time put into the programming job by the programmer from the receipt of program specifications to completion of program testing. That is, Lawrence was interested in measuring the productivity of individual programmers who in turn were developing small programs (50–10,000 lines of code).

He found that programmer productivity increases with better turnaround, but decreases with on-line source code testing and interface to a database. In contrast to Albretch, Lawrence does not define what interface to a database means, nor whether the organizations he studied employed database management systems. Thus, it is not possible to determine whether Albretch and Lawrence agree on the productivity impact of the use of database management systems. However, Lawrence also found that programming experience beyond the first year on the job, structured programming, and walkthroughs contribute little to productivity improvement.

3.6. *NASA/SEL*

Bailey and Basili [4] found higher productivity over the entire system life-cycle to be associated with the use of a disciplined programming methodology, particularly in the early stages of system development. Their findings indicate that productivity measures, as well as other resource utilization estimates must be specific to the organizational setting and local computing environment to provide the most accurate measures. Standard, program-oriented productivity, or cost estimation measures will provide less accurate information than those measures that account for characteristics of the organization and its computing environment. Mohanty [44] and Kemerer [30] also found similar results in their independent examinations of different software cost estimation models.

3.7. *IBM*

Thadhani [54] and Lambert [37] examined the effects of good computer services on programmer and project productivity during application program development. In particular, their studies examine the effects of short response times, programmer's skills, and program complexity on programmer productivity. Thadhani reports that programmers were twice as productive when their system's average response time was 0.25 seconds (or less) than when it averaged 2 seconds or more. However, in a review of this and other similar studies, Conte *et al.* [17] report that average response time is not as critical as a narrow variance in expected response time. That is, programmers should be more productive when their system's response time is fast, consistent, and relatively predictable from the computing task at hand.

Both Thadhani and Lambert assert that unexpected delay in response time to trivial computing tasks (e.g., processing simple editor or shell commands, or compiling a small program) is psychologically disruptive to the programmer. Such delays they argue cause a longer delay than the actual elapsed time. Since LSS development efforts can entail thousands or more of such trivial task transactions, cumulative time will represent a significant cost to the project. Essentially, they argue that response time has an impact on LSS development projects, so that ample processing resources are critical to enhancing software productivity. Subsequently, this could be viewed as evidence in favor of providing individual programmers more processing resources such as through the adoption of powerful personal computing workstations as a way to improve software productivity. That is, if programmers currently must share a small number of heavily loaded computer systems, then providing each programmer with a workstation should improve their collective productivity [43].

3.8. *ITT advanced technology center*

Vosburg *et al.* associates [55] produced perhaps the most substantial study of large-scale software productivity to date. They examined software production data for 44 programming projects in 17 different ITT subsidiaries in nine different countries. Data on programming productivity, quality, and cost were collected from the records of completed projects by means of a questionnaire answered by project managers. Software systems ranged in size from 5,000 to 500,000 coded statements, with a median size of 22,000 statements. Statement counts include language processing directives, macro calls, and file inclusion statements, but not comments or blank lines. Their study covered a variety of software systems including telecommunications switches, programming tools, operating systems, electronic defense systems, and process control. In total, they represent more than 2.3 million coded statements and 1,500 person-years of effort.

The authors focused on classifying productivity drivers according to the ability of a software project manager to control them. They identify two types of factors: *product*-related factors that are not usually controllable by a project manager, and *production process*-related factors that are controllable by managers and thus provide opportunity for productivity improvement.

The product-related factors they identified include:

- *computing resource constraints:* productivity decreases when software being developed has timing, memory utilization, and CPU occupancy constraints.

- *program complexity:* productivity decreases when software is primarily operating systems, real-time command and control, and fault-tolerant applications that require extensive error detection, rollback, and recover routines.
- *customer participation:* productivity increases with customer application experience and participation in requirements and specification articulation.
- *size of program product:* productivity decreases as the number of lines of code increases.

The production process-related factors they identified include:

- *concurrent hardware-software development:* productivity decreases with concurrent development of hardware.
- *development computer size:* productivity increases as computer size (processor speed, main and secondary storage capacity) increases.
- *requirements and specifications stability:* productivity increases with accurate and stable system requirements and specifications.
- *use of modern programming practices:* productivity increases with extensive use of top-down design, modular design, design reviews, code inspections, and quality-assurance programs.
- *personnel experience:* productivity increases with more experienced software development personnel.

Overall, they find that product-related and process-related factors account for approximately the same amount of variance (one-third for each set) in productivity enhancement.

In conclusion, the authors suggest that improving programming productivity requires much more than the isolated implementation of new technologies and policies. In their view, "To be successful, a productivity improvement program must address the entire spectrum of productivity issues. Key features of such a program are management commitment and an integrated approach." [55, pp. 151-152].

3.9. *Australia-80 study*

Jeffrey [26] describes a comparative study of software productivity among small teams in 38 development projects in three Austrialian firms. Each firm used one programming language in its projects, but different from that used by the other two firms. Software systems in the projects ranged from very small (200 LOC) to large (>100K LOC), while their development team size ranged from

1–4 developers for 19 projects, and 3–8 for the other projects. As a result of his analysis, Jeffrey asserts (a) there is an optimal staff level which depends on the language used and the size of the resulting software system, and (b) adding staff beyond the optimal point decreases productivity and increases total development elasped time. However, due to the small sample size (three firms), small team size vis-a-vis individual programmer variations [19], and other common analytical shortcomings in defining input and output measures, the generality of the assertions is limited.

3.10. *Commerical U.S. banks*

Cerveny and Joseph [15] report on their study on software enhancement productivity in 200 U.S. commercial banks. Each bank was required by a change in national tax laws to implement new interest reporting requirements. Thus, all banks had to satisfy the same set of tax law requirements. Cerveny and Joseph found that banks which employed structured design and programming techniques took twice the effort as those banks that used nonstructured techniques, or that purchased and integrated commercial software packages. Effort in their study represents person-hours expended for analysis, programming, and project management activities, which is data apparently collected on a routine basis by the banks in the study. They do not report any measure of source code changes that accompany the measured effort. However, they report that banks that employed structured techniques did so for auditing and control purposes, but generally lacked CASE tools to support the structured techniques. Thus, it is unclear what the net change in software productivity might be if CASE tools that support structured design and programming techniques would have been empolyed.

3.11. *U.S. vs. Japan study*

In a provocative yet systematic comparison of industrial software productivity in the U.S. and Japan, Cusumano and Kemerer [21] argue that Japanese software development capabilities are comparable to those found in the U.S. [20]. Their analyses examined data from 24 U.S. and 16 Japanese development efforts collected from software project managers who completed questionnaires. Their project sample varied in terms of appplication type, programming language used, programming language and application type, and hardware platforms, full-time (versus part-time) staff effort by development phase, percentage of code reuse during development, code defect density, and number of tools/methods used per project. However, the researchers note that their sample of projects was not random, and that the software project managers may have only reported on their best projects. Cusamano and Kemerer employed Fortran-equivalent noncomment source lines of code as the output measure [27], and person-years of effort as the input measure, as well as both parametric and nonparametric statistical tests where appropriate. While they report that software productivity appears on the surface to be greater in Japan than in the U.S., the differences that were observed were not found to be statistically significant.

3.12. *Other studies of productivity and cost evaluation*

Jones [27] at IBM was among the first to recognize that measures of programming productivity and quality in terms of lines of code, and the cost of detecting and removing code defects are inherently paradoxical. They are paradoxical in that lines of code per unit of effort tend to emphasize longer rather than efficient or high-quality programs. Similarly, high-level programming languages tend to be penalized when compared to assembly programs, since modern programs may utilize fewer lines of code than assembly routines to realize the same computational procedure. Cost of code defect detection and removal tends to indicate that it costs less to repair poor quality programs than high quality programs. Thus, Jones' results undercut the utility of the findings reported by Walston and Felix [55] which are subject to these paradoxes. As an alternative, Jones recommends separating productivity measures into work units and cost units, while program quality should be measured by defect removal efficiency and defect prevention.

Chrysler [16] sought to identify some basic determinants of programming productivity by examining programming activities in a single organization. He sought to identify (1) what characteristics of the time to complete a programming (coding) task can be objectively measured before the task is begun, and (2) what programmer skill attributes are related to time to complete the task. His definition of programming task assumes that the program's specifications, "the instructions to the programmer regarding the performance required by the program", must be sufficiently detailed to incorporate the objective variables that can be measured to determine these relationships. Although he studied a sample of 36 COBOL programs, he does not describe their size, nor account for the number of programmers working on each. His results are similar in kind to those of Albrecht, finding that programming productivity can be estimated primarily from:

1. programmer experience at the current computing facility,
2. number of input files,
3. number of input edits,
4. number of procedures and procedure calls, and
5. number of input fields.

King and Schrems [34] provide the classic survey of problems encountered in applying cost-benefit analysis to system development and operation. To no surprise, the "benefits" they identify represent commonly cited productivity improvements. The authors observe that system development costs are usually underestimated and difficult to control, while productivity improvements are overestimated and difficult to achieve. They observe that cost-benefit (or cost-productivity) analysis can be used as:

a. a planning tool for assistance in choosing among alternative technologies and allocating scarce resources among competing demands;
b. an auditing tool for performing *post hoc* evaluations of an existing project; and
c. a way to develop "quantitative" support in order to politically influence a resource allocation decision.

Some of the problems they describe include:

a. identifying and measuring costs and benefits,
b. comparing cost-benefit alternatives,
c. cost accounting dilemmas,
d. problems in determining benefits, and
e. everyday organizational realities.

For example, two cost accounting (or measurement) problems that arise are *ommission of significant costs*, and *hidden costs.* Omitting significant costs occurs when certain costs are not measured, such as the time staff spend in design and review meetings, and the effort required to produce system design documents. Hidden costs arise in a number of ways, often as costs displaced either to others in the organization or to a later time: for example, when a product marketing unit achieves the early release of a software system before the developers have thoroughly tested it that customers find partially defective or suspect. If the developers try to accommodate the marketing unit's demands, then system testing plans are undercut or compromised, and system integrity is put in question from the developers point of view. The developers might later become demoralized and their productivity decrease if they are viewed by others or senior management as delivering lower quality systems, especially when compared to other software development groups who do not have the same demands from their marketing units.

King and Schrems also note that conducting quality cost-benefits has direct costs as well. For example, Jones [28] reports that in its software development laboratories, IBM spends the equivalent of 5% of all development costs on software measurement and analysis activities. More typically, he observes that most companies spend 1.5% to 3% of the cost of developing software to measure the kind of information IBM would collect [cf. 2, 3, 27, 55]. Therefore, this article by King and Schrems can be recommended as background reading to those interested in conducting software cost versus productivity analysis.

Mohanty [44] compared the application of 20 software cost-estimation models in use by large system development organizations. He entered data collected from a large software project, then entered this data into each of the 20 cost-estimation models. He found that the range of costs estimated was nearly uniformly distributed, varying by an order of magnitude! This led him to conclude that almost no model can estimate the true cost of software with any degree of accuracy. However, we could also conclude from his analysis that each cost-estimation model might in fact be accurate within the organizational setting where it was created and used. Although two different models may differ in their estimate of software development costs by as much as a factor of 10, each model may reflect the cost accounting structure for the organization where they were created. This means that different cost-estimation model and, by logical extension, productivity models, lead to different measured values which can show great variation when applied to software development projects. Also, the results of Kemerer's [30] study of software cost-estimation models corroborates the same kind of findings that Mohanty's study shows. However, Kemerer does go so far as to show how function points may be refined to improve their reliability as measures of program size and complexity [31, 32], as well as tuned to produce the better cost estimates [30]. But again, function points depend solely upon program source code characteristics, and do not address production process or production setting variations, nor their contributing effects.

Romeu and Gloss-Soler [48] argue that most software productivity measurement studies employ inappropriate statistical analysis techniques. They argue that the type of productivity data usually reported is *ordinal* data rather than interval or ratio data. The parametric statistical techniques employed by most software productivity analysts are inappropriate for ordinal data, whereas nonparametric techniques are appropriate. The use of parametric techniques on ordinal data results in apparently stronger relationships (e.g., correlations, regression slopes) than would be found with nonparametric techniques. The consequence is that studies of productivity measurement claiming statistically substantiated relationships based on inappropriate analytical techniques are somewhat dubious, and the strength of the cited relationship may not be as strong as claimed.

Boehm [9] reported that productivity on a software development project is most keenly affected by who develops the system and how well they are organized and managed as a team. Following this, Scacchi [50] reviewed a number of published reports on the problems of managing large software engineering projects. He found, to no surprise, that when projects were poorly managed or poorly organized, productivity was substantially lower than otherwise possible. Poor management can nullify the potential productivity enhancements attributable to improved development technologies. Scacchi identified a number of strategies for managing software projects that focus on improving the organization of software development work. These strategies identify conditions in the workplace, and the skills and interests of the developers as the basis for project-specific productivity drivers. For example, developers who have a strong commitment to a project and the people associated with it will be more productive, work harder, and produce higher quality software products. This commitment comes from the value the developers expect to find in the products they produce. In contrast, if they do not value the products they are working on, then their commitment will be low and their productivity and quality of work will be lower. So an appropriate strategy is to focus on organizing and managing the project to cultivate staff commitment to each other and to the project's objectives [cf. 33]. When developers are strongly committed to the project and to team effort [38], they are more than willing to undertake the unplanned for system maintenance and articulation work tasks needed to sustain productive work conditions [6, 7]. Scacchi concludes that strategies for managing software development work have been overlooked as a major contributor to software productivity improvement, and thus require further study and experimentation.

Boehm *et al.* [11] at TRW describe the organization of a software project whose objective was to develop an environment to enhance software productivity by a factor of 2 in 5 years, and 4 in 10 years. The project began in 1981, and the article describes their progress after four years in assembling a software development environment that should be able to support TRW development projects. Surprisingly, their software environment contains many tools for managing project communications and development documentation. This is because much of what gets delivered to a customer in a system is documentation, so tools that help develop what the customers receives should improve customer satisfaction and thus project productivity. However, they do not report any experiences with this environment in a production project. But they report that developers that have used the environment believe it improved their development productivity 25% to 40% [cf. 24, 45]. Nonetheless, they report that this productivity improvement was realized at an additional capital investment of US$10,000 per programmer. Current investigations in this project include the development and incorporation of a number of knowledge-based software development and project management aids for additional LSS productivity improvements.

Jones [28] provides the next study in his book on programming productivity. Jones does an effective job at describing some of the problems and paradoxes that plague most software productivity and quality measures based on his previous studies [27]. For example, he observes that a line of source code is not an economic good, but it is frequently used in software productivity measures as if it were — lines of code (or source statements) produced per unit of time are not a sound indicator of economic productivity. In response, he identifies more than 40 software development project variables that can affect software production. This is the major contribution of this work. However, the work is not without its faults. For example, Jones provides "data" to support his examination of the effects of each variable on comparable development projects. But his data, such as lines of source code is odd in that it is often rounded to the most significant digit (e.g., 500, 10,000, or 500,000), and collected from unnamed sources. Thus, his measurements lack specificity and his data collection techniques lack sufficient detail to substantiate his analysis.

Jones mentions that he relies on his data for use in a quantitative software productivity, quality, and reliability estimation model. However, he does not discuss how his model works, or what equations it solves. This is in marked contrast to Boehm's [9] software cost and productivity estimation efforts where he both identifies the software project variables of interest, and also presents the analytical details of the COCOMO software cost estimation model that uses them. Thus, we must regard Jones' reported analysis with some suspicion. Nonetheless, Jones does include an appendix that provides a questionnaire he developed for collecting data for the cost/quality/reliability model his company markets. This questionnaire includes a variety of suggestive questions that people collecting productivity data may find of interest.

In setting his sights on identifying software productivity improvements opportunities, Boehm [10] also identifies some of the dilemmas encountered in defining what things need to be measured to understand software productivity. In departure from the studies surveyed in the previous section, Boehm observes that software development *inputs* include:

a. different life-cycle development phases each requiring different levels of effort and skill;
b. activities including documentation production, facilities management, staff training, quality assurance, etc.;
c. support personnel such as contract administrators and project managers; and
d. organizational resources such as computing platforms and communications facilities.

Similarly, Boehm observes that measuring software development *outputs* solely in terms of attributes of the delivered software (e.g., delivered source code statements) poses a number of dilemmas:

a. complex source code statements or complex combinations of instructions usually receive the same weight as sequences of simple statements;
b. determining whether to count nonexecutable code, reused code, and carriage returns as code statements; and
c. whether to count code before or after pre- or post-processing.

For example, on this last item, Boehm reports putting a compact Ada program through a pretty printer frequently may *triple* the number of source code lines. Even after reviewing other source code metrics, Boehms concludes that none of these measures is fundamentally more imformative than lines of code produced per unit of time. Thus, Boehm's observations add weight to our conclusion that source code statement/line counts should be treated as an ordinal measure, rather than an interval or ratio measure, of software productivity.

This conclusion is especially appropriate when comparing such productivity measures across different studies.

In a comparative field study of software teams developing formal specifications, Bendifallah and Scacchi [7] found that a variation in specification teamwork productivity and quality could best be explained in terms of recurring teamwork structures. They found six teamwork structures (i.e., patterns of interaction) recurring among all the teams in their study. Further, they found that teams shifted from one structure to another for either planned or unplanned reasons. But more productive teams, as well as higher product quality teams, could be clearly identified in the observed patterns of teamwork structures. Lakhanpal's [38] study corroborates this finding, showing that workgroup cohesion and collective capability is a more significant factor in team productivity than individual experience. Thus, the structures, cohesiveness, and shifting patterns of teamwork are also salient software productivity variables.

In a study that does not actually examine the extent to which CASE tools may improve software productivity, Norman and Nunamaker [45] report on what the software engineers they surveyed believed would improve software productivity [cf. 24]. These software engineers answered questions about the desirability and expected effectiveness of a variety of contemporary CASE mechanisms or methods. Norman and Nunamaker found that software engineers believe that CASE tools that enhance their ability to produce various analysis reports, screen displays, and structured diagrams will have the greatest expected boost in software development productivity. But there is no data available that systematically demonstrates if the expected gains are in fact realized, or to what level.

Kraut *et al.* [35] report on their study of organizational changes in worker productivity and quality of work-life resulting from the introduction of a large automated system. They surveyed the opinions of hundreds of system users in ten different user sites. Through their analysis of this data, Kraut and colleagues found that the system increased the productivity of certain classes or users, while decreasing it for other user classes. They also found that while recurring user tasks were made easier, uncommon user tasks were reported to be more difficult to complete. Finally, they found that the distribution of user task knowledge shifted from old to new loci within the user sites. So what if anything does this have to do with software development productivity? The introduction of new software development tools and techniques might have a similar differential effect on productivity, software development task configuration, and the locus of development task expertise. This effect might be most apparent in large development organizations employing hundreds or thousands of software developers, rather than in small development teams. In any event, Kraut and colleagues observe that one needs to understand with web of relationships between the organization of work between and among tasks, developers, and users, as well as the computing resources and software system designs in order to understand what affects productivity and quality of work-life [35].

Last, Bhansali *et al.* [8] report that programmers are 2-to-4 times more productive when using Ada versus Fortran or Pascal-like languages according to their study data. However, as Ada contains language constructs not present in these other languages, it is not clear what was significant in explaining the difference in apparent productivity. Similarly, they do not indicate whether any of the source code involved was measured before or after preprocessing, which can affect source line counts, as already observed [10].

3.13. *Information technology and productivity*

Brynjolfsson [14] provides a comprehensive review of empirical studies that examine the relationship of information technology (IT) and productivity. In this study, IT is broadly defined to include particular kinds of software systems, such as transaction processing and strategic information systems, to general-purpose computing resources and services. Accordingly, he notes that some studies examine the dollars spent on IT or different types of software systems, compared to the overall profitability or productivity of the organizations that have invested in IT. Furthermore, his review examines studies falling into manufacturing and service sectors within the U.S. economy, or in multiple economic sectors. However, none of the studies reviewed in the preceding sections of this report are included in his review.

The overall focus of his review is to examine the nature of the so-called "productivity paradox" that has emerged in recent public discussions about the economic payoffs resulting from organizational investments in IT. In short, the nature of this paradox indicates that there is little or no measurable contribution of IT to productivity of organizations within an economic sector or to the national economy. His analysis then identifies four issues that account for the apparent productivity paradox. These are:

- *mismeasurement* of IT inputs and outputs,
- *lags* due to adaptation and learning how to most effectively utilize new IT,
- *redistribution* of profits or payoffs attributable to IT, and
- *mismanagement* of IT within industrial organizations.

In a closer comparative examination of these studies, Brynjolfsson concludes

> "The closer one examines the data behind the studies of IT performance, the more it looks like mismeasurement is at the core of the productivity paradox."
>
> [14, p. 74]

Thus, once again it appears that measuring and understanding the productivity impact of new software systems or IT remains problematic, and that one significant underlying cause for this is found in the methods for measuring productivity data.

3.14. *Summary of software development productivity drivers*

From a generous though somewhat naive review of the preceding studies, a number of software productivity drivers can be identified. The generosity comes from identifying the positive experiences or results reported in the preceding studies, and the naiveté comes from overlooking the fact that many of the reported experiences or results are derived from analytically restricted studies, or from dubious or flawed analytical methods. Further, most studies fail to describe how they account for variation in productive ability among individual programmers, which has been systemtically shown to vary by more than an order of magnitude [19]. That is, for very large software systems (500K+ code statements), it seems likely that 'average programmer' productivity dominates individual variations, while in smaller systems (less than 50K code statements) or those developed by only a few programmers, individual differences may dominate. Nearly all of the studies cited above examined small systems to some extent. Nonetheless, if we take a positivist view, we find the following attributes of the software application product being developed, the process by which it is developed, and the setting in which it is develop contribute favorably to improving software productivity. However, we can neither reliably predict how much productivity improvement should be expected, nor how to measure the individual or collective contribution of the attributes.

The attributes of a software project that facilitate high productivity include:

- **Software Development Environment Attributes:**
  - — Fast turnaround development activities and high-bandwidth processing throughput (may require more powerful or greater capacity computing resources).
  - — Substantial computing infrastructure (abundant computing resources and easy-to-access support system specialists).
  - — Contemporary software engineering tools and techniques (use of design and code development aids such as rapid prototyping tools, application generators, domain-specific (reusable) software components, etc., to produce incrementally development and released software products).
  - — System development aids for coordinating LSS projects (configuration management systems, software testing tools, documentation management systems, electronic mail, networked development systems, etc.).
  - — Programming languages with constructs closely matched to application domain concepts (e.g., object-oriented languages, spreadsheet languages).
  - — Process-centered software development environments that can accommodate multiple shifting patterns of small group work structures.
- **Software System Product Attributes:**
  - — Develop small-to-medium complexity systems (complexity indicated by size of source code delivered, functional coupling, and functional cohesion).
  - — Reuse software that supports the information processing tasks required by the application.
  - — No real-time or distributed systems software to be developed.
  - — Minimal constraints for validation of data processing accuracy, security, and ease of alteration.
  - — Stable system requirements and specifications,
  - — Short development schedules to minimize chance for project circumstances to change.
- **Project Staff Attributes:**
  - — Small, well-organized project teams. Large teams should be organized into small groups of 3–7 experienced developers, comfortable working with each other.

— Experienced software development staff (better if they are already familiar with application system domain, or similar system development projects).
— Software developers and managers who collect and evaluate their own software production data and are rewarded or acknowledged for producing high data value software.
— A variety of teamwork structures and the patterns of shifts between them during task performance.

The factors that drive software costs up should be apparent from this list of productivity drivers. Software cost drivers are the opposite of productivity drivers. For example, software without real-time performance should be produced more productively or at lower cost than comparable software with real-time performance requirements.

Also, it should be clear from this list that it is not always possible or desirable to achieve software productivity enhancements through all of the project characteristics listed above. For example, if the purpose of a project is to convert the operation of a real-time communications system from one computer and operating system to another computer-operating system combination, then only some of the characteristics may apply favorably, while others are inverted, occurring only as inhibitors. In this example, conversion suggests a high potential for substantial reuse of the existing source code. However, if the new code added for the conversion affects the system's real-time performance, or is spread throughout the system, then productivity should decrease and the cost increase. Similarly, if the conversion is performed by a well-organized team of developers already experienced with the system, then they should complete the conversion more productively than if a larger team of newly hired programmers is assigned the same responsibility.

Finally, if instead of viewing software productivity improvement from a generous and naive point of view, we seek to understand what affects software productivity in a way that project managers and developers find meaningful, then we need an approach fundamentally different than those surveyed above. To achieve this, we must first articulate some of the analytical challenges that must be taken into account. This challenge is the subject of Sec. 4. We also need to develop analytical instruments or tools that allow us to model and measure software production in ways that managers and developers can employ during LSS projects. This effort may lead us away from numbers and simple quantitative measures, and toward symbolic and qualitative models that incorporate nominal, ordinal, interval and ratio measures of software production. The capacity to accommodate these types of measures is well within the capabilities of symbol processing systems, but generally beyond strictly numerical productivity models. Ultimately, we should articulate an operational knowledge-based model that represents the software production process [22, 23, 40]. Such an operational model could then provide both a framework and compatible computational vehicle for measuring software production, as well as accommodate simulations of how projects work, and what might happen if certain project attributes were altered. This is the subject of Sec. 5.

4. Challenges for Software Productivity Measurement

In order to understand the variables that affect software productivity, people interested in measuring it must be able to answer the following five questions:

a. Why measure software productivity?
b. Who (or what) should measure and collect software productivity data?
c. What should be measured?
d. How to measure software productivity?
e. How to improve software productivity?

The purpose of asking these questions is to appreciate the complexity of the answers as well as to see that different answers lead to different software production measurement strategies. Unfortunately, as we have begun to see in the preceding section, the answers made in practice can lead to undesirable compromises in the analytical methods employed, or in the reliability of the results claimed.

4.1. *Why measure software productivity?*

To date, a number of reasons for measuring software productivity have been reported. In simplest terms, the idea is to identify (and measure) how to reduce software development costs, improve software quality, and improve the rate at which software is developed. In practical terms, this includes alternatives such as:

- increase the volume of work successfully accomplished by current staff effort,
- accomplish the same volume of work with a smaller staff,

- develop products of greater complexity or market value with the same staff workload,
- avoid hiring additional staff to increase workload,
- rationalize higher levels of capital-to-staff investment,
- reduce error densities in delivered products, and decrease the amount of time and effort needed to rectify software errors,
- streamline or downsize software production operations,
- identify possible product defects earlier in development,
- identify resource utilization patterns to discover production bottlenecks and underutilized resources,
- identify high-output or responsive personnel to receive rewards, and
- identify low-output personnel for additional training or reassignment.

Clearly, there are many reasons for measuring software productivity. However, once again it may not be desirable to try to accomplish most or all of these objectives through a single productivity measurement program. For example, different people involved in a large software project may value certain of these alternatives more than others. Similarly, each alternative implies certain kinds of data be collected. This diversity may lead to conflicts over why and how to measure software productivity which, in turn, may lead to a situation where the measured results are inaccurate, misleading, or regarded with suspicion [cf. 25, 36]. Thus, a productivity measurement program must be carefully designed to avoid creating conflicts, mistrust, or other conditions for mismeasurement within the software projects to be studied. Involving the software developers and project managers in the design of the measurement instrument, data collection, and feedback program can help minimize the potential organizational problems as well as gain their support.

4.2. *Who should measure software productivity data?*

The choice of who (or what) should collect and report software production data is determined in part by the reasons for measuring productivity noted above. The choices include:

- Programmer self report,
- Project or team manager,
- Outside analysts or observers,
- Automated performance monitors.

Programmer or manager self-reported data are the least costly to collect, although they may be of limited accuracy. However, if productivity measures are to be used for personnel evaluation, then one should not expect high reliability or validity in self-reported data. Similarly, if productivity measures are employed as the basis of allocating resources or rewards, then the data reporters will have an incentive to improve their reported production values. This is a form of the Hawthorne Effect, whereby people seek to accommodate their (software production) behavior to generate data values they think the data evaluators want to see.

Instead, we want to engender a software production measurement capability that can feed back useful information to project managers and developers in a form that enhances their knowledge and experience over time. Outside observers can often collect such information, but at a higher cost than self report. Similarly, automated production performance monitors may be of use, but this is still an emerging area of technology requiring more insight for what should be measured and how. For example, Irving and associates [25] report that use of automated performance monitoring systems is associated with perceived increase in productivity, more accurate assessment of worker performance, and higher levels of organizational control. However, where such mechanisms have been employed, workers indicate that managers overemphasize such quantitative measures, and underemphasize quality of work in evaluating worker performance. Workers also reported increased stress, lower levels of job satisfaction, and a decrease in the quality of relationships with peers and managers. Ultimately, one would then expect that these negative factors would decrease productivity and increase staff turnover. Thus, the findings reported by Irving suggest some caution in the use of automated performance monitors. Collecting high-quality production data and providing ongoing constructive feedback to personnel in the course of a project is thus a longer-term goal.

Overall, if data quality or accuracy is not at issue, self-reported production data is sufficient. If causal behavior or organizational circumstances do not need to be taken into account, then automated performance monitors can be used. Similarly, if the desire is to show measured improvement in software productivity, whether or not production improves, self-reported or automated data collection procedures will suffice.

On the other hand, if the intent of the productivity measurement program is to ascertain what affects software production, and what alternative work arrangements might further improve productivity, then reliable and accurate data must be collected. Such data might best be collected by analysts or observers who have no vested interest in particular measured outcomes, nor who will collect data to be used for personnel evaluation. In turn, the collected data should be analyzed and results fed back to project developers and managers in a form they can act upon. Again, this might be best facilitated through the involvement of representative developers and managers in the design of the data collection effort.

4.3. *What should be measured?*

The choices over what to measure are many and complex. However, it is clear that focusing on program product attributes such as lines or code, source statements, or function points will not lead to significant insights on the contributing or confounding effects of software production process or production setting characteristics of software productivity, nor vice versa. The studies in earlier sections clearly indicate that different LSS *product, process,* and *production setting* characteristics individually and collectively affect software productivity. However, based on this survey, there are some inconsistencies in determining which characteristics affect the increase or decrease in software productivity. As such, an *integrated* productivity measurement or improvement strategy must account for characteristics of the products, processes, and settings to delineate the potential interrelationships. This is necessary since we cannot predict beforehand which constituent variables will reveal the greatest significance or variance in different projects or computing environments. Similarly, we should expect that software product, process, and setting characteristics will need to be measured using a combination of nominal, ordinal, interval, and ratio measures. As such, consider in turn, the following constituents of software products, production processes, and production settings.

Software products. Software projects produce a variety of outcomes other than source code. Each product is valuable to either the individual developer, project managers, project organization, or the client. Therefore, we should not limit production measurement attention to only one product, especially if comparable effort is committed to producing other closely related products. The point here is that since software projects produce many products along the way, our interest should be focussed on ascertaining the distribution of time, skill, teamwork, and value committed to developing each product. Accordingly, we can see the following kinds of products resulting from a software development project.

- Delivered (new versus modified) *source statements* for successive software life-cycle development stages, including those automatically transformed or expanded by software tools, such as application generators,
- Software *development analyses* (knowledge about how a particular system was produced): requirements analysis, specifications, architectural and detailed designs, and test plans,
- *Application-domain knowledge*: knowledge generated and made explicit about the problem domain (e.g., how to electronically switch a large volume of telephone message traffic under computer control),
- *Documents and artifacts*: internal and external reports, system diagrams, and terminal displays produced for development schedule milestones, development analyses, user manuals, and system maintenance guides, and
- Improved *software development skills*, new occupational or career opportunities for project personnel, and new ways of cooperating in order to develop other software products.

Software production process. LSS are often produced through a multi-stage process commonly understood in terms of the system life-cycle: from its inception through delivery, sustained operation, and retirement. But if requirements are frequently renegotiated, if senior software engineers quit after the preliminary architectural design, or if there are no modern software requirements, specification, or design aids employed, then we might expect that the coding phase may show comparatively low productivity, and that test and integration show comparatively high cost. However, we should observe that none of the studies cited in Sec. 3 collected and analyzed data that addresses such issues.

Since each production process activity can produce valuable products, why is it conventional to measure the outcome of one of the smallest effort activities in this process of developing large software systems, coding. A number of studies such as those reported by Boehm [9] indicate that coding usually consumes 10–20% of the total LSS development effort. On the other hand, software testing and integration consume the largest share, usually representing 50% of the development effort. Early development activities consume 10–15% each. Clearly, delivered software source code is a valuable product. However, it seems clear that code production depends on the outcome and products of the activities that precede it.

In general, software projects do not progress in a simple sequential order from requirements analysis through specification, design, coding, testing, integration, and delivery. However, this does not mean that such activities are not performed with great care and management attention. Quite the contrary. Although the project may be organized and managed to produce requirements, specification, design, and other documents according to planned schedule, the actual course of development work is difficult to accurately predict. Development task breakdowns and rework are common to many projects [6, 7, 41]. Experience suggests that software specifications get revised during later design stages, requirements change midway through design, software testing reveals inadequacies in certain specifications, and so forth [50, 52]. Each of these events leads to redoing previously accomplished development work. As such, the life-cycle development process is better understood not as a simple linear process, but rather as one with many possible paths that can lead either forward or backward in the development cycle depending on the circumstantial events that arise, and the project conditions that precede or follow from the occurrence of these events.

If we want to better estimate, measure, and understand the variables that affect software production throughout its life-cycle, we need to delineate the activities that constitute the production process. We can then seek to isolate which tasks within the activities can dramatically impact overall productivity. The activities of the software life-cycle process to be examined include:

- System requirements analysis: frequency and distribution of changes in operational system requirements throughout the duration of the project,
- Software requirements specifications (possibly including rapid prototypes): number and interrelationship of computational objects, attributes, relations and operations central to the critical components of the system (e.g., those in the kernel),
- Software architecture design: complexity of software architecture as measured by the number, interconnections, and functional cohesion of software modules, together with comparable measures of project team organization. Also, as measured by the frequency and distribution of changes in the configuration of both the software architecture and the team work structure.
- Detailed software unit design: time spent to design a module given the number of project staff participating, and the amount of existing (or reused) system components incorporated into the system being developed,

- Software unit coding (or application generation): time to code designed modules, and density of discovered inconsistencies (bugs) found between a module's detailed design and its source code,
- Unit testing, integration, and system testing: ratio of time and effort allocated to (versus actually spent on) testing, effort spent to repair detected errors, density of known error types, and the amount of automated mechanisms employed to generate and evaluate test case results,

Similar variables for consideration can also be articulated for other system development and evolution activities including quality assurance and configuration management, preliminary customer (beta-site) testing, customer documentation production, delivery turnover, sustained operation and system evolution.

In addition, we must also appreciate that software production can be organized into different modes of manufacture and organization of work, including:

- Ad hoc problem solving and articulation work [6, 7, 33, 41],
- Project-oriented job shop, which are typical for software development projects [50],
- Batched job shops, for producing a family or small volume of related software products,
- Pipeline, where software production is organized in concurrent multi-stage development, and staff is specialized in particular development crafts such as "software requirement analysts", "software architects", or "coders",
- Flexible software manufacturing systems, which represent one view of a "software factory of the future" [53],
- Transfer-line (or assembly line), where raw or unfinished information resources are brought to semi-skilled software craftspeople who perform highly routinized and limited fabrication or assembly tasks.

Accordingly, the characteristics that distinguish these potential modes of software production from one another are their values along a set of dimensions that include:

1. developer skill requirements,
2. ease of productivity measurement and instrumentation,
3. capitalization,
4. flexibility of procedures to accommodate development anomalies, and

5. ability to adopt and assimilate software innovations.

Software production setting. Does the setting where software is produced make a difference on productivity? Do we expect that LSS production at, say, TRW Defense Systems Group is different than at the MCC Software Technology Program Center, the Artificial Intelligence Laboratory at MIT, the Data Processing Center at Aetna Life and Casualty, or the Refinery Software Center at Exxon? Do we expect that LSS production in various development organization departments of the same corporation is different? The answer to all is yes. Software production settings differ in a number of ways including:

- Programming language in use (Assembly, Fortran, Cobol, C, C++, Ada, CommonLisp, Smalltalk, etc.),
- Computing applications (telecommunications switch, command and control, AI research application, database management, structural analysis, signal processing, refinery process control, etc.),
- Computers (SUN-4 workstations, DEC-VAX, Amdahl 580, Cray Y-MP, Symbolics 3670, PC-clone, etc.), and operating systems (Unix variants, VAX-VMS, IBM-VM, Zetalisp, MS-DOS, etc.),
- Differences between host (development) and target (end-user) computing environment and setting, as well as between computing server and client systems,
- Software development tools (compilers, editors, application generators, report generators, expert systems, etc.) and practices in use (hacking, structured techniques, modular design, formal specification, configuration management and QA, MIL-STD-2167A guidelines, etc.),
- Personnel skill base (number of software staff with no college degree, degree in nontechnical field, BS CS/EE, MS CS/EE, Ph.D. CS/EE, etc.) and experience in application area,
- Dependence on outside organizational units (system vendors, Marketing, Business Analysis and Planning, laboratory directors, change control committees, clients, etc.),
- Extent of client participation, their experience with similar application systems, and their expectation for sustained system support,
- Frequency and history of mid-project innovations in production computing environment (how often does a new release of the operating system, processor memory upgrade, new computing peripherals introduced, etc., occur during prior development projects?),

- Frequency and history of troublesome anomalies and mistakes that arise during prior system development projects (e.g., schedule overshoot, budget overrun, unexpected high staff turnover, unreliable new release software, etc.).

4.4. *How to measure software productivity?*

Measuring software productivity presupposes an ability to construct a measurement program comparable to those employed in experimental designs for behavioral studies [18]. This is necessary to insure that the measures employed are reliable, valid, accurate, and repeatable. This in turn implies that choices must be made with respect to the following concerns:

Productivity measurement research design and sampling strategy. Simply put, there are at least three kinds of choices for research design: qualitative case studies, quantitative surveys, and triangulation studies. Qualitative case studies can provide in-depth descriptive knowledge about how software production work occurs, what sort of problems arise and when. Such studies are usually one-shot affairs[a] that are low cost to initiate, employ open-ended anthropological data collection strategies, usually require outside analysts, and produce rich, but not necessarily generalizable findings.

Quantitative survey studies employ some form of instrumentation such as a questionnaire to gather data in a manner well-suited for statistical analysis. The survey sample must be carefully defined to ensure reliable and valid statistical results. In constrast to qualitative studies, survey studies require data analysis skills that are more widely available and supported through automated statistical packages. Consider the following scenario of the sequence of activities entailed in the preparation and conduct of a quantitative study:

1. Develop productivity data collection instrument (form or questionnaire).
2. Pilot test and revise initial instrument to be sure that desired data can be collected from subjects with modest effort.
3. Implement data collection activity and schedule with plans to follow-up on first- and second-round nonrespondents (never expect that everyone will gladly cooperate with your data collection program).

[a]Multiple, comparative case studies are much less common and require a greater sustained field research effort. van den Bosch *et al.* [13] describe comparative, qualitative case study designs for studying software production, while [6, 7] provide detailed examples.

4. Validate and "clean" collected data (to remove or clarify ambiguous responses).
5. Code data into analytical variables, scale, and normalize.
6. Apply selected variables to univariate analysis to determine first-order descriptive statistics, second-order variables, and factors for analysis of variance.
7. Select apparently significant first- and second-order variables from univariate analysis for multivariate analysis, partial correlations, and regression analysis.
8. Formulate an analytical model of apparent quantitative relationship between factors.
9. Formulate descriptive model of analyzed statistical phenomenon to substantiate findings and recommendations.

The chief drawback of surveys is that they usually do not capture the description of process phenomena, and so they provide low-resolution indicators of causal relationships among measure variables. Therefore, surveys are best suited for "snap-shot" studies, although multiple or longitudinal survey studies are also possible but are more costly and less common.

Triangulation studies attempt to draw from the relative strengths of both qualitative and quantative studies to maximize analytical depth, generalizability and robustness. In short, triangulation studies seek to use qualitative field studies to gain initial sensitivity to critical issues, use surveys based on the field studies to identify the frequency and distribution of variables that constitute these issues from a larger population, then derive from these a small select sample of projects/work groups for further in-depth examination and verification. Such research designs are quite scarce in software production measurement because of the cost and diversity of skills they require. This may just be a way of saying that high-quality results require a substantial research investment. van den Bosch *et al.* [13] propose one such study design whose baseline cost is estimated in the range of 1–3 person years of effort.

Unit of analysis. The concern here is deciding what are the critical things to study. As we indicated in Subsec. 4.3, there is a multitude of factors that can potentially affect software productivity. However, it should be clear that all these factors are not simultaneously affective. Instead, their influence may be circumstantial or spread out over time and organizational space. Software products, production processes, and production setting characteristics all can be influential but not necessarily at the same time or with the same computing resources. This leads us to recognize that the subject for our analysis of software productivity should be *the life history of a software project in terms of its evolving products, processes, and production settings.*[b]

Level and terms of analysis. Together with the unit of analysis, the level and terms characterize the basis for determining the scope and generalizability of a software productivity analysis. The level of analysis indicates whether the resulting analysis covers micro-level behavior, macro-level behavior, or some span in between. Given the unit of analysis, should software productivity be examined at the level of individual programmers, small work groups, software life cycle activities, development organization, company, or industry? The level(s) chosen determines the granularity of data needed, as well as how it can be aggregated to increase the scope and generalizability of the analysis. Experience suggests that analysis of data collected across three or more consecutive levels provide very strong results (cf. [13, 40, 41, 51]), as opposed to those cited in Sec. 3 which typically employ only one level. But the greater the desired scope and generalizability, the more carefully systematic the data collection and analysis must be.

The terms of analysis draw attention to the language and ontology of a productivity analysis and the analyst. Assuming the unit and levels for analysis, choices of which analytical vocabulary or rationale to use foreshadows the outcomes and consequences implied by the analysis. Most analysis of software productivity are framed in terms expressing economic "costs", "benefits", and "organizational impacts". However, other rationales are commonly employed which broaden the vocabulary and scope of an analysis. For example, Kling and Scacchi [35] observe at least five different kinds of rationale are common: respectively, those whose terms emphasize

a. features of the underlying technology,
b. attributes of the organization setting,
c. improving relations between software people and management,
d. determining who can affect control over, or benefit from, a productivity measurement effort (addressing organizational politics), and
e. the ongoing social interactions and negotiations that characterize software production work.

[b] An awareness of this also impinges on the choice for research design and sampling strategy.

The point of such diverse rationales and their implied terms of analysis is to recognize that no simple account can be rendered which completely describes what affects software productivity in a particular setting. Instead, what might be the best choice is to interpret an analysis in terms of each rationale to better identify which rationale is most informing in a particular situation. But whatever the choice, the analysis will be constrained by the terms built into the data collection instruments.

4.5. *How to improve software productivity?*

In addressing this question, Boehm [10] identifies a number of strategies for improving software productivity: get the best from people, make development steps more efficient, eliminate development steps, eliminate rework, build simpler products, and reuse components. These strategies draw attention to the development activities or processes that add value to an emerging software system.[c] However, Boehm does not indicate how these productivity improvement opportunities are or should be measured to ascertain their effectiveness, nor can he or anyone else state how much improvement each strategy or a combined strategy might realize.

Clearly, much more needs to be explained in order to begin to adequately answer this question.

4.6. *Summary*

Large-scale studies of software productivity (i.e., across multiple software projects in many different settings) necessitate collecting of a plethora of data. The number and diversity of variables identified above indicate that software productivity cannot be understood simply as a ratio of the amount of source code statements produced for some unit of time. Instead, understanding software productivity requires a more systematic analysis of a variety of types of production measures, as well as their interrelationships. This suggests that we need a more robust theoretical framework, analytical methods, and support tools to address the dilemmas now apparent in understanding and measuring software productivity.

[c] Cusumano [20] independently reports on how these same strategies are regularly practiced in various Japanese software factories to achieve software productivity improvements.

5. Alternative Directions for Software Productivity Measurement and Improvement

We need a fundamental shift in understanding what affects software productivity. In particular, new effort should be directed at the development of a knowledge-based software productivity analysis system capable of modeling and simulating the production dynamics of a software project in a specific setting. In order to develop such a system, it is appropriate to also develop project-specific theories of software production, cultivate software productivity drivers, and develop techniques for utilizing qualitative (symbolic) project data.

5.1. *Develop setting-specific theories of software production*

Standard measures, such as lines of code produced, represent data that are relatively easy to collect. However, they are also the least useful in informing our understanding of what affects, or how to improve software productivity. We lack an articulated theory of software production. This report identifies a number of elements that could be the constituents of such a theory. In principle, these include the software products, the processes which give rise to these products, and the computational and organizational characteristics that facilitate or inhibit the processes. Clearly, developing such theory is a basic research problem, and a problem that must be informed by systematic empirical examination of current software development projects and practices. Such theory could be used to construct new models, hypotheses, or measures that account for the production of large software systems in different settings (cf. [4, 18]). Similarly, such models and measures could be *tuned* to better account for the mutual influence of product, process, and setting characteristics specific to a project. This in turn could lead to simple, practical, and effective measures of software production that give project managers and developers a source of information they can use to improve the quality characteristics of their products, processes, and settings.

5.2. *Identify and cultivate software productivity drivers*

In the apparent rush to measure software productivity, we may have lost sight of a fundamental concern: why are software developers as productive as they are in the presence of many technical and organizational constraints? The potential for productivity improvement is not an inherent property of any new software development technology [35]. Instead, the people who develop software must effectively mobilize and transform whatever resources they have available to construct software products. Software developers must realize and articulate the potential for productivity improvement. New software development technologies can facilitate this articulation. But other technological impediments and organizational constraints can nullify or inhibit this potential. Thus, a basic concern must be to identify and cultivate software productivity drivers, whether such drivers are manifest as new computing resources, or alternative organizational or work arrangements.

Subsection 3.14 identifies a number of productivity drivers that (weakly) follow from a number of software productivity measurement studies. These drivers primarily represent technological resource alternatives. Related research [50, 52] also identifies a set of project management strategies that seek to improve software production through alternative social and organizational work arrangements. These strategies are identified through research investigations into the practice of software development in complex settings (e.g. [6, 7, 35, 41, 52]). These studies are beginning to show that the development project's organizational history, idiosyncratic workplace incentives, investments in prior technologies and work arrangements, local job markets, occupational and career contingencies, and organizational politics can dramatically affect software productivity potential, either positively or negatively [6, 29, 35, 50]. Further, in some cases it appears that such organizational and social conditions dominate the productivity contribution attributable to in-place software development technologies. In other words, in certain circumstances, changing the organization conditions or work arrangements might have far greater an effect in improving software productivity potential than by merely trying to "fix things" by installing new technology. Software productivity improvement will not come from better software development technologies alone. Organizational and project management strategies to improve software productivity potential must be identified, made explicit, and supported.

5.3. *Develop symbolic and qualitative measures of software productivity*

We should develop a rich understanding of how software production occurs in a small number of representative software projects. From this, we can articulate an initial qualitative process model of software production that incorporates subjective and impressionistic data from local software development experts.

Then use this model and data to determine what further quantitative data to collect, as a basis for refining and evolving the process model. Overall, the idea here is to first determine what we should measure before beginning to collect data. Data that is out there and easy to collect, such as lines of code, does not necessarily tell us anything about how those lines of code were produced, what tools were used, what problems were encountered, who wrote what code, etc. Instead, we should seek to be in touch with the people who develop software since it is reasonable to assume that they can identify their beliefs for what works well in their situation, what enhances their productivity, and what improves the quality of their products. Quantitative data can then be used to substantiate or refute the frequency and distribution of the findings described in qualitative terms. Subsequently, this should lead to the development of a family of process models that accounts for a growing range and scope of software production.

5.4. *Develop knowledge-based systems that model software production*

We should seek an integrated approach to capture and make explicit an empirically-grounded understanding of software production in a computational model. This model should embody a computational framework for capturing, describing, and applying knowledge of how software development projects are carried out and managed [22, 40–42]. New software process modeling technology in the form of knowledge-based systems is emerging (e.g. [22, 23, 40]). This technology appears to be well-suited to support the acquisition, representation, and operationalization of the qualitative knowledge that exists within a software development project. Readers interested in a specific realization of this approach should consult [40–42]. However, any software process engineering environment or knowledge engineering system capable of modelling, simulating, and enacting software products, production processes, production settings, and their interrelationships could be employed.

Knowledge acquisition. We can acquire knowledge about software projects by conducting in-depth, observational field studies, e.g., [7]. Ideally, such studies should be organized to facilitate comparative analysis. The data to be collected should account for the concerns described in Sec. 4. This in turn requires the articulation of a scheme for data collection, coding, and analysis. The focus should be directed at gathering and organizing information about the life history of a software development project in terms of its products, processes, and setting attributes described earlier. The goal is to be able to develop a descriptive model of software production such that any analytical conclusion can be traced back to the original data from which it emerged. Subsequently, this descriptive model must capture the knowledge we seek in a form that can then be represented and processed within a knowledge-based system.

Knowledge representation. The area of knowledge representation has long been an active area of research in the field of artificial intelligence. Thus, discussions of topics or approaches can get easily bogged down in debates over implementation technology, philosophy, and the like. Suffice it to say that a knowledge organization scheme is essential, and that such a scheme must again accommodate the kinds software production data outlined in Sec. 5. A suggestive starting point that others are working from is the Schema Representation Language described by [49], and utilized by [47], or the Software Process Specification Language (SPSL) used in [40–42]. For example, in their representation of system development projects, Scacchi and colleagues [22, 23, 40–42, 51] developed a scheme for organizing and representing knowledge about organizational settings, resource arrangements, development plans, actions, states, schedules, histories, and expectations. In turn, they elaborate the relationships between these concepts using data derived from detailed narrative descriptions of system development projects (e.g. [6, 33]) to illustrate their approach. Ultimately, the goal of such a scheme for representing knowledge about software development projects is to facilitate computational analysis, simulation, querying, and explanation [40, 41].

Knowledge operationalization. A knowledge base about software production projects provides an initial basis for developing an operational model of software production. Such a knowledge-based system requires

1. a knowledge base for storing facts, hueristics, and reasoning strategies according to the previous scheme,
2. a question-answer subsystem for retrieving facts stored or deduced from known relationships among facts, and
3. a simulator for exploring alternative trajectories for software development projects.

Suggestive elaborations of such systems are available [22, 23, 40, 47, 49] and recommended. For example, assuming an interesting knowledge base has already been stored, the question-answer subsystem could be used to answer queries of the following kinds:

1. who was the developer responsible for a particular action or situation,
2. what were the project development circumstances during a particular time (schedule) interval,
3. when was a particular circumstance true or when was the action done,
4. where was a specified action performed,
5. how was some software design task accomplished, and
6. why was a certain document produced.

More specific questions such as these can be answered by retrieval from the knowledge base, either by direct retrieval, property inheritance, or by inference rules [22, 40, 49].

5.5. *Simulate and measure the effects of productivity enhancements*

The design of a knowledge-based system that simulates software production requires an underlying computational model of development states, actions, plans, schedules, expectations (e.g., requirements), and histories in order to answer "what if" questions [40]. Ultimately, the operation of the simulator depends on the availability of a relevant knowledge base of facts, hueristics, and reasoning strategies found in development projects.

Consider the following scenario of the simulator use. We have developed or acquired a knowledge-based software production simulation system of the kind outlined above. The simulator's user is a manager of a new project in a particular setting and wants to determine an acceptable schedule for the project (and thus certain attributes affecting productivity). Knowledge about the setting and the project have not yet been incorporated into the knowledge base. The user interacts with the simulator to elicit the relevant attributes of the setting, project, and schedule then enter them into the knowledge base. The user starts the simulation through an interactive question-answer dialog. The simulator would proceed to compare the particular facts related to the user's queries against prior project knowledge already accumulated in the knowledge base and tries to execute the proposed production schedule. This would give rise to changes in the simulated project states, actions, (sub-)schedules, expectations, and histories consistent with those inferred from the hueristics and reasoning strategies. The simulation finishes when the full schedule is executed, or halts when it reaches a state where it is inhibited. Such a state reflects a point in the project where some bottleneck emerges — for example, a key computing resource is overutilized, or some other precondition for a critical production step cannot be met [6, 7, 41, 42]. Analysis of the conditions prevailing in the simulated project at this point helps the user draw useful conclusions about critical interactions between various organizational units, development groups, and computing resource arrangements that facilitate productive work. The simulation may be redone with different settings or project attributes in order to further explore other hueristics for improving productivity in the project.

Ultimately, the simulation embodies a deep model of software production that in turn can be further substantiated with quantified data as to the frequency and distribution of actions, states, etc., arising in different software development projects.

5.6. *An approach*

The approach to developing a knowledge-based software productivity modeling and simultion system described above is a radical departure from conventional approaches to understanding and measuring software productivity. Accordingly, the following sequence of activities could be performed as a strategy for evaluating the utility of such an approach.

- Initiate comparative case studies or surveys of current in-house software production practices. These studies serve to provide an initial baseline data of software project products, production processes, and production setting characteristics.
- Clean and analyze collected data using available skills and tools. This is to provide a statement of baseline knowledge about apparent relationships between measured software production variables. This and the preceding step correspond to the "knowledge acquisition" activity described above.
- Codify subsets of available software project data in a knowledge specification language, such as SPSL [40–42]. This step corresponds to an initial realization of the "knowledge representation" and "knowledge operationalization" activities described above.
- Demonstrate results in the computational language and processor as suggested earlier [40].
- Embed the software productivity modeling and simulation system within an advanced CASE environment in order to demonstrate its integration, access, and software production guidance on LSS development efforts [22, 23, 40–42, 53].

6. Conclusions

What affects software productivity and how do we improve it? This report examines the state of the art in measuring and understanding software productivity. In turn, it describes a framework for understanding software productivity, identifies some fundamentals of measurement, and surveys selected studies of software productivity. This survey helps identify some of the recurring variables that affect software productivity. As a results of the analysis of the shortcomings found in many of the surveyed studies, we then identify an alternative knowledge-based approach for research and practice in understanding what affects software productivity. This approach builds upon recent advances in modeling, simulating, and enacting software engineering processes situated within complex organizational settings. Also, this approach enables the construction of an organizational knowledge base on what affects software productivity and how. Thus, we are optimistic about the potential for developing knowledge-based systems for modeling, simulating, and reasoning about software development projects as a new way to gain insight into what affects software productivity.

Acknowledgements

This work was part of the USC System Factory Project, supported by contracts and grants from AT&T, Northrop Corp., Office of Naval Technology through the Naval Ocean System Center, and Pacific Bell. Additional support to as provided by the USC Center for Operations Management, Education and Research, and the USC Center for Software Engineering. Preparation of the initial version of this report benefited from discussions and suggestions provided by Dave Belanger, Chandra Kintala, Jerry Schwarz, and Don Swartout of the Advanced Software Concepts Department at AT&T Bell Laboratories, Murray Hill, New Jersey, USA. Pankaj Garg, Abdulaziz Jazzar, Peiwei Mi, and David Hurley provided helpful comments on subsequent versions of this report. The collective input of these people is appreciated, but not of their doing if misstated or misrepresented.

References

1. T. Abdel-Hamid and S. Madnick, "Impact of schedule estimation on software project behavior", *IEEE Software* **3**, 4 (1986) 70–75.
2. A. Albrecht, "Measuring application development productivity", *Proc. Joint SHARE/GUIDE/IBM Application Development Symp.* (October, 1979) pp. 83–92.

3. A. Albrecht and J. Gaffney, "Software function, source lines of code, and development effort prediction: a software science validation", *IEEE Trans. Soft. Eng.* **SE-9**, 6 (1983) 639–648.
4. J. Bailey and V. Basili, "A meta-model for software development resource expenditures", *Proc. 5th. Int. Conf. Software Engineering* (IEEE Computer Society, 1981) pp. 107–116.
5. C. A. Behrens, "Measuring the productivity of computer systems development activities with function points", *IEEE Trans. Softw. Eng.* **SE-9**, 6 (1983) 648–652.
6. S. Bendifallah and W. Scacchi, "Understanding software maintenance work", *IEEE Trans. Softw. Eng.* **SE-13**, 3 (1987) 311–323.
7. S. Bendifallah and W. Scacchi, "Work structures and shifts: an empirical analysis of software specification teamwork", *Proc. 11th. Int. Conf. Software Engineering* (IEEE Computer Society Press, 1989) pp. 345–357.
8. P. V. Bhansali, B. K. Pflug, J. A. Taylor, and J. D. Wooley, "Ada technology: current status and cost impact", *Proc. IEEE* **79**, 1 (1991) 22–29.
9. B. Boehm, *Software Engineering Economics* (Prentice Hall, 1981).
10. B. W. Boehm, "Improving software productivity", *Computer* **20**, 8 (1987) 43–58.
11. B. Boehm, M. Penedo, E. D. Stuckle, R. D. Williams, and A. B. Pyster, "A software development environment for improving productivity", *Computer* **17**, 6 (1984) 30–44.
12. B. Boehm and R. W. Wolverton, "Software cost modeling: some lessons learned", *J. Syst. Softw.* **1** (1980) 195–201.
13. F. van den Bosch, J. Ellis, P. Freeman, L. Johnson, C. McClure, D. Robinson, W. Scacchi, B. Scheft, A. van Staa, and L. Tripp, "Evaluating the implementation of software development life cycle methodology", *ACM Softw. Eng. Notes* **7**, 1 (1982) 45–61.
14. E. Brynjolfsson, "The productivity paradox of information technology", *Commun. ACM* **36**, 12 (1993) 67–77.
15. R. P. Cerveny and D. A. Joseph, "A study of the effects of three commonly used software engineering strategies on software enhancement productivity", *Information and Management* **14** (1988) 243–251.
16. E. Chrysler, "Some basic determinants of computer programming productivity", *Commun. ACM* **21**, 6 (1978) 472–483.
17. S. Conte, D. Dunsmore, and V. Shen, *Software Engineering: Models and Measures* (Benjamin-Cummings, 1986).
18. B. Curtis, "Measurement and experimentation in software engineering", *Proc. IEEE* **68**, 9 (1980) 1103–1119.
19. B. Curtis, "Substantiating programmer variability", *Proc. IEEE* **69**, 7 (1981).
20. M. Cusumano, *Japan's Software Factories* (Oxford University Press, 1991).
21. M. Cusumano and C. F. Kemerer, "A quantitative analysis of US and Japanese practice and performance in software development", *Management Science* **36**, 11 (1990) 1384–1406.

22. P. K. Garg, P. Mi, T. Pham, W. Scacchi, and G. Thunquest, "The SMART approach to software process engineering", *Proc. 16th. Int. Conf. Software Engineering*, Sorrento, Italy (IEEE Computer Society Press, 1994) pp. 341–350.
23. P. K. Garg and W. Scacchi, "On designing intelligent software hypertext systems", *IEEE Expert* **4** (1989) 52–63.
24. S. J. Hanson and R. R. Kosinski, "Programmer perceptions of productivity and programming tools", *Commun. ACM* **28**, 2 (1985) 180–189.
25. R. Irving, C. Higgins, and F. Safayeni, "Computerized performance monitoring systems: use and abuse", *Commun. ACM* **29**, 8 (1986) 794–801.
26. D. R. Jeffrey, "A software development productivity model for MIS environments", *J. Syst. Softw.* **7** (1987) 115–125.
27. T. C. Jones, "Measuring programming quality and productivity", *IBM Systems J.* **17**, 1 (1978) 39–63.
28. C. Jones, *Programming Productivity* (McGraw-Hill, 1986).
29. P. G. W. Keen, "Information systems and organizational change", *Commun. ACM* **24**, 1 (1981) 24–33.
30. C. F. Kemerer, "An empirical validation of software cost estimation models", *Commun. ACM* **30**, 5 (1987) 416–429.
31. C. F. Kemerer, "Improving the reliability of function point measurement – an empirical study", *IEEE Trans. Softw. Eng.* **18**, 11 (1992) 1011–1024.
32. C. F. Kemerer, "Reliability of function point measurement – a field experiment", *Commun. ACM* **36**, 2 (1993) 85–97.
33. T. Kidder, *The Soul of a New Machine* (Atlantic Monthly Press, 1981).
34. J. L. King and E. Schrems, "Cost-benefit analysis in information systems development and operation", *ACM Comput. Surv.* **10**, 1 (1978) 19–34.
35. R. Kling and W. Scacchi, "The web of computing: computing technology as social organization", *Advances in Computers* **21** (1982) 3–87.
36. R. Kraut, S. Dumais, and S. Koch, "Computerization, productivity, and quality of work-life", *Commun. ACM* **32**, 2 (1989) 220–238.
37. G. N. Lambert, "A comparative study of system response time on programmer development productivity", *IBM Systems J.* **23**, 1 (1984) 36–43.
38. B. Lakhanpal, "Understanding the factors influencing the performance of software development groups: an exploratory group-level analysis", *Information and Software Technology* **35**, 8 (1993) 468–471.
39. M. J. Lawrence, "Programming methodology, organizational environment, and programming productivity", *J. Syst. Softw.* **2** (1981) 257–269.
40. P. Mi and W. Scacchi, "A knowledge-based environment for modeling and simulating software engineering processes", *IEEE Trans. Knowl. Data Eng.* **2**, 3 (1990) 283–294. Reprinted in *Nikkei Artificial Intelligence* **20**, 1 (1991) 176–191 (in Japanese).
41. P. Mi and W. Scacchi, "Modeling articulation work in software engineering processes", *Proc. 1st. Int. Conf. Software Process* (IEEE Computer Society Press, 1991)

42. P. Mi and W. Scacchi, "Process integration for CASE environments", *IEEE Softw.* **9**, 2 (1992) 45–53. Reprinted in *Computer-Aided Software Engineering*, 2nd ed., ed. Chikofsky (IEEE Computer Society Press, 1993).
43. R. Mittal, M. Kim, and R. Berg, "A case study of workstation usage during early phases of the software development life cycle", *Proc. ACM SIGSOFT/SIGPLAN Software Engineering Symp. Practical Software Development Environments* (1986) pp. 70–76.
44. S. N. Mohanty, "Software cost estimation: present and future", *Software Practice and Experience* **11** (1981) 103–121.
45. R. J. Norman and J. F. Nunamaker, "CASE productivity perceptions of software engineering professionals", *Commun. ACM* **32**, 9 (1989) 1102–1108.
46. A. Pengelly, M. Norris, and R. Higham, "Software process modeling and measurement — a QMS case study", *Information and Software Technology* **35**, 6&7 (1993) 375–380.
47. Y. V. Reddy, M. S. Fox, N. Husain, and M. McRoberts, "The knowledge-based simulation system", *IEEE Softw.* **3**, 2 (1986) 26–37.
48. J. L. Romeu and S. A. Gloss-Soler, "Some measurement problems detected in the analysis of software productivity data and their statistical significance", *Proc. COMPSAC 83* (IEEE Computer Society Press, 1983) pp. 17–24.
49. A. Sathi, M. S. Fox, and M. Greenberg, "Representation of activity knowledge for project management", *IEEE Trans. Pattern Analysis and Machine Intelligence* **7**, 5 (1985) 531–552.
50. W. Scacchi, "Managing software engineering projects: a social analysis", *IEEE Trans. Softw. Eng.* **SE-10**, 1 (1984) 49–59.
51. W. Scacchi, "On the power of domain-specific hypertext environments", *J. Amer. Soc. Info. Sci.* **40**, 5 (1989).
52. W. Scacchi, "Designing software systems to facilitate social organization", in *Work with Computers*, Vol. 12A, *Advances in Human Factors and Ergonomics*, eds. M. J. Smith and G. Salvendy (Elsevier, 1989) pp. 64–72.
53. W. Scacchi, "The software infrastructure for a distributed system factory", *Softw. Eng. J.* **6**, 5 (1991) 355–369.
54. A. J. Thadhani, "Factors affecting programmer productivity during application development", *IBM Systems J.* **23**, 1 (1984) 19–35.
55. J. Vosburg, B. Curtis, R. Wolverton, B. Albert, H. Malec, S. Hoben, and Y. Liu "Productivity factors and programming environments", *Proc. 7th. Int. Conf. Software Engineering* (IEEE Computer Society Press, 1984) pp. 143–152.
56. C. E. Walton and C. P. Felix, "A method of programming measurement and estimation", *IBM Systems J.* **16**, 1 (1977) 54–65.